Wind

Windows® NT Infrastructure Design

Mike Collins

Digital Press
Boston • Oxford • Johannesburg • Melbourne • New Delhi • Singapore

Digital Press™ is an imprint of Butterworth–Heinemann.

The case study of Midas Bank International is fictional, and any resemblance to or implied relation to an actual Midas Bank International is purely coincidental.

Library of Congress Cataloging-in-Publication Data
Collins, Michael (Michael James), 1960–
Windows NT infrastructure design / Michael Collins.
p. cm.
Includes index.
ISBN 1-55558-170-6 (pbk. : alk. paper)
1. Microsoft Windows NT. 2. Operating systems (Computers)
I. Title.
QA76.76.O63C6482 1998
005.4'44769—dc21 97-38048
CIP

British Library Cataloguing-in-Publication Data
A catalogue record for this book is available from the British Library.

The publisher offers special discounts on bulk orders of this book.
For information, please contact:
Manager of Special Sales
Butterworth–Heinemann
225 Wildwood Avenue
Woburn, MA 01801–2041
Tel: 781-904-2500
Fax: 781-904-2620

For information on all Digital Press publications available, contact our World Wide Web home page at: http://www.bh.com/digitalpress

Order number: EY–V447E–DP

10 9 8 7 6 5 4 3 2 1

Designed and composed by ReadyText, Bath, UK
Printed in the United States of America

Trademarks

Microsoft, LAN Manager, MS-DOS, SourceSafe, Visual SourceSafe, Win32, Windows, Windows NT, ActiveX, and Net Meeting are registered trademarks of Microsoft Corporation.
Alpha, AXP, DECnet, DEC, Digital, OpenVMS, and VAX are trademarks of Digital Equipment Corporation.
Ethernet is a trademark of Xerox Corporation.
IBM, IBM-PC, OS/2 are trademarks of International Business Machines Corporation.
Apple, AppleTalk, Macintosh are trademarks of Apple Computer.
NetWare, Novell are trademarks of Novell.
Domain, HP are registered trademarks of Hewlett-Packard Company
UNIX is a registered trademark in the United States and other countries, licensed exclusively through X/Open Company, Ltd.
Lotus Notes is a trademark of Lotus.

All trademarks found herein are property of their respective owners.

This book is dedicated to my daughter, Hannah (6), who decided to demonstrate her support for me by writing a book of magic spells. Her book is not yet finished but it has to be tough competition when it is!

Contents

Preface

Many who are given the opportunity to undertake a technical infrastructure design project are fresh to the challenges it brings. This will continue to be the case as new people enter the industry and advances in technology demand an infrastructure technology upgrade every five years or less. Even when the best technicians or project managers are assigned to such a project they can still be confronted with challenges they are unprepared for.

An important factor in a successful technical infrastructure design project is good design decisions. Good design decisions are based on a sound understanding of how to apply technology. That understanding must be built up from a combination of experience and technical knowledge. It is not sufficient merely to be a technology expert, as the understanding of how to apply the knowledge will be missing. Likewise, to have much experience but to fail to apply it when making a design decision is to risk making the same mistakes again.

Technical knowledge can be built up by reading technical literature, investigation or training. Indeed, there is a large collection of published technical literature from which to choose and many good training courses available. Unfortunately experience can't be bought and neither can understanding. All too often understanding is replaced by faith in knowledge, which in the case of a technical infrastructure design may well lead to a technically sound decision but one that fails to serve the business well.

It is possible however to assist the development of understanding by providing a framework for developing experience and knowledge. Such a framework needs to clarify the subject matter by distilling its essence, allowing the development of arguments and their clear communication. In the way that paintings are discussed in terms of color, light and texture, the subject of technology infrastructure design needs its own framework of concepts.

This book was written to present a suitable framework of concepts for use on a technical infrastructure project. Having personally been through several such projects I chose to write the book I would have wanted to buy at the outset. It provides guidance for the beginner as well as techniques for the more experienced technician or project manager looking to enhance their approach. The essence of this book is a structured approach to the key aspects of a Windows NT technical infrastructure design project, from technology through to project management.

The framework consists of analysis tools and a project roadmap. Using the concepts presented here will not guarantee the right design decisions are always made, far less the best designed technical infrastructure possible. What they will do is provide a way for decisions to be analyzed, questioned and discussed and act as a guide through such a project.

By creating a book that is neither a technical manual nor a project management manual, but something in between, there has been no benchmark against which it could be judged. I am satisfied that the book is how I want it to be and so am optimistic that others too will see it as a valuable addition to the available Windows NT literature.

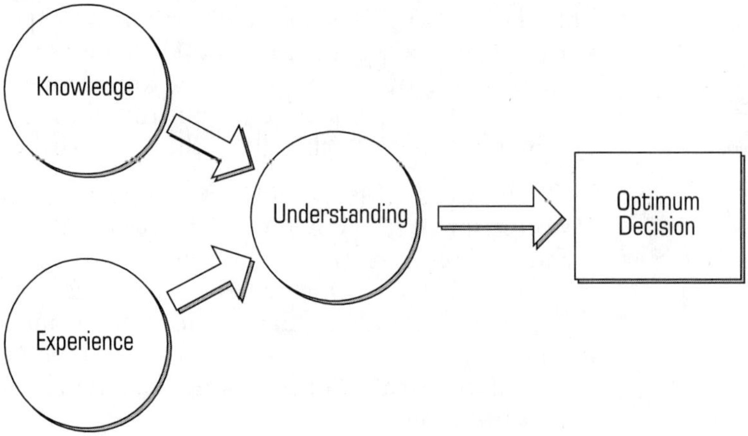

Thanks

Thanks are due to the many people who shared my belief that a book of this type was needed. Due a special mention is Jon Buxton, who found the time to plough through reams of draft manuscript to offer advice about the structure of the book. Thanks also to the reviewer retained by the publisher whose challenging style strengthened my belief that this type of book was badly needed.

Thanks are due to my wife who saw the activity as a useful sink for my energy. Her support in giving me the space to get on with it was essential.

Liz McCarthy and Mike Cash at Digital Press deserve recognition for adopting just the right mix of encouragement, trust and a sense of proportion. This is particularly commendable as my proposal to them was that I write a type of book that had not yet been published.

1

Introduction

This book is a guide to the execution of a Windows NT based infrastructure analysis and design project. The fundamental rationale behind the book is that each technical infrastructure project comprises broadly the same set of activities and faces the same set of issues. By defining those activities and showing how the issues may be addressed, it encapsulates the re-usable components of a technical infrastructure analysis and design project.

This book complements project management literature by applying the theory of the subject to a particular type of project. It complements technical literature by providing a framework in which to make design decisions. The tools and techniques presented are independent of technology so they will apply as well to a design that uses future products.

In summary it is about:

- Applying standard project management techniques to a technical infrastructure project
- Using proven tools to ensure a quality analysis of the technical infrastructure requirements
- The creation of a design that can be shown to support those requirements

The book is organized in two parts, the first introduces tools and concepts and the second is based on their application to a general case study.

While focusing on a Windows NT 4 based technical infrastructure, the techniques and project activities described here are equally applicable to a Windows NT 5 based technical infrastructure.

Why Read This Book?

Make a quick and confident start to your project	By providing a template project plan and guidance on resourcing, roles and responsibilities, a quick and confident start can be made to a Windows NT technical infrastructure project.
Ensure your project delivers what the business needs	For a technical infrastructure design to be successful it is essential that the full set of business intentions are captured as well as all the requirements on the system. Tools are provided for: ▪ defining the scope of the project ▪ capturing the intentions of the business ▪ gathering user requirements ▪ gathering application requirements.
Keep control over the design process	A way is presented that will speed the process of making key design decisions and allow you control over how a design is created to meet the needs of the business.
Many worked examples	Examples in a variety of technical areas show how the tools presented in this book may be practically applied.
Learn how to use proven Tools and Concepts	The tools and concepts have all been developed on real technical infrastructure projects. They have been proven to be flexible and successful.
Be prepared for Windows NT 5 and the Active Directory	Use of the project roadmap and tools presented in this book will be even more valuable when applied to a Windows NT 5 infrastructure project. Windows NT 5 presents far more configuration possibilities than Windows NT 4. So to build a successful Windows NT 5 based technical infrastructure will need a far greater understanding of the target organization resulting in a more complex project.

Intended Audience

This book is aimed at those who either have to manage a Windows NT based technical infrastructure design project, have to contribute to one technically, or have a need to understand the nature of such a project. Typically this includes:

- Project managers

- Line managers
- Consultants
- Technical staff
- Solution architects

Scope

The scope of this book is focused on the activities associated with a Windows NT technical infrastructure analysis and design project, these include:

- Defining the project scope
- Planning
- Managing the project
- Capturing the business intentions driving the project
- Gathering the user and application requirements on the technical infrastructure
- Gathering information for planning
- Analysis and design (taking account of impending Microsoft products)
- Testing, training, and procurement
- Windows NT4 and moving to Windows NT5

The following are *outside* the scope of this book:

- **System Installation**

  In most organizations system installation is a well understood logistical process.
- **Provision of Technical Reference Material**

  This book is not intended to be a technical reference text. Where technical details of Windows NT have been mentioned it is to illustrate analysis methods and points of note only. In every case, the reader should refer to the latest reference material on the subject for definitive information.
- **Project Management Reference Material**

  Although the basic concepts of project management are covered, this book is not a work on project management theory. There are plenty of such books available, however the challenge of applying the theory to a real project will be with the reader.

- **Product Selection or Endorsement**

  The purpose of this book is to provide you with the tools to arrive at the best design decision for your project. Technology advances so rapidly that a product deemed the best one day, will be superseded by a better one within months so product recommendations would rapidly become useless as they date.

- **Systems for the Management and Operation of the Technical Infrastructure**

  The approach outlined in this book acknowledges the importance of this aspect of technical infrastructure design by accounting for the needs of the IT Support organization in the requirements gathering activity. The design of systems for the management and operation of the technical infrastructure is out of scope as the focus is on the design of the technical infrastructure itself.

- **Hardware**

  Choice of hardware can clearly affect both the overall performance and the reliability of a technical infrastructure. Differentiation between different hardware options tends to be vendor specific and changes rapidly over time. So rather than include in this book partisan information that will date, it is recommended that the market is surveyed for suitable hardware at the right time and decisions are made using the same processes advocated in this book for software oriented design decisions.

Because the scope of this book is far reaching and covers several disciplines it is unrealistic to expect every reader to get the same level of benefit out of every chapter. Rather, it would be typical to expect someone to concentrate on the first part of the book which covers tools and management or the second part which covers application of the tools to a design, depending on which one complemented their existing skills and experience.

Where technologies have been omitted through lack of space or through their immaturity, the tools and approach advocated here can be easily adapted, making this book an equally valuable guide on projects that use different or new technologies.

Methodology

Central to the approach recommended in this book is a practical methodology based on concepts tailored to the process of designing a Windows NT based technical infrastructure:

Project Model

To provide a framework for the project a model is introduced showing how all the key project activities and tasks relate to each other. A traditional approach is taken to sequencing the activities of the project which has the advantage that it will be intuitive and familiar. It is an approach that places emphasis on analysis and design as a means of getting the system right first time. The project model consists of four main phases, this book concentrates on the first three, omitting the Implementation phase. A summary of the project model is shown below:

Figure 1.1 *Summary Project Model*

Design Preparation includes establishing project scope, determining the business forces driving the project and gathering requirements on the technical infrastructure. The Design phase is the process of developing a design to meet the requirements. Implementation Preparation is about proving the design as well as carrying out supporting activities such as training, testing and installation planning. This model will be referred to later in this chapter and throughout the book. The structure of the book is based around the model.

Service Based Technical Infrastructure

Over recent years applications have come to rely more on functionality provided by common services either provided by the operating system or layered products. This allows the designer of an application to focus more on the actual business functionality of the application and less on developing supporting services. The set of services relied on are collectively referred to as the technical infrastructure, with typical services being file, print, time, etc.

Describe a System by its Attributes

Each technical infrastructure service can be characterized by a set of attributes. For example, we can describe a file service as secure or scalable. It is also possible to explain the effect of a design decision using the same attributes. If the same attributes are used to describe system requirements then it is possible to see a direct link between a design decision and how it affects the service's ability to meet a particular requirement.

Represent Intentions of Business with Business Principles

The need to capture the way the corporation intends to apply information technology to solve business challenges is satisfied by a formal construct called a business principle.

Represent Key Design Decisions with Design Principles

Key design decisions are captured in another formal construct called a design principle. The design principle states a design decision, policy or rule, and backs it up with a reason for the principle, the implications of adhering to it and any problems associated with it.

Use of the Book

This book should be used as a source of:

- Guidance in the structure and processes of a technical infrastructure project
- Tools for analysis and design
- Examples of those tools in action

Do not expect to find the answer in this book to what the correct Windows NT domain design should be for each circumstance. Do expect to find an explanation of the means of arriving at the correct design for your project.

Expect to find some aspects of the book more useful than others. Successful deployment of just a few of the tools will pay handsome dividends. The project model, activity and tasks descriptions and checklists presented in this book should be treated as starting points. You should tailor them to meet the unique needs of your project.

The tools and methods advocated for technical infrastructure analysis and design are strong enough to be:

- Unaffected by advances in technology
- Used on a project where there is either no infrastructure or what is there is being completely replaced as well as one where there is a need to integrate with existing systems

This book should not be seen as a substitute for any other. Sources of technical material such as the Windows NT Resource Kits will provide data that will be essential when carrying out the design. Books on project management methodologies will provide useful tips, processes and templates to complement the approach recommended here.

Use of a Case Study

A single case study is used throughout the book for illustrating the tools and concepts introduced. It is entirely fictitious though it has many features in common with a real project. Any relation between the case study and a particular organization is entirely coincidental.

The case study is based on a multinational corporation called Midas Bank International (MBI) that has a number of organizational problems caused by the recent acquisition of three subsidiaries. The leadership of the bank has initiated a project to create a major new global application built to run on Windows NT. The case study focuses on the project to design the global Windows NT based technical infrastructure that will be required to support it.

The multinational banking marketplace is rife with competition, it has many legal constraints and the pace of change is increasing. As such, it represents what might be described as a worst case scenario for the creation of a pervasive technical infrastructure. The intention is that there will be significant elements in the case study that apply directly to organizations in other industries.

The purpose of the case study is to illustrate the process of moving from business objectives to a design for a technical infrastructure that would effectively support the business. With this in mind, the actual design arrived at is of less importance than the way it is arrived at. Clearly the reverse will be true for the reader!

The greater the amount of detail an example includes, the more specific it gets, demanding more background material to substantiate it. More background material would dilute the content of the book and be tedious to read. For that reason, the examples in the book in many cases will not go to the level of detail found on a real project. For this reason the approach to the use of examples should be one of seeing them as a starting point.

The reader's focus should be on the process being used throughout the design. Instead of being concerned about whether the design being developed for the case study is correct, consideration should be given to how the tools used in the process can be employed on a real project.

The case study concentrates on the technologies most commonly found in a Windows NT technical infrastructure, in most cases focusing on the Microsoft implementations. For example, there are several implementations of the DNS naming service available the text concentrates on the Microsoft version.

Because the emphasis of the book is on the process and tools used to arrive at a design, it is not necessary for the case study to address every technology likely to be found in the typical corporate IT environment. At the business level the issues are the same regardless of underlying technology. Once the basic tools have been grasped, the reader should be able to apply them to alternative or emerging technologies.

Organization of Text

The book is divided into two parts:

- **Part I** Background and the Design Preparation phase of the project model
- **Part II** The Design and Implementation Preparation phases of the project model

The chapters in Part I cover project management and the project model in detail along with concepts central to the book. The chapters in Part II are aligned to each technical infrastructure service under design, except for the Implementation Preparation phase activities which are grouped into a single chapter.

Part I

2 *Elements of a Technical Infrastructure*	The concept of a technical infrastructure as a set of services is defined, along with a means of describing service characteristics in business terms.
3 *Running the Project*	An introduction to the basic techniques of project management, concentrating on practical issues relevant to a technical infrastructure project.
4 *Project Planning*	Identifies the basic activities and tasks involved in a technical infrastructure project.
5 *Business Principles*	The concept of a business principle is proposed as a tool for capturing how an organization intends to use technology to support its business objectives. Business principles are used to directly influence key design decisions. A set of business principles are developed for the case study.

6 *Design Principles*	Design principles record key design decisions. They are justified by references to requirements and to business principles. Design principles are used throughout Part II of the book in the development of a technical infrastructure design for the case study.
7 *Developing Principles*	Recommendations for how to go about developing business principles and design principles in circumstances that may not be ideal.
8 *Requirements Gathering*	Describes the process of gathering the user requirements, application requirements and the data necessary for supporting the design with information about the existing systems. Requirements gathering also supports the development of installation plans.

Part II

9 *Network Services*	The design of the network is outside the scope of a technical infrastructure design, though the networking capabilities of Windows NT make it appropriate to consider how certain services may be designed to work within the context of an existing network.
10 *Naming Services*	A fundamental link between the network and the technical infrastructure, naming services contribute to the usability and flexibility of a technical infrastructure.
11 *Domain Design*	Essentially the design of management and security services of a technical infrastructure, the domain design is the basis for the rest of the technical infrastructure.
12 *Windows NT Groups*	An adjunct to the management and security service provided by Windows NT domains, groups are an important means of structuring a user population.
13 *File and Print Services*	The original networked technical infrastructure services, file and print form an important part of any technical infrastructure solution serving both users and applications.

14 User Environment	Although not a service, the user environment can't be overlooked as it provides the interface to file and print services as well as being affected by naming standards. The user environment also plays an important part in realizing several types of business objective.
15 Time Services	Making sure the clocks on all the computers in the infrastructure have the same time can be important to certain types of application. It can also be required for regulatory reasons.
16 Naming Standards	Describes the role of names and the advantages of standardization. Distinction is drawn between the aspects of a name that are determined by the design of the subject of the name and the aspects that are discretionary.
17 Implementation Preparation	Just as the design phase of the project is closing, several activities need to be initiated to prepare for the implementation of the new system. Among them are developing and testing the design, purchasing equipment and training.

Appendices

A Example Business Principles	A selection of business principles are listed, from which suitable examples may be chosen and developed to apply to a real project.
B Example Design Principles	A selection of design principles are listed, from which suitable examples may be chosen and developed to apply to a real project.
C User Logon Scripts	The logon script implementing the design developed in the chapter on User Environment is listed in full here.
D Case Study Gantt Charts	The activities and tasks typical of a technical infrastructure analysis and design are shown in Gantt chart form.

Assumptions

The assumptions will be different depending on the background of the reader and what he or she intends to get out of this book. It is assumed the reader has:

- An awareness of networks
- An awareness of PC technology
- Access to technical documentation (TechNet or the Windows NT Resource Kit)

Part I

The Design Preparation Phase

The chapters in Part I of the book concentrate on the Design Preparation Phase of the project. They cover:

- An introduction to a Windows NT based technical infrastructure and how to characterize it
- A project roadmap detailing the activities and tasks behind the project phases in the diagram below
- Identification of the scope of the project
- Introduction of the concept of a Business Principle as a means of capturing key business drivers for the project
- Introduction of the concept of the Design Principle as a means of capturing key design decisions
- The gathering of requirements for the project
- Project documentation

Figure I.1 *Design Preparation Phase*

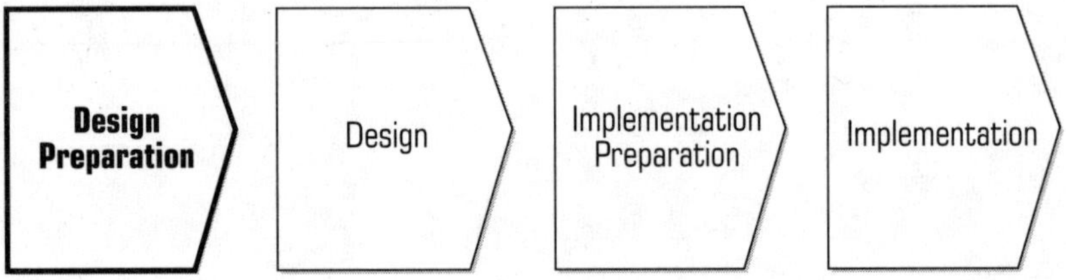

2

Elements of a Technical Infrastructure

The emergence of a technical infrastructure as a key component in the delivery of distributed applications has been boosted by the uptake of Windows NT. Understanding the technical infrastructure and its role is key to building a system for the business. This chapter introduces the elements of a technical infrastructure as services and provides a framework for describing their individual characteristics.

The basic proposition of this chapter is that all components of a system, not just the application itself, make a contribution to how well it addresses the broad business need of an organization. Therefore, to effectively design a system requires us to be able to describe in business terms how the various components change their behavior as a result of design decisions.

To support this proposition two key concepts are introduced:

- Applications are supported by a set of infrastructure services, collectively termed a technical infrastructure.
- The infrastructure services can be described in business terms using a set of attributes.

Those readers who may be familiar with the concept of a technical infrastructure and its component services should at least read the section Defining a Technical Infrastructure to acquaint themselves with terminology and definitions specific to this book.

The objective of this chapter is to introduce a way of thinking about the underlying components of a distributed computer system that will contribute to their successful deployment.

Structure of Chapter

Table 2.1 shows the topics covered in this chapter.

Table 2.1 *The Structure of Chapter 2*

Topic	Contents
The evolution of client-server computing	The chapter begins with a review of how modern client-server, or distributed computing evolved out of technology constraints and business pressures. We then see how a client-server system can be characterized by a set of *attributes*, allowing us to describe the business impact of different technical choices.
The evolution of technical infrastructure services	A closer look at how technology has developed to enable distributed computing identifies a distinct layer of software components used by an application, which are introduced as *infrastructure services*.
Introduction to the elements of a technical infrastructure	Several of the common infrastructure services are then examined to illustrate how they support a distributed application.
Defining a technical infrastructure	Following the introduction to attributes and infrastructure services a distinction is drawn between those services that are designed to be utilities and those that are designed to incorporate application logic. The components of a Windows NT based technical infrastructure are defined for the purpose of this book.

The Evolution of Client-Server Computing

The evolution of computing which has its beginning with traditional mainframe computers with dumb screens, has been guided by a mix of business needs and technology's ability to meet those needs. For example, pressure to produce a more scalable system encourages the development of technology to offer a solution. That solution is usually an incremental step forward, building on solid, proven foundations. Sometimes there are revolutionary breakthroughs but they are rare.

This section plots the evolution of client-server computing in terms of business pressures and technology's attempts to relieve them. This approach is important when we come to look at the underlying technology of client-server computing later in the chapter, focusing then on how foundations need to be built to allow a complete system to deliver benefits.

The Pressure for Client-Server

The roots of computing are in the storage and processing of data where both were undertaken by the same computer. Over time, basic networks were established which allowed the transfer of data from one computer to another and gave remote user access to certain computer functions. The processing carried out was sometimes complex involving statistical calculations and sometimes simple like sorting and printing. We will see later on how the simple capability of transferring some data from one computer to another embodies many of the characteristics of modern client-server computing.

The initial functions carried out over early networks were developed as convenience measures. For example, when once it may have been necessary to transfer a file of data from one computer to another via a magnetic tape, it was becoming easier to use a network. It isn't until the use of two computers connected together by a network became a deliberate architecture for solving a computing problem that the concept of client-server computing became real.

Let us use an example to illustrate how client-server computing was encouraged as a result of business pressure. Consider a traditional mainframe run by an insurance company to store life insurance details for several million people. Originally, the only way to query that information was to carefully design a query and submit it for batch processing. The result often took many hours to arrive. Often many iterations would need to be performed before the query produced the correct results. Then, the results might prompt additional batch queries to refine the data. Days could have elapsed before the required results were obtained. The time overhead is a tremendous constraint when important commercial decisions depend upon the results of these queries.

Moving a subset of the data to a smaller, personal computer for analysis offers a dramatic speed advantage that can provide a competitive advantage. It was this pressure that led to the development of tools that allowed a personal computer to be used in conjunction with a mainframe for more expedient data processing.

This style of processing demands only simple communications between two computers. In fact, this simple architecture is capable of supporting many types of networked client-server applications. Here are three more simple examples:

- By providing easy, on-line access to data many users can benefit from the same information, potentially enhancing productivity.

- Measurement data collected from an experiment by a small computer is buffered up and then sent periodically to a more powerful computer for statistical analysis.
- Distribution of a price list file to a computer in a car sales showroom enables local production of quotations.

Thus, the original pressure for client-server computing was the promise of the business advantages that might be possible if the constraints of central computing could be overcome.

The Development of Client-Server

Initial client-server systems tended to be split as shown in Figure 2.1, using the new power of the user's workstation. *Presentation* typically included some sort of data entry interface based on windows or forms. Often elementary field validation was also carried out at the client.

Figure 2.1 *Original Client-Server Architecture*

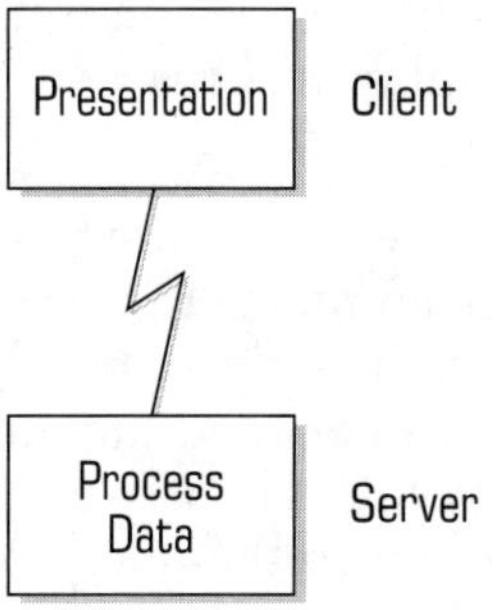

Over time, additional schemes for distributing the main components of a whole application were developed, as shown in Figure 2.2:

Figure 2.2 *Versions of Clent-Server Architecture*

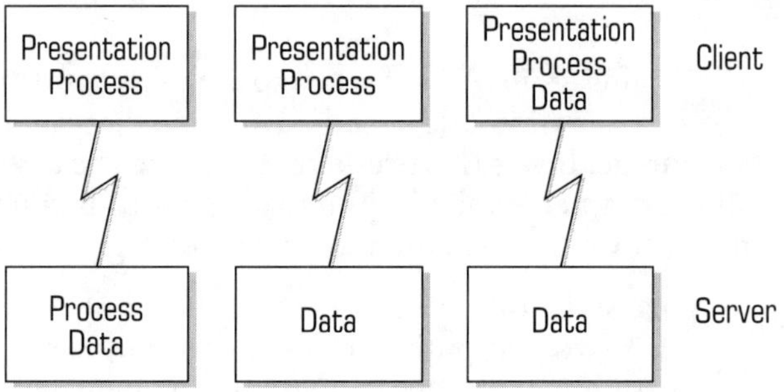

In the version of client-server architecture showing processing being carried out at both client and server, the early implementations used basic data transfer mechanisms. It wasn't until later that processes remote from each other began communicating using more powerful techniques. This type of client-server computing allowed businesses to exploit the low cost of desktop processing power. In another version, nearly all processing was taken off the server hosting the data and moved to the client. This was done when businesses saw the advantage of speedy, on demand processing. The final version of client-server architecture illustrated shows all processing and presentation functions as well as a portion of the application data having moved off the server system, relegating the server to archiving or protecting important data.

Observations on Two Tier Client-Server Architecture

The distributed computing architecture discussed so far is often referred to generically as two tier client-server, the total processing being split into two principle components each running on a different computer. Among its advantages are that it lends itself well to many clients sharing a small number of server services. It is also relatively simple to implement using the tools on the market today.

The principle problem with a two tier client-server architecture is achieving adequate performance as the number of client systems increases. The reason for this is that the server and network components eventually become overloaded as the increased number of clients causes a corresponding increase in overall work.

For example, most people will have experienced the scenario where their file server takes a long time to serve a file, or it takes a long time to log in to the network. What is happening is that a component in the client-server system is struggling to cope with the load. It could be the network or it could be the server computer. At a finer granularity, it could be any component within the network such as a router or any component within the computer such as a disk. The net effect is that due to a bottleneck, one component of the client-server system is stopping others from doing any useful work (you can include the human being waiting for the file if you wish).

This scenario occurs when the distribution of work between clients and servers is inappropriate for their respective processing capacities, or perhaps the way the application has been designed leads to excessive communications traffic. Ideally, an application designer would create a client-server system such that this didn't happen, however there are usually too many unknowns to be able to reliably achieve this objective. Compounding this is that a lot of the early tools available for building client-server systems rigidly dictated the computers upon which processing, presentation and data were to reside. Recent developments in tool technology now make it possible for the components of a distributed system to be allocated to computers after the application has been created, allowing the system to be tuned.

The problem is most severe from the users' perspective when the delay appears to be caused by components other than their desktop computer, as there is an element of unpredictability and the feeling that someone else is causing a problem in the system. It is this type of user reaction that has led to pressure to enhance overall system performance.

Several methods can be adopted to tackle the problem of overloaded client-server components. Of the five potential solutions listed below, those numbered 1, 2 and 5 are primarily designed to address a server bottleneck and solutions 3 and 4 are designed to alleviate a network bottleneck. Each solution is discussed in more detail following the list.

1. Operate duplicate servers
2. Increase the power of the server
3. Increase the capacity of the network
4. Re-balance the processing split between client and server
5. Split the serving functionality amongst a set of servers

Option 1 appears straightforward but only works if the serving software has been designed to work over multiple servers. In the case of a file server, splitting the serving of files between two servers so that half the clients access one and the other half access the other can work well. If, however, the users needed to share all their files then this may prove too impractical. Methods such as clustering are designed to address this problem.

Option 2 is a common and relatively simple operation until the expansion capability of the computer is reached and is often used to avoid having to implement options 4 or 5.

Option 3, increasing network capacity will work if the bottleneck is the network, however it can be an expensive exercise both in terms of initial and ongoing costs. Increasing network capacity should normally only be considered if the application has been designed to minimize network usage or the application is fundamentally network bandwidth hungry. An example of a bandwidth hungry application would be a video server.

Option 4, as has been noted, is often difficult to do due to constraints imposed by tools. Option 5 has proven to be a practical option that is gaining popularity. Another way of looking at option 5 is to see it as the use of servers dedicated to specific tasks. For example, one server would be the database server and another the processing server. Thus, if the multiple serving tasks of one server were to be distributed one task to a server then there would be a net increase in serving capacity without placing any special requirements on the serving software. If this solves the client-server performance imbalance then fine. An added bonus is that it is a highly scalable option.

However, once the client-server balance of the application has been optimized and the servers have reached their maximum capacity, to scale further requires resorting to duplicate servers per task. As discussed earlier, running a serving task across multiple servers places constraints on the design of the software due to issues of co-ordination between servers. On the other hand there is an opportunity presented here to offer a resilient configuration. Thus, if in a duplicated server configuration one server were to fail and there was some way of switching client access over to a remaining server, either automatically or manually, then the service could be kept going for all users.

A simple example of this would be to employ two print servers, both accessible from all clients. Should one print server fail, the client users can manually connect to a printer via the surviving print server.

Figure 2.3 *Server Scalability*

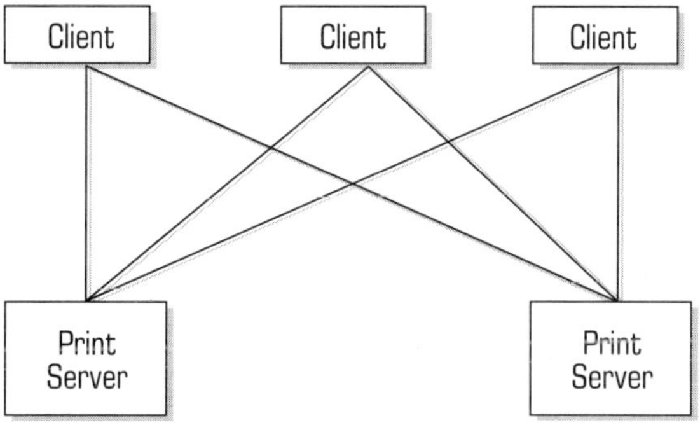

An implication of a client computer accessing multiple specialized or dedicated servers is that the complexity of the application rises as the functionality is split between client and server. This has important consequences:

- As applications have grown and tools become more complex, the client workstations need more power.
- Every time there is a change in the business logic of the application, all the client computers need to be upgraded.
- Should server database schema be modified, all the client computers need to be upgraded.

Peer to Peer Computing

It is usual to classify the types of conversation the client computers and the server computers have between each other to characterize their roles. This can be helpful in understanding the working of a distributed application.

There are two basic classes of conversation:

- Client-server
- Peer to peer

A client-server conversation is of the form request-response, where one software component always issues the requests and the other always issues the response. A peer to peer conversation is where each component can issue both requests and responses. Another way of looking at it is that with peer to peer computing each partner in a conversation can adopt the role of both client and server. Peer to peer computing is commonly used to enable programs to synchronize data or to cooperatively process data.

It is important to note that by looking at distributed computing in terms of software components communicating between each other, client-server or peer to peer relationships become independent of the underlying hardware configuration. This is significant because it means that the client and server portions of an application or service may reside on the same computer or different computers and still function in the same way.

Three Tier Client-Server Computing

To solve these problems with two tiered computing and yet continue to exploit the successful concept of client-server computing, there has been a move in the industry to shift the business logic of an application into a new class of server, the application server. This class of server, or servers, would then access dedicated database engines. The client systems are relegated to information consumers, offering a user interface service for the user to communicate with the application server.

The resulting architecture of the application has three layers:

- Information consumers
- Application servers
- Database engines

Figure 2.4 illustrates this three tier client-server architecture. Communication between elements of the architecture is client-server between the three layers. Between the application servers there can be peer to peer communication to perform synchronization duties or exchange of data. While the architecture is well defined in purely software terms, not mandating three separate types of computers, it is usual to find in practice that the three layers are broadly represented by PCs at the client end, mid-range servers for business processing, and high powered new or traditional mainframes serving the data.

Figure 2.4
Three Tier Client-Server Architecture

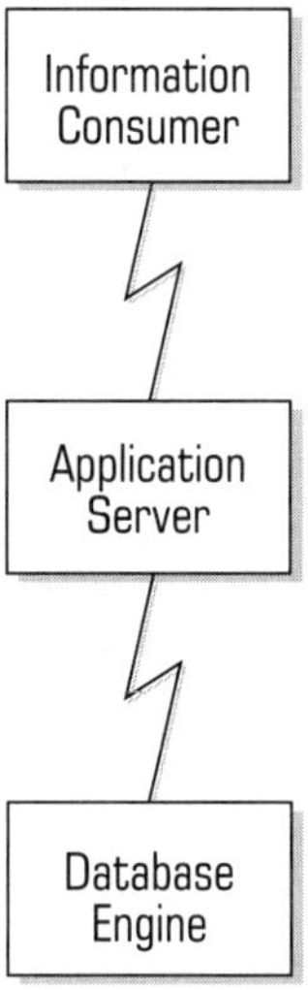

This is commonly known as *Three Tier Client-Server Architecture.* The following sections of this chapter discuss the basic networked services necessary for a three tier client-server application to function.

Observations on a Three Tier Client-Server Architecture

Before going any further we will summarize what we know about client-server computing. As all the observations we made were expressed in terms of the attributes of a system, the observations have been categorized according to system attribute.

Attribute	Observations
Complexity	Distributing function across several computers has the effect of increasing the number of elements of the system, software, hardware and networking. The complexity of a distributed application system will always be higher than that of an equivalent one tier or two tier system.

continued ▸

Attribute	Observations
Software Development	Testing a distributed application is harder than testing a non-distributed one for two reasons: ▪ there are more components in the system to test ▪ more factors affect the run-time environment, making exhaustive testing of every scenario impossible.
Support	Problem diagnosis can be much harder as the application is usually more complex than an application confined to a single computer.
Capacity	Distributed systems with greater total capacity for processing and data storage than a single computer can certainly be built. The capacity of a given distributed system configuration will be limited by the first component to reach its own capacity limit. Careful design is required to ensure no one component seriously limits the overall system capacity.
Reliability	The greater number of components involved in a distributed computing system enhances the probability of a system component failure, which may lead to system failure, in turn reducing the overall system reliability. If a goal of the system is high reliability it can be designed to ensure that the failure of any one component does not cause the failure of the complete system.
Availability	For a given level of reliability, the availability of a system is governed by the speed with which a repair is carried out after a failure and the amount of planned down-time necessary. If a goal of the system is high availability it can be designed to ensure that repairs can be carried out quickly and components of the system can undergo planned down-time without affecting the overall availability of the system.
Flexibility	Partitioning an application by architecting it to run across multiple computers offers the flexibility to be able to replace parts of the application with minimal impact on the overall system.
Scalability	The preceding sections introduced three tier client-server computing as a means of solving the scalability problems of two tier client-server computing. Scalability remains one of the strongest attributes of the three tiered computing architecture.
Performance	One of the main motivations for three tier client-server computing is the way its architecture lends itself to addressing performance problems. It is general enough to allow optimum distribution of processing across computers without incurring network bandwidth problems.

continued ▸

Attribute	Observations
Security	Distributing an application, particularly in a heterogeneous environment, will usually mean it does not fall within the security domain of any single operating system. Other methods of security then have to be found. The transmission of data over a network between client and server may pose a security hazard though its more likely to be the threat of inadvertent corruption that is greater rather than anything malicious.
Manageability	Now that an application consists of multiple programs on multiple computers it becomes difficult to ascertain whether all the components are running. There are new challenges in the area of restarting remote components of applications, being alerted to error conditions and logging activity.

Characterizing Client-Server Systems

By demonstrating in the preceding sections how distributed computing has evolved as a result of business pressures, we are now in a position to define how well a distributed system addresses those pressures in business terms. For example, we can characterize a system by stating how secure it is or how scalable it is.

Why would we want to do this? The reason is because the ability to characterize a distributed system in business terms allows us to compare different design decisions in a way that relates directly to how well each system meets a business need. The benefit is that the business implication of a design decision can be brought into more focus.

The attributes used to categorize the observations made of three tier client-server computing in the previous section provide us with a list of possible business terms. The design chapters of this book will use seven of these attributes when analyzing the implications of different design decisions. They are defined in Table 2.2 and will be referred to as *common attributes,* as each is applicable to most elements of a system.

Table 2.2 *Defining Common Attributes*

Attribute	Definition
Scalability	The ability to be deployed in an increased network of computers or to accommodate greater throughput without experiencing any architectural or implementation constraints.
Reliability	The frequency with which a service becomes unavailable. Also, the measure of the accuracy with which its task is executed.

Table 2.2 *Defining Common Attributes (continued)*

Attribute	Definition
Availability	The percentage of time a service is available.
Manageability	The degree to which a service needs to be managed or it is possible to manage.
Security	The degree to which a system is protected from deliberate or accidental violation. This ranges from protecting corporate data from access or change through to ensuring system parameters can't be modified.
Capacity	The measure of how much work a system can cope with.
Performance	The speed with which a system executes work.

It should be noted that there are many candidates for being common attributes; the ones chosen here are a set that have seen successful use. The reader is of course free to choose his or her own set of common attributes. The main check should be whether they are a broad and reasonably complete set with respect to the business needs they have to describe. For example, if an organization had an effective set of IT standards then a suitable attribute to include might be Standards, prompting consideration of the degree to which our design adheres to the stated standards.

Evolution of Technical Infrastructure Services

If we stop for a moment and take stock of what we have discussed, it all began with a look from the business needs perspective at how client-server computing was born, then we tracked its development to modern distributed computing, and proposed that by using a set of common attributes the key characteristics of a distributed system can be described. What we have not yet examined is how distributed systems are built and what technical challenges need to be overcome.

Subsequent sections of this chapter analyze more closely the workings of a distributed system by discussing how the various stages of client-server evolution have been addressed by the underlying technology. This underlying technology is described collectively as the *technical infrastructure* and is made up of a set of *technical infrastructure services*.

We shall begin by observing how functionality becomes abstracted from applications over time and migrates into the operating system. In the past application developers would have had to develop code to carry out functions that today are carried out by other components of the system. An example might be that in the early days of IBM compatible PCs, for a high resolution display adapter to be used, a software developer had to write a display handler for the application to use it effectively. Another application on the same computer may well have a slightly different display handler written for the same device. Thus there was duplication of effort leading to increased cost. If we forget the DOS based PC and imagine that the two applications were built to run on a multitasking operating system then we have an even bigger potential problem. If the applications were unaware of each other there would be unpredictable consequences as they both drove the display as if they had exclusive access. If the driver software provided by the display manufacturer or supplier of the operating system had been offered at a more abstract level, providing arbitration for a multitasking operating system, less application specific code would need to be written, leaving the developers to concentrate on the business functionality of the application.

On a computer running a modern operating system it is now possible to purchase the equivalent of the display system in the example with a high level programming library supplied and the operating system arbitrating simultaneous access to the display resources. The hard work of getting the display to work for the application has shifted away from the application developer and into the operating system.

Over time other functionality has migrated from the application to the underlying operating system leaving application developers to focus more on addressing the business functionality and less on managing system resources, as illustrated in Figure 2.5

Figure 2.5 *Growth of System Functionality*

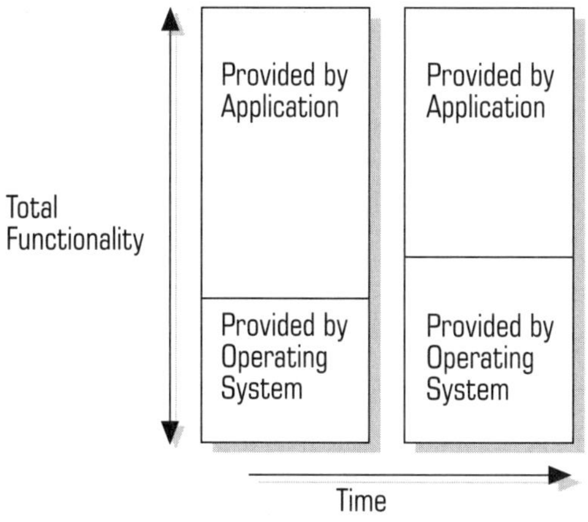

In fact, the example above simplifies the matter somewhat. While functionality has been migrating out of applications, there are two places it has been going. One place is the operating system itself and the other is a middle layer between the operating system and the application. Perhaps one of the most obvious examples of this is the emergence of the database. Whereas once each application created would have had to include the storage mechanism for the application's data, today, a commodity database is used to provide various data storage and manipulation services leaving the designer to concentrate on the format and use of the data.

Examples of services that have migrated from the application to the operating system or a middle layer are shown in Table 2.3.

Table 2.3 *Service Migration*

Service	Migrated to:	
	Operating System	Middle Layer
Transaction Management	✓	✓
Workflow		✓
Data Management		✓
Security	✓	✓
Remote procedure calls	✓	✓
Queuing		✓
Mathematical functions		✓
Threads	✓	
Networking	✓	
File management	✓	
Locks	✓	
Memory management	✓	
Management of IO devices	✓	

Some of the services in the middle layer are now migrating to the operating system and in some cases the operating system already has a version of the service. A service may also be supplied by a third party as an alternative to an existing operating system service for reasons such as full adherence to a standard or additional functionality.

So far the discussion has centered on the case of a single computer but today networked systems are common. Windows NT in particular is designed as a networked operating system offering a wealth of services. The following sections concentrate on those services related to Windows NT.

Figure 2.6
Emergence of Middle Services Layer

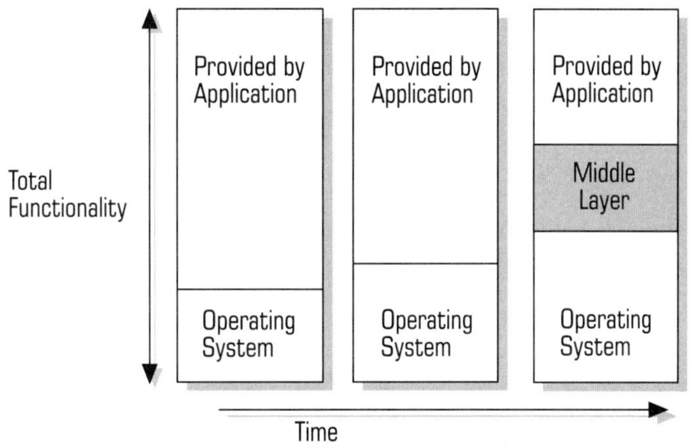

To develop a clear understanding of the nature of a technical infrastructure, we need to consider the emergence of networked applications and the types of services they require. A simple distributed computing architecture is illustrated in Figure 2.7. The application programs communicate with each other using a protocol defined or selected by the application designer and typically private to the application. Such a protocol might support queries against a customer's bank account or instructions to transfer money from one account to another. The application programs interface to the middle layer services through an application programming interface (API).

The middle layer services communicate with each other using protocols that are either based on standards defined in the industry or that are proprietary to a number of vendors. Middle layer service protocols are used to support common functions such as the storing of a file on a remote computer. The network layer represents standard network protocols such as TCP/IP or IPX/SPX which are used to carry the messages of the higher level protocols.

The important point to note about this mechanism is that for any two software components to inter-operate they must implement the same protocols. In most cases, protocols are designed to be computer architecture and operating system independent so computers and operating systems of differing types can still inter-operate. The use of standard protocols and standard interfaces introduces some homogeneity into a heterogeneous network of systems by hiding underlying differences.

Figure 2.7 *General Distributed Computing Architecture*

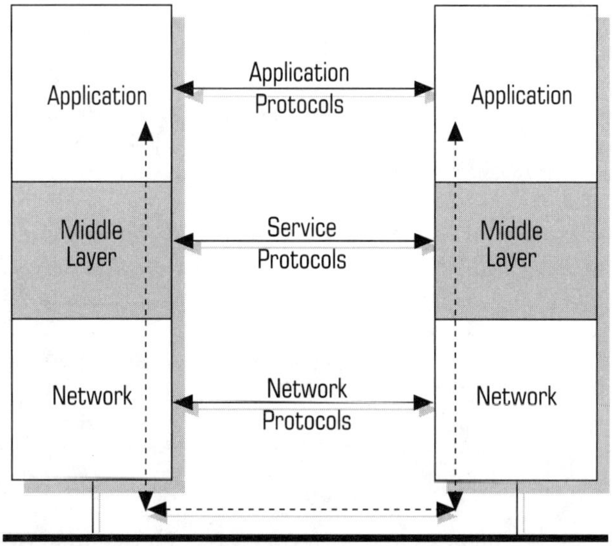

The design of a technical infrastructure focuses on the middle layer and its service protocols.

Supporting Role of Infrastructure

As infrastructure is a fundamental part of a whole system, it follows that its attributes have a strong bearing on the attributes of the whole system. The following examples emphasize how the role of the technical infrastructure is to support the delivery of an application service by ensuring its characteristics meet the business needs.

Infrastructure is all around us in our daily life. One example might be a network of gas stations. We assume they will be there when we need them and we assume they will have the right type of gas along with some means of metering and paying. Thinking a bit further, we assume that the tanker trucks have planned their regular arrivals at the gas stations to maintain the underground tanks and we assume that the refinery has stocks of the gas for the tankers to load up with. At the risk of taking things too far, for the refineries to have produced stocks, they must have been supplied by crude oil from perhaps an international oil field. Our government must maintain a friendly trading relationship with the nation owning the field.

While little to do with IT, the example does illustrate the complex elements underlying the provision of the apparently simple service of issuing gas to a car. The complexities become even more apparent if we examine the example to see how manageable it is if something goes wrong. Perhaps a tanker truck breaks down on the way to a delivery? Its breakdown must be notified, it must be recovered or repaired, and an alternative tanker truck may need to be scheduled urgently. Problems we may encounter are communication delays, lack of resources to provide an alternative vehicle or driver, and cost of recovery.

Another example of infrastructure at work would be the supply of bread to the consumer. Many societies have progressed to the point that the supply of bread is carried out through retail outlets after having been manufactured by bakeries. In the past, families would bake their own bread with the implication being that each undertook to procure the necessary ingredients and each knew the process of manufacture. Now, the purchaser of a loaf of bread in a supermarket has little interest in where the bakery got the ingredients from or how the bread was made. The principle interest of the consumer has now switched to the quality of the bread, its price, and its value for money. The ease of access to the supermarket may also be a factor.

In both these entirely non-IT examples it should be apparent that behind a relatively simple function there can be a complex infrastructure that is delicately tuned for optimum performance. This infrastructure can face many challenges if things go wrong or the pattern of user demand changes. Thus, for a supermarket company to build a chain of supermarkets requires that an entire manufacturing and distribution infrastructure needs to be created to not only supply groceries to the supermarket under normal circumstances but it should be optimized for the environment. For example, it may need to scale, so there would be no point in building a factory to bake 100,000 loaves a week if the anticipated demand will be 200,000 in six months time.

In computing terms, the infrastructure is everything that needs to be in place to support the delivery of an application to a user community in the manner required, reliable, scalable, manageable, and so on. We may immediately think of such things as printing, file transfer and computers. Subsequent sections examine exactly what a technical infrastructure consists of and how these components contribute to a complete distributed system capable of supporting a business.

Introduction to Elements of a Technical Infrastructure

This section looks at how a technical infrastructure can be split into a number of distinct services that support both applications and higher level services. For each service, the basic computing problems presented by operation in a distributed environment are introduced. The services we focus on are:

- Name Resolution
- Time
- File and Print
- Security and Management

Additional services could have been included. However, as an introduction, the objective of this section is to focus on the key services and encourage a way of thinking about them that will be important as we proceed through the project.

Name Resolution

Consider a small courier firm. This firm only took deliveries between different locations in the same town so at the source location the courier needed to know who to pick the package up from and at the destination who to hand it to. Therefore, for each location the courier need only know the name of a person, the street name and building number.

In order to expand, the firm began to offer their service between local towns. At once, the courier needed to know the source town and destination town for each delivery. There are two reasons this is the case, one is compelling and the other mere convenience. The compelling reason is that the courier needs to know which town's *John F Kennedy Avenue* the address refers to. The second reason is for convenience in either picking up the correct town map to find the location or setting off in the right direction.

Computers present the same issues when it comes to naming or addressing things. All the time an application is confined to one computer all it needs to know about locating its data is the directory and file name. Once the application becomes distributed among many computers it has to have some way of identifying in which computer the directory and file name it requires resides. In Microsoft terminology this is the *Universal Naming Convention* (UNC) name which has the form *\\computer-name\share-name\directory-path\file-name*. A more general term for a unique name containing every possible name element is *a fully qualified name.*

The fundamental need is to be able to refer to any resource within the network of computers with a unique name, avoiding any possible conflict or error. The most common way of structuring names to achieve simplicity yet retaining flexibility is in a hierarchical manner. This has the advantage of allowing elements of the fully qualified name to be duplicated in other fully qualified names as long as each in their entirety was unique. The complete set of valid unique fully qualified names is called the *name-space*.

Returning to UNC notation, the following names are all acceptable in a single name-space:

```
\\cpu1\reports\report1.doc
\\cpu1\reports1\report1.doc
\\cpu2\reports\report1.doc
```

We now need to examine what has actually changed in the extension of the name-space from being local and confined to a single computer to one that spans a network of computers. Access to files is governed by the operating system so when asked to open a file it has to translate a text string of the type *directory-path\file-name* into something that uniquely identifies that file to the operating system. Thus, the operating system operates a look-up service to resolve textual names to something more meaningful for the computer. This works very well within the context of a single computer, however if the complete UNC name is used, how is the operating system to locate the remote computer just by using its computer name? It's like having the name of the town the courier should deliver to but no map or instructions how to get there. For a computer to get to another computer it needs to know the network address of the other computer, which is a unique number in the network of computers. Thus, there needs to be a generally available means of translating a computer name into a network address.

A typical solution involves the computer with the need to resolve a name querying another computer on the network that is known to offer a name resolution service. The name resolution service undertakes to map the name to a network address which is then used by the requesting computer to establish a network connection to the computer referenced in the UNC string.

The diagram shows how a name resolution service resolves a name to an address. Computer A must have been configured to know the address of the computer offering the name resolution service, which is 3.0. To find the network address of Computer B it would send a name resolution request containing Computer B's name to the computer with address 3.0. The name resolution service would return the address 3.6. For this to work, the name to address mapping would either have had to be loaded into the name resolution service manually or Computer B would have had to have informed the service of its name and address automatically.

Figure 2.8 *Name Resolution*

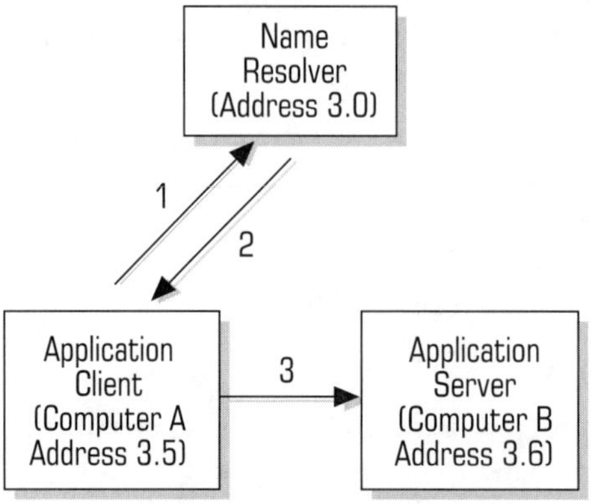

Among the challenges of a name resolution service are the need to cope with computers that have not been designed to register their name to address mapping with the name service, interoperability with other types of name resolution service and the need for accuracy and high availability.

Time

The notion of time is used throughout a computer to synchronize events occurring within both the operating system and applications. Perhaps the events reported from an application are noted in a log file where their chronological order is important for diagnosis purposes. For certain applications the exact sequence of events will be important for legal or regulatory reasons. Thus, a computer runs a clock which is accessible from applications via a programming interface.

In many cases the computer clock only needs to increment a counter on a regular basis to be useful, this being enough to provide relative timings. The clock will normally be binary, counting up in fractions of a second. For it to be useful to a human, the binary number representing the time has to be translated to yield year, month, day, hour, minutes and seconds.

Within one computer, all applications that make use of the clock are guaranteed to have the same time. When extending the concept of a time service to a network of computers a problem arises. While each computer has its own clock they may not all tell the same time, making it difficult to know just by looking at time stamps in a log file or creation dates of files on different computers which log entry or file creation preceded the other. Clearly this could be calculated if the difference in times between the clocks was known. However, this is rarely a practical calculation.

The problem of unsynchronized clocks becomes very important if one considers a hypothetical distributed financial application executing a transaction. A deal is struck on the client computer at t=5 as indicated by the client's clock. A log of the deal is recorded in a file on the client. The client sends a message to a server that proceeds to debit an account, this is logged at t=4 as indicated by the server's computer.

An audit of these log files would show an account being debited with no deal having been struck. There are of course ways round this problem in specific cases; in the example above an improvement could be made by including the client's time stamp in the message to the server, which would then be recorded in the server log file when the debit is made.

Figure 2.9 *Clock Synchronization*

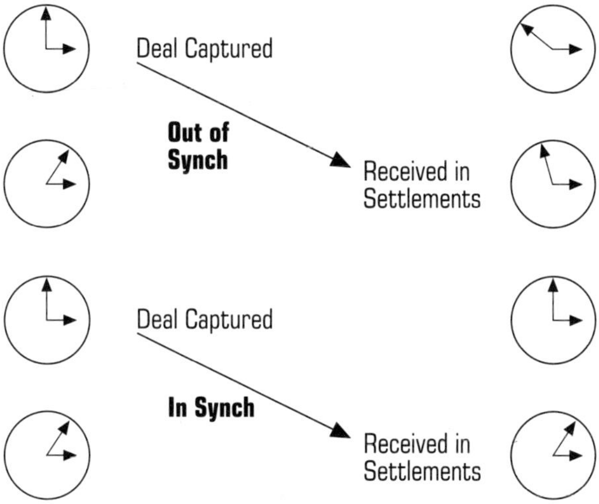

A better solution is to ensure all the clocks on all the computers in a network have the same time. How are they to be synchronized? The common method for clock synchronization involves the use of a time server on the network. The time server responds to requests for the time and is usually a computer with an accurate clock. When it is sufficient to achieve time synchronization across a network, how accurate that clock is is not very important (as long as all clocks have approximately the same degree of accuracy). Sometimes it is important to be extremely accurate and this is when an external time source would be used. Typically the accurate time source is an atomic clock accessed over a dial-up connection initiated by a device attached to the time server computer. There are several accurate, or authoritative time sources available for public use, usually operated by national or governmental agencies.

Upon boot up at regular intervals, a computer might inquire of the time server the current time and using the result, set the clock of its own computer. For both computers to translate this number to the same date and time, they both must have the same concept of when time began. It's no good the time server responding with the number 3473265 seconds, if one computer thinks this is the number of seconds that have passed since the year 1900 and the other thinks it is the number of seconds that have passed since the year 1930. For this reason each "time system" has its own concept of when time began. This is known as an *epoch* time.

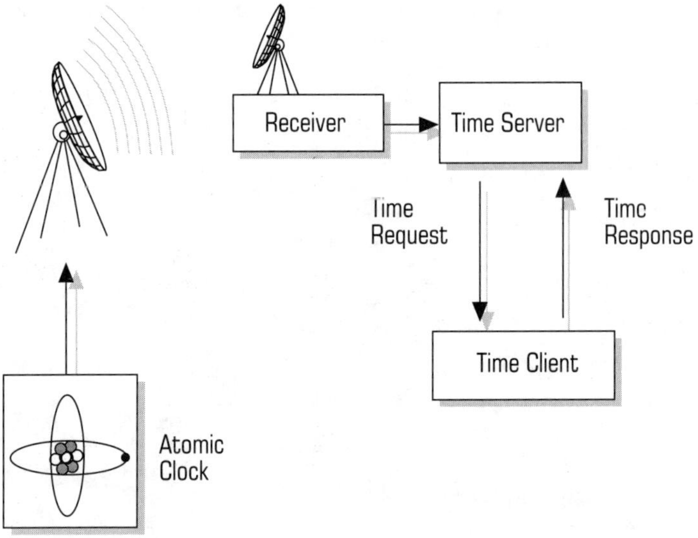

Figure 2.10 *Time Synchronization Using External Source*

The above explanation of how computers synchronize time across a network overlooks one important physical phenomenon which threatens the elegance of the solution. When a computer inquires of a server the current time, the server duly returns a number. The packet containing the number then takes a finite and usually unpredictable amount of time to return to the inquiring computer, the time service client. Thus, the client sets its clock with the value of time, as measured by the time server a fraction of a second ago. Time services will typically implement mechanisms to minimize the impact of this, though an explanation of how they work is beyond the scope of this book.

Files and Printing

Most people are familiar with the concept of a file and print server, hence their treatment here together, though in practice there is no reason to group them. A file server is a computer that has the task of providing storage for files that can be accessed from remote computers. The files can be dedicated to one user or, as is common, the files can be shared, allowing many people to access them. The benefits of a file service are:

- Files can be shared more easily
- Operational overheads are lowered as many files are backed up in one go by an operator, avoiding the reliance on individuals to back up their own computers
- More efficient use of storage media.

Although simple in concept, an example will show some of the basic problems a shared file service can introduce. Continuing the courier firm example (begun in the Name Resolution section), suppose one of the administrators has compiled a list of frequent customers showing their names, addresses, phone numbers, a contact name and discount rate. This document is known to be left in a particular drawer for all to use. On one occasion confusion arises as to who is to make a copy of the list, take the copy away, update it and return it. Worse, the two people who think it is their duty copy it a day apart where in the intervening time a regular customer has defected to another courier firm. Thus, we have two updates being generated, each different. As each updated version is placed in the drawer, the previous version is removed and scrapped. One of the two updated copies will be more up to date than the other, though there is a risk, without co-ordination that this later version, having already been put in the drawer is then replaced by a less up to date version.

This is exactly the type of problem that can arise when two people are editing the same shared file.

Consider additional implications of a shared file service. Suppose that someone removed the frequent customer list from the courier firm's special drawer and accidentally disposed of it. Now, several people are denied access to this list, so prudence would suggest a copy needs to be maintained. Alternatively, the list is returned to the wrong drawer, how are others to find it now? These examples parallel the problems associated with corrupted (or deleted) or relocated files stored on a shared file service.

Thus, in summary, a simple file service has to address the following problems:

- With no arbitration mechanism, two users accessing the same file can corrupt each other's work.

- Single point of failure. If the file server goes down, many users may not be able to work.
- If an application accesses files on a file server how is it to locate them? If the location (UNC) is hard-coded into the application and the location changes the application is broken.

Over time, methods of addressing these shortcomings have been developed. Arbitration of the access to a file by multiple users is usually done by requiring the file system to be informed how a file is being accessed. A user can open a file to read it or write to it. Clearly there is no conflict if many users wish to read a file at the same time, however there is if many users want to write to the file at the same time. This is solved by limiting the number of users able to open the file for write at any time to one. Single points of failure can be avoided by duplicating hardware and methods of keeping identical copies of files, though such solutions are not without cost and complexity. The need to allow a user or application to always refer to a file using the same UNC but to actually change the location of the file, can be achieved using a level of indirection where a logical UNC is mapped by the operating system to a physical UNC.

The advantages of sharing printers are equivalent to those of sharing file storage. By sharing printers we can make a large pool of resources, perhaps many different types of printer, economically available to a large number of people.

Printer sharing is highly scalable as printers can be added to *pools* of identical models to increase capacity and slower printers can be replaced by faster ones, in each case without the user being aware of anything other than an increase in service. The use of printer pools also enhances the overall availability of a shared printer implementation through the use of redundant devices. The failure of the print server computers themselves can be mitigated by using redundant computers to serve the same or equivalent printers.

As printers differ they all require their own specific program to turn a word processor document, spreadsheet or some other file type into a printable file. This program is called a printer driver and typically resides on the computer creating the print job for sending to a server. Thus, the print client needs to have a suitable driver for the target printing device on the server. Management of this situation can get difficult as the client population grows and the diversity of printers in use increases. Management of the printer devices themselves can also present issues in a large population as manual intervention is sometimes essential.

Security and Management

The topic of security has many aspects including data access control, physical system security, and application access. In this section we shall focus on computer resource access control where a resource might be a file, printer, computer or even an administrative utility.

The usual approach to computer resource access control is to treat the process in two parts. The first part is user authentication, where upon submission of a correct username and a password combination to the computer operating system the user is logged on and granted some sort of identifier. The second part is authorization where a user is either granted or denied access to a requested resource. Typically the identifier is compared against a list on the resource, maintained by the operating system, detailing who gets what level of access. This list is often referred to as an *access control list*. Using this mechanism, one user may, for example, only be able to submit files to a printer while another might be able to perform operations on the printer device, depending on the access control list on the operating system printer resource.

The management of computer resources is thus carried out by users who have been granted sufficient rights to carry out management activities such as adding a user or upgrading the operating system. The corollary to this is that the domain of management extends as far as the security domain supplied by the set of operating systems.

All the time computers were considered as standalone systems, there was a security and management domain per computer. As the need for users on one computer to access resources on another arose out of the development of client-server computing there became a need to extend the security domain to avoid the need for logging on to each computer involved. This was accompanied by a need to extend the management domain to make it easier to manage a set of computers.

In general terms the needs are:

1. How to control access to resources in an efficient, network transparent manner, regardless of where they are located.
2. How to manage any computer remotely without needing to re-logon.

The solution to the first need is to allow people to logon to a network of systems instead of just logging on to one computer. To do this requires a single user account database either shared or replicated throughout a set of computers. Extending the security domain like this means the management domain is also effectively extended, partially satisfying the second need. To complete the picture it is necessary for administrative tools to be true client-server applications allowing the user to work at one computer and manage several remote computers.

Defining a Technical Infrastructure

A definition of what a technical infrastructure is can help clarify our approach to its design and our understanding of its role in a complete system. We stated earlier in this chapter that a set of infrastructure services can be collectively referred to as a technical infrastructure. However, the discussion also noted that the services comprising a technical infrastructure are always changing, with new ones emerging from applications and, after a time, disappearing in to the operating system.

For this reason, the most appropriate way to define a technical infrastructure is to define what a technical infrastructure service is. That way, the definition will stand the test of time, while the constituents of the technical infrastructure may change. The remaining sections of this chapter propose a definition for a technical infrastructure service and for the purpose of this book, draw up a list of services typically found in a current Windows NT technical infrastructure.

Categories of Service

A major step towards a definition of a technical infrastructure service is to draw a distinction between it and another type of service, the *application* infrastructure service. The rationale for this distinction is that the configuration of an application infrastructure service is closely related to the design of the application it is there to serve, whereas the configuration of a technical infrastructure service is independent of applications.

Figure 2.11 *Application and Technical Infrastructure Service Layers*

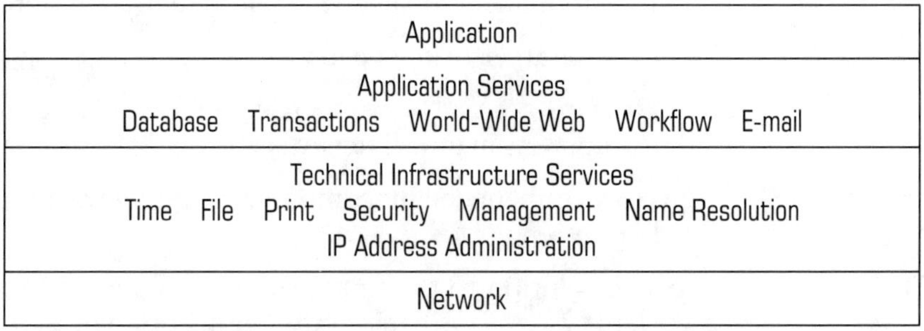

Figure 2.11 makes the distinction apparent. In general, an application will directly use the application services which in turn will use the infrastructure services. Another way of looking at it is to say that the infrastructure services provide important capabilities for building a dis-

tributed application. Application services represent the fertile ground where functionality is being abstracted from the applications to appear as new application services and application service functionality is migrating out into an infrastructure service.

The higher level services will, as the architecture diagram illustrates, make use of the lower level services. It is usual for one high level service to make use of a number of the lower level services.

Application Services

Let us clarify what we mean by an application service. Most business applications use one of three styles to address a business problem:

- Data
- Transactions
- Messages

Each one reflects the fundamental nature of a business need. For example, a management information system will likely be data oriented, a ticket reservation system would be transactional and an insurance claims processing system, messaging based.

Application Infrastructure Services provide the basic general purpose interfaces to support these processing styles. The data service would provide transparent access to any source of data, the transactional service would provide two-phase commit, preferably across a number of resource managers and the messaging service would provide access to e-mail and workflow services.

To define an application service we can say that it must satisfy these criteria:

- Can express application logic or manage application data
- Configuration of the service in a network is determined directly by the needs of an application
- Is available through an Application Programming Interface

Consideration of application services is beyond the scope of this book as it impinges on application design.

Technical Infrastructure Services

We can now define a technical infrastructure service as satisfying these criteria:

- Doesn't express any application logic or manage any application data
- The service protocol is transparent to the calling program
- Is available through an Application Programming Interface

From the perspective of a technical infrastructure service, it matters little whether it is being used directly by an application or indirectly via an application service.

A Windows NT Based Technical Infrastructure

Having defined a technical infrastructure in terms of generic services we can list the typical technologies found in one based on Windows NT:

Table 2.4 *Windows NT and Related Technical Infrastructure Services*

Service	Implementation
Naming	Windows Internet Naming Service (WINS) Distributed Name Service (DNS)
Network	TCP/IP, DHCP, NetBEUI, IPX/SPX
Time	Windows NT Time Service Network Time Protocol (NTP)
File	LAN Manager Network File Service (NFS) NetWare
Print	Windows NT Print Services, UNIX Print Services
Security	Windows NT Domains
Management	Windows NT Domains

The Ones That Got Away

As distributed computing is an evolving landscape, the technologies which are available as technical infrastructure services will change. Indeed, at any point in time, views will differ regarding which technologies can be treated as technical infrastructure services.

For example, it might be argued that e-mail or Web technology should have been included as it satisfies in the most part our definition of a technical infrastructure service. The reader is free to make up his or her own mind which services comprise a technical infrastructure. The author chose a common, core set, known to be broadly applicable.

Summary

In the past an application simply ran on a standalone computer with access to the various resources being managed by the operating system. What functionality wasn't supplied by the operating system was supplied by the application. It was common for applications to contain a large portion of code to cope with non-business processing, the provision of basic functionality such as data management and input/output.

Over time, common functionality has been abstracted out of applications into generally available services and tools. This process was accelerated by the introduction of networked applications, which have come to be known as client-server applications.

The set of services commonly found in a distributed computing environment now form a significant part of the overall delivery of the application, to the extent that when an application needs to be resilient, the services it depends on need to match that resilience. To allow different distributed computing services to be characterized in a way that describes how well they meet a business need, the use of common attributes was proposed.

A technical infrastructure was defined as a set of services which were completely independent of business logic or business data. These services were shown as distinct from application services, which provide the basis for building the business logic or business data into an application.

3

Running the Project

A successfully completed project may lead to praise for the project team, however, a failed project will lead to criticism of the project manager. Effective techniques for managing a team of people towards an objective will pay dividends by assisting in the identification and management of issues that can cause failure.

Many of the tasks involved in planning, designing and building a technical infrastructure are common from one project to the next, as are the risks and dependencies. Variations arise when we consider resourcing, interfaces with other groups and logistical matters.

The purpose of this chapter is to describe the basic roles, responsibilities and processes involved in the successful management of a typical technical infrastructure project. It will not teach a professional project manager anything new about project management and neither does it propose a project methodology.

Structure of Chapter

The chapter is structured as follows:

Table 3.1 *Structure of Chapter 3*

Topic	Contents
Project Components	The basic components of a project that allow the work to be structured, progress monitored, resources estimated, dependencies identified and risks managed are introduced.
Managing for Success	Steps are recommended for ensuring the project is perceived as successful. Among them are the way people need to be kept informed and the correct identification of the customer to the project.

Table 3.1 *Structure of Chapter 3 (continued)*

Topic	Contents
Project Administration	A project will eventually acquire its own documentation, commercial contracts, procedures and routine events. The responsibility for administering these aspects of a project are outlined as tasks for a project administration function.
Getting Started	Getting a project begun can be awkward. Advice is given for getting the project off to a good start.
Using Consultants	Consultants are retained to satisfy a short term demand for resources and experience. This section examines the pros and cons of different ways of using consultants.
Project Documentation	Unless considered in advance, project documentation can be a project casualty. Recommendations are put forward for: ▪ The documents that need to be produced ▪ How to map content to a document

Project Components

While there are several established project methodologies in use, most have the following basic concepts in common:

- **Elements of Work**—the way the work involved in a project can be repeatedly broken down into smaller, more manageable parts.
- **Milestones**—the way project progress can be measured using a series of planned accomplishments.
- **Dependencies**—is the need for something external or internal to the project to occur for an element of project work to be able to proceed.
- **Risks**—things that threaten quality, timescales or budget.

Each of these concepts is examined below.

Elements of Work

To understand a project it is useful to break it down into a sequence of logical stages or *phases*. Attention can then be focused on the individual phases and the work that needs to be done within them. Different project methodologies advocate basic phases that differ little except in name. The phases used in the case study technical infrastructure project throughout this book are visible on the project roadmap diagram in the introductory chapter. They are:

- Design preparation
- Design
- Implementation preparation
- Implementation

Activities are the units of a project that are the next level down from phases. A well chosen activity will have a natural and well defined objective. It will also have a low number of links to other activities and will be straightforward to manage as a single exercise. Activities can be broken down into smaller units of work called *tasks*. This is particularly useful if the activity has a number of elements to it or is being undertaken by several people. We will use the structure in Table 3.2 to describe both activities and tasks.

Table 3.2 *Activity and Task Description Definition*

Feature	Overview
Activity or Task Overview	This should be a summary of what needs to be carried out for this activity or task.
Prerequisites	Everything that has to be in place before it can start.
Deliverable	It might be a document, a relationship or a piece of physical infrastructure.
Resources	Who is going to work on the activity/task, when and for how long.
Start/Finish	When the activity/task starts and when it finishes. This represents the elapsed time.
Activity or Task Owner	Who is responsible for the deliverable from this activity/task. This person also provides the project manager with estimates of resources needed to complete activity.
Deliverable Sign-off Authority	This is this person who is interested in the deliverable and formally accepts it.
Reviewers	These are the people who are going to review progress and deliverables at various stages. They could be other members of the project team, someone designated as a technical design authority or any other party with a valued opinion.

Deliverables

An activity or task is not worth doing unless it produces something that contributes to the project. That something is termed a deliverable and can take many forms. It could be a CD-ROM with a software kit on it or it could be a document describing a design. It should always be possible to identify a deliverable for an activity.

Deliverables can help us ensure that there is value to a piece of work. They can also help us know when an activity or task is complete, as the risk of not knowing can cause the continued commitment of resources beyond the point where they are necessary. When the deliverable is complete, so should the activity be. Many of the activities and tasks in the MBI case study plan (see Chapter 4, Project Planning) have documentation as a deliverable.

The activity or task owner is responsible for production of the deliverable.

Sign-off

In cases where there is a contractual style of arrangement the process of the recipient or customer signing-off a deliverable is a declaration that both parties agree that task or activity is complete. If contractors are being used this can be the trigger for payment.

Even if contractors are not involved, the sign-off is an essential tool for managing commitment to a project and ensuring all parties are satisfied.

Milestones

Milestones are key events that represent achievements along the route to project completion. Their main purpose is to act as an indicator of progress but they also have a powerful psychological effect. Milestones can be used to focus a project team on an objective, raising motivation and, when achieved, instill a sense of satisfaction.

Correct identification of milestones can, therefore, have an important effect on the running of a project. First, they must be realistically achievable or people will get disenchanted through a sense of failure. Second, they must be sufficiently near in terms of time, for people to not mentally set them aside for later, causing a last minute panic.

As a rule of thumb, a project lasting ten weeks would have milestones set at weekly intervals. A project lasting six months would use monthly or two-weekly intervals. A project of a year would set milestones a month apart.

It would be normal to identify a milestone with every activity or task deliverable, though following on from the observations just made additional milestones may be identified if it is convenient. The characteristics of a good milestone are:

- It has an owner
- It occurs on a certain date
- It must be possible to state whether the milestone has been achieved or not
- A deliverable is produced upon achievement of the milestone.

Dependencies

A prerequisite may need to be satisfied before an activity can start. This prerequisite will be a deliverable from another activity or some agency external to the project. The timely satisfaction of prerequisites is clearly important in determining the smooth progress of work. In this way project activities are related to each other and dependencies are introduced.

Example dependencies are:

- The laboratory testing cannot proceed until the design document is complete.
- Installation cannot begin until the new computers have been delivered.

Another important type of dependency is the availability of people. It is quite common to find that an activity can be held up through the non-availability of a suitably skilled person. Perhaps they are on vacation or otherwise engaged in another of the project activities.

The important thing about dependencies is that they are the links through which a delay in one activity can have a corresponding effect on other activities. Delays cost money as they cause idle resources, so we should always try to minimize the effect a dependency has on our use of resources and on the project as a whole. It is for this reason we should add contingency time to our estimates for when a deliverable can be made available. In other words, give the activity longer than an "expert" might think it would take.

A Gantt chart is an effective tool for developing an understanding of the effect different dependencies will have on the overall resource utilization of a project. A Gantt chart for the MBI project is shown in Appendix D.

Risks

A risk is anything that is outside the direct control of the project team that could adversely impact the project. For example, a particular project may involve use of a recently released software product to gain access to certain important new features, the risk is that there might be problems with this new version that will take unplanned time to overcome. Many risks can of course be anticipated, in which case their potential impact can often be lowered by planning for some contingency time or an alternate approach.

A risk is essentially a gamble. If the gamble comes off, everything is fine, if it doesn't, the unwanted outcome will immediately threaten the project by demanding more time and resources than planned.

The fact that coping with a risk may involve extra time and resources means risky activities should not be put on the critical path of the project. It is also worth considering carrying out risky activities early in the project plan to allow more scope for recovery if things should go wrong.

Risks should be identified at the start of the project and constantly re-evaluated as circumstances change. To allow us to manage a reduction in risk we should aim to record the following information about each risk identified:

1. Its likelihood of occurring. A good way to do this is to assign it a rating of high, medium or low.
2. Its impact, should it occur. This helps us judge how important the risk is. Again, rate the effect of the impact high, medium or low.
3. What is to be done to lower or remove the risk. This will be in the form of a strategy for action. It is advisable to assign responsibility to someone for executing this strategy.
4. What is to be done should the risk occur. This is the contingency plan and will describe how the project should recover from such an occurrence.

Experience will alert you to a number of risks. To identify the rest it is helpful to consult other people involved in the project and to think through the project from start to finish. Look for risks where there are dependencies on other parties or assumptions are being made.

Managing for Success

Managing a project has a strong prescriptive side to it in that there are well understood processes to carry out, many of which are described in this chapter. However, project management has another side to it born out of the responsibility a project manager carries, that of the success of the project.

A project is all about change and change in an organization brings new responsibilities for some people and removes them from others. It crosses line management boundaries and compels the project manager to operate in the murky world of corporate politics. Thus, to achieve success, the project manager has to be politically adept.

Faced with the likelihood that requirements will change, people's ideas will change and there will probably be at least one organizational re-structuring during its lifecycle, the project manager needs to organize the project to ensure it doesn't fall victim to these strong currents.

Experience pays the most dividends when up against odds such as these. However there are a few things every project manager should do to manage the success of their project:

- identify who the customers are
- set expectations accurately
- create the project team carefully
- manage at the task level
- keep people informed.

We look at these aspects in the following sections.

Who is the Customer?

A project to replace the technical infrastructure has the potential to impact many areas of IT in an organization. We can safely assume someone decided the project needed doing and is paying for it. We can also assume someone will have to live with the result and someone else will have to support it. It is worth giving some thought to who it is we are trying to satisfy out of the list of interested parties. Are some interests more important than others? If we can work out who we are trying to please we can begin to plan for their satisfaction and our success.

From the IT department's perspective, such a project will of course improve the infrastructure. It will be likely to represent a major technological step forward so can only be seen as a good thing.

From a support team's perspective it may bring opportunities to gain experience in the latest technology. It may also bring many support headaches as the new infrastructure settles in. Over time, the support team would be looking to see a new technical infrastructure bring benefits in terms of supporting more users with the same number of support staff, or bringing the time to fix figures down. The new technical infrastructure should be more reliable and more manageable.

Users have no need to be aware of the technical infrastructure and so should be indifferent to its upgrade or replacement. Indeed, we should endeavor to make any changes at this level transparent to the user community. If anything is noticed we should ensure it is an improvement. For example, a user community being upgraded from Windows 3.*x* to Windows NT will notice a few basic improvements such as the less frequent need to reboot out of a hang. However, we should be aware that these people are not going to thank the technical infrastructure project for anything, in fact the only time they will comment is if they get inconvenienced in any way.

The business at one level will have a simple view of technical infrastructure which is that it is there to enable the delivery of business applications. This may include e-mail or spreadsheets but certainly the key applications necessary for the corporation to carry out its business. At another level we may hope for a view that says the technical infrastructure can have some strategic value as a platform for building enterprise-wide applications quickly and running them reliably and cheaply.

The application developers will be interested in the technical infrastructure as a means to deliver their application. They will understand the technology and are the group least likely to be inconvenienced by its installation.

This all seems rather negative but it does emphasize the need for the project to recognize the diverse interests at work in the target environment. We should plan to minimize any problems that might ensue and accept that we are unlikely to be perceived as heroes on this project.

Set Expectations Correctly

It is critical that the technical infrastructure project explains exactly:

- What it will be doing
- Who will be impacted and when
- What people will end up with

It is also important that the project keep explaining these things again and again. It is too easy for memories to fade, and expectations to drift.

If expectations aren't set with careful explanations, people will make inaccurate assumptions about what your project is planning to deliver, which will only become apparent when it is too late. Careful judgment is also required to avoid over commitment and hence expectations set in excess of what can be delivered. In other words, be careful not to set yourself up for failure.

Include People

At some point in the project, usually in the run up to installation, co-operation of the interested parties will be needed to make sure everything goes smoothly. In particular, we need the people who have to sign-off the project to feel able to do so without hesitation, or our project could slip and we will end up failing.

Reasons not to co-operate might be that the system doesn't work as advertised or perhaps it does work but it is clear things could have been done differently in some areas. If the system doesn't work then we have made a serious mistake and we shouldn't expect sign-off. If, however, we have made decisions about matters that were not prescribed in the specification and not consulted those who would be affected by these decisions then we have stacked up problems for ourselves. It is often difficult accepting decisions that have been made on your behalf, particularly if you feel that the decisions have been made by someone not qualified to make them.

It is advisable to include representatives from each interested party on the project team and consult them to ensure all decisions made that might affect their interests are supported. In this way we can avoid surprises near the end of the project when things are more costly to fix.

Having said all that, it may be that the consultative approach outlined as a solution does not fit with the culture of the corporation. Perhaps certain affected parties have to accept what they are delivered. In some cases, it can be very difficult to gain an effective contribution from the business as a result of mistrust instilled through earlier projects. Whatever the culture of an organization, the need to bring other people along into the decision making process cannot be understated.

Who Should be Included?

There are two main reasons why additional people would need to be included in the project. One is that they have expertise or experience to impart and the other is that their co-operation is needed. The first reason usually looks after itself if the core project team has been identified appropriately. The second reason has political overtones which need to be accounted for by the project manager in the evaluation of who should be included in the project.

Table 3.3 *Organizational Groups and Their Responsibilities*

Responsibility	Group	Potential Contribution
Security (physical and electronic)	IT Security	Guidance on corporate security standards (e.g., minimum password length, etc.).
Processing support	IT Operations	IT Operations will end up running the system. Their co-operation with its deployment is clearly important.
Application support and platform support	IT Support	This group will end up supporting the infrastructure. This group needs to be prepared for a smooth handover of support from engineering once the system is installed.
Software quality	Change Control	Processes for managing change control and software release procedures.
Application development	Software Development	Assistance with migrating applications to the new infrastructure.
Support of cabling, telephones, network backbone, routers, hubs, etc.	Networks	Corporate WAN topology information, testing WAN and LAN traffic, and diagnosing network related problems.
Physical infrastructure	Facilities	Making space for the laboratory and planning the machine room environment.
Hardware and software purchasing	IT Purchasing	Getting a good deal. Knowledge of corporate supply policies such as preferred vendors. Supply of equipment to overseas locations.

As organizations vary in size they will each have the various routine functions allocated to different groups with different responsibilities. For example, a small company may employ an odd job person who does everything from hanging a whiteboard to delivering the mail. The larger organization may employ a team to attend to office furniture and a small army to deliver the mail. Thus, generalizing who needs to be involved, in terms of the groups they work for can be difficult. Table

3.3 makes some suggestions for who needs to be involved, focusing on the responsibilities they and have and the contribution they might make.

Creating Project Team Structure

The creation of a project team will involve getting three key things right:

- A good mix of people who are able to work together
- An appropriate project team structure
- Clear identification of people's roles and responsibilities.

Achieving a good mix of people can only be done based on experience. Unfortunately, choosing people for a project based on whether they can work together effectively or not is not practical as options will usually be limited.

Choosing an appropriate project team structure will have a significant effect on the chances of success. Two basic structures are illustrated in the second of the two following sections.

Clear identification of people's roles and responsibilities within the project structure is also critical. This allows people to operate more effectively when these parameters are fully understood.

It is difficult to be prescriptive about creating a project team structure because so many unquantifiable factors have a bearing on it. The recommended approach is to begin by considering a standard project team structure and its associated roles and responsibilities then base the rest on experience.

To build on experience review some projects you have been involved with or have observed in terms of the roles and responsibilities people adopted, the project team structure and how successful they were. Try to identify their successes and failures.

Learning from Other Projects

It is easier to learn from where projects have failed than where they have succeeded. This section sketches out three scenarios that illustrate some of the common ways projects go out of control or fail.

Example 1

The project team in this example comprises many groups all with different but related responsibilities. Project management is weak and tends more towards project administration. There is no one with formal responsibility for the technical lead but there is an individual who is very strong technically who sees the project as a chance to realize their own technical objectives.

The project begins to slip very early on as there is constant re-evaluation and re-assignment of project tasks on a minor scale between groups. Much time is spent analyzing what might need to be done and little time spent actually doing. The mechanism for getting something agreed is undefined and so progress stagnates.

This project is never going to complete on time and under budget at this rate. So what is wrong? Well, there are some observations that can be made:

- This sort of situation will go on until the first or second serious deadline is missed or someone works out that the budget will over-run far too early. Strong project management should ensure the contributors are working to realistic timescales for the different phases of the project. Requests for regular re-assessments of time needed to complete activities should reveal a slipping project earlier than might otherwise be apparent.
- Someone without authority is influencing the project to serve their own agenda. This agenda has nothing to do with project deadlines or budgets and can only cause wasted effort and delay.
- When the project does get going, there will be many issues to resolve between the different project groups as there is a lack of intellectual cohesion which could have been present had the project manager assigned a solution architect.
- Issues raised will in many cases be late in getting resolved through lack of effective project management.

The case for strong project management is clear in this example. Less clear is what can be done about the lack of technical progress. One suggestion already mentioned might be to install someone as the solution architect for the whole project. This person would be responsible for the technical integrity of the solution and would act as an intellectual focus for all matters technical. This alone is not enough to guarantee progress. The solution architect needs to have personal traits that include leadership and the desire to achieve an end result.

Example 2

The project team has been populated by the best technical brains the corporation has at its disposal. The collective mentality is "just do it."

Most of the individuals have been experimenting with Windows NT for some time, having taken part in numerous beta test programs. There are already several Windows NT domains in use.

Progress is very fast, though many technical aspects of the project change quickly. There is some documentation but it is out of date almost as soon as it is written due to the high pace of change. Decisions are made with a view to creating the most technically elegant solution.

In this type of project it is anyone's guess what will be delivered to the users. They will almost certainly receive something that works though with a few quirks. A project for updating the infrastructure will need to be instigated straight away to cope with a functionality shortfall.

What went wrong this time? Did anything go wrong at all?

Let's answer the second question first. From one perspective, the project can be considered a success. It delivered something quickly and took the head of steam out of the pressure on the IT department to satisfy users by supplying Windows NT.

From another perspective, it may be that:

- No one is really sure what was installed
- Of the 50 workstations installed, 35 were found to have unique installations (differing service pack levels, different drivers, non-standard names, etc.)
- Fault calls take longer to fix because of the non-standard environment
- The support department didn't have time to get trained on Windows NT resulting in a fix to one problem storing up another for later
- As a result of the diverse configurations, the system failed its audit
- A user could delete all system files on the application server
- Analysis has shown that an upgrade is impractical and the next version of the infrastructure needs to be a complete new installation.

The list could go on. The project wasn't as successful as it could have been but would you bet your business on it? In this example no one was looking after the interests of the support organization and no one was ensuring that the end users got exactly what they wanted.

Example 3

The project team consists of a line manager with no experience of Windows NT and two technicians, both reasonably familiar with Windows NT though this is their first project to deploy it into a business critical environment. In fact, it is not treated as a project by anyone involved.

The main characteristic of this "project" is the prolonged discussion over technical design matters between the two technicians. Resolution is based on technical elegance and strength of character. The manager is not very familiar with Windows NT and so can't contribute to their resolution. The technicians are unable to articulate in a way the manager can understand, what the implications of each design option are.

This situation can result in stalemate but it can also result in design decisions being made without taking into account all factors. For example, the technicians on this project may be arguing over whether or not to provide local backup domain controllers from the master domain, ignoring, or unaware of the importance of speedy login and access to resources by users in remote locations connected over slow WAN links.

It would seem clear from this example that there should have been someone whose job it was to make sure design decisions took account of all factors, particularly those of the business. This person may have been a technically aware project manager or perhaps a solution architect capable of bridging the divide between technology and business.

Project management theory points to the need to have a balanced team with different individuals contributing different qualities. In total, these qualities maximize the chance of a successful project.

Finally, in most successful projects there will be one or two people whose contributions stand out as exceptional. With hindsight much credit for the project's success can be laid at the feet of these few people. Supporting people like this on a project, while recognizing their possible shortcomings can be a recipe for success.

Project Team Structure

In this section we will look at a typical project team structure and how, in a large scale design and implementation, several individual projects are brought together under a program structure. In the simple project team structure shown (Figure 3.1) the project manager is accountable to a steering committee, reflecting the fact that the project is sponsored by the business. The solution architect would work with the project manager assisting in the planning function and also providing technical leadership for the design and development activities.

Figure 3.1 *Simple Technical Infrastructure Project Team Structure*

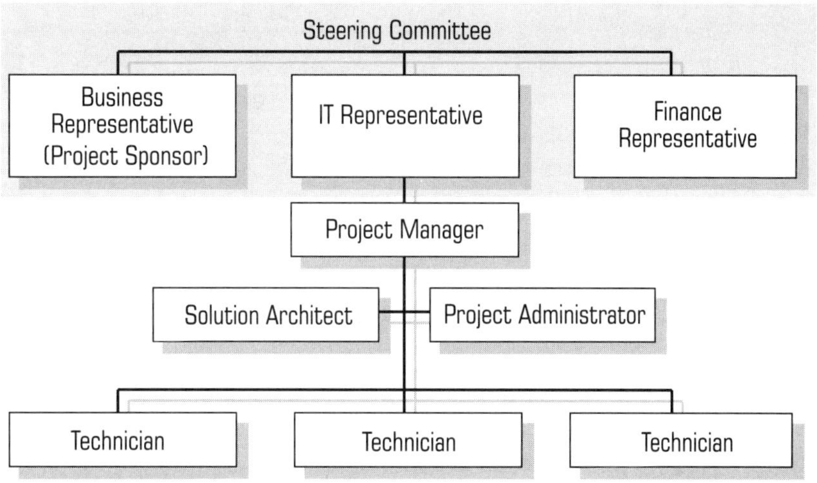

The technical infrastructure project may be running in parallel with other projects to:

- Port applications to the new technical infrastructure platform
- Install seating and desks
- Install/upgrade the network
- Application development for the new technical infrastructure

In such circumstances the logical structure of the whole program would look like Figure 3.2.

The program manager has the responsibility for managing the combined timescales and budgets for all sub-projects. This person depends upon the quality of the information reported by the project managers.

The role of technical design authority is that of independent consultation and review. This would normally be a person who has acknowledged authority in the technical domain of the project. Not having any project task responsibility, their expertise is exploited in design review meetings and the review of documentation.

For a modest sized project having a separate individual for each of the roles identified in the structure diagrams, particularly the program team structure, would be unnecessary. The important thing is that the roles are understood and executed by someone. For example, the same individual might carry out both the role of project manager for the network project and at the same time the role of program manager.

Figure 3.2 *Simple Program Structure*

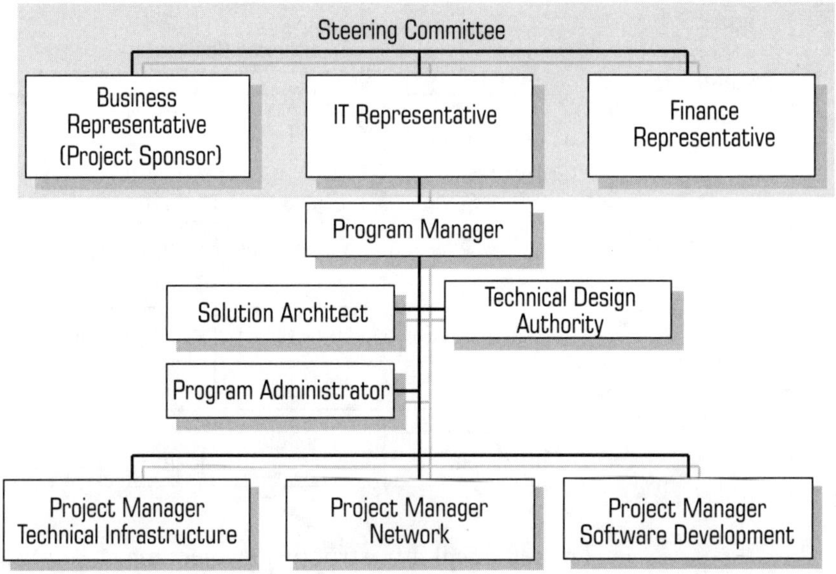

The responsibilities associated with the roles we have identified so far are listed in Table 3.4 along with those of some important supporting roles.

Table 3.4 *Roles and Responsibilities*

Role	Responsibilities
Project Manager	▪ The deliverables of the project ▪ Reporting to the steering committee ▪ Identification and management of risks ▪ Budget control ▪ Resourcing ▪ Day to day management of subcontractors ▪ Day to day monitoring of allocated tasks ▪ Allocation of tasks to individuals
Program Manager	▪ Program strategy ▪ Coordination of all subordinate projects ▪ Project management methodology ▪ Program reports to steering committee ▪ Management of subcontractors
Technical Design Authority	▪ Expert design input ▪ Expert review of documentation content

Table 3.4 *Roles and Responsibilities (continued)*

Role	Responsibilities
Solution Architect	▪ The overall technical integrity of the solution ▪ Assist the project manager in the identification of tasks, risks and milestones ▪ Team leading technicians
Technician	▪ Execution of technical design and development tasks
Quality Manager	▪ The overall quality of the solution ▪ Effective communication with other groups ▪ Adherence to project processes
Support Representative	▪ Reviews documents for support implications
Business Analyst	▪ Ensures business needs are met
User Representative	▪ Reviews plans and documents for user implications ▪ Ensures user's interests are represented at all stages of the project ▪ Sign-off of final system
Project Administrator	▪ Collation of project documentation ▪ Presentation, grammar and consistent style of project documentation ▪ Taking and circulating meeting minutes ▪ Circulation of meeting agendas

Assigning Tasks

The nature of the design phase and to a greater extent the implementation preparation phase is such that the project is peaking in number of people and the pace of development is greatest. Progress will be visible on a daily basis and problems can bring everything to a halt very quickly. It is therefore important to put in place a mechanism for monitoring progress that is practical for the task.

The quantity and frequency of events makes it very difficult to use a Gantt chart style project management tool as it can take too long to bring it up to date. It is also not very easy to use a Gantt chart to illustrate progress clearly. The Gantt chart is best reserved for planning work such as estimating timescales and determining resource requirements. It can also be useful as a prop for discussing contingency arrangements and for coordinating with other projects.

The most practical method of managing progress in these two phases of the project is the task list. Each person on the project should be given a task list by the solution architect or project manager that makes it very clear what their responsibilities are. A section from an example task list is illustrated in Table 3.5 showing task number, priority, description, expected completion date and actual completion date.

Table 3.5 *Task List*

Name: Joe Technician				
#	**Priority**	**Description**	**Planned**	**Actual**
1	2	Create SMS package for TopSoftware V7.5	12/12/97	
2	2	Add printer connections to logon script	12/12/97	
3	3	Document logon script logic flow	4/1/98	

Keeping People Informed

Underlying the efforts we need to make to include the interests of those not directly involved in the project should be good communications. This means accurate and speedy imparting of project information to make sure:

- No one feels left out.
- No one is left out.
- No one has a surprise. Some people react very badly to surprises!
- People are up to date and in a position to contribute to the whole project.
- No one can say "You didn't tell me that was happening..."

To address these points it is necessary to target the information to the recipient and proactively bring it to their attention. That means focused reports distributed by internal post or e-mail. Merely placing the reports on a Web page or public directory will not be sufficient as it depends on people making the effort to regularly check for new information.

Project Administration

The administration of a project is a responsibility that is split between the project manager and a dedicated project administrator. Project administration concerns itself with the mechanics of a project, those aspects that are unrelated to the project content. The purpose of project administration is to make sure everyone knows what is going on around them, that they have a mechanism for formally raising issues and resolving them and that all project activity is recorded and indexed.

Additional project administration responsibilities may include reviewing project documentation for grammar, standards of production, and conformity to a chosen style. This complements the expert review which examines the content of the documentation. We will examine the following project administration activities:

- Reporting on project progress
- Organizing and running regular meetings
- Creating and publicizing meeting agendas
- Taking and publishing minutes
- Issue management
- Project team communications
- Running a document library

Reporting

A formal process, reporting has two principle purposes:

- To inform
- To record

Regular written reporting should be used when one party has obligations to the other. For example, a subcontractor should submit a regular written report on progress to the customer. In the case of a technical infrastructure project, the project manager would issue written reports to the project sponsor and program manager. This would normally be enough in a straightforward project. If, however, there are other parties that need to be kept informed then additional tailored reports may be produced. Table 3.6 outlines the structure of a project manager's report.

Table 3.6 *Project Manager's Report to Program Manager*

Section	Explanation
Executive Summary	This should be no longer than one page and should summarize the key points of the rest of the report.
Progress this reporting period	Summarize the progress made since the last report was submitted. This should be put in the context of the overall project plan with a statement on whether the progress is ahead, on or behind schedule. For each activity, there should be a new estimate for when it will be completed. Reasons for variance should be given.

Table 3.6 *Project Manager's Report to Program Manager (continued)*

Section	Explanation
Progress to date	A summary of the progress since the start of the project. Should record significant milestones achieved and past reasons for variance from the plan.
Finances	Progress against budgeted expenditure.
Open issues	All currently open issues should be reported here. For each issue there should be a description of its impact, who owns its resolution and steps being taken to resolve it.
Closed issues	A summary list of all issues closed. This list need only include the issue, its resolution and date of resolution.
Changes this reporting period	Changes to the project plan should be summarized. These may include revised estimates to completion, substitution of contractors, revised deadlines, new resources and so on.
Changes to date	Major changes that have occurred since the project began must be listed along with a brief description of their effect on the project.
Resource Utilization	For each individual used on the project there should be a record of how much time they have spent, how much time they planned to spend, and how much time will be required of them for completion.

Regular Meetings

The need to have project meetings can be seen by some as an unnecessary overhead and it is perhaps true that many project meetings are a waste of time because there is no clear understanding of what they should achieve. A well planned project meeting can be used to:

- Gain consensus for decisions
- Challenge assumptions
- Address issues
- Review performance
- Verbally update people
- Report progress

Care should be taken not to allow the meeting to be a substitute for written progress reports. To maintain its value it should focus on those things that benefit from human interaction and discussion. On the other hand, the project meeting is not the place to carry out project work such as working on elements of the design. It is appropriate, however, to bring key design decisions to the meeting for comment when they have an impact on other areas of the project.

At suitable junctures in the project, including phase boundaries, the focus of the regular meeting should be a review of progress to date, the purpose being to take a high level of view of how well the project is moving towards its goals. It can be useful to include a member of the steering committee or a suitable senior representative at this type of meeting.

Agenda

Here is a proposed agenda for a regular technical infrastructure project meeting:

Technical Infrastructure Project
Weekly Meeting Agenda

Date and Time:	Friday 2nd August 1996, 2 p.m.
Attendees:	Attendee 1 Attendee 2 Attendee 3 ...
1. Project Manager's Report	The project manager would give a summary of the key points of the report.
2. Progress to Date	Summary by the key individuals and project manager of progress since the last meeting.
3. Actions from Last Meeting	Review of progress against actions outstanding from the last meeting and from previous meetings.
4. Issues Outstanding	These are the issues on the issue list maintained by the project administrator. They will have been summarized in the project manager's report.
5. New Issues	A review of new issues and an opportunity to raise new issues.
6. Any Other Business	An opportunity for anyone to raise anything deemed important but not captured by the previous agenda items.

The agenda can vary from week to week to include additional items. Those shown in the example above should really be considered the minimum items necessary for a complete meeting.

Minutes

The proceedings at each meeting should be recorded to:

- act as a record for future reference
- capture decisions
- record actions

It is recommended that the project administrator take the minutes to allow the other attendees to focus on the meeting itself.

The minutes should always be written up in a timely manner after the meeting and circulated to all attendees including absentees. A copy should also be sent to various interested parties who don't regularly attend. Accompanying the minutes should be a note inviting people to identify any errors and submit corrections, as it is important for all who attended to agree that the minutes are a fair and accurate representation of proceedings.

As a minimum, the minutes should include the following sections:

- Who the minutes were taken by
- Location, date and time of the meeting
- Attendees and apologies
- Circulation list
- Introduction and meeting proceedings
- Logistics for next meeting
- Actions arising and actions still open

Issue Management

On a technical infrastructure project we must expect there to be issues raised. Issues are things that either need a resolution or a decision made about them. All too often issues remain unaddressed, subsequently developing into problems which then begin to impact the schedule of the project.

Issue management is not about making decisions, it is about ensuring that decisions get made. The project administrator should run an issue log, published for all to see, that records the details of each issue. As with other project material, groupware can make it straightforward to keep the issue log up to date and available on-line.

The details it should record are:

- Issue reference number
- Date issue was logged
- Issue description
  - Impact of issue
  - Proposed course of action
- Who logged the issue
- When the issue needs to be resolved by
- Name of the person allocated to resolve it

The issue log should be reviewed on a regular basis by the project manager who would allocate the task of resolving each of the outstanding issues to members of the project team.

Issues and tasks must not be confused. Issues are distinct from tasks in that they are specifically to do with something that needs to be resolved, whereas tasks are straightforward things that need to be done. For example, an issue might be:

- *An item of software recently identified as essential to progress now has a four week lead time from the suppliers.*

A task would be:

- *Create the logon script for the workstation.*

The MBI project manager decided to maintain a list of current issues to monitor their resolution. The issues list is shown in Table 3.7.

Table 3.7 *Example MBI Issue Log*

#	Date Logged	Issue/Impact/Action	Logged By	Owned By	Resolution Needed by
1.	12/8/97	**Issue**: Length of lead time for software **Impact**: Project delay **Action**: Use earlier version	M.C.	L.S.	12/24/97
2.	13/8/97	**Issue**: The server RAID controller hangs intermittently **Impact**: System not production worthy **Action**: Investigate alternative RAID controller	L.S.	M.C.	

Table 3.7 *Example MBI Issue Log (continued)*

3.	13/8/97	**Issue**: A key member of staff has just resigned **Impact**: Project delay through lack of required skills **Action**: Recruit contractor	H.V.C.	R.T.C

Project Team Communications

Communication between project team members is essential to the exchange of information, rapid resolution of issues, the forming of consensus, and engendering a sense of project identity. Clearly lack of communication is going to hinder a project. It could even be damaging as the grapevine fosters cliques and divisions in the team.

A typical technical infrastructure project team may well include members in different time zones, some may even work for different organizations. This can present a challenge when it comes to communications, both verbal and written.

It should be a high priority to set all project team members up with effective electronic communications at the onset of the project. Tools that can help are:

- Lotus Notes
- Microsoft Net Meeting
- World-Wide Web

Running a Documentation Library

A large project will produce many documents, particularly if it is being run using a typical project methodology. A function of project administration is to collect, collate, and file all project documents, keeping them accessible for reference.

Many of the project documents will need to go through review stages before being signed-off and distributed to the target audience. Use of a groupware tool can facilitate this process by allowing the document production process to be implemented as a workflow.

Where documents have been signed-off they should be filed as is along with an electronic copy. It is recommended that a source control system be used as a tool for enforcing revision control.

Getting Started

It is rarely possible to say exactly when an intention to do something becomes a project. Perhaps it is when a budget has been allocated? Some methodologies require a project registration form to be completed and approved before a project officially exists. A practical indication of when a project begins to exist is when someone is allocated the responsibility of managing it through to completion.

It is crucial at this early stage that expectations are set correctly and that everyone who is involved has a common understanding of what the project is about. The person holding the budget will be wanting confirmation of whether it is realistic, the technical community will want to know if and how they may be involved and the recipients of the technical infrastructure will want to know how the change is going to impact them.

For these reasons it is advisable that the project manager carries out some basic steps to get the project off onto a sure footing. What follows are some recommendations for these basic steps.

Identify Key People

On the assumption that the project manager has already been identified by management, this individual should then identify and recruit:

- Solution Architect
- Design Authority
- Project Administrator

These people should be assigned their responsibilities as described in Table 3.4 on page 60. It is important that a commitment is given by the line manager of each of these people for the time that they will need to spend on the project. For example, it is not good if the first time an emergency arises, the Solution Architect is pulled off the project to solve the pressing problem. Always try to have people committed on a full time basis to the project. If they are part time it becomes a constant battle to ensure their efforts are sufficiently focused on your project's objectives.

Two Page Project Flyer

The theme of good communication should run through every project. To this end it is worth getting the project off on a good footing by advertising it to all who may be concerned at the earliest opportunity.

Because we have a project and two or three people assigned to it there is already something we can usefully say about it. No more than a couple of pages should suffice, covering these aspects:

- Project name
- Project objective
- Sponsor
- Timescales
- Contact names and numbers
- Anticipated approach
- Who will be affected

The contact names and numbers should be those of the project manager and the line manager responsible for instigating the project. It may be that not much is known about the anticipated approach for the project. However, it may already have been decided that, for example, the project will be evolutionary in nature and only install the new technical infrastructure one site at a time. If so this could be stated. Be careful not to make any commitments or alarm people. Such a document is useful only if it is informative, it should not be a warning.

Report Initial Resource and Budget Estimates

Estimating resource requirements at such an early stage may not seem worthwhile as the error factor could be rather large. The main use is for budgeting, as corporate fiscal processes demand to know how much something is going to cost before the money is committed. A secondary purpose is to set expectations correctly. It is obviously better to justify a request for 250 days of a consultant's time at the outset rather than present a bill for the fees to the manager who assumed we would only have used 30 days.

Both these reasons make it important to have an estimate of some sort. To serve our interests we should estimate high. Then add more time to the estimates. Then add even more even time for contingency purposes. Do not under estimate a project's ability to consume resources.

Kick-off Meeting

If most of the team members are already identified at this early stage then it is worth organizing a kick-off meeting. Such a meeting would be an opportunity for introductions and a discussion about aspects of the project. If done properly it can instill a sense of purpose and the feeling of identification with the project.

What Next?

Once the initial tasks have been completed and the project is seen to be underway, attention should turn to the many things that need to be done next. These are nearly all tasks that should be initiated or carried out by the project manager as the leader of the project. Here is a summary of what could happen next:

#	Task	Comments
1.	Plan scoping and business analysis workshops	Interviews may be substituted for the workshop
2.	Get agreement on which sites the infrastructure will be deployed to first and initiate site surveys	The survey questionnaire will need to be developed and individuals in those target locations contacted
3.	Set up regular project meetings	Useful to give advance warning to attendees for a series of meetings
4.	Contact purchasing department to establish preferred suppliers, contacts and discount levels	Product evaluation activities may be underway for products that will be needed for the technical infrastructure
5.	Recruit additional people to the project	Always getting commitment from their line management for the time they will spend on the project
6.	Research whether there are any other projects in the organization that could affect the technical infrastructure project	For example, it would be a waste of effort planning to install the technical infrastructure in an office that was about to be closed!

Using Consultants

Some of the project team members may not be directly employed by the corporation but consultants brought in for their specialist skills or experience. As use of external consultants is quite common it is worth considering how it might affect a project.

There are three main reasons for using consultants:

- To bring expertise in particular technologies
- To bring relevant experience
- To cope with a short term demand for extra resources

Other benefits of consultancies are their ability to substitute consultants on a project to bring new skills, consultant training is at the expense of the consultancy firm and bringing people onto a project can usually be done more quickly using consultants than having to recruit. On the down side, the daily rates of consultants can cause a doubletake, though when put in the context of the overall project cost their fees are easier to justify.

Another potential drawback of using consultants, particularly if they are brought in to compensate for a lack of experience, is that they will boost their experience further, not that of the corporation's staff. Careful allocation of people to project tasks can help to overcome this.

Risk Sharing

Related to the benefits and drawbacks of using consultants is the matter of risk. Whether they are being brought in for their experience or knowledge and wherever they are used, the underlying motivation for employing them is to lower the risk on the project.

The essence of successful risk sharing is when the *risk to a third party, and hence the overall project,* of carrying out an activity is lower than the risk associated with keeping the activity in-house. We shall see in the following example how this type of arrangement works.

Risk Sharing Example

Suppose you have decided your house needs an addition. You clearly have several options as to how you go about getting it designed and built. You could:

1. Design it yourself and subcontract the building to a builder's firm
2. Commission an architect to design it and still subcontract the building to a builder's firm
3. Design it yourself and employ hourly labor (recruited from the sidewalk) to build it
4. Commission an architect to design it and employ hourly labor to build it
5. Do it all yourself

6. Subcontract the whole job to a specialist company

How do we choose? Well it can depend on:

Cost — The cheapest would be option 5.

Time — If we had no time we would go for option 6.

Experience — If we had none we might go for options 2 or 4 or 6.

Confidence — Whether we use hourly labor or subcontract the work may depend on how confident we felt in managing a construction labor force.

Maybe the job is particularly difficult for some reason. Under normal circumstances we may have chosen to do it all ourselves but go for option 6 instead so that if anything goes wrong we have a come back on the single company. Option 2 is almost as good in this case though if something does go wrong there is the risk the architects will blame poor materials or workmanship and the builders may blame poor design, leaving you to arbitrate and get one party to accept the blame. In fact this risk is present to some degree in all options except 6.

We may decide that as we designed and built the house ourselves many years earlier we couldn't trust anyone else to design and build an addition. In this case we would choose to employ hourly labor to mix cement and dig the foundations under our supervision.

This scenario and the associated options are directly analogous to the situation a corporation faces when embarking on a technical infrastructure project and knowing that it has neither the experience or expertise to carry it out without professional assistance.

If we distill the options in the above scenario and apply it to the subject of this book we are left with two modes of engaging consultants. One is where they are retained as hired hands. The other is where they undertake part of or all of the project on your behalf. The principle difference is where the buck stops should anything go wrong.

Time and Materials

Using hired hands, the bulk of the risk remains with the employer. If one of the consultants does under perform there is little that can be done but to replace that person with someone else. It is important to remember though that even in this situation, risk can be reduced if the consultant engaged has valuable experience or knowledge. This style of engagement is normally termed "time and materials" meaning that the customer is charged for the consultant's time plus any additional expenses such as travel and accommodation that might be incurred carrying out the assignment.

Subcontracting

If consultants are retained to undertake a portion of the project an amount of risk passes to them in exchange for their customer's money. Thus they are given a specification to deliver to. When they have done the job they get paid. This type of engagement is sometimes called subcontracting.

The heading for this section is Risk Sharing and so far we have talked of offsetting risk through use of consultants. Perhaps there has been an implication that the consultants take on the risk? This need not necessarily be the case if to the consultant the task is viewed as low risk. This is when the arrangement of using consultants works best.

Consultancy Pricing

The starting point that most consultancies use for calculating a price for a job is the daily charge out rate. This rate will vary according the seniority of each consultant used and have associated with it an internal cost from which their profit margin will be calculated. The consultancy's internal cost will be a blanket cost covering all their combined overheads.

Daily Rates

If the job is being done on a time and materials basis the rate offered can either be discounted using a previously agreed formula or a discount can be negotiated for that deal only. Discount will be more likely to be forthcoming if there is a competitive situation or the prospect of a long term commitment to their consulting services. The latter situation is very desirable from a consultant's point of view as they do not have to keep expending pre-sales effort, usually non-revenue earning, to secure extensions to their contract. If the consultancy will be gaining expertise through participating in the project then it can be possible to negotiate a lower price.

Subcontractor's Perspective

From the subcontractor's perspective, estimating the price that should be charged for a job is complex as there is a cost that needs to be applied to compensate for the risk element. For example, a consultant might estimate a job as taking 100 days if all goes well. Cross examination by a project manager might reveal that several things could go wrong causing up to 200 days to be expended. With that estimate the subcontractor might then price the job based on 200 days time usage. Unfortunately, while fully protecting themselves, the subcontractor will not have arrived at a competitive price.

Closer analysis might lead the subcontracting project manager to conclude that there is only a 40% chance of things going wrong so they may be tempted to reduce the price to one based on 140 days. There is still a risk being taken on at that price, though one calculated to ensure a high chance of profit and of winning the business. A corollary of this is that companies will sometimes decide not to bid for the types of business where, based on the risk calculation, they cannot achieve the desired balance of competitiveness and commercial viability.

Using Project Management to Reduce Risk (and Cost)

How can we reduce the chance of things going wrong? This is where project management comes in. Effective project management should be able to reduce the risk appreciably, though there is of course a cost to employing a project manager.

Taking the pricing example introduced above further, suppose that the 140 days is just for technicians managing themselves. The subcontractor might judge that by including a project manager on the job for 15 days the chance of something going wrong is reduced, making a cost based on 115 days technician time an acceptable risk. Thus, the total resource requirement is now 130 days, 10 less than before, allowing the subcontractor more flexibility with price and profit margin.

The main method of getting a competitive price from a potential subcontractor is to make them compete for your business. While consultancies will be tempted to tolerate different profit margins this alone might not affect their total price much, however, they may also take a different view of the risk they are incurring or their ability to manage it, making much more of an impact on the price.

The Risk of Subcontracting Risk

A customer should be suspicious of a consultancy bidding for a subcontract with a price significantly lower than their competition. It may point to a faulty analysis of the situation which will cause that company difficulties once things start to go wrong. While legally the responsibility lies with the subcontractor, it is not in the customer's interest to have their subcontractor go out of business so care should be taken to choose a consultancy that will get it right.

The subcontractor will obviously aim to make a profit on any deal. One way they do this is to conveniently ignore risks outside of their scope of influence for the purpose of pricing and present a very tight contract, the purpose being to charge extra every time the customer, that is you, forces a change or delay on the subcontractor. This is where the subcontractor will be making the majority of their profit. Thus, the subcontractor that submits the lowest bid might not end up being the lowest cost choice over the duration of the project.

Defining the Interface

The key to an effective consulting engagement or subcontract is the interface between the customer and the consultants. Good practice is for both parties to agree to a document describing what the interface should be. The following shows the basic sections of a consulting engagement document with recommended contents:

Section	Content
Executive Summary	A summary of the key points of the rest of the document.
Project Particulars	▪ Project reference number ▪ Project Name ▪ Start/End Date
Purpose	To record the agreed aspects of the consulting engagement.
Scope	This is the scope of the document, not the scope of the consulting engagement. It would state whether this interface document was restricted to a single project, part of a project or many projects. It would name the projects within its scope.
Intended Audience	Typically this would include the project sponsor, the consultancy management, and all other people with an interest in the contractual arrangements.
Work Schedule	A definition of the work to be undertaken by the consultancy. This should also include a description of any deliverables arising.
Resource Estimates	How much time will be used by each consultant.
Costs	Details of daily rates, discounts and a total. Note whether this is an estimate, fixed price, or capped at a particular value.
Interfaces	Should say who in the customer organization (suggestion in brackets) deals with the following consultancy personnel on a day to day basis: ▪ Project Manager (customer project /program manager) ▪ Solution Architect (customer senior solution architect) ▪ Technicians (customer technicians)

continued▸

(continued)

Section	Content
Customer Responsibilities	The obligations the customer has to the consultancy. This will depend to a large extent on where the risk lies and who is supplying project management. Suggestions to choose from are: ▪ Timely review of documentation (e.g., 24 hrs) ▪ Working facilities (e.g., desk, phone, etc.) ▪ Resolution of issues ▪ Detailed project plan ▪ Access to necessary people ▪ Accuracy of data ▪ Timely supply of data
Consultant Responsibilities	The obligations the consultant has to the customer. Again this depends on the risk sharing, suggestions are: ▪ Detailed project plan ▪ Regular reports of progress including resources used, estimates to completion, charges incurred to date.
Problem Resolution	This section describes the process for dealing with problems should they arise. It should include an escalation procedure calling for more senior people to contribute to finding a resolution.

Food and Shelter

Once consultants are engaged they will be billing for their time. It therefore makes sense to ensure they are fully effective, working on their assigned task rather than being hindered by any logistical constraint.

A theory proposed by Maslow states that an individual has a hierarchy of needs. At any point in time focus will be on satisfying the lower needs before the higher needs can be addressed. Thus, in simple terms, food is the most basic need, above that is shelter and warmth and so on up to ego. Only when all needs are satisfied does an individual become fully contributing and creative.

Perhaps a little dramatic, but it does point to sorting out the following for a consultant:

- Electronic cash card for food and drink
- Electronic card key or identity badge
- Telephone
- Desk

- E-mail
- Internet/intranet Web access
- Laptop connection to the network (security permitting)
- PC (if laptop not supplied or allowed)

Project Documentation

The ultimate deliverable from a project to design and implement a technical infrastructure is of course the properly working technical infrastructure. However, there are good reasons why deliverables from the various activities should include high quality documentation:

- Once implemented, those who planned and designed the infrastructure will move on leaving the task of supporting it to others. A reference of exactly what was implemented then becomes important to sustain continued engineering and development work.
- Documentation can be used to assist the process of arriving at agreement between a number of parties by being a vehicle for communication.
- Technical Support will need operational documentation to assist the diagnosis of problems, the maintenance of a consistent and predictable system and configuration details. For example, their documentation should include details on how to create a new workstation from the standard engineering kit.

This section examines:

- The documents one might expect to be produced from a complete technical infrastructure design project.
- How to decide what information to put in which document.
- What documents are needed?

Tables 3.8 to Table 3.10 are lists of project documents organized by the phase in which they should be produced. We will see in Chapter 4, Project Planning that a number of these documents represent the main deliverable from each phase.

While not all projects will require all the documents listed in Table 3.8, Table 3.9, and Table 3.10, some may produce substantially more including:

- Process oriented documents related to the project methodology
- Whitepapers (technical discussion documents)

- Product evaluation reports
- Business cases (to obtain funding)
- Job descriptions (for recruiting and reference)

It is recommended that the project manager and solution architect draw up a list of the documents that will be required to support the project, making sure they are all clearly identified as deliverables from the relevant project tasks.

Table 3.8 *Design Preparation Phase Documents*

Document	Overview
High Level Plan	A document embracing all the topics covered in this chapter (including a plan for the documentation the project will produce!)
Two page project flyer	A document to broadcast the inception of the project.
Site Surveys	The set of survey results from the Planning Requirements activity.
Business Principles	The scope and business principles of the project.
Requirements Specification consisting of the following two documents:	
Application Requirements	The requirements placed on the project by applications.
User Requirements	The requirements placed on the project by the business users and the support users.
Functional Specification	A statement of what will be delivered by the project.

The Requirements Specification and Functional Specification are both described in more detail in Chapter 8, Requirements Gathering.

Table 3.9 *Design Phase Documents*

Document	Overview
Logical Design(s)	The document should contain all high level design work. In a large project this document may be split up into sections based on technology area.

Table 3.10 *Implementation Preparation Phase Documents*

Document	Overview
Implementation Detail	This could be one document or several: ▪ Description of how to create a workstation kit for distribution ▪ How to create software installation packages ▪ Description of how to create any other product from this phase.
Workstation Installation	Procedure for creating a standard workstation installation.
Server Installation	Procedure for creating a standard server installation.
Procurement Specification	Details of all purchasing requirements for both production and development usage.
Implementation Plan	Plan for implementing the technical infrastructure at a particular site.
User Acceptance Test	A document containing tests used to validate user oriented functionality.
System Acceptance Test	A document containing tests used to validate system oriented functionality.
Operations Procedures	Routine operational tasks for operators of the technical infrastructure (e.g., adding a user to the system).
System Guides	Describing how to create the software product deliverables from the Implementation Detail activity.
Recovery Procedures	Procedures for recovering from system failures.
Site Detail (one per site)	This document will contain the definition of how technology is applied to a particular site. It represents an application of the Design Phase logical design documentation. For example, the logical design would provide guidelines as to how many file servers to use for a given size of site. The Site Detail document would state exactly how big the site was and how many file servers are to be used.

Mapping Content to a Document

The intended content for most of the documents listed in the three tables earlier should be clear. Where it can get difficult is deciding exactly what goes in the design related documents, or rather, which documents will have to be written to convey the design from high level architectures through to implementation detail.

It is important to work this out before beginning any documentation to avoid wasting time later on editing. Getting this right can lead to an easier set of documents to maintain and use. For example, the detailed design for a site might specify use of Service Pack 4. This obviously has no bearing on the logical design, so it would be convenient if this information were in a separate document as it is likely to change as soon as Service Pack 5 is released.

The two main factors that influence how the design documentation is structured are the scale and the diversity of the implementation environment. For example, a small project may get away with one document covering all aspects of design while a large project may require several documents just to cover the logical design. A diverse implementation environment may also call for several documents to reflect the variations of configuration necessary.

Table 3.11 summarizes three basic documentation strategies designed to offer a suitable alternative for a range of scenarios.

Table 3.11 *Design Documentation Strategies*

Option	Documents	Content
1	*Logical Design*	High level architecture of the technical infrastructure. This document should focus on the fundamental design decisions. For example: ▪ Domain model ▪ How file and print services will be delivered ▪ Flow diagrams for scripts ▪ User environment ▪ Service architectures ▪ There may even be individual documents for each of the elements of the design.
	Implementation Detail	This document should record details about the design that may change as the technology details change. For example: ▪ The contents of the workstation "build" ▪ Logon scripts ▪ Configuration requirements for applications ▪ Acceptance tests ▪ Failure analysis and recovery

continued ▸

Table 3.11 *Design Documentation Strategies (continued)*

Option	Documents	Content
	Site Detail	There should be one of these documents per site. Its contents should record unique aspects of that site. For example: ▪ IP address allocation ▪ Names of computers ▪ User groups and privileges ▪ Which services are allocated to which servers ▪ Any customizations needed causing a variation from the design.
2	*Design*	In this option, the Design document includes everything that would have gone into the Logical Design and Implementation Detail documents listed above.
	Site Detail	As shown above.
3	*Design*	All design information goes into this document.

Summary

While there are several different established project methodologies in use, most have the following basic concepts in common: elements of work (activities and tasks), milestones, dependencies and risks. Managing a project for success involves identifying who the customer is, setting expectations accurately, creating the project team carefully, management at the task level and keeping people informed.

Project administration concerns itself with the mechanics of a project, those aspects that are unrelated to the project content. The purpose of project administration is to make sure everyone knows what is going on around them, that they have a mechanism for formally raising issues and resolving them, and that all project activity is recorded and indexed. Getting a project started will involve identifying key people, issuing a notice that the project has begun, reporting initial budget estimates and staging a kick-off meeting.

There are three main reasons for using consultants: expertise, experience, or to cope with a short term demand for extra resources. A drawback to using consultants is that the daily rate can seem high, though when put in the context of the overall project cost their fees can often be easier to justify. Consultants may be retained to share risk or to simply provide extra resources. How they are retained will determine their pricing structure.

A well run technical infrastructure design project will generate a large quantity of documentation. It is recommended that the project manager and solution architect draw up a list of the documents that will be required to support the project, making sure they are all clearly identified as deliverables from the relevant project tasks.

4

Project Planning

Project planning is an exercise in estimating the future. It is an art as much as a science, resting heavily on experience. However, without a plan we cannot justify judgments regarding resourcing, time scales, or progress to date. As a project evolves, we use the project plan as a tool with which to manage that change. Each project is different, requiring a unique project plan, however when two projects share the same problem domain their project plans will share the same broad structure and parts.

Using the project model presented in the introductory chapter and the project management concepts from Chapter 3, Running the Project, we develop a simple project plan for the MBI case study. The result can be used for making a quick start on the development of a plan for a comparable project.

This chapter is intended to be a source of reference for the project manager embarking on a Windows NT based technical infrastructure project by providing an insight into the content of the key activities. For a technician, much of the value found here will be the structure applied to those activities. Whether read by a technician, a project manager, or a hybrid of the two, presented here are the reusable elements of a technical infrastructure project plan. A complex project offers many opportunities for success, and using this solid planning foundation will help to maximize those opportunities.

Structure of Chapter

Table 4.1 summarizes the structure of this chapter.

Table 4.1 *Structure of Chapter 4*

Topic	Contents
The project model	A phased project model is introduced as the basis for understanding the relationship between the high level components of a project.
Project activities	A full definition is provided for each activity identified in the project model. These are the foundation of a technical infrastructure design project plan.
Enhancing the project plan	This topic addresses the need to complement an activity view of a project with milestones, dependencies, and an understanding of the risks.
Project tasks	Summary descriptions of the tasks involved in each activity are provided.
Completing the project plan	The project is completed with the addition of resources and a review of the milestones, dependencies, and risks.

The Project Model

The model illustrated in Figure 4.1 and introduced in Chapter 1, shows the complete set of high level activities involved in a technical infrastructure project divided into four project phases.

Figure 4.1 *Technical Infrastructure Project Model*

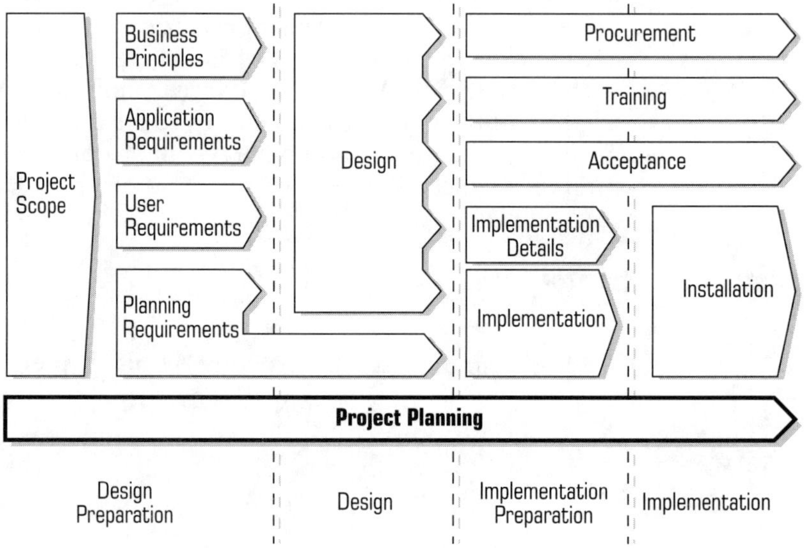

Rather than being a project plan, the model should be seen as more like a data flow diagram, showing how one activity provides information to another.

This section examines each of the phases in detail, the subsequent section entitled Project Activities defines each of the constituent activities. The highlighted activity in the figure is of course the subject of this chapter.

It should be noted that the size of a box bears no resemblance to the scale of its associated activity! For example, Implementation Details is one of the largest project activities.

The four phases are:

1. Design Preparation
2. Design
3. Implementation Preparation
4. Implementation

This book concentrates on the analysis and design of a technical infrastructure, the supporting activities for which are to be found in the first three phases of the project. The fourth phase, Implementation, is illustrated for completeness as several activities span it and the previous phase.

If the project model were to illustrate the full lifecycle of the technical infrastructure, it would include a support phase following the implementation phase. While clearly very important, coverage of support activities is beyond the scope of this book.

Design Preparation

The objective of the design preparation phase is to ensure all necessary information is accumulated prior to the logical design commencing. The first activity is to establish the scope of the project, then the user and application requirements can be gathered in parallel with the identification of the business principles that apply to the project. To aid planning and to complement the user and application requirements, the current state of the technical infrastructure must also be determined.

The key deliverables from this phase of the project will be:

1. A statement of project scope.

2. A set of business principles defining how the corporation intends to apply IT to solve the business challenge.
3. A *Requirements Specification* defining the user and application requirements.
4. A *Functional Specification,* developed from the Requirements Specification. In practice (in the case of a technical infrastructure) this requires the design process to be started but the creation of this document is dealt with in the design preparation phase for convenience.
5. A document detailing the state of the current technical infrastructure.
6. A high level project plan.

Design

This is the phase of the project where the bulk of the design work is carried out and principles of design identified. The deliverable from the design phase is a set of documentation describing how the system is going to work, which we will refer to collectively as the *Logical Design.*

In practical terms the Logical Design is a more detailed version of the Functional Specification. The reason for this is that the function of a Windows NT based technical infrastructure is essentially defined by the configuration details of the products chosen to implement it. The audience for the Logical Design will not be the same group of people who provided the system requirements but the broad technical community within the corporation.

Implementation Preparation

The logical design is not going to leave us in a state where we are ready to plan an installation. There are several additional things that need to be done before we can start, such as:

- Test the design
- Train support staff
- Train the users
- Port software
- Write scripts
- Create installable software kits and packages
- Write implementation and operation documentation

The objective of the implementation preparation phase is to get us to the point where we are ready to complete the planning of an installation. Note that the implementation preparation phase includes a more detailed project planning activity, effectively a sub project to the plan described in this chapter, geared towards the detailed tasks necessary for getting the system into production at a particular location. Deliverables from this phase of the project include a wide set of documentation as well as software products such as installable kits and scripts.

Implementation

This comprises the tasks of installation, physically setting computers up, formatting disks and installing software kits and packages. It also includes execution of training and user acceptance testing.

Project Activities

This section defines each of the high level project activities shown in the technical infrastructure project model. The details of these activities are covered in other chapters of this book. The activities are each defined using the activity definition structure detailed in Chapter 3, Running the Project.

The activity definitions mention a variety of job roles; Table 3.4 in Chapter 3, Running the Project, summarizes the key ones. The activity definitions listed in this chapter do not carry resource estimates as they must be evaluated on a project by project basis. To arrive at resource estimates for the activities, begin by applying resource estimates to the tasks comprising each activity and then summarize for the activity. The constituent tasks for each activity are listed later in this chapter.

Project Planning

Table 4.2 *Project Planning*

Activity:	Project Planning
Activity Overview	The development of a project plan for the technical infrastructure project. It will identify the key project activities and tasks, assign resources to them, and identify milestones, risks and dependencies.
Prerequisites	Project scope activity complete

Table 4.2 *Project Planning (continued)*

Activity:	**Project Planning**
Deliverable	A high level project plan showing project structure and the main activities. This will be in the form of a document that includes a Gantt chart. The plan should also show milestones, dependencies, and risks.
Resources	▪ Project manager ▪ Solution architect
Activity Owner	Project manager
Deliverable Sign-off Authority	▪ Project sponsor on behalf of steering committee ▪ The managers responsible for all resources participating in the project
Reviewers	▪ Project sponsor ▪ Solution architect ▪ Any people representing departments likely to be affected by the project

Scoping

Table 4.3 *Scoping*

Activity:	**Scoping**
Activity Overview	Identification of the scope of the project using a workshop or interview technique. Attendees/interviewees: ▪ Project sponsor ▪ Key business managers ▪ IT managers representing Architecture, Strategy and Support functions
Prerequisites	Project go ahead
Deliverable	Brief document detailing the agreed project scope
Resources	▪ Solution architect ▪ Project manager ▪ Workshop facilitator (to run workshop and write up afterwards)
Activity Owner	Project manager
Deliverable Sign-off Authority	Project sponsor

Table 4.3 *Scoping (continued)*

Activity:	Scoping
Reviewers	▪ Project sponsor ▪ Project manager ▪ Any people representing departments to be affected by the project

The resources listed above assume a workshop as the medium for determining the project scope. If interviews were used instead, the resources identified would probably need to increase the time they allocate for this activity.

Business Principles

Note: Business principles are introduced in Chapter 5.

Table 4.4 *Business Principles*

Activity:	Business Principles
Activity Overview	Identification of the business principles of the project using a workshop or one or more interviews. Attendees/interviewees: ▪ Project sponsor ▪ Key business managers ▪ IT managers representing Architecture, Strategy and Support functions
Prerequisites	Agreed set of project scope areas as output from the Scoping part of this activity
Deliverable	Document detailing the agreed business principles
Resources	▪ Solution architect ▪ Workshop facilitator
Activity Owner	Project manager
Deliverable Sign-off Authority	Project sponsor
Reviewers	▪ Project sponsor ▪ Project manager ▪ Any people representing departments likely to be affected by the project

Application Requirements

Table 4.5 *Application Requirements*

Activity:	Application requirements
Activity Overview	Determine the requirements that existing or new applications will place on the planned technical infrastructure
Prerequisites	▪ List of applications that need to be supported ▪ List of sites and contact names targeted
Deliverables	Both deliverables are shared with User Requirements activity ▪ Technical Infrastructure Requirements Specification ▪ Technical Infrastructure Functional Specification
Resources	▪ Solution architect ▪ Business analyst ▪ Site representative ▪ Application experts
Activity Owner	Solution architect
Deliverable Sign-off Authority	Project manager, business analyst, site representative and applications expert
Reviewers	Technical design authorities, site representatives, project manager, business analyst

User Requirements

Table 4.6 *User Requirements*

Activity:	User Requirements
Activity Overview	Determine the requirements of business users and IT Support on the planned technical infrastructure
Prerequisites	List of contact names for targeted sites
Deliverables	Both deliverables are shared with Application Requirements activity ▪ Technical Infrastructure Requirements Specification ▪ Technical Infrastructure Functional Specification

Table 4.6 *User Requirements (continued)*

Activity:	User Requirements
Resources	▪ Solution architect ▪ Business analyst ▪ Site representative ▪ Application experts
Activity Owner	Solution architect
Deliverable Sign-off Authority	Project manager, business analyst
Reviewers	Technical design authorities, site representatives, project manager, business analyst

Planning Requirements

Table 4.7 *Planning Requirements*

Activity:	Planning Requirements
Activity Overview	▪ Development of planning requirements gathering tools ▪ Survey the sites targeted for the new technical infrastructure
Prerequisites	List of contact names for targeted sites
Deliverables	Documented planning requirements results
Resources	▪ Solution architect ▪ Business analyst ▪ Site representative ▪ Application experts
Activity Owner	Solution architect
Deliverable Sign-off Authority	Project manager, business analyst and site representative
Reviewers	Technical design authorities, site representatives, project manager, business analyst

When attempting a survey of a remote site that may be in a different time zone and involve a different native language allow for a reasonable amount of contingency as much time can be lost trying to identify the right people, making contact and traveling. Costs for travel and accommodation should be included in the project budget.

Design

Table 4.8 *Design*

Activity:	Logical Design
Activity Overview	▪ Determine and gain agreement for the technical scope of the design ▪ Carry out design of all technical elements ▪ Regularly issue draft design for review ▪ Determine product requirements ▪ Conduct design reviews
Prerequisites	▪ Business principles ▪ Site surveys ▪ User requirements ▪ Application requirements
Deliverables	Logical technical infrastructure design
Resources	▪ Solution architect ▪ Design technicians ▪ Project administrator
Activity Owner	Solution architect
Deliverable Sign-off Authority	Project manager
Reviewers	▪ Technical design authorities ▪ Project manager

Don't underestimate the amount of time the solution architect will devote to task managing contributing technicians, preparing a consistent design document and driving the resolution of technical design issues.

Procurement

This activity will vary tremendously from project to project making it very difficult to estimate resources. In situations where the corporation has an effective set of existing purchasing agreements and processes, the amount of resource the project will have to fund to cope with this activity will be low.

Table 4.9 *Procurement*

Activity:	Procurement
Activity Overview	▪ Requirements identification ▪ Product evaluation and selection ▪ Product purchasing
Prerequisites	Logical design complete
Deliverables	▪ Product evaluation reports ▪ Receipt of goods
Resources	▪ Project manager ▪ Technician ▪ Project administrator
Activity Owner	Project manager
Deliverable Sign-off Authority	Combined with sign-off of a complete installation
Reviewers	▪ Technical design authorities ▪ Solution architect

If this activity can be started before the logical design is complete then it should be, as the process of product evaluation and purchase can take a long time.

Training

Table 4.10 *Training*

Activity:	Training
Activity Overview	Train local users and local technical support in the operation of their new systems
Prerequisites	▪ Stable technology content to technical infrastructure ▪ User environment implementation detail complete
Deliverables	▪ Training materials ▪ Trained users ▪ Trained IT support staff
Resources	▪ Technical author ▪ Instructors ▪ Project administrator
Activity Owner	Project manager

Table 4.10 *Training (continued)*

Activity:	Training
Deliverable Sign-off Authority	■ Local technical support manager ■ Local business manager
Reviewers	Technical design authorities

Acceptance

Table 4.11 *Acceptance*

Activity:	Acceptance
Activity Overview	■ Implement the logical design under laboratory conditions ■ Create system and user acceptance tests ■ Carry out system and user acceptance tests ■ Test bandwidth requirements ■ Test computer capacity
Prerequisites	Logical design
Deliverables	■ User acceptance test ■ System acceptance test ■ Signed-off tests
Resources	■ Solution architect ■ Technicians
Activity Owner	Solution architect
Deliverable Sign-off Authority	Project manager
Reviewers	Technical design authorities

Implementation Detail

This is the activity where the logical design is progressed to a state where the configuration of each site is defined in detail. The principle behind splitting the design process into two activities (and in two different project phases) is to make distinction between the content that should rarely change, recorded in the Logical Design Document, and the content that could change more frequently as technology advances and site details change, recorded in the Implementation Detail Documents.

Table 4.12 *Implementation Detail*

Activity:	Implementation Detail
Activity Overview	▪ Create software products (e.g., workstation installation kits, application installation packages, logon scripts, etc.) ▪ Write documentation to support software products ▪ Carry out testing ▪ Carry out a pilot implementation ▪ Manage the release of software products ▪ Capacity planning ▪ Reviewing the design
Prerequisites	▪ Logical design complete ▪ Target sites identified
Deliverables	▪ Workstation and server installation kits ▪ Application installation packages ▪ Supporting documentation describing how to install the software on a new workstation or server and operate the system. The target audience will be the IT Support Group. ▪ Documents recording the implementation details. The target audience will be Engineering. ▪ Documented recovery procedures showing what to do in the event of a system failure ▪ Report from laboratory ▪ Report from pilot
Resources	▪ Solution architect ▪ Technicians ▪ Site representatives ▪ Project administrator
Activity Owner	Solution architect
Deliverable Sign-off Authority	Project manager
Reviewers	Technical design authorities

Implementation Planning

The overall project plan is geared towards the creation from scratch of a complete technical infrastructure. At the point when the logical design is complete and the project moves into the implementation preparation phase, focus will tend to shift towards the needs of the locations that are destined to receive the new infrastructure. This is to be expected, but it creates a situation where the goal of the overall infrastructure project overlaps and in some cases competes with the goal of getting systems installed.

The recommended approach is to treat the implementation of the system in a particular location as a distinct sub-project of the overall project. It would not be uncommon to find several distinct sub-projects running in parallel each with the goal of achieving an installation at a different location.

It is beyond the scope of this book to go into detail about location implementation planning as the details will vary considerably from project to project. Chapter 17, Implementation Preparation, provides an overview of the tasks involved in implementation planning.

Table 4.13 *Implementation Planning*

Activity:	Implementation Planning
Activity Overview	▪ Co-ordination with other parties ▪ Setting expectations ▪ Milestones ▪ Dependencies ▪ Risks ▪ Resourcing
Prerequisites	Complete and tested technical infrastructure design
Deliverables	Implementation plan
Resources	▪ Implementation project manager ▪ Solution architect ▪ Application specialist
Activity Owner	Local project manager
Deliverable Sign-off Authority	▪ Technical support ▪ Business representative
Reviewers	Representatives from IT support and the business from the target deployment locations

Enhancing the Project Plan

Now we have identified the main project phases and their activities and we can begin to enhance the project plan by:

- identifying milestones
- scheduling around dependencies
- highlighting risks and developing contingency arrangements

These will provide a basis for breaking the activities down into tasks. Once we have done that we should use the extra level of detail to enhance the plan again by revising the milestones, dependencies and risks.

Please refer to Chapter 3, Running the Project, for an introduction to milestones, dependencies and risks.

Milestones

Milestones will be of most value in Implementation Preparation and Implementation, though they are essential for all phases. For the purpose of illustration we shall look at the milestones used in the Implementation Preparation phase of the MBI project.

The MBI project manager decided to set milestones in the implementation preparation phase at a week apart, each to be completed on a Friday. In most cases, there is more than one milestone due for achievement each Friday. To make people aware of which milestones fell in which week, the list was published promptly after each progress meeting. To make the milestones relevant, the project manager chose to base them on the deliverables of the implementation detail activity. The list was presented as in Table 4.14.

Table 4.14 *Implementation Preparation Phase Milestones*

Date	Milestone	Details
wk 1	▪ Group 1 CPS Build T0.01 ▪ Group 2 CPS Build T0.01	Released for trial
wk 2	▪ Group 3 CPS Build T0.01 ▪ Group 4 CPS Build T0.01 ▪ Group 1 CPS Build T0.02 ▪ Group 2 CPS Build T0.02	Released for trial
wk 3	▪ 1st draft of all installation and configuration documentation	Issued for review
wk 4	▪ 1st draft of all engineering documentation ▪ Installation packages for top five applications created and tested	Issued for review
wk 5	▪ Group 3 CPS Build T0.02 ▪ Group 4 CPS Build T0.02 ▪ Group 1 CPS Build T0.03 ▪ Group 2 CPS Build T0.03	Released for trial

Table 4.14 *Implementation Preparation Phase Milestones (continued)*

Date	Milestone	Details
wk 6	▪ Group 1 CPS Build V1.0 ▪ Group 2 CPS Build V1.0	Basic build passed acceptance test in UAT lab
wk 7	▪ Group 3 CPS Build V1.0 ▪ Group 4 CPS Build V1.0 ▪ Installation packages for all applications created and unit tested	Basic build passed acceptance test in UAT lab
wk 8	▪ Finished complete build testing	Complete build passed UAT and SAT
wk 9	▪ Installation & configuration documentation complete ▪ Engineering documentation complete	

Note: CPS is Computer Profile Setup, a tool from the Windows NT Resource Kit used for automating initial system installation. SAT and UAT stand for System Acceptance Test and User Acceptance Test respectively.

A milestone list need not be any more complex than this, but be careful not to invent milestones for the sake of it. A bad milestone is shown in Table 4.15.

Table 4.15 *An Example of a Bad Milestone*

Date	Milestone	Details
wk n	Logon script design document 50% complete	Intermediate review

This is a bad milestone because it is difficult to judge when a document is 50% complete, leaving it open to interpretation as to whether the milestone has been achieved or not. Most important though, nothing actually happens if this milestone is achieved, nor does anything happen if it is not achieved. The milestones listed for the MBI project can all be shown to trigger something or mark something as completed.

In the case of the CPS builds, the achievement of the Group 3 CPS Build T0.02 may be marked by the dispatch of a tape or CD with the build on to all parties involved in the test program. In the case of documentation, the milestone may mark the release of a bound copy for review. The important thing is to to pick milestones that team members can identify with a sense of achievement.

Dependencies

The following list identifies a selection of basic project dependencies between activities and tasks. Creating such a list is an ideal starting point, however, a Gantt chart offers a more practical vehicle for developing and recording the complete set.

1. High level planning and business principles must both follow scoping as it is important to understand the extent of the project before committing any resource.
2. Business principles must be agreed prior to design work beginning.
3. The design also needs input from requirements gathering as it will be necessary to incorporate aspects of current systems in the new design.
4. Once the design is nearing completion implementation preparation can begin. It is at this point that we know both what we have got (site surveys) and we know where we are going (logical design).
5. Procurement should begin as soon as the required equipment is known to avoid lead times or product evaluations becoming the critical path.
6. Implementation detail, that is, taking the design through to the level of detail needed for an installation, can run in parallel with the laboratory work. Both can't start before the design is finished.

   Note: Any procurement for laboratory equipment should have been initiated a lot earlier. Lack of lab can seriously impact a project schedule.
7. Training of the staff who will have to support the installation can begin as soon as the key technologies are chosen. They should be trained prior to the installation.
8. Installation can only begin once the workstation installation and associated software installation packages have passed all acceptance tests and been signed off for release.

Some of these dependencies are implied in the general layout of the project model diagram shown at the beginning of this chapter. The

Gantt chart in Appendix D completes the set. As external dependencies vary considerably from project to project they have been omitted from the Gantt chart.

Risks

As a project progresses additional risks will become apparent, however the initial risks and their avoidance strategies are identified for the MBI project in Table 4.16.

Table 4.16 *MBI Project Risks and Avoidance Strategies*

#	Risk	Impact	Avoidance	Contingency
1	Diverse nature of organization means that it will be hard to arrive at firm decisions. **Probability**: High	Work will be slowed and the integrity of the project objective will be compromised. **Impact**: High	A high level project committee should be set up with representatives from the various organizational groupings, chaired by the MBI CEO with the purpose of facilitating corporate-wide project decisions.	Narrow scope of project so fewer people need to be involved in the decision making process. Project could be split into an initial limited implementation to be followed, if successful, by the full implementation.
2	Many of the resources allocated to the project have support responsibilities. Their work on the project will come second place to support demands. **Probability**: High	Delays due to diversion of project resources. **Impact**: Medium	The management of these resources should commit to supporting the project. Additional resources should be contracted in to the project to reduce the importance of any conflict of interest.	Eliminate use of resources with support responsibilities by retaining contractors and consultants.
3	The project depends on the ongoing network upgrade project. **Probability**: Low	Delays in that project will cause delays in this technical infrastructure project. **Impact**: Medium	Schedule technical infrastructure project to allow for network project slippage.	Re-schedule technical infrastructure project.

The Project Plan So Far

We have now successfully defined each of the top level activities and identified the following project characteristics:

- Milestones
- Dependencies
- Risks

Appendix D, Case Study Gantt Charts, shows the dependencies between the activities. The correct stage to add resources to the plan is after the tasks have been identified, which is the next step in development.

Project Tasks

To make the project plan more useful we will now go to the next level of detail down from activities and identify their constituent tasks. This book treats tasks as smaller scale activities. Before starting, let us briefly review the objectives of breaking the project down like this.

One of the powerful aspects of a project plan is the way it can be used as a resource and time scale estimating tool. By identifying all tasks and each of their resource requirements and dependencies we can arrive at overall resource requirements and time scales. Through this approach we can see the resource requirements and time scales for each of the activities and project phases too. By breaking the project into tasks we gain a clearer understanding of inter-task and inter-activity dependencies.

As each project is unique, involving different tasks and different constraints, each will have different rolled up resource and time scale values. It is therefore important that this process be performed for your project, though use the MBI case study information as a starting point and a reality check.

The tasks in the MBI project are listed below on a per activity basis in this chapter, each with brief explanatory text.

For brevity we have not listed complete task definitions in the same way we did for the activity definitions listed earlier, but have enumerated the tasks under each activity and provided a short description. It is highly recommended that a full task definition be drawn up for each task being delegated to another project team member. Using a concise method of communicating what the task involves and in particular, what its deliverables should be is important if misunderstandings are not to arise. This will be essential for the design tasks and the implementation detail tasks. The chapters in this book addressing the design phase and the implementation preparation phase provide much of the detail that will be required to define the tasks listed here.

Project Planning Tasks

Table 4.17 *Project Planning Tasks*

Task	Description
Establish external dependencies	Find out which tasks are dependent on factors beyond the scope of the project
Establish internal dependencies	Find out which tasks are dependent on the output from other tasks
Estimate resource requirements	Identify how many people will be needed, when and with what skills
Identify milestones	Mark the output of key deliverables or achievements as milestones
Identify risks	What risks threaten successful completion of the project? Make necessary contingency plans
Start project off	Kick off project with announcement, meeting and project summary document

Scoping Tasks

Business principles are introduced in Chapter 5, design principles in Chapter 6.

Table 4.18 *Scoping Tasks*

Task	Description
Workshop preparation	▪ Meet with project sponsor to explain scoping/business principle/design principle process you intend to use ▪ May require production of a document to explain process
Run workshop	Would include project sponsor, may include a small number of additional relevant people
Write up scope	Document agreed project scope and circulate for comments and confirmation

Business Principle Tasks

Table 4.19 *Business Principle Tasks*

Task	Description
Workshop preparation	Confirm who needs to attend Send each memo or meet them explaining purpose of workshop and what preparation is advisable
Run workshop	Facilitate creation of complete set of business principles An off-site workshop is worthwhile considering it can reduce interruptions
Write up principles	Document workshop proceedings and circulate for comments and corrections

Application Requirements Tasks

Table 4.20 *Application Requirements Tasks*

Task	Description
Establish required applications	Find out which applications are required by consulting the business
Analyze each for infrastructure requirements	For each application, requirements in terms of technical infrastructure services need to be established
Documentation	▪ Record requirements in Requirements Specification Create Functional Specification ▪ Task is shared with the equivalent User Requirements task

User Requirements Tasks

Table 4.21 *User Requirements Tasks*

Task	Description
Define scope of user requirements	By considering scope of project and way in which it will affect user population, establish information that will be required from users
Determine source of user requirements	Identify people who have authority, knowledge and time to provide the required information

Table 4.21 *User Requirements Tasks (continued)*

Task	Description
Create user requirements tool	Design format and wording of questions that will need to be put to users, to ensure answers are in a usable format
Gather user requirements	▪ Send a copy of questionnaire in advance of visit to allow for preparation ▪ Site should then be visited and questionnaire worked through
Documentation	▪ Record user requirements in the Requirements Specification ▪ Create Functional Specification ▪ Task is shared with equivalent Application Requirements task

Planning Requirements Tasks

Table 4.22 *Planning Requirements Tasks*

Task	Description
Define scope of planning requirements	By considering scope of project and plans that will need to be made, establish information that will be required
Determine source of planning requirements	Identify people who have authority, knowledge, and time to provide required information
Create planning requirements tool	Site survey questionnaire is main tool for gathering information for implementation planning activity
Gather planning requirements	People should be sent a copy of questionnaire in advance of visit to allow for preparation Site should then be visited and questionnaire worked through
Check and document results	Results of survey should be checked, written up, and circulated for confirmation

Design Tasks

Table 4.23 *Design Tasks*

Task	Description
Establish scope of technical design	Identify technologies and technical challenges that fall within scope of design
Domain and/or Active Directory	Create design for security and resource administration
Naming services	Create naming service design
Naming standards	Define and gain agreement to set of naming standards
Groups	Define Windows NT group usage strategy
File and print services	Create file and print service design
Time services	Create time service design
User environment	Create design for user's working environment
Network	Plan IP address management strategy and define network requirements

Note that the tasks of domain design and naming standards are of a highly sensitive nature and consequently can take a lot of time and effort to bring to a conclusion. Any resourcing estimates for these two aspects of design should include a large degree of contingency.

The scope of this book extends as far as the design tasks listed in the table above. On a full scale project there may be a number of additional design tasks to address areas such as:

- Workstation configuration
- Systems monitoring
- Backup/restore
- Software distribution

The exact list of design tasks will reflect the scope of the project as there is no one definitive list.

Procurement Tasks

Table 4.24 *Procurement Tasks*

Task	Description
Identify requirements	List products that need to be purchased for both laboratory and production environment
Organization of loans	Negotiate with suppliers for loan of products
Agree on evaluation criteria	Agree on a set of criteria by which products will be selected—important as it is an attempt to minimize subjective arguments after evaluations
Evaluate products	Carry out evaluations and record results
Recommend and agree products	Document and circulate recommendations Seek confirmation to proceed with recommendations
Purchase products	Talk to purchasing department to acquire the goods (Don't forget to negotiate a discount on loaner you have as it is now used goods!)

Training Tasks

Table 4.25 *Training Tasks*

Task	Description
Needs analysis	Conduct interviews to establish current skill levels among users and technical support
Prepare training program	Comparing skill levels against skill requirements, prepare training schedule
Deliver training	Conduct training (or organize for an agency to do it), including tests for competence at end

Acceptance Tasks

Table 4.26 *Acceptance Tasks*

Task	Description
Create User Acceptance Test (UAT)	■ Task should be carried out by representatives of user community ■ Should include responsibility for enhancing test based on problems fixed and features added
Create System Acceptance Test (SAT)	■ System acceptance test is intended for use by technical support group, however, as infrastructure is designed by engineering, SAT is ideally created by that group ■ Should include responsibility for enhancing test based on problems fixed and features added
Execute UAT	Carry out UAT noting any failed tests
Execute SAT	Carry out SAT noting any failed tests

Implementation Details Tasks

Table 4.27 *Implementation Details Tasks*

Task	Description
	Software Delivery Strategy
Design software delivery strategy	Determine how initial installations and software upgrades are to be implemented
Create initial installation mechanism	Design, implement and test mechanism for initial installation
Create software upgrade mechanism	Design, implement and test mechanism for software upgrade and installations
	Product Deliverables
Create workstation installation kit	The "kit" of software along with documented instructions for installing a new workstation
Create server installation kit	The "kit" of software along with documented instructions for installing a new server
Create application installation packages	Create the automatic installation packages for various layered software applications and tools

Table 4.27 *Implementation Details Tasks (continued)*

Task	Description
Create system guides	▪ This is documentation describing scripts, how to create an installation kit and how to create an application installation package ▪ This documentation is targeted at a system engineering audience
Application porting	Porting of applications to new platform Includes testing of application compatibility
UNIX integration	Testing all aspects of UNIX integration method
Novell NetWare integration	Testing all aspects of Novell NetWare integration method
Recovery procedures	Analyze deployment configurations for purpose of designing, testing and documenting recovery procedures to be executed in event of a component or system failure
Remote computer management	Create remote computer management environment
Create logon scripts	Write user logon scripts and any other scripts needed to support infrastructure
	Development Testing
Set up development laboratory	Plan and install systems and software for use as a laboratory
Volume testing	Using laboratory or (with caution and agreement) part of production environment, to measure system behavior under a load
Installation testing	Using laboratory to test workstation and server installation kits
Software unit testing	Testing of all software components individually
Software integration testing	Testing of all software components. For example, testing whether terminal emulator is compatible with other installed products
Laboratory management	Ongoing administration of laboratory

Table 4.27 *Implementation Details Tasks (continued)*

Task	Description
	Pilot Implementation
Identify suitable pilot	Decide whether pilot is appropriate and why
Plan pilot	Create project plan for pilot ensuring users are fully aware of objectives and risks
Manage pilot	Manage implementation of pilot systems, training of users and recording of results
Review pilot	Carry out joint review of how well pilot met its objectives and publish results
	Software Release Management
Run acceptance tests	Run tests that allow product to move from engineering to User Acceptance Test status
Software release administration	Manage process of change control and quality control for software and documentary project products
Software production	Creation and issue of releases of software for beta testing
	Capacity Planning
Translate business workload into hardware requirements	For given business workload identify hardware configuration required to deliver certain level of performance
Incorporate business plans	Consulting with business to establish how workload is likely to change over an agreed planning horizon
Size the systems	Based on planned business workload changes and knowledge of what configuration delivers what performance with what particular workload, calculate required system configuration
	Reviewing the Design
A design review	Carry out one or more design reviews for each component of technical infrastructure to check that design will meet requirements laid down in Functional Specification

Implementation Planning Tasks

Table 4.28 *Implementation Planning Tasks*

Task	Description
Define the scope of the installation	If the installation project is effectively several small projects, define in detail the scope of technical infrastructure sub-project
Identify roles and responsibilities	Who is responsible for success of the project? What parts of project are various team members responsible for?
Recruit core project team members	Identify who will be needed and get a firm (written) commitment from their management that their priority is your project
Publish project terms of reference	Advertise objectives of project and how you plan to achieve them
Identify milestones	There could be some milestones in common with overall project
Identify dependencies	One dependency will be timely delivery of released infrastructure builds
Identify risks	Consult widely on likely risks as there will be many things over which you have little influence
Identify and secure local resources	▪ At stages of project there may be a need for ad hoc local resources ▪ Make sure they are identified up front and have necessary skills

Completing Project Plan

Now that the tasks involved are understood we can start to apply resources to the plan. The starting point should always be to take each task in turn and consider how long it should take to accomplish and what skills are required. We won't go to this level of detail with the case study; instead, the Gantt charts assume unlimited resources of sufficient skill. A more realistic outcome is that the project plan will show dependencies on the availability of appropriate resource. In other words, two or more activities that could overlap might have to be carried out in sequence as there is only one person available with the skill to do them all.

We already have a list of milestones, dependencies and risks, produced based on the project phasing and activity plan. We should now check to see whether our work identifying tasks has highlighted any more suitable candidates for milestones, introduced new dependencies (e.g., resourcing), or risks. Again, this is beyond the scope of the case study, largely because these aspects will vary significantly from project to project.

It is very important that the plan be realistic and achievable. To make sure it is, each person undertaking a project task and each person responsible for someone who is, should agree that the time scales are appropriate for what is being asked. The plan should therefore be presented to each interested party for their approval. Once approval is gained, those parties will be working for the plan and not against it.

Appendix D shows the project Gantt chart down to task level with several generic task dependencies.

Summary

Each project is different, requiring a unique project plan. However, when two projects share the same problem domain their project plans will share the same broad structure and constituent parts. The project plan presented in this chapter is broadly applicable to a technical infrastructure design project.

A project model is proposed, based on a phased approach beginning with design preparation, followed by design, then implementation preparation and finally implementation. The focus of the book is on the first three phases.

Each phase is divided into activities which are clearly defined units of work. Once these activities have been defined for a project the plan may then be enhanced through the addition of milestones, dependencies and risks.

To realize the power of the project planning process and in particular the Gantt chart technique, the project is further broken down into tasks. Tasks may be allocated to individuals to carry out. To complete the plan, resources should now be applied and all milestones, dependencies and risks re-evaluated.

5

Business Principles

The investment an organization makes in Information Technology should always be justified in terms of the benefits it brings to the business. It may be to gain a competitive advantage, or to deny that advantage to others. Whatever the reason, we must strive to build a system that supports the business, not impedes it.

We saw in Chapter 2, Elements of a Technical Infrastructure, that it is important to give the design of a technical infrastructure as much consideration as the design of any applications that may run on it. Specifically, if the characteristics of the technical infrastructure do not match those required by the business then we may see a number of implications:

- An application may be over-engineered to implement functionality that should have been provided by the infrastructure.
- The technical infrastructure may become a barrier to change.
- Unilateral solutions will be developed to solve shortcomings in the technical infrastructure.
- Management costs may be higher than necessary if the infrastructure has not been designed for manageability.
- If the complexity is too high, reliability may suffer and the time to fix may be too long.

This chapter and the next (Chapter 6, Design Principles) are about how to apply the same rigor to the development of a technical infrastructure as would be done for a well thought out, well planned application development. The process described here emphasizes analysis and documentation. Most projects tend to be weak in these areas, however there is no more work involved in following this design method than any other. Indeed, one of the reasons this approach is so powerful is that it produces a stable, agreed result quickly, avoiding protracted discussions on points of design that can be difficult to conclude.

The first stage of the process, covered in this chapter, is to capture key business decisions that are within the scope of the project. The next stage, covered in Chapter 6, is to make design decisions supported by the business decisions. Figure 5.1 shows the activities this chapter applies to in the overall project model.

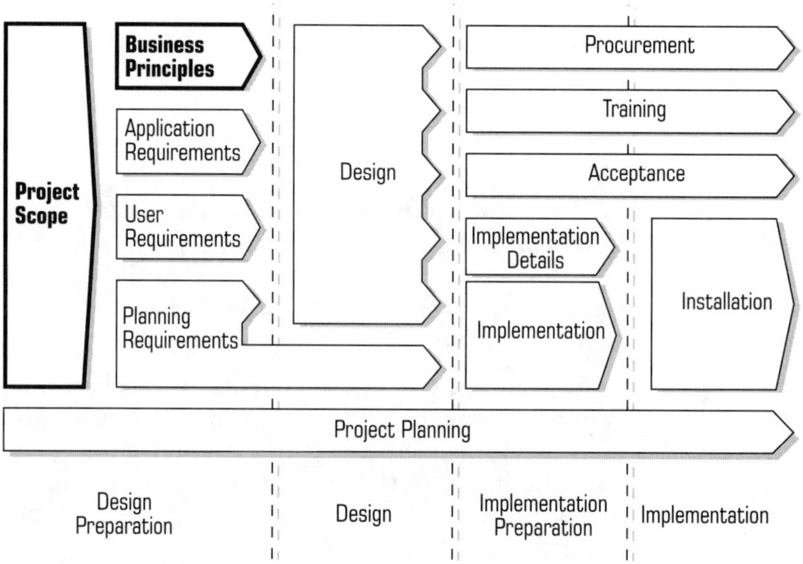

Figure 5.1 *Scoping Business Principle Activity in Project Model*

This chapter makes heavy use of the case study to provide examples. It is important to keep in mind that their purpose is to illustrate the tools introduced; the actual content of the examples is secondary.

Structure of Chapter

Table 5.1 *Structure of Chapter 5*

Topic	Content
Concepts	Introduces the key concepts that will be used in this and subsequent chapters to structure the approach to the design of a technical infrastructure.
Scope of the Project	Examines the forces acting on a technical infrastructure project and shows how they can be used as cues for defining its scope. Five areas of project scope are then developed for the fictitious Midas Bank International (MBI) case study.

Table 5.1 *Structure of Chapter 5 (continued)*

Topic	Content
Principles of the Business	Shows how the principles governing the way a corporation intends to apply IT to its business can be written down as a formal argument and then used to support the design of a technical infrastructure. Five principles of the business are developed for the MBI case study based on the five areas of project scope identified in the previous section.

The examples produced in this chapter are used extensively later on in the chapters focusing on technical infrastructure design.

Concepts

The relationship between the concepts about to be introduced can be illustrated as a three tiered analysis model, as shown in Figure 5.2:

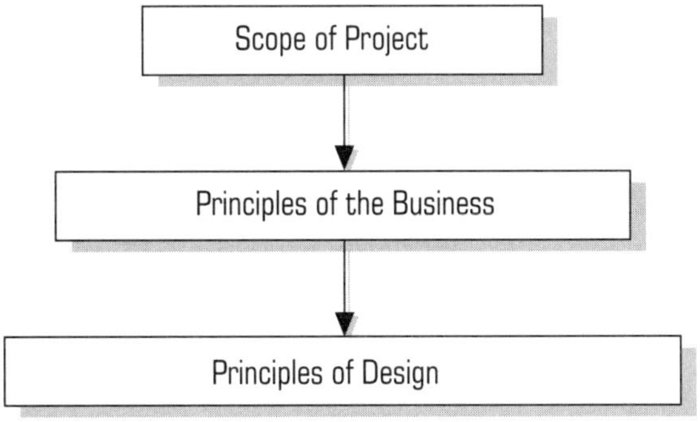

Figure 5.2 *Top Down Approach to Technical Infrastructure Design*

The analysis model allows us to take a top down approach to defining key parameters of the project. The first stage is to identify the bounds of the project by defining the areas within scope.

Once the areas of project scope are defined we come to the critical element of the model which helps us represent the needs of the business as a set of principles. These principles are non-technical in nature and are used to guide subsequent technical design decisions. These Business Principles represent the crucial bridge between business and technology by capturing succinctly the policies governing how the corporation intends to apply technology to solve business problems. Business principles are created for each of the areas of project scope.

The final element of the model is a means for justifying key design decisions in terms of business principles. A statement of this kind is called a Design Principle. Design Principles are covered in Chapter 6.

The strength of this approach is in the way it leads logically from a business oriented statement of scope through to a solid set of practical guidelines for making technical design decisions. Thus, each design decision can ultimately be justified in terms of how it contributes to the business goals, though as we will see later in the chapter, it is not possible to *derive* a subsequent stage of the model from an earlier stage. Thus, there is no formula for automatically moving from analysis to a design.

Chapter 7, Developing Principles, offers recommendations on practical means of identifying scope areas and business principles, such as use of workshops or interviews. The following sections in this chapter will describe the first two stages of the model in more detail making extensive use of the MBI case study. The intention is to illustrate the use of the concepts so the readers may develop sufficient understanding to be able to apply them to their project. The actual content of the examples in terms of project type and business segment is entirely secondary to the purpose of the example.

Project Scope

To focus project effort it is important to confine its scope to only those areas that are necessary for the project to be completed. This will avert time being spent on matters that may be perfectly valid in their own right, but do not contribute to the achievement of the project's objectives.

Projects with an ill-defined scope, or a scope that is too ambitious, can fail because there is no clear understanding of what should be included and what shouldn't. This is often compounded by there being no sense of priority between competing needs. The identification of areas of project scope is therefore an important step that needs to be carried out right at the beginning of a project.

Identifying Project Scope Areas

The scope of a project will be the result of trading of business priorities against available resources. Because of this, scope may change throughout the life of a project as business priorities change and the resources available vary. We should be prepared for this and always maintain an accurate set of statements defining the scope of the project.

Some scope areas will be immediately apparent, for example, a project to replace UNIX office servers with Windows NT servers will be likely to have as a scope area *Remote file and print services*. Others will be less apparent, requiring more concerted thought about what the project is trying to achieve and what will be affected by it. We should always try to develop as complete a set of scope areas as possible as they will be the foundation for the business principles for the project. A missing scope area may cause the planning of an aspect of the project to be overlooked.

A good scope area statement will not pre-judge anything, as its objective is to identify where decisions, or business principles, are necessary, not to make them. For example, a bad scope area statement might be *Development of an IT Strategy* as it assumes an IT strategy is needed. A better statement might be *IT Strategy*, leaving the job of deciding what to do in this scope area for later.

Figure 5.3 *Forces Acting on a Project*

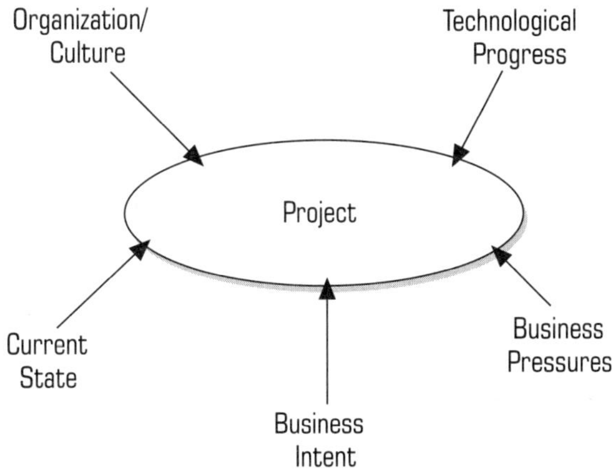

In Chapter 7, Developing Principles, there is a comprehensive checklist for assisting in the identification of scope areas. At this stage we will look at the basic forces operating on a project that provide a source of project scope statements.

Table 5.2 *Project Forces*

Project Force	Definition
Business Intent	▪ The way in which the corporation intends to achieve its goal of commercial success. ▪ Could be based on a business strategy but need not be formal. This captures the vision of how the leadership see the corporation evolving in the future in more detail than a mission statement.

Table 5.2 *Project Forces (continued)*

Project Force	Definition
Organization/ Culture	▪ How the organizational structure and cultural aspects of a corporation affect its ability to strive for, or accommodate change. ▪ The ability of an organization to absorb change or work in a particular way will have a bearing on how a business intent can be realized. This has direct implications for how IT can be used to realize the business intent.
Technological Progress	▪ The constant improvement in technological capability. ▪ Too much consideration of IT at the stage where we are trying to establish and document the intent of the business risks constraining our thought processes. On the other hand, ignoring it completely denies the opportunity to consider its potential to give competitive advantage.
Business Pressures	▪ The internal and external factors affecting the corporation's ability to remain competitive. ▪ Chances of success will be enhanced if the business intent is developed with a full understanding of the pressures on the business.
Current State	▪ The current state of the IT infrastructure, organizational structure, business processes, financial condition, etc. ▪ Attempts to change the current state, such as those that would be caused by a technical infrastructure project, will frequently result in resistance, reflecting a natural inertial force.

It would be usual for a project to include areas of project scope relating to each one of the five project forces, though where this is not the case it is important to be confident of the reason why not.

Create as many scope areas as necessary. A typical large scale project will have up to about 15. If you find that you have more than this, consider whether some could be combined into a more high level statement. A large number of scope areas or a set that can be easily grouped into different categories may indicate that the project should be broken down into two or more sub-projects with narrower scope.

Example Project Scope Area

We shall take an example in the Business Intent category: The creation of a new technical infrastructure is often triggered by the need to deploy a new application. A valid question is whether the technical infrastructure is there to support the deployment of that one application or there to support a set of future applications as well.

The benefit of designing the infrastructure to support potential future applications should be clear, as it allows more infrastructure stability and consequently is likely to need less overall investment. To support this approach the business needs to take a long term view of the return on infrastructure investment.

On the other hand, financial and time imperatives frequently confine the scope of technical infrastructure to the minimum required for supporting the application driving the project. In such a case we must accept that the business intends to take a short term view of the investment and keep costs down.

This is clearly an area where there needs to be one or more business principles developed to guide the project, so it is a natural candidate for a scope area. We state it as follows:

Scope Area:	Suitability of the Technical Infrastructure to support a broad range of future applications.

Notice how the scope area records a topic that requires further consideration from the business perspective without pre-judging the outcome. This is precisely what we are looking for as it prompts the creation of business principles to resolve the question prior to design work beginning.

Case Study

The case study which will be used throughout the book was mentioned in the introductory chapter. We use it for the first time here to develop a set of project scope areas for the fictitious organization Midas Bank International, or MBI.

Clearly, the effective identification of project scope areas is something that can require a large amount of contextual information such as the market the organization trades in, its size, geographic distribution and so on. We will need to provide some contextual information for the case study to be effective, though every effort will be made to keep it to the minimum necessary. It is an artificial case study, contrived to illustrate the use of project scope areas, so some aspects of it may appear implausible!

For the purpose of this exercise we will analyze the relevant background material for a single project scope area in each of the five categories of force on a project, as introduced earlier in this chapter. If this were a real project we might create more scope areas, however, for practical reasons we are limiting the extent of the case study. As we follow the case study throughout the book the reader is welcome to conclude that had we identified additional scope areas at this stage, the additional business principles that would have been created for each of those scope areas would have been valuable. First we will review some background information.

MBI Background

The business of MBI includes all aspects of banking. The company has grown recently through acquisition though the management have not been able to successfully integrate the new subsidiaries, precipitating a very fragmented organization. Each subsidiary retains a large amount of autonomy with the attendant differences in organizational structure, technology, and skills. It is a goal of MBI that it rapidly becomes a fully integrated organization.

MBI has a total population of around 8,300 distributed among the locations around the world where MBI and its three subsidiaries, the Red Bank, Green Bank and Blue Bank have offices. The New York and London offices are substantially larger than any of the others with Buenos Aires being the smallest.

- ***Project Force 1: Business Intent***

The CEO has recently initiated a project to develop a new global settlements system aimed at allowing settlements processing to be carried out anywhere in the world. It will be built to run on a Windows NT platform. The IT division of MBI has responded to this by initiating a project to create a global Windows NT based technical infrastructure for the entire bank to support the new application.

Our case study focuses on the technical infrastructure project with the application development project being a key driver for its creation. The global settlement system project clearly represents the intent of the business so we should consider it as within the scope of the project. This is sufficient to write:

Scope Area 1:	The needs of the planned settlements system.

- ***Project Force 2: Organization/Culture***

The organizational structure of MBI and its subsidiaries brings with it a number of difficulties when the holding company attempts to treat the group as one company. This is recognized by the CEO as one of the main challenges to MBI.

More specifically, the project manager for the technical infrastructure project and some of the business heads of department have expressed a concern that the radical changes likely to be brought about by the new application could impact customer service as the organization struggles to cope with the relatively high degree of change. This is sufficiently important for the scope of the project to encompass consideration for coping with the necessary organizational change.

Scope Area 2:	The need for MBI to cope with change.

- ***Project Force 3: Technological Progress***

  The autonomy MBI subsidiaries have has led to a diverse set of IT systems. There are small areas where modern technology is in use but there is no cohesion regarding its usage. For the organization to succeed in using modern technology, it needs to be clear about how best to harness it in its unique and changing political structure. The choice for MBI can be distilled down to the question of the degree to which different parts of the corporation are free to determine aspects of their own use of technology. If there is a high degree of freedom the end result will inevitably be a lack of consistency throughout the bank. This has the potential to seriously impact any project to create a new technical infrastructure, so the issue should be within scope.

Scope Area 3:	Corporate-wide consistent deployment of technology.

- ***Project Force 4: Business Pressure***

  Faced with declining profits, the institutional shareholders recently forced a management review of business at MBI. A firm of management consultants were retained and after a short analysis, recommended a process of strategy setting for MBI.

  The objective of this strategy setting would be to define a strategy for making MBI a profitable organization. The board of MBI would own the strategy and the success of its subsequent implementation.

  At the point the technical infrastructure project began, there had been no strategy developed yet, so the decision was made to include within the scope of the project the topic of flexibility on the basis that the exact business requirements were unknown.

  Note that at this stage it is not necessary to consider whether flexibility is required in the technical infrastructure design or not. That comes later with the business principles. It is merely necessary to mark the question as being within the scope of the project.

Scope Area 4:	Flexibility of the Technical Infrastructure.

- *Project Force 5: Current State*

  The two aspects of the current state of MBI that are clear are the control each subsidiary is used to exerting over its IT systems and the consequent diversity of IT systems. The subject of IT diversity has been addressed in scope area 3, technology progress, so we can declare a scope area covering subsidiary control over IT systems. Of course at this point we don't know what level of control can be provided with the new system or what the problems might be, but based on our knowledge of Windows NT we should know that we will need guidance from the business regarding who controls what resources and administrates users.

Scope Area 5:	Distributed IT administration and control.

Review of Project Scope Areas

Identification of project scope areas must be the first step in the process of relating business needs to technology. Only business principles that fall within these scope areas will be relevant to the project. The scope areas can be arrived at by studying the implications of each of the five principle forces on a project:

1. Business intent
2. Organization/culture
3. Technological progress
4. Business pressures
5. Current state

Business Principles

Businesses vary considerably in the degree to which they contemplate and document their plans for the future. However, a project which aims to solve a business problem using technology must begin by capturing the intentions of that business. Once captured, they can be used as the basis for further analysis and deduction, ultimately leading to a technical design. Thus we can show how the business need has been taken into account for each key design decision.

It is important to keep in mind that the parameters for making key design decisions are ultimately derived from the business. For example, there might be several design options presented for locating and managing user accounts on a computer system. One option might be to use a single central accounts database and another might be to split the accounts database into three parts with a third of the user population in each. Resolving this design decision is a sterile academic exercise not guaranteed to deliver the correct result unless it can be linked to a business requirement. Such a requirement might be expressed as: "any type of system unavailability should affect no more than one third of the user population."

It is this type of business oriented statement, expressed in such a way as to guide the application of IT, that we should capture as a business principle. Alone, no matter how valid a business principle statement might be, it is vulnerable to constant questioning which acts to devalue the extensive discussions that may have gone on to identify it. To avoid this the reasons for the choice of business principle statement should be recorded along with any implications there may be for it to be adhered to. Lastly, where problems can be foreseen with the adoption of a business principle these should be listed as well.

A set of business principles, along with their associated arguments, developed for a particular project can be a very powerful guiding force, making the process of moving towards a design more efficient by providing a framework for decision making. By their nature they are business statements and so it is very important they should be developed and agreed on by representatives of the business who have the necessary understanding and authority.

Business principles created for one project may apply to other projects, encouraging a consistent approach and reducing the work required to develop new business principles as each new project is undertaken. As many business principles should be created as there are principles guiding the application of IT, as long as they are within the scope of the project defined by the project scope areas.

Scope of a Business Principle

Our primary objective for developing business principles is to guide the creation of a technical infrastructure. It will become apparent however, that of the business principles we will develop, many will apply to the applications as well. While we are not substituting the business analysis process that determines the shape of a new application we should recognize that some of the business principles will say as much about the characteristics of an application as they do about the technical infrastructure.

Let us consider a business principle that states that users should be able to carry out their jobs from any computer in the corporation. From a technical infrastructure perspective we might begin to interpret this in terms of ensuring users could always gain access to their home drive and always log on with the same user identification.

From an application perspective it may drive certain architectural decisions, such as where to locate configuration files. Locating them on a server may make them more accessible from alternate workstations. Locating them on a workstation makes them relatively inaccessible. Locating application configuration files on a server will in turn generate requirements placed by the application on the technical infrastructure.

Thus, while a business principle was directly applicable to the technical infrastructure, it was also applicable to an application, which in turn placed requirements on the technical infrastructure. This highlights the importance of combining the influence of business principles with the requirements applications place on a technical infrastructure. Identifying the needs of applications is addressed in Chapter 8, Requirements Gathering. One of the skills of the technical infrastructure architect is to know to what degree a business principle drives the technical infrastructure directly and to what degree indirectly via applications.

Definition of a Business Principle

A business principle states how a corporation intends to apply IT to support its business. Each business principle statement will have associated with it the following three elements:

Justification	Why the principle is valid
Implications	What will happen or need to happen should the principle be adopted
Issues	The problems that will need to be overcome for its adoption

To be consistent we will write down a business principle using a convention:

Business Principle
This is the business principle statement
Justifications
1. Justification number one 2. Justification number two
Implications
1. Implication number one 2. Implication number two
Issues
1. Issue number one 2. Issue number two

The business principle statement and each of the three associated elements are defined in the following sections.

Business Principle Statement

A business principle statement should say something positive and constructive about the corporation's approach to business, it should not just be a statement of fact. Generic statements should also be avoided unless they happen to have direct relevance in a specific case.

Business principle statements should be future oriented because they will be used to guide the process of moving to a future state. They are not intended to be a record of what is current or what has happened in the past.

For every principle statement it should be possible to construct one or more valid contradictory statements as a test of its strength. If the principle statement doesn't tell us anything or is too vague, creating a contradictory statement will be very difficult. For example:

Business Principle
All new servers will be sourced from the same manufacturer.

A valid contradictory statement might be:

Business Principle
The choice of server manufacturer for new systems will be left to local country policy.

Both of these are good business principle statements. A bad one would be:

Business Principle
The Bank has been organized to use the same business practices in each customer facing office.

A business principle should be rejected if it:

1. **Mentions a future date:** If it does it should probably be an objective of the project.
2. **States a fact:** If it does so it probably has its place providing context for the project.
3. **Fails to record a decision:** A business principle that fails to record a decision is of no use as a principle.

The bad business principle in the previous example offends on the second and third points.

Business Principle Justification Statements

The justification of a business principle statement should answer the question why? This is a way of linking the statement to a strategic intent, documented, or otherwise. The justification may reference the mission statement. There may be any number of justifications for a given statement. Following on with the previous example:

Justifications
1. Global consistency of server technology lowers support costs. 2. Enables a cost-effective volume based corporate purchasing agreement to be struck. 3. Easier to arrange global support.

Justification for the alternative statement:

Justifications
1. Allows choice of a server manufacturer that can deliver the required level of local support. 2. Allows choice of most cost-effective manufacturer as the relative cost of servers from different manufacturers varies from country to country.

Notice how although the principle statement mentions technology, the justification statements are all business oriented. This emphasizes the business impact choice of technology has.

Business Principle Implications Statements

The implications of a business principle statement describe the effect adherence to it will have. In most cases it will be a change or action of some sort which can be expressed as a prerequisite for the business principle to be realized. The list of implications for a given statement could be extensive if it were to attend to detail, however the number of implications should be kept to the minimum necessary and they should focus on the business impact. Our example continues:

Implications
1. A corporate standard server manufacturer must be chosen.

Implications for the alternative statement:

Implications
1. Each country must agree on a local standard server manufacturer. 2. Guidelines must be provided to each country indicating the criteria for choosing a server manufacturer (e.g., cost, support, etc.)

Implication statements may express benefits or drawbacks.

Care should be taken to not express a design decision in an implication statement. Instead, it should identify the need for a design decision. The correct place for a design decision is in a design principle. Notice how in the example above it does not say which server manufacturer should be chosen, only that the decision needs to be made.

The implication statements will have a much more powerful effect on guiding design decisions than either the business principle statement or it justifications. It is therefore very important that the implications of a business principle are thoroughly considered and agreed on before being written down.

Business Principle Issue Statements

The issues related to a business principle statement are the problems that need to be addressed. Finishing the example:

Issues
1. There will be resistance from some parts of the organization to adoption of a corporate standard. 2. It may not be possible to choose a single manufacturer capable of offering the necessary level of support in all the countries where MBI currently operates, or might operate in the future.

For the alternative principle:

Issues
1. It will not be possible to use the same system recovery procedures in each country.

At the stage business principles are being developed there may not be enough facts available to be precise about some of the potential issues. In such cases we should be content to record it as a speculative issue with a note that clarification is required.

There can be difficulty deciding whether something should be an implication or an issue, as it may often be a matter of degree. The test that should be applied is to ask whether a practical solution is immediately obvious. If it is, it's an implication, if it isn't, it's an issue.

We would expect all issues to eventually acquire a solution, or to be proven unfounded if they were of a speculative nature. An issue that cannot be resolved will effectively be a show stopper, making it impossible to adhere fully to the business principle.

Case Study Business Principles

We will now apply the concept of business principles to the case study we began earlier. There are several possible processes for developing business principles and each is described in Chapter 6, Developing Principles. For the purpose of this case study we will develop a set of proposed business principles based solely on the information we have discovered so far, detailed earlier in this chapter. In a real project this is not the preferred approach; ideally they would be developed with direct input from representatives of the business.

In every case of business principle development, particularly when developing them with minimal business input, it is critical to ensure they are verified by the business. The process we will go through in this example is to take each project scope area in turn and to create a single business principle based on our knowledge of MBI and its technical infrastructure project. In a real project we would not confine ourselves to a single business principle per scope area, we might develop two, or three, or possibly more, depending on what needs to be said.

In each case we will be looking to distill the intentions of the business into principles that we know will assist the task of designing the technical infrastructure. How can we predict whether a business principle will assist or not? This is very difficult. To help we can recall one of the more practical reasons why we develop business principles, which is to guide decisions in areas where there are options. Thus, we can look for areas we know will require a decision to be made for design work to proceed. We will see that it is not always the business principle statement that contains the useful information for design work but the associated implications and issues statements.

An Important Comment on the Case Study

The business principles chosen in the following case study are relatively high level and oriented towards applications. This is consistent with the situation at MBI where a technical infrastructure is being created in response to the need to deploy a single new application.

Throughout the design chapters of the book we will identify the need for additional business principles that are less high level but could be argued are more useful to us in the development of a technical infrastructure. This discovery mirrors what you will experience when first attempting to use business principles. We will find, when carrying out the design, that the value they bring is very sensitive to the level at which they are pitched. Too high a level and they don't say anything specific enough to be useful. Too low a level and they unnecessarily constrain the design. Bear in mind this observation throughout the book to help you develop a feel for what makes a useful business principle.

Business Principle for Scope Area 1

Scope Area 1:	The needs of the planned settlements system.

One of the reasons for the initiation of a project to create a new global settlements application was the need to be able to operate the settlements process competitively. The way to doing this is seen by MBI as being able to carry out that processing in a country where the wage costs are low, as settlements processing is a labor intensive operation.

The implications of this approach for the technical infrastructure and the new settlements application are potentially far reaching. To trade in one country, process the settlements in another and settle the trade (i.e., communicate with relevant stock exchange) in another implies the need for a complete communications infrastructure. This is important from the perspective of the technical infrastructure as a complete network doesn't exist in MBI. By stating the business intent in a business principle and drawing this out the inadequacy of the network as an issue allows us to gain recognition of this challenge early.

To see how this argument might guide us later we can think through what this implication statement might mean to a design. Looking at name resolution for example, the implication more or less mandates that any computer should be able to resolve the address of another computer on the network, which apart from having a network, is a minimum basic requirement for computer communication. We will see this as a design principle later.

Business Principle 1
It must be possible to use the settlement processing component of the system from any MBI office in the world.
Justification
1. If another country promises lower labor costs then to improve the bank's profitability, settlements processing should be able to shift to that country. 2. There will be only one global settlements system so it must be possible to use it from anywhere (see business principle 3).

continued ▸

continued

Implications
1. The technical infrastructure must support communications between the settlements processing component of the application which may be in any office and the trading components of the application which must be in MBI offices local to stock exchanges. 2. As it is known that the settlement application requires a single security environment in which to function, an implication of this business principle is that the entire MBI technical infrastructure should be a single security environment.
Issues
1. The network infrastructure in MBI cannot sustain reliable communications in some regions of the world.

So how does this business principle help us? Consider if we hadn't proposed the principle and were in the process of designing the technical infrastructure naming resolution service. It is conceivable that there could be discussion around naming service design with one argument being for a partitioned name space along MBI subsidiary lines. This business principle makes it quite clear that a partitioned name space does not support the business intentions.

Business Principle for Scope Area 2

Scope Area 2:	The need for MBI to cope with change.

This scope area was born out of the recognition that change within MBI may be difficult to accomplish. That alone is not sufficient to resolve any design decisions; what we need to know is the deployment strategy that will be employed for implementing the new application. We can then start to consider the implications and issues that arise with the design of the technical infrastructure.

The CEO is considering two options for deployment strategy:

1. Implementing the complete technical infrastructure and running the new application alongside the existing systems for an agreed period throughout the bank before switching over completely to the new system within one day.
2. A phased approach taking in groups of offices at a time. In each case there would be a period of parallel running prior to complete dependence on the new system.

Assuming the second option has been chosen we can see immediately that by adopting a strategy of phasing in the application we are in a position to phase in the technical infrastructure. Another implication might be that as there will be some parts of the bank using the new application and technical infrastructure at the same time others are using the old systems, there may be a temporary need for a level of integration between the new systems and the old.

Business Principle 2
The new settlements system will be phased in to MBI taking in groups of offices at a time.
Justification
1. The settlements process as it is currently carried out in MBI is fragile. Any problems with switching over to a new system will increase the risk of the Bank incurring fines for late settlements and errors. This phased approach minimizes that risk. 2. The new settlements system and the technical infrastructure should only be implemented over suitable WAN connections. As many of these need upgrading, with the work taking place over the next 18 months a phased rollout is the only option if the system is to be available anywhere soon.
Implications
1. There will be a degree of integration needed between the new system and the old if they are to run in parallel for a period of time (e.g., use of existing non-preferred file servers). 2. A wider range of support skills will be needed at offices during their parallel running phase. 3. There may be a need to implement integration solutions to enable parallel running that will be redundant once the old systems have been de-commissioned. 4. Phasing in the new settlements system presents an opportunity to implement the technical infrastructure in a similarly phased manner. 5. The support organization must phase in a globally integrated approach to supporting this application.
Issues
1. Management of the costs incurred to fund parallel running that must be written off after the transition. For example, purchase of an extra computer to satisfy temporary additional processing requirements.

Business Principle for Scope Area 3

Scope Area 3:	Corporate-wide consistent deployment of technology.

Knowing the current federated structure of MBI and the likely need for each subsidiary or office to have control over their own resources (see business principle 5), it is possible there will be pressure to provide duplicated applications, services and systems so each political entity can have a "full set." From a technical perspective this is not likely to be ideal, neither is it likely to be cost effective.

For example, in some cities where MBI is represented by more than one constituent Bank, each office may demand its own application servers or servers dedicated to infrastructure functions. A policy for dealing with this eventuality would make it easier to reach design decisions relating to architecture, scalability and management.

Taking this example one step further, suppose that two offices were to each demand their own server where, from a technical standpoint, one would be sufficient. A business principle opposing such a demand might state that there should be no more servers than technically necessary. Such a principle would allow design work to proceed without the designer needing to heed political demands that have no technical basis. MBI chose a business principle based on a generalized version of the example above.

Business Principle 3
Where there is no sound reason for their existence duplicate applications, structures, services and systems should be removed and avoided.
Justification
1. Guards against compromising the design. 2. To make the corporate goal of integration of MBI into a single organization easier. 3. To support the corporate goal of lowering IT support costs through economy of scale.

continued▸

continued

Implications
1. One of the greatest areas of duplication is IT Support. To address this principle the multiple disparate IT Support organizations must be merged into one. 2. May require subsidiaries to accept a reduced level of control over IT resources compared to that which they have been used to. 3. A set of corporate standard applications and systems should be published to resolve the issue of which system should be used where alternatives exist. 4. Some subsidiaries or offices will need to migrate away from their existing system to the standard system.
Issues
1. Resistance to giving up current systems.

Business Principle for Scope Area 4

Scope Area 4:	Flexibility of the Technical Infrastructure

A discussion with the CEO reveals that in addition to lowering costs, the new infrastructure must enable the Bank to be more agile in terms of where and how it does business. MBI is under pressure from its customers to trade in countries where it does not have a presence, offering new services as it does so.

Banks that can move into these new markets swiftly can be more effective at attracting customers and retaining them. Manual based systems make the lead time to set up an operation in a new country very long. The CEO is looking for the new technical infrastructure to assist such expansion, not to be an impediment.

This is clearly what we are looking for as a business principle statement. Now we need to think through what the implications and issues are likely to be.

Again we should think in terms of identifying the things we anticipate being valuable when it comes to supporting technical decisions. For example, in a developing country that has just opened up a stock exchange or bond market, the communications infrastructure might be very poor, indeed it may take months to get a high speed leased line organized. This can be critical if the application demands high bandwidth. Temporary technical infrastructure solutions like dial-up links may need to be considered. These will have attendant problems such as bandwidth (capacity), reliability and security. It is conceivable therefore that the technical infrastructure should be required to offer automatic data encryption, error correction and compression over dial-up WAN links.

The business principle MBI chose to address this scope area states the type of situation the technical infrastructure needs to be flexible enough to cope with. The implication statements draw out the attributes of such a system.

Business Principle 4
The IT systems must support the business goal of rapid establishment in additional countries.
Justification
1. New markets are emerging rapidly. Early presence in these markets is essential for establishing market share and retaining customers. 2. MBI may take over another bank with a differing IT infrastructure. Integration between the two banks should be a case of extending the MBI infrastructure.
Implications
1. The new settlement system must be scalable. 2. The technical infrastructure must be scalable. 3. The technical infrastructure must have spare capacity (capable of accommodating an increased workload without additional hardware). 4. The management requirements of the components of the technical infrastructure must be minimized to make them practical for use in offices with limited local support capability. 5. Remote manageability will be necessary to support new offices that have no technical support capability.
Issues
1. Communications links to countries with emerging markets can take months to organize. 2. The offices opened to deal with new markets may not have access to system support staff and communications to support them may be difficult.

Business Principle for Scope Area 5

Scope Area 5: Distributed IT administration and control.

Knowing MBI to be a set of distinct organizations we should consider how the existing structures in place to control their own users and manage their own resources will impact the phased deployment of a global cross-organizational IT system.

MBI saw the best strategy for success as allowing the existing distinct organizations to participate in the management and support of the system from the beginning, allowing for a migration of responsibilities as the organization gradually integrates its structures.

How to do this, and what the implications are, raises many questions. For example, how do we integrate a local support capability into a global one? How are language difficulties overcome? How can the system be built to facilitate local control of resources? How can availability targets for a global system be achieved with a fragmented support organization?

Because there are a wealth of important questions linked to the initial observation on control of users and resources we have an ideal candidate for a business principle. The implications and issues give us the opportunity to begin to build the arguments we will need later in the design process.

We know that MBI intends to move from its current fragmented state towards a single, integrated structure as quickly as possible, in the process, replacing the practice of local control of users and resources with one where all such control is exercised from one point on the network.

We know that it is only the new technical infrastructure that will be capable of offering this sort of central control, making its presence a critical dependency for organizational change. What we need to establish is whether organizational change should be a critical dependency for the technical infrastructure. In other words, should the organizational change coincide precisely with the implementation of the new technical infrastructure? If it should, then we need only demand that the new technical infrastructure allow central control of resources and users. If we require the technical infrastructure to be implemented in advance of the organizational change then we may demand that it offers the same level of local control of resources and users that the current system does, in addition to allowing central control for when the organization integrates.

We can see that the strategy chosen has a strong bearing on the functionality that needs to be offered by the new technical infrastructure. A business principle stating the strategy to be adopted will play an important role in guiding design decisions related to control of resources and users.

MBI decided that although it would be likely to make the system more complex, the freedom created by requiring that the local control available in the old system should be retained in the new, would be important as a catalyst for change by allowing the implementation of the new global settlement system in advance of organizational integration.

Business Principle 5
The new technical infrastructure should allow subsidiaries and regional offices to have the same level of local control over their own users and IT resources as the existing technical infrastructure.
Justification
1. The existing organizational structure of MBI will take some time to change so we must put in place a means of recognizing the current organizational authority of subsidiaries and regional offices pending migration to a new organizational structure.
Implications
1. The security system will need to facilitate each subsidiary or regional office to control access to their own IT resources or provide a suitable administrative procedure to do so. 2. The security system will need to facilitate each subsidiary or regional office to administer their own user population or provide a suitable administrative procedure to do so. 3. The security configuration of the technical infrastructure will be more complex than had MBI been a single administrative unit. 4. While local authority must be recognized, there will need to be certain standards that subsidiaries and offices will need to adhere to so corporation-wide capabilities can be delivered (e.g., the ability of deals captured in one office to be settled in another).
Issues
1. Difficulties integrating local administration and support organizations into a global support infrastructure could present a risk to system availability. 2. By allowing a high degree of local control in the initial design it may prove politically difficult moving to a more centrally controlled organizational structure where some of this control may be revoked.

Note that this business principle touches on a critical subject for domain design, that of control of users and resources. It is recommended that you take care to encourage the construction of business principles that you know will resolve domain design decisions. This will draw on the skill of the solution architect to lead the process of business principle development in non-technical terms.

Review of Case Study Business Principles

The business principles chosen for the MBI case study can be described as fairly high level. They are definitely driven by the business and are related intimately to the project underway.

In another example we could have chosen, the requirement for a new Windows NT based technical infrastructure would not have been so clearly driven by the need to deploy an application. In which case we would see business principles that applied more directly to the technical infrastructure. As it is, the case study is application oriented and some of the business principles are more relevant to an application architect than a technical infrastructure architect. However, the application will end up placing demands on the technical infrastructure, effectively translating business requirements into technical requirements.

In an organization that is not attempting such radical change as MBI we would expect to see some business principles that linked business to technology more closely. For example, "Users should be restricted from changing a workstation's configuration." The justification for this might be based on the belief that support costs are minimized if supporting a known configuration. The technical implications and issues for such a principle should be easy to derive.

Business principles are high level and while they are an excellent starting point we need to go to another level of detail if we are going to successfully make technical design decisions that can be justified as supporting the business. The gulf between a business principle and a decision around, for example, how many name servers to implement is currently too large. The tool we will go on to use was mentioned at the beginning of this chapter as the design principle, the subject of Chapter 6.

Summary

This chapter has described a powerful tool for representing policy information which relates to the needs of the business. Business principles should speak in terms of the business and nothing else. As a complete set for a company they are a powerful statement about how it is plotting its course for the future. Their strength is in the fact that they can be used to guide decisions around how to design and implement systems and processes.

A particular business principle may apply to several projects, offering the possibility that work involved in developing business principles at the beginning of a project may be reduced as several are chosen for re-use from previous projects. Some business principles will turn out to be more useful than others though it is very difficult to predict at the creation stage which they will be. In nearly every case it is the implication statements that carry the most value when it comes to guiding design decisions.

6

Design Principles

Many important design decisions need to be made during the creation of a new technical infrastructure, each of which must be justified as the most appropriate. By adopting a standard method of structuring the argument behind a design decision we have a powerful tool for communicating the reasoning behind each choice.

This chapter describes how technical decisions that are made during the creation of a technical infrastructure design can be captured using the concept of a design principle. A design principle is similar to a business principle in that it is a justifiable statement with associated implications and issues. The difference is that it is sufficiently technical to be able to resolve a design decision. Just like a business principle, a design principle is an argument, but in this case the argument must clearly be supported by a business principle or business need, enabling us to link the business through to technology.

For example, a business principle might state that application traffic has absolute priority over infrastructure traffic on the corporate WAN. A design principle chosen to reflect it might say that all software kit distribution over WAN links less than T1 or equivalent is to be by CD-ROM. If the design principle were to be challenged on technical grounds we could show that it is fully supported by a statement of business priority.

Use of design principles throughout a technical infrastructure design will make it stronger and more defensible. The structure of a design principle provides a standard way of justifying a design decision that is clear to read and avoids the need to represent precise technical matters in unstructured text. The design principle as defined in this chapter is used throughout the design chapters of this book. This chapter supports the design activity within the overall project model as illustrated in Figure 6.1.

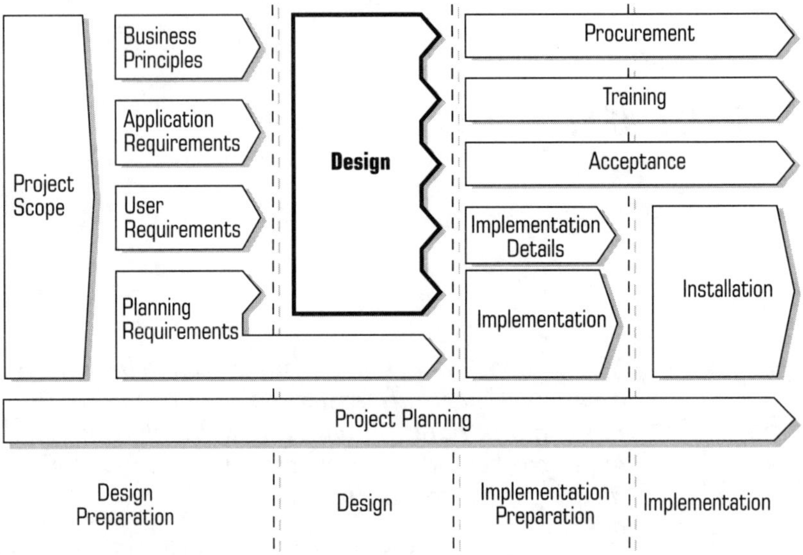

Figure 6.1 *Design Activity Within Project Model*

Structure of Chapter

Table 6.1 shows the structure of this chapter.

Table 6.1 *Structure of Chapter 6*

Topic	Contents
Design Process	For the value of a design principle to be recognized it is important to know what a technical infrastructure design should convey. This topic examines what constitutes a good technical infrastructure design and then introduces the constraints and requirements influencing design decisions.
Definition of Design Principle	A design principle is defined and illustrated with two examples.

The chapter closes with a summary that includes rules of thumb for creating design principles.

Design Process

What constitutes a technical design, how to create one and the influences over it are topics rarely analyzed in the context of a Windows NT technical infrastructure. We shall refer to them collectively as the design process. Without an understanding of the design process, a designer can be likened to a craftsman attempting to fashion a detailed carving with a blunt instrument. Worse, each member of a design team, unless sharing the same concepts, will have different views of the design process, denying the team a common set of concepts upon which to base design discussions.

By developing an understanding of the design process the value of the design principle as a tool for expressing key aspects of a design can be appreciated. The following subsections give an overview of the three aspects of the design process.

What Constitutes a Technical Infrastructure Design?

A technical infrastructure is built from off the shelf software components plus a small number of custom made components such as logon scripts and custom utilities. A technical infrastructure design must specify:

- Which software components are used
- How software components must be configured to achieve the required behavior
- How each software component relates to another
- The functionality of custom components
- How the design meets the needs of the business

The document(s) that specify the technical infrastructure constitute its design.

A good design should have these characteristics:

- **Completeness**—A technical infrastructure design that is complete should stand alone and not require any supporting documentation. It should include all aspects of design necessary to determine how to build a technical infrastructure that can support the business according to stated requirements. Another important aspect of completeness is the degree to which arguments supporting design decisions are fully recorded. The design should not depend on unwritten assumptions or associated documentation to justify design decisions. It should all be spelled out within the technical infrastructure design document.
- **Clarity**—A technical infrastructure design that lacks clarity will be vulnerable to misinterpretation, potentially leading to a failure to support the business in the way intended. Clarity is diffi-

cult to achieve unless there is a suitable convention used for recording design decisions.

- **Durability**—Technology will continue to advance and organizations will always be restructuring, making it a challenge to create and document a technical infrastructure design in such a way that it will survive its shifting context. The best approach is to create a design in terms of rules and policies, with an argument for each. When done in this way, it becomes easier to change the implementation details without affecting the rationale for a design decision.

The design chapters of this book show how to design the various technical infrastructure services according to the guidelines above. We will see that design principles help make the task significantly easier.

Creating a Technical Infrastructure Design

Producing a technical design to meet a set of requirements is a creative activity bounded by various constraints. Each design option must be resolved and the decision justified. To create a quality design we must be certain that the process we use allows us to consider all the arguments.

The diagram in Figure 6.2 illustrates the six most important influences on a design, including the business principles. By considering each of these influences when making a design decision we can be confident of having entertained all critical factors.

Figure 6.2 *Design Principles Influences*

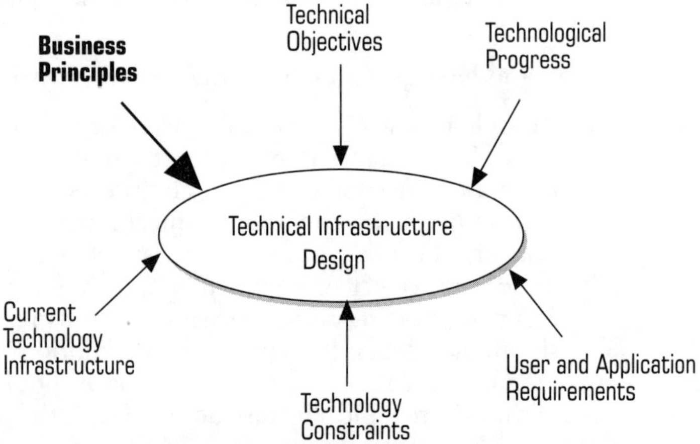

To examine how a design decision is made let us consider the need to design a file service. If we have no other information to guide us, this is a task with many possibilities, only bound by what is possible with technology. By considering the influences in turn we can narrow down the design possibilities to the point where the business principles can help us make the final decision.

- *Technical Objectives*

  We could reduce the number of possible solutions by conforming to a technology strategy if one were in place. This would restrict our choice of technology. For example, a technical strategy may dictate the use of LAN Manager protocols for file services, ruling out Novell NetWare or NFS.

- *Technological Progress*

  The future plans as laid out by a vendor for a product that may form part of the technology strategy could influence our choices by opening up potential possibilities or again restricting our options. Perhaps a higher capacity disk array will shortly become available?

- *Current Technology Infrastructure*

  A need to accommodate an existing technical infrastructure may constrain us further. At this stage, our set of options for a file service may have been reduced to manageable proportions. However, we are now faced with the need to choose the most appropriate options. When considering the current technical infrastructure we should be looking at aspects such as levels of user mobility supported, the protocols in use, or the control users have over their own files.

- *User and Application Requirements*

  Users and applications will be the users of a file service so we should look at what their needs are. For example, it may be critical to the application that the file service is always present, suggesting a resilient design based around a clustered server.

- *Technology Constraints*

  The file service design will ultimately have to be implemented out of contemporary technology which will have limitations determined by what is technically possible at the time. For example, a file server will have a maximum serving capacity and a network a fixed bandwidth. In practice, the technology constraint on a project is determined less by what is possible with technology alone, than what is possible with the level of technology that can be purchased for a given cost.

- *Business Principles*

  Importantly, the file service is only implemented to serve the needs of the business, either directly or indirectly through an application. We have already seen how we capture the needs of the business using business principles. Our design must therefore take them into account to complete the set of factors we need to consider.

  The input from Business Principles is critical to the traceability of the ultimate business reason for making a design decision. It is this component more than anything else that distinguishes the approach to creating a technical infrastructure advocated in this book.

It is not necessary or practical to go through a formal process such as we have just seen for every decision that needs to be made. The value of recognizing the influences is that it can form a mental checklist for use when creating or reviewing a design.

Requirements and Constraints on Design

An influence on a design can work in either of two ways, either as a constraint or as a requirement. Recognizing the difference can lead to a clearer understanding as to how to account for each. For example, in order to obtain guidance from the business on a particular design decision you may wish to show how a set of *requirements* are met in differing degrees for two alternate designs *constrained* by the existing technical infrastructure. Explaining the constraints would be a less successful approach.

Requirements are the things that are gained by consulting other people and tend to be specific to a business. For example, a requirement might be to load balance access to file servers using duplicate hardware. Constraints are those things that restrict the design in some way, usually by dictating what is possible and what is not. For example, a constraint could be that Windows NT does not implement load balancing over two network adapters.

Table 6.2 categorizes the influences shown in Figure 6.2 into constraints and requirements:

Table 6.2 *Constraints and Requirements*

Constraints	Requirements
Technical Objectives (strategy)	Business Principles
Technological Progress	User and Application Requirements

Table 6.2 *Constraints and Requirements (continued)*

Constraints	Requirements
Technology Constraints	
Current Technology Infrastructure	

Thus, the process of arriving at design decisions from a set of design options is summarized in Figure 6.3. It is these design decisions that we capture as design principles.

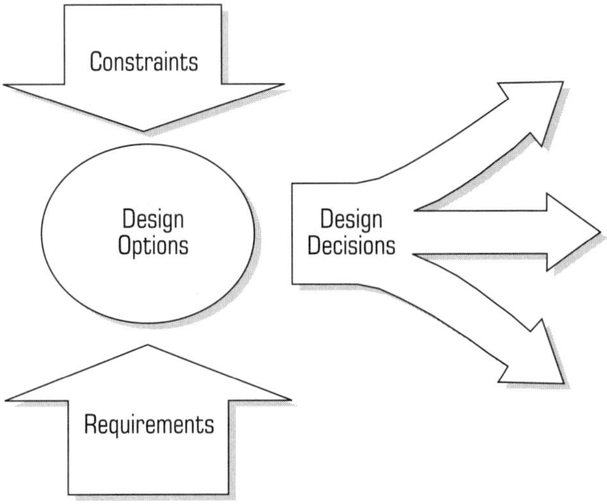

Figure 6.3 *Constraints and Requirements on Design*

We will see in the chapters dealing with the design phase of the project that requirements are frequently mentioned while constraints less so. The reason for this is that the constraints as defined here are easier to ascertain and agree on than the requirements, so the book places more emphasis on the tougher aspect of the design challenge.

Definition of Design Principle

Here we define a design principle and illustrate its usage with a single example. The chapters dealing with the design phase of the project introduce many more design principles based on the case study running throughout the book. There are also a number of examples given in Appendix B, Design Principles.

A design principle has the same structure as a business principle and is written in the same way:

Design Principle
This is the design principle statement
Justification
1. Justification number one 2. Justification number two
Implications
1. Implication number one 2. Implication number two
Issues
1. Issue number one 2. Issue number two

There is no automatic process for generating design principles, they must be a product of the standard design activity. They are a tool for making our design more readable, understandable and powerful.

To that end, a design principle may embody:

- design rules
- policies
- decisions

You may consider some of the design principles shown in this book incomplete, or you may disagree with a statement used. This is to be expected as they are used primarily as examples and will need to be tailored to each individual project.

Statement

As with the business principle, this statement should be strong enough for it to be possible to argue one or more alternatives, though experience and common sense should tell us that many of them are inappropriate. We should aim to apply technical knowledge to ensure the design principle says something that contributes to defining our design. We would expect to create as many design principles as necessary to complete a design as their nature is to clarify a design document rather than obscure it.

Here is an example design principle statement continuing the file service design example. It is difficult to point to a typical design principle, so the one chosen here has been picked because it links closely to two of the business principles developed for MBI. For comparison, a more technically focused design principle addressing the same design topic is shown at the end of this section.

Design Principle
The technical infrastructure will *facilitate* the use of existing Novell NetWare and UNIX file servers but will be designed to achieve *maximum benefit* when using Windows NT Server in this role.

A possible alternative design principle:

Design Principle
All file services will be provided by Windows NT servers.

Justification

As with business principles, justifications answer the question why? This is the critical part of the design principle as it allows us to demonstrate the compelling reasons for our choice of principle statement.

Business principles are the strongest source of support for design principles and should always be referenced where possible. The technical reasons for a principle should also be stated along with any other significant supporting arguments.

Justification statements should be concise, however they should not require any leaps of understanding by the reader or they would lose impact. A practical way to construct a justification statement is to write in one sentence or clause the ultimate justification and then in a following phrase explain the link to the design principle statement. This type of construct can be seen in each of the three example justification statements.

The justifications on the next page follow on from the first of the two design principle statements above.

Justification

1. The new settlements system should be phased in to MBI (Business Principle 2), making it necessary to use the existing file servers during the transition period.
2. MBI should be treated as one organization. As such, duplicated applications or systems should be avoided (Business Principle 3). This design principle facilitates a future move to use only one type of file server.
3. The client systems will be Windows NT. Optimum technical fit will be achieved if the file servers are also Windows NT.
4. IT support has few people with Windows NT skills so Windows NT systems should be introduced slowly to avoid availability issues through lack of support.

Implications

This section lets us note some of the implications of the principle statement. The best way to develop the implications is to think one stage beyond the principle statement and consider the benefits, savings, drawbacks, prerequisites, and general effects of the design principle. The benefits and savings would be spin-off reasons that would support the principle but which may not be significant enough to be classed as a justification.

The drawbacks are important to mention because we need to capture both sides of the argument for the design principle to be complete. The justification records the main reasons supporting the principle, drawbacks record the reasons detracting from it. Typically, the drawbacks mentioned as implications would not be serious problems. If they were, they would be categorized as issues, explained below.

In the example, we should be concerned that if we are to be using an existing system that it measures up to our particular requirements. It would not be acceptable if it were not secure enough, or perhaps was already overloaded. We should also consider overcoming potential incompatibilities such as different file systems.

The implications are things that have to be done or that will happen if the principle is carried out.

Implications
1. Can use tactical solutions for exploiting Novell NetWare and UNIX platforms. 2. Design need not be constrained by having to work with Novell NetWare and UNIX file and print services. The priority is for Windows NT optimized design. 3. Automatic username and password synchronization between different security domains may still need to be addressed to allay user complaints where more than one type of file service is in use.

Care needs to be taken not to nest design principles using the implications statements. Taking the example above, we may have thought ahead and be tempted to state as an implication that Gateway Services for NetWare will need to be used. This type of statement is clearly a good candidate for a design principle in its own right. Unless this is the only option, which is rare, we should instead state the need for a solution, for example, a means of accessing Novell NetWare file and print services needs to be determined. We are now free to create another design principle specifically around the design decision regarding access to non-Windows NT file and print services.

Issues

Issues are the problems or things that will need to be resolved for the design principle to be adhered to without compromise. As with Business Principles, what separates an issue from an implication is that an issue is something for which a solution is not immediately apparent.

The choice of a good design principle normally involves the consideration of negative implications and issues balanced against the principle and its justification. Thus it is unlikely that we will have arrived at this stage to find any show stopper issues.

If show stoppers are found then this suggests either of two reasons:

1. The design issue the design principle is attempting to address needs re-examining to determine whether there are any alternative approaches.

   In cases like this it is important to consider the overall sense of the argument developing in the design principle. Finding a show stopper issue will mean the design principle argument goes something like the following:

   ⇒ this is the assertion,

   ⇒ this is why it is chosen,

⇒ these are the implications, and

⇒ this is why it can't be done.

A less than convincing argument!

2. The design principle should stand because it is being used as a statement for some political purpose and there is every intention of removing the show stopper. Carrying out the design principle will of course be difficult until the show stopper is resolved.

The process of design should by its nature be thorough so we must ensure all statements in a design principle are precise. This is in contrast to a business principle where we could accept issues that were vague because sufficient detail wasn't available at the time, or statements intended to be warnings.

Concluding the example:

Issues
Where optimizing support for Windows NT clients in a mixed Windows NT and UNIX or Novell NetWare file server environment requires the use of an additional computer this will incur extra cost.

A More Technical Version of the Example

Design Principle
Novell NetWare based file services will be accessed via Microsoft Directory Services for NetWare running on Windows NT server.
Justification
1. Only one file service protocol need be run on the Windows NT workstations. This will make the client configuration more simple, supportable and hence reliable. (The goal of a simple, supportable and reliable client configuration would be expressed as one or more business principles.) 2. Facilitates migration to a complete Windows NT file server environment with minimum impact on the Windows NT client population. As file services are consolidated onto the Windows NT server platform there need be no changes to the workstations.

continued ▸

Implications
1. Lack of a single security environment while non-Windows NT file servers are in use. The file service design must provide configuration and operational guidelines for achieving a desired level of file service security. 2. The architecture of the Directory Services for NetWare gateway is such that without sufficient consideration the Windows NT server hosts can present a bottleneck. The file service design must provide guidelines for configuring the gateway software to avoid performance problems.
Issues
1. The corporate audit department has determined that using a Windows NT server system as a gateway to Novell NetWare file services is an unacceptable security risk for certain environments.

Summary

For a technical infrastructure design to be complete, clear, and durable, it needs to:

- Take into account all requirements and constraints.
- Make sure design decisions are written in a way all can understand.
- Be expressed in terms of policies and rules.

The design principle offers a convention for writing down design decisions that allows for common understanding and their expression as rules or policies.

The following rules of thumb should be adhered to when creating design principles:

1. The design principle statement should be strong, positive and concise.
2. The design principle statement can state policy, design decisions and rules.
3. At least one justification statement should reference a business principle.
4. Justification statements should explain clearly how they support the design principle statement.
5. Implication statements can be positive or negative.

6. If there is no apparent solution to an implication then it should be an issue.
7. Design decisions should not be expressed in implication statements.
8. Issues should not be so serious as to invalidate the design principle.

7

Developing Principles

Several methods are available for identifying project scope and creating principles. It is important that the method which is best suited to the organization and culture of the corporation is chosen. Support for the principles is essential if they are to be of value, making it important to involve the right people in their creation, review, and approval.

Three important concepts were introduced in Chapters 5 and 6:

- Project Scope
- Business Principles
- Design Principles

The first allowed us to write the scope of the project, the second provided a way of representing the needs of the business, and, the third, a way of representing a design decision with a structured argument. The purpose of this chapter is to offer recommendations for methods of creating business principles and design principles that will ensure they are of value to the project and supported by all parties.

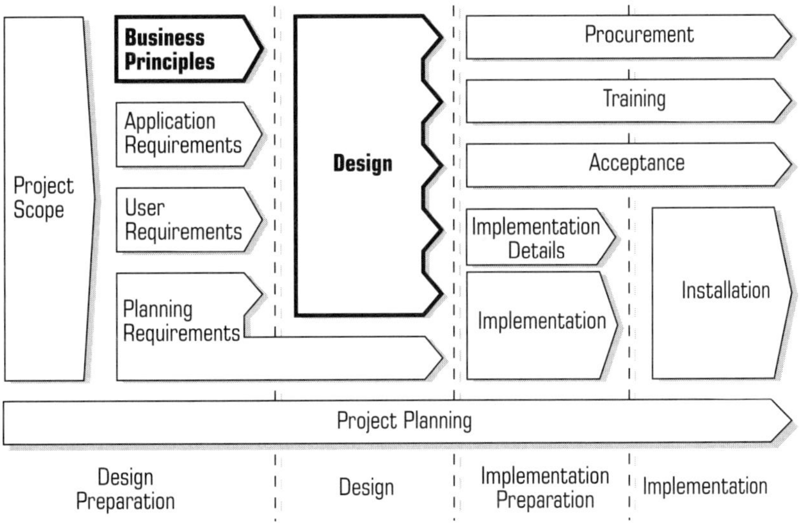

Figure 7.1 *Developing Principles in the Project Model*

If some of what is covered in this chapter appears prescriptive, it is because it is necessary to convey the processes involved in a straightforward fashion. In practice, the solution architect or workshop facilitator needs to be flexible and adaptive, applying a sound framework of concepts in a complex environment.

Figure 7.1 shows the activities in the overall project model to which this chapter applies.

Structure of Chapter

Table 7.1 shows the structure of this chapter.

Table 7.1 *The Structure of Chapter 7*

Topic	Contents
Process Overview	The basic sequence of events for identifying project scope and principles is outlined. Recommendations for ensuring success are given.
Developing Project Scope Areas Business Principles Design Principles	Different methods for developing project scope areas and principles are described along with their relative benefits and drawbacks. Recommendations are made for how to address different project situations.
Relating Requirements to Design	A method of expressing required system attributes in the wording of a principle is examined with the intention of strengthening the linkage between requirements and design.
Ensuring the Principles are Used	How to ensure that the business principles and design principles are adhered to throughout the project.

Process Overview

Three simple rules govern the process of getting to the point when design can begin:

1. Start identifying Project Scope Areas only after sufficient background material has been reviewed.
2. Don't start developing Business Principles before the Project Scope Areas have been agreed to.

3. Don't start the design before the set of Business Principles have been agreed to.

Identifying Project Scope Areas and Business Principles are iterative processes, as illustrated in Figure 7.2. Each must be complete before moving on to the next stage.

Figure 7.2
Project Scope and Business Principle Development Sequence

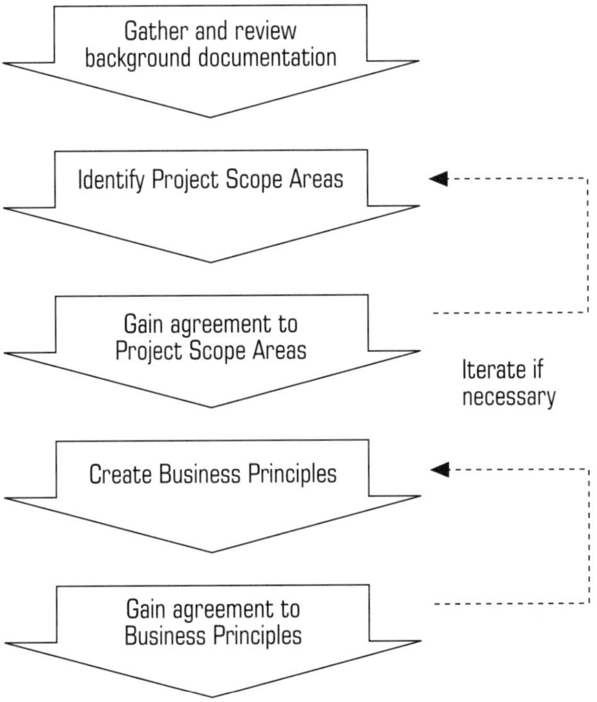

The creation of Design Principles will also be an iterative process but it extends throughout the Design phase of the project into the Implementation Detail activity of the Implementation Preparation phase.

Developing Project Scope Areas

The identification of scope areas for a project should be clearly distinguished from the creation of business principles. If carried out as a joint activity there is the risk of constant revision of the scope areas as business principles are developed.

For example, consider an organization building a new Windows NT technical infrastructure. A scoping only meeting might identify "System and network management" as one of the project scope areas. A combined meeting to identify project scope and business principles may start by identifying the same project scope area but then when discussing business principles the question of whether the project scope area should be revised to include application management may be raised.

It is tempting in circumstances like this to accommodate the new point of view. This creates a creeping scope for reasons of personal preference and technical convenience. Ultimately this will dilute resources and the project will lose focus on what its original objectives were. Thus, the choice of scope areas should be carried out in an initial project scoping meeting attended by a small number of key project individuals. The minimum recommended participants are:

- Project sponsor
- Project manager
- Solution architect

Choosing the Project Scope Areas

The following table provides a checklist of candidate project scope areas. In some cases the word(s) in the list will be sufficient, however it would be more usual to qualify them more. For example, the word Reliability may be qualified by focusing on what needs to be reliable so the project scope area could become "Reliability of network."

Table 7.2 *Potential Areas of Project Scope*

■ Access to Data	■ Future-Proofing
■ Access to Systems	■ Integration
■ Accuracy	■ Reliability
■ Applications	■ Management
■ Capability	■ Tradition
■ Change	■ Multinational
■ Communications	■ Operations
■ Competitiveness	■ Organization
■ Cost	■ Processes
■ Culture	■ Products
■ Customers	■ Responsibility
■ Efficiency	■ Scalability
■ Expertise	■ Security
■ Flexibility	■ Service

It is preferable to let people identify the project scope areas themselves if they can, with the minimum of prompting. If those present at the project scoping meeting are experiencing difficulty identifying project scope areas, or are uncertain whether they have arrived at a complete set, it can be helpful to use the items in Table 7.2 as prompts.

For the process of creating business principles to be practical we should aim to choose no more than about a dozen project scope areas. Less would be acceptable. If more appear to be necessary it may reflect the fact that the project needs to be split into sub-projects, each of which can be treated as a separate exercise.

Developing Business Principles

A business principle is a statement of business intent that we intend to use to support key technology design decisions represented in the form of design principles. Thus, knowing in advance what key design decisions will need to be made will obviously help us craft candidate business principles, as we seek to include statements that we know we will need to support a future design decision.

For example, the MBI solution architect had been aware of constant debates regarding whether the several alternate file and print server types should remain in place alongside Windows NT servers. By encouraging a business principle dealing with the issue of duplicate functionality provided by different types of system, the required design decision can be made. The solution architect should be constantly thinking along these lines throughout whichever process is used to develop the principles. One word of caution is necessary. It is important for the solution architect to resist any urge to "reverse" the existing systems into the business principles. Thus, we shouldn't consciously look to create business principles that support the existing infrastructure as this would defeat the purpose of the whole process.

The business principles must clearly be created using knowledge of the business. The challenge is, how is that knowledge elicited and how are the principles formed? There are two main options for getting business principles created:

- Stage a workshop
- Consult people

Workshop

The purpose of a workshop is to carry out work as a group activity. So, for it to be successful, it must be attended by all the people who need to contribute to its planned output. A workshop should operate to an agenda that will include use of techniques for harnessing group creative activity and distilling that output. Workshops benefit from having one or two people acting in the role of facilitator. In this role they focus on the processes of the workshop and are responsible for capturing the output. They do not contribute to the content of the workshop.

In many cases the workshop approach is the best option because with the right people in attendance we can include contributions from authoritative representatives of the business and reach agreement to the final list of principles all in one exercise.

The drawback to workshops is that they are often hard to stage logistically and in some cases the "right" people needed to participate may not value the exercise sufficiently to lend their support. It is also very important to note that for a workshop to be run successfully, it requires an experienced facilitator, someone who can guide the creative and decision making processes to ensure the output is of the form required. In summary, use a workshop when:

- The right people are available
- You have an experienced facilitator available

What goes on before and after a workshop is as important as what goes on in the workshop. We will now look at preparatory activities, the workshop itself, then what needs to be written up and carried out as actions afterwards.

Preparing for the Workshop

The first thing to establish is who the attendees need to be. Once the project sponsor is familiar with the process you intend to go through they should be in a position to decide who needs to contribute to the development of business principles.

We should always be conscious of the fact that different people will approach developing a new system from different angles and to many, the value of the techniques described in this book will not be instantly apparent. To ensure we gain the maximum contribution from anyone who participates in the workshop we must therefore provide an adequate explanation of the process and its objectives.

At a minimum we should contact all identified attendees either in person or using a memo, to explain:

1. Why the workshop is being staged
2. Nature of workshop—how it will be run
3. What a Business Principle is, including examples

4. The objective of the workshop is to create a complete set of business principles that everyone agrees with
5. Who will be attending and what their roles will be
6. Why it is important that this individual should attend
7. When the workshop will be staged and how long it will go on for

The Workshop

The first item on the workshop agenda should be to review all the items on the preparatory memo with the priority being to ensure the attendees know what a business principle is and what it is for. For some attendees benefit it will be useful to provide some more background to the project itself.

The workshop should be run by two people ideally, one to ensure the workshop objectives are met by keeping proceedings on schedule and explaining process where necessary and the other to assist with content. Both should be comfortable assisting in the production of good business principles by encouraging the rewording or rejection of those that are poor.

A useful technique for developing business principles with consensus support is as follows:

1. Get everyone to write on separate pieces of card what they think business principles should be. At this stage only ask for the business principle statement itself.
2. Stick all the cards on the wall and group them into similar statements. Get agreement for the grouping.
3. Attempt to consolidate the statements in each group into one statement. You should be aiming to end up with between one and three statements or candidate business principles for each of the scope areas.
4. For each business principle statement, in open forum invite justifications for the statement. This should be easy to get started as it is probable that some of the arguments that came out when deciding principle statement groupings will be suitable justifications.
5. The attendees should then be split into groups of two or three. The business principles statements and justifications should then be divided across the groups and each group set the task of identifying implications and issues. The reason for splitting into groups is that this stage can be time consuming and provoke

much discussion. By using smaller groups working in parallel, the workshop can be more productive.

6. Bring the groups back together to share the findings and agree on each other's work.

After the Workshop

The most important thing to do after the workshop is write it up. If the exercise went successfully we will have a full set of business principles each with associated justifications, implications and issues. These should be put into a document that includes the following information:

- Introductory explanation of the project itself
- The project scope areas, to provide more context (identified earlier in a more select meeting)
- An explanation of the process being used to capture the business intent—business principles
- Example business principles
- The business principles themselves

The draft version of the document should be circulated to all workshop attendees, along with those who were invited to the workshop but couldn't attend, requesting each person confirm the principles listed accurately reflect those developed in the workshop. It should be made clear that the document will be issued as version 1 at a certain date and from that point onwards the principles will guide the project.

Consulting

If it is not possible to run a workshop, an alternative is to use a series of interviews with the same people who would have attended a workshop. The main difficulty with using a consulting technique to arrive at a set of business principles is gaining consensus. Consider the possibility that one interviewee disagrees with a business principle developed in conjunction with another interviewee. How is this situation to be resolved? One option is to stage a meeting to discuss and reach agreement, however that may be impractical for the same reason you are not using a workshop.

The recommended way to avoid this difficulty is to identify one person in advance as having the authority to resolve such matters on behalf of all contributors. Thus, once all proposed business principles have been developed in one to one interviews, the list can then be reviewed for consistency and quality with the decision making authority. The project sponsor may choose to adopt this role or to nominate someone for it.

The Consulting Process

The consulting process can be considered a variation on that used for a workshop. The following sequence summarizes the recommended process for using a consulting technique to establish business principles:

1. Identify set of contributors and agree with project sponsor who will be the decision making authority.
2. Notify interviewees of the impending process and arrange interviews. Employ a modified version of the memo used to notify people of the workshop. See section Preparing for the Workshop above.
3. Construct a draft set of business principles with each interviewee.
4. Consolidate all proposed business principles by combining where necessary and removing overlaps.
5. Review the list with the decision making authority to resolve conflicts and remove any that are inappropriate.
6. The remainder of the process is the same as that used to deal with the output from a workshop. See section After the Workshop above.

Choosing the Business Principles

In using either the workshop or the consulting process it can be difficult to get started or, near the end of the process, to be satisfied the set of business principles is as near to completion as it can be. The tool shown in Table 7.3 Business Principle Prompts can be used to provoke ideas for business principles and to confirm the set produced is complete.

The category column of the matrix lists the project scope areas introduced earlier in Table 7.2. Using the three arbitrary qualifiers of human, business and technology as column headings, suggestions for business principles can be developed across the matrix.

To use the tool, combine an entry from the first column with a choice from the other three columns from the same row to arrive at the basic elements of a business principle. For example, suppose the project scope area was *change,* we could combine this with the heading *business* and then choose *type* from the common box. Possible business principles arising might be:

Business Principle	Change should be evolutionary
Business Principle	Change should be revolutionary
Business Principle	Change should be avoided

It is very important to keep in mind that the main purpose of this tool is to provide a source of *ideas*. It should already be clear that the prescriptive creation of business principles unique to a particular project is plainly impractical. The tool is not intended to be rigorous in any way. So it doesn't matter how it is used. For example, it is not necessary to be confined to constructing a potential business principle statement out of elements from a single row.

Categories matching the common attributes have been highlighted in italics to emphasize their importance. It is not essential to create a business principle in each italicized category but thought should be given to the potential value in the design phase of a business principle that makes a strong reference to a common attribute. For example, if you know there is already a debate around whether some form of high availability solution such as clustering should be used for critical file servers, development of a business principle in the category of *Availability,* with the intention of resolving that debate would be natural.

Table 7.3 *Business Principle Prompts*

Category	Human	Business	Technology
Availability	▪ Geographical ▪ Skills	▪ Business differentiator	▪ Applications ▪ Continuity ▪ Communications
Service	▪ Style	▪ Customer service	▪ Internal Service Level Agreement
Access to Data	▪ Restrictions ▪ Rationale	▪ Business need ▪ Geographical ▪ Temporal	▪ Security system ▪ Authentication ▪ Authorization
Access to Systems	▪ Restrictions ▪ Rationale	▪ Business need ▪ Geographical ▪ Temporal	▪ Security system ▪ Physical access ▪ Authentication ▪ Authorization
Applications	▪ User Interface ▪ Usability	▪ Flexible ▪ Dependencies ▪ Usage	▪ Resilience ▪ Availability ▪ Performance ▪ Manageability

continued ▸

Table 7.3 *Business Principle Prompts (continued)*

Category	Human	Business	Technology
Capability	▪ Support groups ▪ Help desk ▪ Business process	▪ Weakness ▪ Constraints ▪ Strengths	▪ Quality of systems ▪ Speed of migration ▪ Spare capacity ▪ To change
Capacity	▪ Peak demand	▪ Customer demand ▪ Efficiency	▪ Spare ▪ Utilization levels ▪ Planned increase/ decrease
Change	▪ Cope with ▪ Resist	▪ Type (evolutionary, revolutionary, avoided, encouraged...)	▪ Migrate ▪ Substitute ▪ Flexibility
Communication	▪ Language	▪ Standards	▪ Speed ▪ Reliability ▪ Bandwidth
Competitiveness	▪ Sense of ▪ Identification with success	▪ Survival ▪ Dividends ▪ Agility	▪ Asset or Liability
Cost	▪ Hiring ▪ Redundancy ▪ Wages	▪ Opportunity ▪ Expense	▪ Software ▪ Hardware ▪ Networks
Culture	▪ Ability to change ▪ Value ▪ Service	▪ Dealing with customers ▪ Culture of customers	▪ Role of IT ▪ Value of IT ▪ Power of IT function
Suppliers		▪ Costs ▪ Lead times	▪ Viability
Customers	▪ Interface	▪ Treat	
Efficiency	▪ Training	▪ Profit/Loss ▪ Measurement	▪ PCs / Support person ▪ Utilization
Expertise	▪ Training	▪ Business	▪ Technical
Flexibility	▪ Roles ▪ Responsibilities	▪ Processes	▪ Change ▪ Scalability
Future-Proofing	▪ Culture of change	▪ Continued support ▪ Cost of change	▪ Technology choice ▪ Planning for change
Integration	▪ Organizational units	▪ Processes	▪ Applications ▪ Legacy systems ▪ Framework ▪ Tactical/strategic

Table 7.3 *Business Principle Prompts (continued)*

Category	Human	Business	Technology
Management	▪ Level of ▪ Responsibilities	▪ Structure ▪ Presence	▪ Systems ▪ Network ▪ Applications
Market Share	▪ Skills ▪ Return per employee	▪ Plans	▪ Vendor
Multinational	▪ Language ▪ Customs ▪ Costs	▪ Customers ▪ Trading partners ▪ Currency	▪ Language support ▪ Purchasing
Operations	▪ Routine ▪ Service	▪ Support to business	▪ Processes ▪ Automation
Organization	▪ Power structure ▪ Decision making ▪ Authority	▪ Competitive orientation ▪ Staffing levels	▪ Relationship between IT and the business
Processes	▪ Training ▪ Routine ▪ Accuracy	▪ Core ▪ Re-engineer ▪ Optimize	▪ Automate ▪ Change control ▪ Software development
Products	▪ Human component ▪ Selling ▪ Knowledge ▪ Experience	▪ Competitive ▪ Range ▪ Profit ▪ Lead time	▪ Choice ▪ Strategy ▪ Technical fit ▪ Dependence
Responsibility	▪ Individual ▪ Definition	▪ Profit/Loss ▪ Entrepreneurial	▪ Competitive advantage
Scalability	▪ User population	▪ Market share	▪ Planned capacity ▪ Utilization
Security	▪ Integrity ▪ Authorization ▪ Authentication	▪ Confidentiality ▪ Damage	▪ Access ▪ Consistency ▪ Data ▪ Applications
Support	▪ Skills ▪ Language	▪ Speed of Response ▪ Economy ▪ Criticality	▪ Local ▪ Remote ▪ Access
Tradition	▪ Values	▪ Differentiator ▪ Opportunity	▪ Constraint

Developing Design Principles

The majority of design principles will emerge early in the design phase of the project and they will be instrumental in shaping the project's technical characteristics. For this reason it is important that the technical design community, that is, all who have a say in design decisions, not just the project team, agree with the design principles.

The two main approaches to creating design principles and gaining agreement for them are:

- to stage a workshop
- to let the designer create them during the design process

We discuss both below.

Workshop

If a workshop is used to create an initial set of commonly agreed upon design principles then it should be carried out at the beginning of the design process. It is very important that the key individuals with responsibility for design are present at the workshop.

In preparation, each individual should have reviewed all available scope, requirements, and business principle material relevant to the project. In such a workshop it is important to have a cross section of expertise and interests present to ensure as many arguments as possible are considered.

One approach to structuring the workshop is to have the facilitator or solution architect initiate and guide the development of principles for each technical area. This relies heavily on the ability of the solution architect to be able to think clearly on his or her feet on all design topics and to have prepared seed design principles prior to the workshop.

Another approach is to directly address the requirements specification by developing a principle for each requirement or set of requirements. The drawback here is that it doesn't accommodate the free thinking necessary for creating a complete design. It does however make for a quality functional specification because rather than using simple statements in it such as "A means of optimizing disk performance will be provided," we can record a technical decision on the subject, mentioning a method of optimizing disk performance with reasons for its choice. If possible such an exercise should be followed by a more free format design session to cover the areas not explicitly stated in the Requirement Specification. However the workshop is structured it will only be effective if it is led by an experienced workshop facilitator who can make sure it stays focused on objectives and completes on time.

Please refer to the guidelines for staging a workshop given in the earlier section Developing Business Principles for how to prepare for the workshop and how to document it.

Solo Design

As with the workshop, the real focus of the exercise is to begin the design process. In this approach, technicians designing a part of the technical infrastructure would begin work, creating design principles as they proceeded. The design chapters of this book record the production of design principles in this manner.

Agreement to the design principles is now gained through reviewing the design itself, which is built around the design principles. The solution architect should work with the design technicians to ensure a consistent approach to the pitch and wording of the design principles as, left to their own devices, different people will develop their own concepts of how to use them. Not all will be wrong, but on a large project consistency of usage is critical for fostering common understandings.

Creating design principles as part of the design activity is the recommended approach as it ensures the design principles are all directly relevant to the design, allowing clear exposition of the key design decisions.

Relating Requirements to Design

We saw in Chapter 2, Elements of a Technical Infrastructure, that the technical infrastructure services can be characterized in terms of a set of common attributes, such as performance or availability. To strengthen the link between business policy and design it is useful to think about overall system requirements in terms of the same set of attributes the corresponding services must have to satisfy them. The rationale behind this is based on the assumption that the attributes used to characterize a business requirement will be the ones we need to consider when designing the underlying technical infrastructure service.

By adopting this approach we can:

1. See more clearly how the business requirement can be met by particular service configurations.

2. Check whether the requirement says enough for us to make the necessary design decisions.

For example, a general requirement might be for the new system to give users access to a remote mainframe. The requirement as it stands says nothing other than the basic functionality required. It says nothing about the attributes important to that connection. Thus, we could implement a dial-up link over a 1200 baud modem that took a user five minutes to log on if we wished and satisfy the requirement as stated. To stand a chance of getting it right we really need to know what level of *performance* is required, how *secure* should the connection be and so on. Only then can we develop the solution from infrastructure services that offer the appropriate degrees of performance and security.

Some of these required attributes may have been stated in a blanket fashion elsewhere, for example, all communications will be encrypted. Nevertheless, we can benefit from developing an understanding of the system requirements in terms of attributes, as they will then form a common link with the technical infrastructure services.

Attributes

The attributes we have discussed so far were termed common attributes to reflect their general applicability to a variety of services. This chapter introduces the concept of *specific attributes* to characterize the particular behavior of a technical infrastructure service where the common attributes are insufficient. As a reminder, the common attributes used in this book are:

- Scalability
- Reliability
- Availability
- Manageability
- Security
- Capacity
- Performance

Specific Attributes

Choosing different design options for some infrastructure services can have a significant influence that can't be characterized by one of the project's common attributes. In this situation we should look for a specific attribute to serve our purpose.

For example, if we choose the infrastructure services provided by the Windows NT Domain Model then we can identify three specific attributes:

- Organization
- Geography
- Administration

To understand why "organization" is a specific attribute, consider how different Windows NT domain designs are more suitable to different organizational structures. Looking at it another way, by specifying the organizational structure to be supported we can begin to measure the suitability of each possible domain design.

Using Attributes to Specify Characteristics of a Requirement

Here we take a brief look at the means by which attributes can be incorporated into the three categories of requirement statement (see Chapter 4, Project Planning). Note that in all cases it is more important to ensure the requirement is correctly stated rather than contorted to include reference to an attribute.

Remember that eliciting requirements that are accurately characterized in terms of common or specific attributes is always going to be a matter of skill for the technical architect. For example, one person's interpretation of highly available might be continuous service 8 hours a day during working hours and another person's might be service 24 hours a day but minor downtime can be tolerated. The same problem is clearly present with all the other attributes.

Business Principles

The creation of business principle statements should not be fettered in any way. However, it is more practical to include reference to attributes in the justification, implication and issue statements. If the attributes that have been chosen are relevant to the corporation then it should be natural to include references to them.

The attribute list can be used in the workshop or during a review as a check to see whether all the angles have been considered. For example, we can test the implication statements for a business principle to see whether all the implications relevant to the organization have been noted.

User Requirements

This analysis category has us looking for factors affecting our design that arise from the end users and IT support users. User requirements are gathered using a questionnaire and it is here that we have the opportunity to capture requirements in such a way that they are described in terms of the common or specific attributes. For users the two most important common attributes will be availability and performance, with security important in some cases. Simplicity will also be an issue if the system becomes too complex.

Crude availability requirements can be established by asking when users need access to systems and applications and how long they can be unavailable before their job is impacted. While it is a fair assumption that users will always say adequate performance is mandatory, we should try to identify where the infrastructure might cause delays for a user. Questions seeking information about regulatory deadlines, regular data transfers and intensive processing can lead to information expressed in the way required to directly influence infrastructure design.

Application Requirements

When consulting application developers or application documentation, care must be taken to uncover any assumptions being made about the technical infrastructure. For example, suppose one statement about an application says it sends 50MB of data every night at 9 pm from Hong Kong to Chicago and another statement says that the data is processed in Chicago to be made available as reports by 9 am Hong Kong time the next morning. These two statements are rich in assumptions, which, with assistance from an application expert, we should be able to turn into requirements on the technical infrastructure expressed in some part in terms of attributes.

Continuing the example, a consultation with the application expert may reveal the following infrastructure requirements:

1. The network bandwidth should be capable of guaranteeing the transfer of this quantity of data by 3 am Hong Kong time as it takes 6 hours to process the data. Examining the requirement in more detail should reveal specific needs in terms of reliability, availability and performance.
2. If the transfer fails before 80% of the job is complete it should be possible to restart it remotely. A specific manageability need would be to be able to monitor the transfer remotely and generate an alert if it failed. There should also be the ability to restart the transfer remotely.

Ensuring the Principles are Used

Once the principles have been developed their value will only be retained if they are adhered to. This statement may seem obvious but we must take steps to ensure that people are comfortable with them or our good work will be wasted.

For the principles to be adhered to they must be accepted by all necessary parties. That means everyone must agree that the discussions and arguments over their creation have been concluded. To reach this agreement there needs to be a formal, inclusive process for accepting the principles.

The recommended process is that the business principles and design principles are formally reviewed and then signed off by the following people:

- *Business Principles*

  All who contributed to their creation, including:

  - Representatives of the sections of the business concerned
  - Business analysts
  - Project sponsor
  - Project manager

- *Design Principles*

  All who contributed to their creation, including:

  - Representatives of the sections of the business concerned
  - Infrastructure architect
  - Application architects
  - Support manager
  - Business analysts
  - Project sponsor
  - Project manager

Summary

Identification of project scope should be completed prior to development of business principles or there can be problems. Business principles can be developed in a workshop, attended by all interested parties and run by a facilitator whose job it is to focus on workshop agenda and methodology. They can also be developed by using a series of interviews where the emerging business principles are repeatedly confirmed with all contributors until complete agreement is reached. A workshop is recommended for the speed with which it produces a result.

Design principles can be developed in a workshop in the manner of business principles or they can be developed by the designer at the time the design work is being carried out. A workshop will produce a consistent set of design principles. Designers embedding design principles in their design work may lead to more relevant principles. However, their consistency will need to be monitored closely by the solution architect. Creating principles as part of the design activity is the recommended approach.

To strengthen the link between business policy and design it is useful to think about overall system requirements in terms of the same set of attributes the corresponding services must have to satisfy them. The rationale behind this is based on the assumption that the attributes used to characterize a business requirement will be the ones we need to consider when designing the underlying technical infrastructure service.

Once the principles have been developed their value will only be retained if they are adhered to. For the principles to be adhered to they must be accepted by all necessary parties. The recommended process is that the business principles and design principles are formally reviewed and signed-off by all the people involved in their creation and representatives of those who will be affected by their use.

8

Requirements Gathering

Only by capturing and confirming the complete set of requirements on a system can we confidently begin a design. The requirements will come from a variety of sources with some changing over time. Here we describe a method of gathering a set of requirements in such a way that we can have confidence in their quality.

The purpose of Requirements Gathering is to determine the needs of the new technical infrastructure. We must gather three types of requirement:

1. Application Requirements

   An application's requirements must address the dependencies it has on the infrastructure services and on other applications. It is also important to identify the characteristics of an application in terms of the common and specific attributes as identified in Chapter 2, Elements of a Technical Infrastructure (e.g., availability, scalability, performance).

2. User Requirements, Business and Support

   A business user's requirements must address the user's environment and their working practices, for example the degree of mobility they need and how the system needs to be supported. A support user's requirements will be concerned with how the infrastructure may be managed and repaired.

3. Planning Requirements

   The application and user requirements, along with other factors such as the business principles that have been developed in the initial stage of the project will allow the desired state to be defined. Planning how to get to that state requires that we first determine the current state. To do that we must gather the technical and logistical details of the current technical infrastructure. The process of gathering these planning requirements is sometimes referred to as a *current state analysis*. Determining the current state is important for two reasons:

- It provides a benchmark against which the new infrastructure may be compared.
- It provides valuable information to the design process, particularly in cases where the new technical infrastructure will have to incorporate elements of the existing one.

The gathering of the three types of requirement are all dealt with in this chapter for the following reasons:

- Each type of requirement needs to be gathered at the same phase in the project.
- The source of both user and planning requirements will in many cases be the same.
- The same requirements gathering tool or process can be used to gather user and planning requirements.

Once gathered, the requirements must be documented in a Requirements Specification to which all contributors must agree. This will form the basic input to a document called a Functional Specification which will describe the planned functionality of the new technical infrastructure.

The requirements gathering process is identified as three separate activities in the planning phase of the project roadmap in Figure 8.1 (highlighted).

Figure 8.1
Requirements Gathering Activities

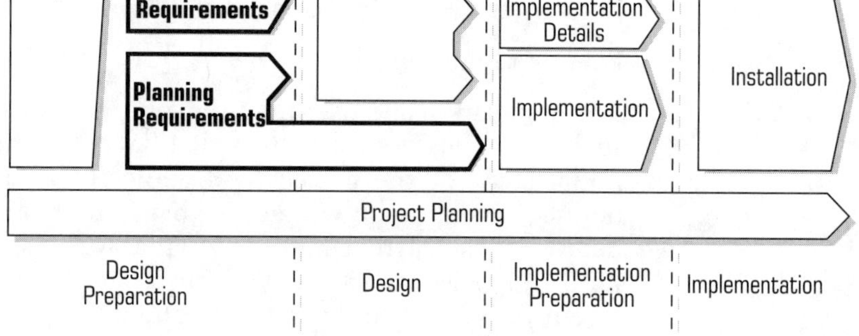

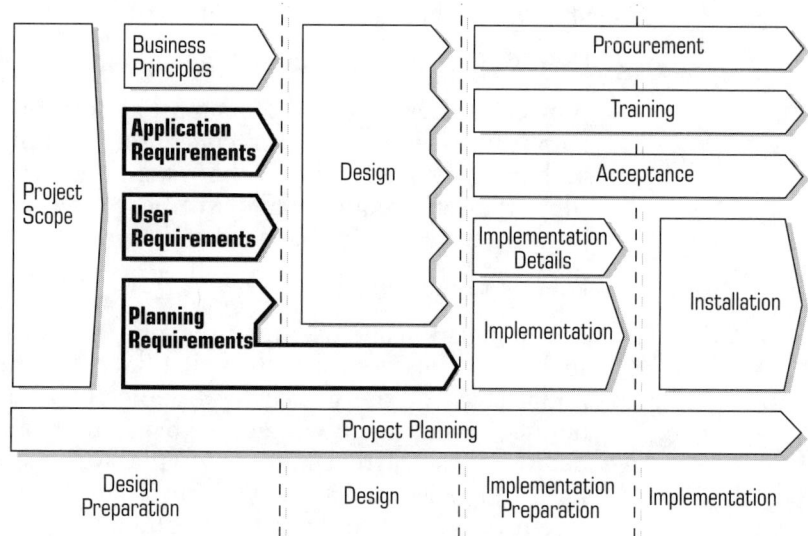

The MBI case study will be used to show what is involved in each of these activities.

Structure of Chapter

This chapter includes the topics shown in Table 8.1.

Table 8.1 *The Structure of Chapter 8*

Topic	Contents
The Gathering of Requirements	▪ Rules of thumb for ensuring the efficient gathering of requirements.
Application Requirements	▪ Determining the requirements an application places on the technical infrastructure by examining its functionality, architecture, and dependencies on other applications
User Requirements	▪ Capturing new requirements for the system ▪ Requirements imposed by the existing technical infrastructure
Planning Requirements	▪ Surveying the existing systems. ▪ Identifying and Surveying the sites targeted for deployment. ▪ Checking the data for accuracy and completeness.
Documenting the Requirements	▪ Consolidating the user and application requirements into a Requirements Specification document. ▪ Storing and maintaining the results of the Planning Requirements activity. ▪ Documenting the requirements that will be met by the planned technical infrastructure along with any additional functionality in a Functional Specification.

The Gathering of Requirements

Each of the three Requirements Gathering activities detailed in this chapter may involve use of either of the following two techniques for gathering information:

- A questionnaire to be filled in independently
- An interview based on the questionnaire

In each case the quality of the information gathered and the ease with which it is gathered will depend on how the people who need to supply the information are briefed. Use the following rules of thumb:

- **Explain why.** It is important to explain the purpose of the requirements gathering activity and why it is important to cooperate with the process.

- **Include logistical details.** Include information about:
  ⇒ how long a questionnaire should take to fill in
  ⇒ when it should be completed by
  ⇒ who it should be returned to
  ⇒ how long an interview should last
  ⇒ who will do the interview
  ⇒ when the interview will occur
- **Explain who.** Getting the right person to attend the interview or fill in the questionnaire is critical to the quality of the response you will receive. Make the skills and knowledge required of the person clear. It is recommended that the person be contacted in advance for the purpose of confirming that they are likely to be able to respond with the required level of detail and quality.
- **Target the audience.** Try to minimize the number of people that need to respond to the questionnaire or be interviewed. Each person that needs to be dealt with will take an investment in time and effort to get them through the process. These are commodities that are under pressure.
- **Reason for asking questions.** Explaining why a question is being asked can encourage empathy for the objective.
- **Be concise.** If someone can misinterpret a question, they will.
- **Give plenty of warning.** The people you will be asking to fill in the questionnaire or participate in an interview will be busy, so plenty of advanced warning of the requirements gathering activity will give them a chance to make the time available.

The above information should be included in a letter sent out in advance of the questionnaire or interview.

Once the Requirements Gathering questionnaire has been created it is recommended two tests be carried out:

- A "walk through" be carried out for the purpose of testing the completeness of the set of questions. This is a technique whereby the process of using the information gathered from the questionnaire is simulated. For example, in the case of a questionnaire designed to gather planning information a simulated planning exercise should be run to check whether the questions covered all the information needed to complete a plan.
- A trial run to check that the way questions are phrased elicits the correct type of response. This will reveal where questions are

ambiguous or unclear. The recommended approach is to identify a site close to home to pilot the questionnaire.

Application Requirements

The set of requirements an application places on the technical infrastructure is one of the key influences on how it is designed. We must begin by obtaining from the development manager responsible a specification of the services and their associated attributes required by an application. These would then be documented and then we would proceed to ensure the technical infrastructure delivered.

In practice, things don't always work out like that. We will often need to deduce the requirements based on a sketchy collection of evidence. To be confident of revealing all requirements, the process of working out the needs of an application should include examining three categories of information:

- **Application Functionality** will give us an overview of the application and allow us to make some initial observations on its likely requirements.
- **Application Architecture** will provide an understanding of how the different components of an application depend on each other, determining its overall attributes.
- **Infrastructure Dependencies** that exist will help us understand how the attributes (e.g., scalability, capacity, etc.) of an application are directly affected by the technical infrastructure.

The first two categories will provide supporting information for the third, which is ultimately where our interest lies for understanding the requirements an application places on the technical infrastructure. We will be looking to understand each of the requirements not only in straight forward functional terms but as they are characterized by the common attributes. For example, a requirement might be to send a file from one site to another overnight. We should aim to understand how critical it is that file gets there, by what time? Will the application retry?

Note that the following sections use the concept of application architecture in a way that may not be fully supported by a purist on the subject. The purpose of dealing with it this way here is to encourage the reader to distinguish between internal application links and external links as a means of structuring the analysis of an application's behavior in a system. Documenting the application requirements and creating the Functional Specification is covered in a separate section in this chapter.

Application Functionality

A functional specification for an application, if available, can provide a valuable starting point for gaining insight into what will be needed from the technical infrastructure. This type of document expresses what an application does from the perspective of the user, not how it does it so although useful, we should be conscious of its limitations.

Its main value lies in providing a sketch of what we are dealing with. Our knowledge of the business or similar applications will allow us to make reasonable starting assumptions regarding its likely technical infrastructure requirements. To establish application functionality, the questionnaire should ask for a copy of the functional specification or, if unavailable, a written overview of the application functionality.

Application Architecture

The functional specification describes the *what* of an application; what we really need to understand is the *how*, such as:

- Inter-process communication methods
- Location of data
- Management of data (replication, extracts, backups)
- Client processing / Server processing
- User access—local/remote?

These items are aspects of application architecture which if not to be found in a functional specification are usually to be found in the detailed design specification. Application architecture, in very general terms, describes internal interfaces and dependencies. In the same way one application can be dependent on either another application or a component of the technical infrastructure, one component of an application may be dependent on another component of the same application.

Figure 8.2 illustrates the relationship between the various types of dependency.

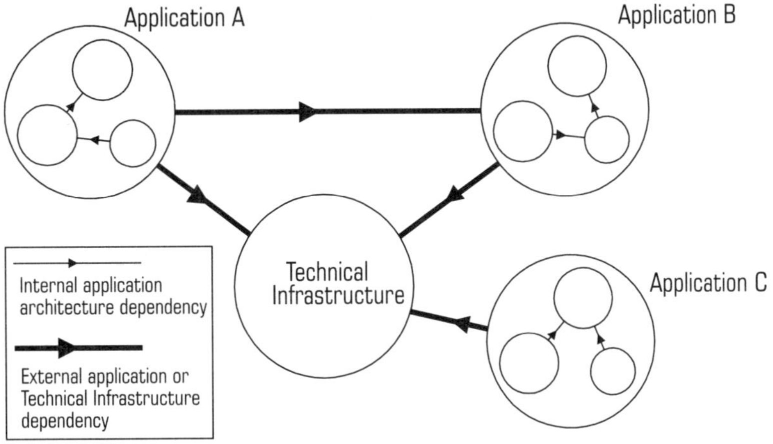

Figure 8.2 *Architecture, Application, and Technical Infrastructure Dependencies*

Infrastructure Dependencies

Applications depend on the technical infrastructure in two contexts:

- To communicate with another application. For example the infrastructure dependency might be the network or the naming service.
- When using the technical infrastructure is an end in itself (e.g., printing, or storing a file).

Both are based on the premise developed in Chapter 2 that the characteristics of an application must be reflected in the characteristics of the technical infrastructure services it depends on for it to be able to meet its overall business requirements. This is regardless of whether the services are used to communicate with another application or as an end in themselves. Some examples of both contexts are shown below.

Communicating with Another Application

In this example the need for a network link with a suitably high level of availability is illustrated.

Suppose a critical application were dependent on another application for some data but attempts to make a connection to get that data frequently failed. To the dependent critical application it is unimportant whether the other application is unavailable or whether it is the infrastructure services used to establish communication to that application that are unavailable. The infrastructure services must therefore offer a suitable level of availability matching that of the application if overall availability is not to suffer.

A technical infrastructure designer has limited power to influence the way in which one application depends on another but can definitely influence how dependencies on the technical infrastructure can impact the attributes of an application. Considering the example above, it must be the job of the technical infrastructure designer to ensure that the services used to enable the exchange of data between the two applications offer a level of reliability to match the requirements of the business.

Using a Technical Infrastructure Service

Examples of ways an application can depend on the technical infrastructure alone:

- **Characteristics of the dependency:** *Availability and performance*

  The ability to print a high quality report on demand from an application might be very important. Perhaps it is a statement of account balance for a high net worth individual, or a quotation of price for some business. It is the responsibility of the technical infrastructure to provide this capability. A well designed technical infrastructure will have recognized the need for availability and performance and placed two identical printers in a pool for resilience and served them from a lightly used computer.

- **Characteristics of the dependency:** *Availability*

  To enable mobile workers arriving at any office to be able to plug their laptops into the network and begin work, the infrastructure services responsible for providing the network connection must offer a suitable level of availability. The applications or services the user needs to use will be inaccessible if the basic network connectivity infrastructure services are not functioning.

- **Characteristics of the dependency:** *Capacity*

  An application that uses temporary disk space to create output data must rely on the infrastructure to ensure the necessary disk space is available or the application may not work properly. Use of quota management may allow the technical infrastructure to manage the capacity of the disk subsystem.

Application Requirements Questionnaire

The Application Requirements questionnaire tables in this section show a typical set of questions that are designed to elicit all the critical information we need to know about an application's use of the technical infrastructure. It is always worth checking whether any of this information is detailed in existing documentation.

Some of the information requested here may be irrelevant for a particular project or it might be appropriate to ask additional questions. If in any doubt as to whether all the necessary information is being requested about an application the recommended approach is to review the application architecture and functionality asking how the application interfaces to the environment it functions within.

Categories of information collected include:

- General application details
- Application functionality overview
- Application architecture
- Links and dependencies
- Technical infrastructure service needs

Table 8.2 *General Application Details*

Instructions: Complete this table for each application.	
Information	**Details**
Name of application	
Application version	
Type—application, productivity tool, utility	
Operating system & version	
Prerequisite layered software	
Supplier	
Manufacturer	
Support agreements	
Dedicated computer requirements	
Memory requirements	
Disk space requirements	
Language	

Table 8.3 *Application Functionality Overview*

Instructions: Complete this table for each application. Detail key application functionality mentioning: ▪ Why it is important to the business ▪ What alternatives there are (if any) ▪ Legal implications
Name of application:
Overview text

Table 8.4 *Application Architecture*

Instructions: Complete this table for each application.	
Information	**Details**
Name of application	
Who supports the application?	
Does the client software have to be installed on the local workstation?	
Can a network copy be used?	
Interprocess communications protocol	
Network protocols required	
IP port numbers used (if applicable)	
What constraints are there on the location of the server?	
What hardware architecture is the application available for?	
Does the application use any built-in database replication?	
List all dependencies on other applications	

Table 8.5 *Links and Dependencies*

Instructions: Complete this table for each dependency listed in Table 8.4, Application Architecture.	
Information	**Details**
Dependency	
Description	
Interface	
Protocol	
How critical	
Volumes	
Resilience	
Frequency	
Contingency	

Table 8.6 *Tehnical Infrastructure Service Needs*

Instructions: Complete this table for each application component.	
Application Name:	
Component Name:	
File and Print Services	
List drive mappings.	
List UNC connections.	
Define directory structures required.	
Printing requirements (e.g., page rate, paper size, fonts, etc.)	
Printer type needed/preferred.	
Naming Services	
Does it use host names or NetBIOS names or both?	
What is the maximum name lookup rate generated by this application component? When is this rate experienced?	

Table 8.6 *Tehnical Infrastructure Service Needs (continued)*

Does it use hardcoded IP addresses to reference other computers?	
Security (Domain)	
Does the application component run as a Windows NT service? If so provide name and rights.	
List local and global groups required.	
List directory permissions.	
List share permissions.	
Provide details of special accounts.	
Time Services	
Where does it obtain time from?	
Does this application component require time to be synchronized with:	*Provide details below:*
All computers hosting components of the application?	
Another application?	
Any external agency?	
An external time source?	
Operating System	
List all run-time environment shared files required (include size, version and date for each).	
List all known incompatibilities with either other applications or operating system components.	
Are any special keyboard mappings used?	
Are any OS or layered product patches required?	
Management and Operations	
How is the application managed?	
How often are updates supplied?	
Does it depend on Windows NT security in any way?	
Does it generate log files? How are they managed?	

Table 8.6 *Tehnical Infrastructure Service Needs (continued)*

What is the shutdown/restart procedure?	
Does it generate Windows NT events or SNMP traps? If so provide details.	
Additional details.	

User Requirements

The purpose of user requirements gathering is to establish the demands that will be placed on the new technical infrastructure by users. User requirements should be gathered for two communities, the business users for whom the system is being built and the support users who will manage and operate the system.

The following list shows the steps involved in gathering user requirements. Each step is detailed in the following sections:

1. Define scope of user requirements
2. Determine source of user requirements
3. Create the user requirements gathering tool (questionnaire)
4. Gather user requirements

Documenting the user requirements in a Requirements Specification and creating the Functional Specification is covered in a separate section in this chapter.

Define Scope of User Requirements

Defining the scope of the user requirements that need to be gathered is important for two reasons. One is that it ensures questions aren't asked for which the response won't be used. This saves time and effort but the more important reason is that it avoids mis-setting expectations with the user community regarding what they will be getting out of the new technical infrastructure. Asking a user whether they need a feature or not tends to imply that if they do need it they will get it.

The scope of the user requirements questions should be governed by the overall project scope, which was identified at the beginning of the project. If the project scope statements are not specific enough to determine precisely whether or not a question should be asked then it is recommended that the question be asked anyway as the response may become important later.

Determine Source of User Requirements

Business user requirements of the technical infrastructure must ultimately reflect the requirements of the individual users themselves, though in highly structured environments it is practical to treat a group of users as having identical requirements. In cases like this a single representative should be nominated to respond to the questions on behalf of the group. If this can't be done then there is no alternative but to address each user individually.

In cases where the new technical infrastructure will represent a major advance in technology bringing many new possibilities, the frame of reference of a user familiar only with the existing system may not allow them to entertain requirements they have no idea are possible. Business principles overcome this to some extent as they are used to guide a solution architect in the application of new technology. However, there will likely be people within the IT and business communities who have a sound understanding of how new technology can be used to the advantage of the business. These people should be sought out for their input to the User Requirements Gathering activity.

Identifying the source of support user requirements will be a case of finding the person who can define the management and operations needs of the support function. In some cases these needs will be written down though in most cases they are embodied in the existing support systems.

Note that whereas the new technical infrastructure is being created to satisfy the requirements of the business, which has no dependence on the technology, the requirements of the support function will have a dependency on the new technical infrastructure. In that sense their management and operations needs are likely to change to reflect the requirement to support a user population on new technology. For this reason it is unrealistic to expect the support users to be able to know, at the requirements gathering stage of the project, exactly what their requirements will be. Two strategies for addressing this are:

- to focus on service level agreements as a summary of the support user requirements.
- begin a pilot at an early stage as a means of familiarizing the support users with the technology that will have to be managed and the tools that can be used to manage it.

Create User Requirements Tool

If the new technical infrastructure is replacing an existing one then the user requirements for the new system will comprise:

- functionality provided by the current infrastructure, and
- additional functionality.

The natural tendency for anyone who is asked to state their requirements will be to focus on the additional functionality needed. While this is a start, to establish the full set of requirements we must make sure we identify all the functionality that must be retained.

The recommended approach is to pose questions about the need for current and new functionality, leading the respondent by the subject of the question. There are two things to note about this method:

- The requirements gathered will be constrained by the scope of the questions, in other words, if a topic isn't asked about, a requirement won't be revealed.
- The fact that a technical infrastructure already exists can be taken advantage of by asking questions that aim to confirm the continued need for existing functionality. One way of doing this is to ask users to identify the good features and bad features of the current infrastructure.

To develop the set of questions it is recommended you consider matters from the point of view of a user, not from the point of view of a technician or architect. This way you won't be constrained by your knowledge of technology and you will begin to focus on the needs of the user. A business analyst may be enlisted to help in the construction of the questionnaire as they would be expected to be able to develop a thorough understanding of the needs of a user. There is no formula for arriving at the complete questionnaire. Start by considering things such as:

- What does the user produce on a regular basis?
- What do they depend on the IT systems for?
- How do they communicate with other users?
- What do they do to compensate for shortcomings in the existing IT systems?

The type of question posed will have a large influence on the quality and usability of the responses they elicit. An open question, which is one that leaves the responder free to decide the content and structure of the response, will result in answers of different style and content from each person. This has two drawbacks, one is that it is hard work for the person answering the question and the second is that it is extremely difficult to consolidate all the responses to a particular question if there is no common structure. Asking a closed question is the recommended approach for gathering user requirements because such a question only demands that the responder select an answer from a predefined set of options.

The most straightforward type of closed question is one that demands a yes or no answer; other types demand a choice from a set of options which let the user identify a scenario or make a value judgment. Examples of closed questions requiring a judgment:

Circle chosen response				
1. What is the business impact if the system is unavailable for 30 minutes?	Low	Medium	High	
2. What time of day does the system need to be available from?	6am	7am	8am	9am
3. How many pages do you usually print per day?	<10	<50	<100	>100

There is still a place for the open question but it should be used judiciously. The most appropriate use for it is as a "catch all," asking for requirements to be volunteered that have not been covered by the rest of the questions.

In every case questions should be phrased carefully to avoid setting user expectations as it is not the task of the requirements gathering exercise to say anything about what will or will not be delivered in the new technical infrastructure. There is no suggestion that questions should be omitted in order to evade supplying a function necessary for users to carry out their jobs. What must be avoided as far as is possible is any reference as to how they might require a certain product or technology to carry out their job, unless the question happens to be within the scope of the project.

Consider the following alternatives:

"Do you need an ISDN line to your home?"

Compared to...

"Do you ever need to work from home?"

The second question is preferable to the first in cases where it is advantageous to establish the need but reserve the decision on technology to the design phase of the project. A design decision on behalf of the user can be made by asking more questions to establish exactly what they need to do from home.

Gather User Requirements

It is helpful to think of gathering the requirements as a two stage process:

1. Preparing the users
2. Gathering the requirements

The process of gathering requirements from users will trigger feelings of concern in many which can prejudice the timeliness or quality of the information gathered. This makes it important that any fears are dealt with by a full explanation of the process being undertaken and the benefits that will accrue. The most effective way to communicate these points is in a meeting staged prior to distribution of the questions. The meeting will also provide an opportunity for the users to ask questions about the project.

It is always preferable to meet with the person responding to the questions to gain the chance to clarify any issues they may have, particularly if their first language is different to that of the questionnaire. If a meeting is not possible, a telephone call, or video conference may be used to almost as good effect. A large project will call for requirements to be gathered from many people so it will not always be practical to discuss responses with each person on a one to one basis. In such cases it is recommended that for each group of users a local representative be identified who is given the responsibility for the completion of the questions by their group. Clarification of issues should then be carried out through this representative.

Case Study User Requirements Questionnaire

The following tables of questions are appropriate to the MBI case study and will be relevant to most technical infrastructure projects. However, it is important that the list of questions be tailored to each project.

Categories of information MBI collected include:

- Business user

  ⇒ details

⇒ mobility

⇒ printing and data sharing

⇒ productivity application

⇒ application priorities

- IT Support Requirements

Satisfying some user requirements will be more difficult than satisfying others and the users will have no notion of which requirement will be more difficult than another. They will know, though, how important each requirement is to them. If we know the importance attached to each requirement we can prioritize the design and development work, placing the low priority items that are difficult to deliver at the bottom of the list.

The user requirements questionnaires shown below may be enhanced to request that each requirement is graded in terms of its importance. For example, High, Medium or Low.

Table 8.7 *Business User Details*

Instructions: A copy of this table should be filled in for each user.	
Information	**Details**
User name	
Telephone contact number	
Business group	
Supervisor's name	
Manager's name	
Assistant's name	

Table 8.8 *Business User Mobility*

Instructions: A copy of this table should be filled in for each user.		
Does the user need to be able to work from any workstation?		
⇒ In the same office (other than their usual one)	Yes	No
⇒ In another office in the same city	Yes	No
⇒ In another office in the same country	Yes	No

Table 8.8 *Business User Mobility (continued)*

⇒ Anywhere in the corporation	Yes	No
Does the user work from a portable computer?	Yes	No
Is this in addition to a desktop workstation?	Yes	No
Does the user need to work from a laptop in their usual office?	Yes	No
Does the user need to work from a laptop?		
⇒ In another office in the same city	Yes	No
⇒ In another office in the same country	Yes	No
⇒ Anywhere in the corporation	Yes	No
⇒ From home	Yes	No
⇒ From hotels	Yes	No
⇒ From the offices of another corporation	Yes	No

A more detailed version of Table 8.8 would include questions asking what application and data sharing needs a user had when working at a different workstation.

Table 8.9 *User Printing and Data Sharing Requirements*

Instructions: A copy of this table should be filled in for each user.		
Does the user potentially need to share data with . . .		
Members of the same business group?	Yes	No
Any other business group?	Yes	No
Members of specific business groups only?	Yes	No
If the answer is yes, please list those groups here:		
Does the user need to share data with users in other countries? If the answer is yes, please list those users and countries here:	Yes	No
Is access needed to any public directories?	Yes	No

Table 8.9 *User Printing and Data Sharing Requirements (continued)*

Printing		
List the applications the user needs to print from:		
Paper sizes required: A3 A4 A5 Labels A4 envelope Small letter envelope		
Does the user need to print confidential documents?	Yes	No
How many pages per day (on average) does the user print?		Pages/day

Table 8.10 *User Productivity Application Requirements*

Instructions: A copy of this table should be filled in for each user.		
Does the user need use of a . . .		
Word processor?	Yes	No
Spreadsheet?	Yes	No
Database tool?	Yes	No
Presentation tool?	Yes	No
Personal organizer?	Yes	No
Web browser?	Yes	No
Electronic mail?	Yes	No
Graphics creation tool?	Yes	No
Does the user schedule activities between members of a group?	Yes	No
If the user requires a Web browser do they need to access internal corporate pages only?	Yes	No

Table 8.11 *Business User Application Priorities*

Instructions: A copy of this table should be filled in for each user. List all applications used along with business priority (1–5, 1 = highest priority)	
Application	**Priority**
1.	
2.	
3.	
4.	
5.	

Table 8.12 *IT Support Requirements*

Instructions: A copy of this table should be filled in for each distinct support group.	
Information	**Details**
Name of support group	
Manager of support group	
Service level agreements in place	
List all functions that need to be carried out remotely	
List all management tools in use	
Backup	
Volume of data to backup	
Window in which to backup data	

It is recommended that Table 8.12, IT Support Requirements, be designed in conjunction with IT Support rather than trying to anticipate too much regarding their environment and needs. The version shown above is far from complete.

Planning Requirements

The planning requirements activity must collect all the information about the current environment that will be required for the design and implementation planning of the new technical infrastructure. The list shown below sets out the steps involved in gathering planning requirements. Each step is detailed in a subsequent subsection:

1. Define scope of planning requirements
2. Determine source of planning requirements
3. Create planning requirements tool
4. Gather planning requirements

At the end of this section is an example questionnaire used to gather the planning requirements on the case study MBI project. The Gathering of Planning Requirements is often referred to as carrying out a Site Survey.

Define Scope of Planning Requirements

The project scope statements developed at the beginning of the project should be used to define the broad areas of information to include in the survey. Be careful they don't limit its scope too much as it is common to need information unrelated to the project but related to the system undergoing change. If in doubt about whether something should be included, err on the side of safety and include it.

Determine Source of Planning Requirements

Where to get information from will clearly depend on what information is required. Information sources include:

- IT Support
- Users
- Facilities
- Corporate standards group
- Audit department
- Networks group
- User representatives
- IT Security/Audit
- Legal department

Create Planning Requirements Tool

To determine the information that will need to be gathered it is recommended that a simulated planning exercise be carried out. By stepping through the creation of a plan for the installation or upgrade of a technical infrastructure noting all the information required to execute the plan, the key questions that need to be asked in the Site Survey should be identified.

Where technical infrastructure projects include the upgrade and installation of new hardware it is common to need an accurate hardware and software inventory. Automatic inventory tools are available for gathering much of this data and should certainly be considered where the computer population is high.

Use of an Automatic Inventory Tool

Such a tool will typically comprise a client component that needs to be installed on each computer and a server component responsible for storing the data sent to it by the clients. The client component will be set to send inventory information to the server on a regular basis so the information gathered by the automatic inventory tool is kept up to date.

Automatic inventory gathering tools will usually gather software information as well, though care should be taken to be sure the tool can correctly recognize all software likely to be installed. The thing it won't reliably tell you is whether the software installed is ever used. That is when you must resort to a questionnaire.

Use of the Manufacturer's Inspection Tool

A more reliable method of gathering hardware configuration information can be to use tools supplied by the manufacturer of the hardware. In most cases, however, these tools have to be invoked from the computer itself and the data generated is only available as a text file. Use of these tools is best restricted to the first pass at gathering an inventory where they can be used to verify the data gathered by the automatic tool.

An Inventory Database

It is important to note that an automatic inventory tool will only gather a subset of the information required for planning. For example, it won't gather information about the business unit a user belongs to or the name of the user of the computer. It won't gather the user's telephone number and it won't gather the computer's asset number.

The complete inventory database needs to include the information gathered by the automatic inventory tool as well as additional information entered manually. In some cases the automatic inventory tool allows the entry of key information such as asset number at the time the client component is installed. This is useful though it is information that cannot be updated automatically.

The creation of a complete inventory database may be possible by extending the database provided with the automatic inventory tool. Where it cannot be extended to be complete it may be necessary to feed the data from the automatic inventory tool into a new database.

Tracking Change

When the client base runs into hundreds and thousands it is common to find that there is constant change in the computer population. People will be upgrading system components, replacing old computers with new, and moving desks, taking their workstations with them. An inventory gathered one day will therefore be out of date the next unless all the changes can be captured on an ongoing basis. An automatic inventory tool will not be able to keep track of all types of change.

A way of keeping track of changes is to use a change management process. It should be designed to capture every change that affects the value of data stored in the inventory database. As the changes may be carried out by different groups it is important that all the groups likely to effect change are identified and instructed on their responsibility to follow a process that ensures an up to date inventory. Typical changes having an effect on inventory are:

- Purchase and installation of a new computer—the automatic inventory tool client will need to installed as part of the commissioning process.
- De-commissioning an old computer.
- Moving a computer and user to another desk or building.
- Installation or upgrade of software.
- Upgrade of computer.

The inventory database must be owned by a single group to ensure changes are made with the right level of authority and control. It is commonly owned by the help desk as the usual way to initiate change is to lodge a call with the help desk. Thus, they are able to track a change from initiation to completion.

Conclusion

The gathering of Planning Requirements may be accomplished using the following tools:

- Installation and regular use of an automatic inventory monitoring tool
- Use of the manufacturer's system inspection tool to verify the information gained by the automatic inventory monitoring tool
- Interview
- Questionnaire

Finally and most importantly, once the inventory is gathered it must be kept up to date. This should be done using a change control process that allows each inventory change to be captured.

Gather Planning Requirements

There may be many difficulties to overcome in acquiring the data that can't be collected automatically including language barriers, ignorance and cost. A number of approaches to gathering the data are possible. Here is a summary, starting with the most preferable:

1. **Have the solution architect personally interview site representatives**—The solution architect should know exactly what is required from the survey and should be able to judge whether the information being returned in the questionnaire is of value.
2. **Have a technician personally interview site representatives**—A good technician will understand when a response makes sense but they may not have the strength of personality to gain sufficient serious commitment from the site representatives.
3. **Have the project manager personally interview site representatives**—Such a person should be able to command the commitment necessary but may not appreciate the quality of the responses.
4. **An interviewing team**—The combination of the project manager and a technician or the solution architect will provide an optimum combination of skills to gather requirements on a site visit.
5. **Conduct telephone or video conference interviews**—This will often work well though lacks the flexibility for consulting other people during interview. For this method to be successful, the interviewees must be willing participants. If they are not, the medium makes it difficult to rectify the situation.

In every case, the questionnaire should be sent out in advance of the interview so the interviewees may have time to prepare. Do not expect to get questionnaires filled in without requiring intervention from the project team. Without anyone available to clarify questions or to judge the quality of information being returned, the results will be disappointing and of low value to the planning process.

Planning Requirements Questionnaire

The survey questionnaire presented in this example is designed to gather planning requirements from a single office incorporating several business groups.

The following categories of data should be gathered to cover the Planning Requirements:

- General IT Overview
- LAN Details
- WAN Details
- User Details
- Server Details
- Local Support Capability

Table 8.13 *General IT Overview*

Instructions: This table should be filled in once for the office.	
Information	**Details**
Preferred suppliers	
Preferred network protocols and NOS	
Planned changes	
Current status of IT infrastructure	
Geographic dispersion of site	
Support organization capability	
Site specific comments	

Table 8.14 *User Population Overview per Office*

User Group	Power Users	Average Users	Casual Users
Administrators			
Managers			
Traders			
Settlements			
Total			

Knowledge of the user structure of the location will give us an indication of overall scale. Without this knowledge misunderstandings can arise.

Table 8.15 *LAN Details*

Instructions: This table should be filled in once for the office.	
Information	**Details**
List names of all permanent computers on the office LAN	
List names of all laptops that regularly connect to the office LAN	
If DNS is used detail the name space design	
Number and type of LANs	
Is structured cabling in use?	
What different LAN types are in use?	
Are FDDI / ATM / Frame Relay in use?	
What technology is the office network backbone?	
What cabling is used from the LAN segments to network backbone?	
Provide details on LAN utilization levels	
Hubs: type in use, ports available, cabling supported, spare slots	
Routers, make, model, ports free and used	
Bridges, make, model, ports free and used	

Table 8.15 *LAN Details (continued)*

Number and type of terminal servers	
Network protocols supported on the LAN?	
NIC registered subnets used?	
Network management tools used?	
Please supply a diagram of the LAN	
Are there any plans to upgrade the network within the next n months? If so when?	

Table 8.16 *WAN Connections per Office*

Instructions: This table should be filled in once for each existing and planned WAN connection from the office.	
Information	**Details**
Destination of WAN connection	
Does this WAN connection exist or is it planned?	
Line type	
WAN speeds	
WAN protocols	
Communications lines suppliers	
Communications hardware	
Encryption type in use	
IP network number for WAN connection	
List the protocols used over each WAN connection	
Are there any planned changes for this WAN connection? If so what and when?	

Table 8.17 *User Physical Environment*

Instructions: 1. A copy of this table should be filled in for each user. 2. If the user will be moved to a different desk within the next n months add the new details to the items marked *	
Information	**Details**
User name	
Telephone extension	
* Desk number	
* Network port number(s)	
* Power outlets free/used	
Group supporting user	

Note that Table 8.18 is designed for an IBM compatible PC. A modified table would be necessary for an alternative type of workstation.

Table 8.18 *User PC*

Instructions: A copy of this table should be filled in for each PC a user has.	
Information	**Details**
Network details:	
NetBIOS name	
Host name	
IP address	
MAC address	
Port number	
Address of default gateway(s)	
IP addresses and host names of DNS server(s)	
IP addresses and computer names of WINS server(s)	
Network segment type (shared ethernet, FDDI, etc.)	

Table 8.18 *User PC (continued)*

Computer Details:	
Manufacturer	
Model	
Age	
BIOS manufacturer and revision level	
CPU manufacturer, type and speed	
Memory quantity, type and # slots free	
Disk size	
Monitor manufacturer, model and size	
Operating system type and version	
What OS patches are installed?	
Software Details:	
List the applications and tools installed on the PC (include manufacturer and version number)	
1.	
2.	
3.	
List file share connections from PC:	
1.	
2.	
3.	
List printer connections from PC:	
1.	
2.	
3.	

Table 8.19 *Terminal Connection*

Instructions: This table should be completed for each terminal or terminal emulator connection required by the user.	
Information	**Details**
Host type	
Host name	
Network protocol	
Terminal type	
Current terminal emulator used	
Maximum number of connections	
Applications accessed	

Table 8.20 *Computer Details*

Instructions: A copy of this table should be filled in for each server accessed by the user population or that is relevant to the planning of a new technical infrastructure.	
Information	**Details**
Server name	
Model	
Manufacturer	
Supported by	
Memory	
Disk configuration	
Operating system type and version	
Network connections	
Role	
List applications hosted	

Table 8.21 *Support Skills per Office*

Instructions: A copy of this table should be filled in for each office.			
Quantity of support skills	**Aware**	**Competent**	**Expert**
Windows NT 4 WS			
Windows NT SVR			
Windows NT 3.x			
Windows 95			
Windows 3.x			
TCP/IP networks			
Information		**Details**	
Support organization structure (Please attach structure chart)			
Supply details of training program			
Supply details of recruitment plans			

Care should be taken to customize Table 8.21 for the particular project. As it stands it is largely incomplete, though valid as a basis for a more comprehensive questionnaire. MBI chose to end the Site Survey questionnaire with a general application audit simply to get an overview of all the applications relevant to a location. Table 8.22, Application Audit per Office, shows the table used.

The application audit for a location should include all applications that will be relevant to the future Windows NT installation there. Some will already be in use at that location or another and may need to be ported, others might be being created specially for the new infrastructure and not yet be deployed. The location application audit should be cross-checked with the applications revealed by the User Requirements gathering activity.

It makes sense to consult the business and IT for this information. The business manager at a location is more likely to be aware of future application needs whereas the IT staff are likely to be more aware of what is actually in use. It would not be uncommon for the findings in this section to undergo several amendments as people remember applications that will be needed, or decide that some won't be required after all.

Table 8.22 *Application Audit per Office*

Instructions: Complete this table for each application in use or planned for use at the office.	
Information	**Details**
Product or Application Name	
Manufacturer	
# Users	
Business Area	
Gateways to other systems	
Intentions to change?	

Documenting the Requirements

Once all the requirements have been gathered we need to consider how to use them in the design and planning process. Before we can do that we need to do two things:

1. Confirm the requirements are accurate.
2. List those requirements that will be satisfied in the design.

In both cases a document will be produced, recording the final agreed information. The production of each of these documents should be treated as an overall project milestone.

Confirming the Application and User Requirements

In traditional analysis and design methodologies geared towards software development it is common to define the output of the analysis phase as a Requirements Specification. Such a document is a useful vehicle for summarizing what has been asked for from our project, however we must be clear that at this stage what has been asked for, may not necessarily be delivered.

The Requirements Specification will comprise:

- Application requirements
- User requirements
  ⇒ Business user requirements
  ⇒ Support user requirements

After gathering requirements we are likely to have a wealth of demands with widely varying validity.

Several statements of requirement will overlap. Some "requirements" will be expressed as solutions, though we may wish to solve the particular problem another way.

The task we have to accomplish is to turn these raw requirements into a set of consolidated requirements by merging overlapping requirements statements and removing any references to solutions. The risk in this process is that some requirements are overlooked or misinterpreted so it is critical that the consolidated set is distributed for approval to those who were originally surveyed to check that their requirements have survived the consolidation.

When circulating the consolidated Requirements Specification for review take care to ensure no one assumes the document is stating what will be delivered. The final Requirements Specification will have statements such as:

- The system must be available for 18 hours/day
- Time to repair should be under four hours
- Must support remote distribution of new applications

The Requirements Specification document should include a sign-off sheet for each reviewer to add his or her signature to indicate approval.

Confirming Planning Requirements

Errors are cheaper to correct sooner rather than later so it is important the data is confirmed as early as possible. The difficulty with confirming the type of data returned from the Planning Requirements activity is that it implies the need to gather the information again for comparison. This is impractical so the recommended approach is to examine samples. For each site, examine in detail the information gathered on one server, one workstation, one user, and so on. Any discrepancies should trigger a more thorough examination to see whether there is a consistent error throughout the information. For example, it may be that the tool used to establish the amount of memory installed in a workstation produced inaccurate information.

However the Planning Requirements were gathered, the recommended approach is to use a spreadsheet or database rather than keeping them in a document. Now, as the environment changes it is easier to keep the Planning Requirements information up to date.

Creating the Functional Specification

Once the Requirements Specification has been agreed on as an accurate record of what was asked for we should then consider which of those requirements are going to be satisfied in our design. We will find that:

- Some will be outside the scope of the project
- Some will be impractical to deliver for reasons such as cost or sheer impossibility

The document stating what will be delivered is referred to as a *Functional Specification.*

The effort needed to produce the Functional Specification from the Requirements Specification may be substantial. On a large project it is common to have to deal with hundreds of requirements, each of which must be examined to ascertain whether it can be delivered. The only practical way involves the chief architect and other technical architects thinking through the first stages of a design to satisfy themselves which requirements can be safely met and which can not.

Two approaches can be taken for documenting the Functional Specification. One is to put a check mark by the requirements that will be satisfied and a justification for those that won't. The other is to record the Functional Specification, which is actually a fledgling design, as a set of Design Principles.

As each principle is asserted, its justification would include supporting statements for one or more of the requirements. This is particularly powerful as it not only specifies the functionality to be delivered but it says something about how it will be delivered along with the implications and issues of a particular solution. Note that this approach will take a lot of effort before a Functional Specification is available, though a number of key design decisions would have been made during its development. The use of a workshop to create the initial set of design principles for the Functional Specification is described in Chapter 7, Developing Principles.

Preparing for a Phased Delivery

The scope of the Functional Specification may be too large for practical delivery in one go. When this is the case it is recommended that the technical infrastructure be delivered in two or more phases. The Functional Specification should be the place where the functionality to be delivered with each phase is identified.

If the requirements gathering questionnaire elicited a priority rating for each of the requirements then that may be used to guide which are met in which phase of delivery. For example, suppose user mobility between adjacent offices was rated as High, then the features listed in the Functional Specification necessary to deliver this level of user mobility should be delivered in Phase 1.

The Functional Specification should be distributed to all relevant parties for approval and sign-off again, though care must be taken to explain:

- why certain things will not be delivered
- the phased delivery of requirements

Obtaining agreement to the Functional Specification is critical as this document describes what will be delivered in the technical infrastructure. This should be made clear to those reviewing it. Once design work is underway, changes to the contents of the Functional Specification will cost money and potentially slip the project.

Summary

The purpose of Requirements Gathering is to determine the needs of the new technical infrastructure. There are three sources of requirements, one is the set of applications that will run on it, another is the users that will use and support it and another is the planning requirements.

The set of requirements an application places on the technical infrastructure is one of the key influences on its design. The process of working out the needs of an application should include examining three categories of information: functionality, architecture and dependencies.

The purpose of user requirements gathering is to establish the demands that will be placed on the new technical infrastructure by two communities of users, the business users for whom the system is being built, and the support users who will manage and operate the system. A questionnaire is the most appropriate tool for gathering requirements. Questions should be closed, ensuring the results are of a consistent quality and that they can be managed effectively.

The planning requirements activity should collect all the information about the current environment that is likely to be required for the design and implementation planning of the new technical infrastructure. It may be possible to use an automated tool for gathering much of the factual planning data. Though, again, a questionnaire is often required to capture the more imprecise items of data.

The user and application requirements should be documented in a Requirements Specification. This document should be reviewed and agreed upon, however, the existence of a requirements does not commit the project to satisfying it. A Functional Specification should be produced based in a large part on the Requirements Specification, detailing the functions that will be implemented by the new technical infrastructure.

Part II

The Design and Implementation Preparation Phases

The chapters in this part of the book concentrate on the Design Phase and the Implementation Preparation Phase. Part II builds on the concepts and the case study introduced in Part I.

What follows in this preamble are some notes on the chapters relating to the Design Phase. By reading these notes the purpose and structure of these chapters will become apparent. The single chapter addressing the Implementation Preparation Phase of the project needs little introduction here as it deals with each of the activities in that phase in a self-contained way.

Figure II.1 *Design and Implementation Preparation Project Phases*

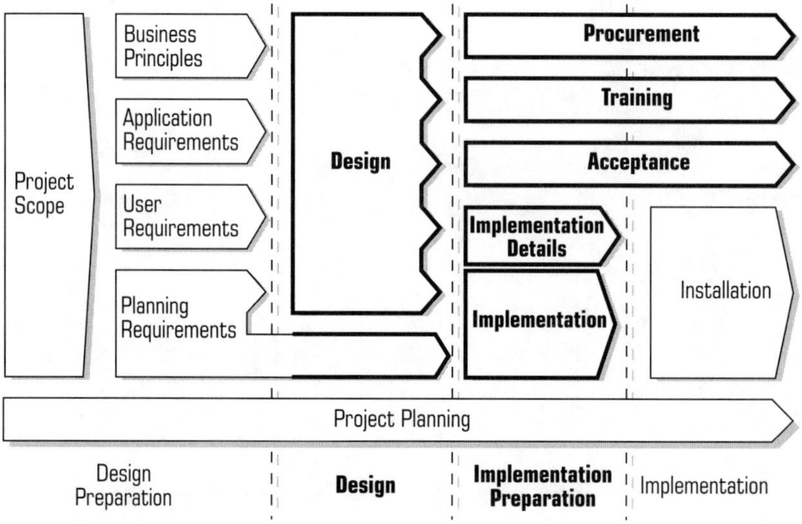

Design Chapters Purpose and Structure

1. The purpose of the design chapters is to illustrate how a technical infrastructure design can be developed using business principles for guidance and design principles to capture the key design decisions. It is not their purpose to show a correct design for a particular scenario.

2. During the course of creating the design there are several points where it is acknowledged that had a business principle been available, a design decision might have been resolved more easily. This is what happens on a real project. If a complete set of business principles had been created for the case study in Part I of the book it would have been unrealistic and therefore misleading.

3. Where new business principles are identified they are listed at the beginning of Appendix A.
4. The scope of the case study design can never hope to be as far-reaching or as detailed as would be expected on a real project. The best approach is not to consider it as a definitive design but as a framework from which parts may be removed and other parts added to arrive at a complete design for your project.
5. Appendix B contains a selection of design principles. Appendix A lists additional business principles which may be used as a source of ideas.
6. Design principles created during the design are numbered as Design Principle <chapter #>-<principle number>, for example, Design Principle 9-2. Business principles are numbered in a similar fashion except for the five created specifically for the case study in Chapter 5. These are numbered MBI Business Principle <principle number>. Most of the statements within a design principle will be of a generic nature though some will be examples of how the principle could be tailored to a specific project.

Design Chapter Structure

The structure used in each design chapter is:

Introduction

An overview of the main issues facing the task of designing the particular technical infrastructure service. The scope and goals of the chapter are summarized.

Technology Review

A review of the Windows NT related technology relevant to the service under design.

Its purpose is to provide the non-expert reader with sufficient technical background to be able to gain benefit from the following Technical Infrastructure Service Design section of the chapter. It is also intended as a refresher for those with more experience of the technology. It is not intended to be a reference text on the technology and as such will not provide an exhaustive coverage.

In many cases the concepts behind the infrastructure service described in a design chapter will be apparent from the technical review section, however an introduction to the basic concepts of most of the technical infrastructure service is provided in the chapter Elements of a Technical Infrastructure.

Technical Infrastructure Service Design

- *Scope of design*

  A definition of the elements that must be included in the service design.

- *Requirements on the design*

  The user requirements and application requirements are chosen to support the case study design. Only a small number are used so as to avoid detail that has little relevance to other projects.

- *Common attributes*

  The service under design is discussed in terms of how it can be characterized by the common attributes. In some cases not all the common attributes are relevant so they are omitted from the discussion.

- *Specific attributes*

  Where specific attributes exist for a service they too are discussed in terms of how they can be used to characterize the service.

- *Design topics*

  The design of each service will vary in its approach, which leads to the structure of this section differing from one chapter to the next. The overall objective is to create a design for the case study by addressing each element within the design scope defined earlier in the chapter. Design issues are resolved using business principles and decisions are recorded using design principles.

Extending the Book

Although this book focuses more on the process of developing a design than the technology itself, a time will come when advances in technology make new design chapters appropriate. The following steps illustrate how an additional chapter dealing with a new technical infrastructure service may be developed.

Note that when documenting a design for a technical infrastructure service it is recommended that exactly the same approach is followed.

1. Review the technology. In particular, look for the characteristics that make it a technical infrastructure service. If its configuration is tied to the demands of a specific application then it is an application service and its configuration should be handled with the design of the particular application.

2. Decide which attributes apply and analyze the technology in general terms. Try applying the common attributes first. To discover any specific attributes consider the words you would use to compare one design with another for that infrastructure service.
3. Define the scope of the design. List all the items that must be specified for the design of this service to be complete.
4. Review the user requirements, application requirements, and business principles for anything they say that has a direct bearing on the design. This need not be exhaustive at this early stage of design but it sets out some basic parameters that allow the reader to follow early key decisions.
5. Develop the design creating design principles and taking guidance from the business principles. Consider the following:
   - Be sensitive to areas of design where the business should have a final say.
   - Don't over-specify the design. It should focus on rules, policies and principles. The implementation details can obscure a design and in the end, they tend to change, invalidating the design document. The design should be able to tolerate certain changes in the environment without needing to be rewritten.
   - If new business principles are necessary they should be created. It will be a design decision that prompts the need for a business principle. However, be careful not to reduce the business principle to a design principle or it will lose its value.

9

Network Services

Networking a small number of Windows NT systems together is very straightforward with the tools supplied with the operating system. However, a number of issues become important when the need is to implement a larger scalable network of systems that must combine flexibility with manageability. Addressing those issues will demand co-operation between those creating the technical infrastructure and the network group.

This chapter examines the relationship between the network and the Windows NT technical infrastructure running upon it. It shows how, in an ideal world, one would design the Windows NT technical infrastructure first and then the network second. In many cases, however, this is not practical but it is important to know the demands such an infrastructure places on the underlying network that may lead to a change being necessary and conversely the restrictions an existing network can place on the Windows NT infrastructure.

The design and management of a network infrastructure is traditionally the responsibility of a distinct group within an organization. As Windows NT offers more and more basic networking functionality, the boundary between the network group and the Windows NT technical infrastructure group may eventually break down. Until it does it will remain beyond the scope of a book such as this to cover network design. For the purpose of this chapter the network is something we assume to be there and working correctly.

Design of the technical infrastructure network services is part of the design activity shown on the project roadmap in Figure 9.1.

Figure 9.1 *The Design Phase*

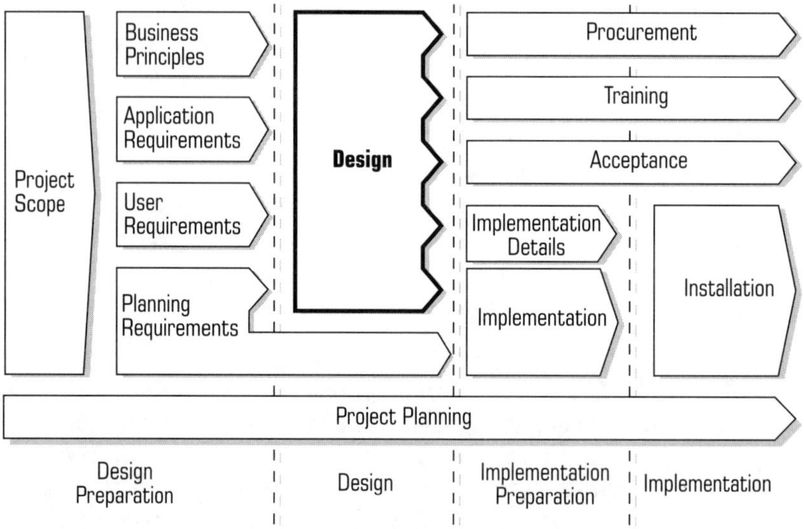

Structure of Chapter

This chapter divides itself into two main sections as shown in Table 9.1.

Table 9.1 *Structure of Chapter 9*

Section	Overview
Technology Review	A review of the technologies involved in the provision of network services in a Windows NT environment including: ▪ Network protocols ▪ Network address management ▪ Benefits and drawbacks of routing ▪ Dial-up communications
Network Services Design	A network address management system is designed for the MBI case study along with a system for using dial-up networking to satisfy the business need for rapid establishment of business in a new location.

Technology Review

This section of the chapter reviews Windows NT technology associated with the underlying network. Later sections address the application of this technology to the MBI case study. For a more detailed description of Windows NT networking technology, please refer to the Networking Guide volume in the Windows NT Server V4.0 Resource Kit.

Windows NT Network Protocols

The following network protocols are provided for use on Windows NT:

- NetBEUI
- IPX/SPX
- TCP/IP

NetBEUI was originally created to allow small workgroups of computers running DOS to communicate for the purpose of sharing nework resources. This protocol is not routable and is therefore impractical to deploy in a large corporate network as the primary network protocol. NetBEUI has the advantage that it is an efficient protocol, facilitating fast local communications. The most likely use of NetBEUI is to retain backward compatibility with DOS or Windows systems not running IPX/SPX or TCP/IP.

IPX/SPX is provided for compatibility with NetWare networks. The name of the software component providing this protocol is NWLINK and on its own will support basic inter-process communications with other computers running the same protocol.

The following additional functionality can be provided over NWLINK on Windows NT computers:

- For a Windows NT server to offer file and print services to a NetWare client it must run FPNW (File and Print services for NetWare).
- A server can re-serve NetWare server shared services to Microsoft (non-NetWare clients) using GSNW (Gateway Services for NetWare).
- A Windows NT workstation can access NetWare server based shared resources by running CSNW (Client Services for NetWare). Novell offers an equivalent component.

To overcome the limitations of NetBEUI, Windows NT offers a comprehensive implementation of IP, the obvious choice for a corporate Windows NT networking protocol.

Each of the three *protocols* so far mentioned can be used through the NetBIOS application programming *interface* (API), which was originally used as the API for NetBEUI. This is the interface most Windows NT utilities use by default. A Windows Sockets interface is also provided as an alternative for the IP stack to make it easier to support applications and utilities that have a UNIX genealogy or that were designed for TCP/IP on Windows NT. An example of the former would be the file transfer utility FTP.

An additional, less general purpose protocol available on Windows NT is DLC or Data Link Control, which enables:

- Use of Hewlett Packard network printers
- Communications with IBM SNA systems

Finally, Windows NT Server Services for Macintosh provides file and print services for Apple Macintosh clients. No special client software is needed on the Macintosh.

Other networking protocols are available for Windows NT from third parties. Notable among them is DECnet from Digital Equipment Corporation. For the remainder of this chapter we shall concentrate on IP, as in a large corporate environment this is the most important protocol of the three.

Basic TCP/IP Concepts

IP Address Management

Considerable effort will go into the development of a large IP network including planning the:

- Logical topology
- Redundant paths (physical topology)
- Bandwidth required
- Media types (FDDI, Ethernet, etc.)
- Network costs
- Management tools
- IP network allocation
- Routing
- IP address allocation (within each IP network)

The last three on this list directly affect a Windows NT technical infrastructure based on IP. As we will see, we may well want to influence the decisions regarding routing and IP network allocation but they tend to remain areas "owned" by those responsible for the corporate network. IP address allocation to computers from a set of IP networks, on the other hand, is a task most network groups are happy to delegate to other IT groups.

For example, given a particular network with one or two addresses reserved for routers, the IT group may decide which addresses are allocated to which computers. One block of addresses might be allocated to servers perhaps and another block to workstations. In a network where there is constant change of computers and maybe some mobile users with laptops computers, the administrative overhead of IP address allocation can become a burden.

This challenge is increased when we consider that each computer will need to be configured with several network related parameters, for example, the default router address. A change to one of these parameters can mean updating every computer on one or more subnets.

To meet this challenge the IETF (Internet Engineering Task Force) has defined a protocol called DHCP (Dynamic Host Configuration Protocol) for automating the management of IP address allocation. It is based on the concept that the relationship between a computer and its IP address is essentially temporary, allowing a DHCP server to maintain a pool of addresses that are used on an as requested basis. Addresses can be re-used by different computers after they have been released by another.

Tools based on DHCP are implemented by a number of different vendors including Microsoft, with each offering slightly different functionality. The Microsoft DHCP tool is bundled with Windows NT Server. The following sections summarize the basic concepts of the DHCP mechanism.

Leases

A lease is the term used to describe the temporary assignment by a DHCP service of an IP address to a computer. The starting point for a lease acquisition is where the client has no IP address and does not know the IP address of any DHCP servers. Figure 9.2, Successful Acquisiiton of an IP Address Lease, illustrates the process whereby a client acquires an IP address lease.

Other important aspects of the leasing process are as follows: The IP address is normally leased for a finite duration. At set times during this period, beginning after half of it has expired, the client begins a process of lease renewal. This is essentially a repeat of the DHCPrequest and DHCPack conversation but not using broadcasts.

If a lease can't be granted or renewed by a DHCP server it will respond with a DHCPnack (negative acknowledgment), forcing the client to begin lease acquisition again. When a client boots up it confirms it can still use the lease it had before last shutdown with the DHCP server.

Figure 9.2
Successful Acquisition of an IP Address Lease

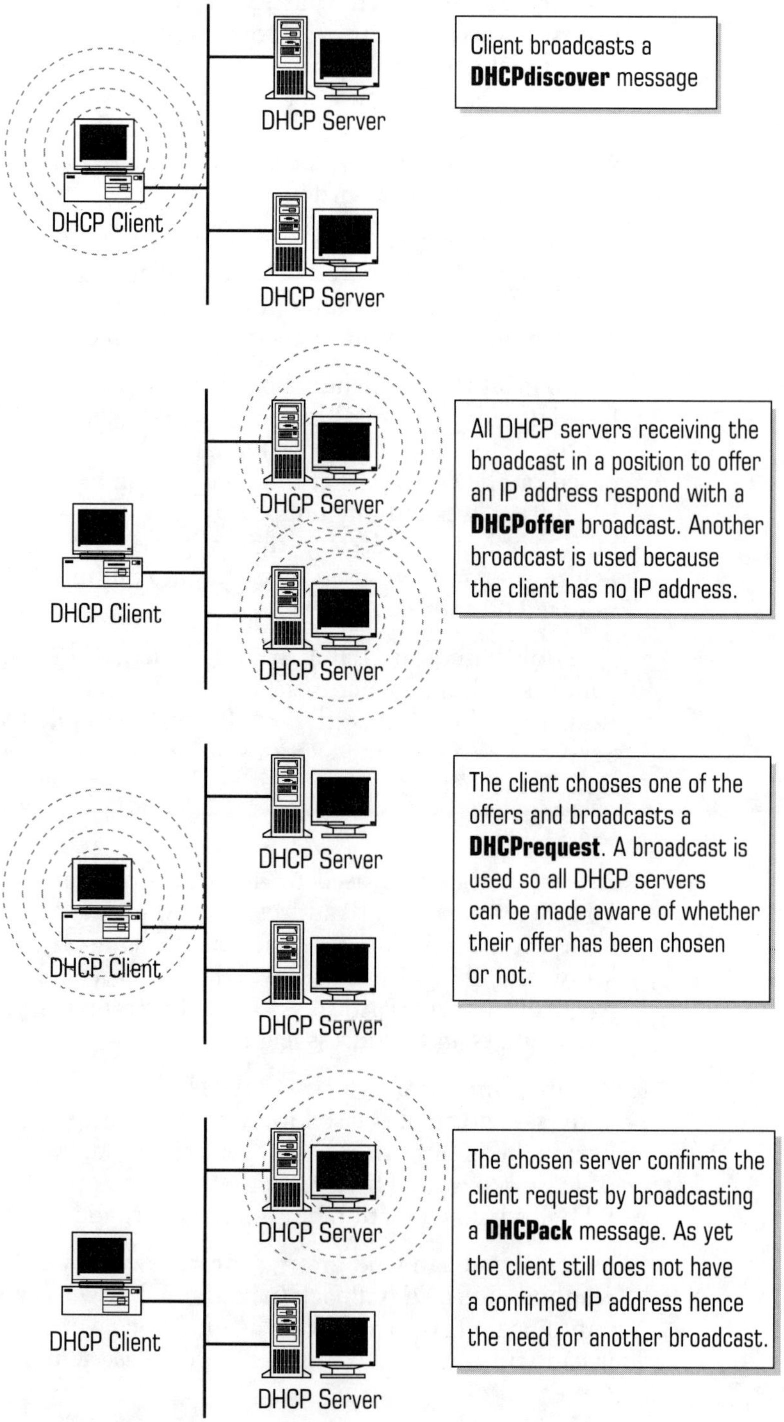
DHCP Server
DHCP Client
DHCP Server
Client broadcasts a **DHCPdiscover** message
DHCP Server
DHCP Client
DHCP Server
All DHCP servers receiving the broadcast in a position to offer an IP address respond with a **DHCPoffer** broadcast. Another broadcast is used because the client has no IP address.
DHCP Server
DHCP Client
DHCP Server
The client chooses one of the offers and broadcasts a **DHCPrequest**. A broadcast is used so all DHCP servers can be made aware of whether their offer has been chosen or not.
DHCP Server
DHCP Client
DHCP Server
The chosen server confirms the client request by broadcasting a **DHCPack** message. As yet the client still does not have a confirmed IP address hence the need for another broadcast.

If there are new network parameters (see the sections on Scopes and Scope Options later in this chapter) available when the boot up confirmation takes place, the client will be informed. In a long lease a reboot can update client network parameters before a routine update would at half lease expiration. If the client can't contact the DHCP server that granted it its lease it will continue to use the IP address anyway.

Reservations

A reservation differs from an indefinite lease by declaring a particular IP address to be used exclusively on a designated computer. That is, if the reserved address is not currently leased, it is not available for any other computer to lease. One reason why this might be advantageous is where a particular application depends on a computer always having the same IP address.

The Microsoft DHCP server allows reservations to be configured based on MAC address, that is the unique address on the network interface card. Thus, when a DHCP server finds that it can match the MAC address contained in a broadcast DHCP Discover with a MAC address of a reservation, the DHCP server will DHCPoffer the reserved address.

Non DHCP Clients

Not all systems are able to obtain an IP address or IP configuration details from a DHCP server, so it is important that we ensure their manually configured addresses don't get automatically leased by a DHCP server. The solution is to add an *exclusion* to the set of addresses available for lease. The exclusion might be one address or a block of contiguous addresses.

Scopes

A scope is the artifact through which leases are managed using DHCP Manager. A scope is defined as a range of IP addresses in a subnet with certain characteristics:

- Scope name
- Subnet mask
- Lease duration—applies to all leases in the scope
- IP address exclusion ranges (see section Non DHCP Clients)

In addition to these characteristics, each scope has a set of optional network parameters (scope options) which can be downloaded to the DHCP client during a lease acquisition or renewal conversation.

Scope Options

A Windows NT DHCP client will accept the following scope options:

- List of routers
- The client's DNS domain name
- List of DNS servers
- List of WINS servers
- NetBIOS node type
- NetBIOS scope ID

(Chapter 10, Naming Services, contains a description of WINS, DNS, NetBIOS and node types.) As an administrative convenience, options can be set to apply to all scopes on a DHCP server by setting them as global options. Global options can be over-ridden by scope options or local client settings.

The Routed Network

The complete IP address space is divided by convention into a set of smaller IP address spaces, each of which is referred to as a *network* or *subnet*. A group of linked networks is called an *internet*, which is distinct from *the Internet,* the internationally accessible IP based network. Subnets are connected together using routers which have the task of taking a communication packet from one subnet and forwarding it, sometimes via several other routers and subnets, to the subnet of the target computer.

Broadcasts and Routers

Most routers will route a variety of protocols such as IP, Novell IPX, and DECnet, allowing highly scalable networks to be planned and built. However, the way a router handles non-routable protocols must also be planned for if a network is going to provide the correct service to a Windows NT technical infrastructure. A non-routable protocol is one that typically involves a broadcast (a message intended for all computers, rather like a radio transmitter broadcasts to listeners), which when used in a network consisting of a large number of computers can take up considerable bandwidth as broadcast messages flood around the network.

The usual way to limit this adverse effect of broadcast traffic is to confine it to a subnet. Unfortunately this has the obvious drawback of limiting the number of computers that will receive a particular broadcast, impacting the functionality of whatever is employing a broadcast protocol.

The following methods can be employed to limit broadcasts yet allow the protocol to be used effectively:

- Forward broadcasts between subnets on a LAN but restrict them from the WAN. The component of a router that does broadcast forwarding is referred to as a Relay Agent.
- Use a router to forward a broadcast packet directly to a target computer. The router will have had to be configured in advance to know which computer to forward the packet to. The prime example of an infrastructure service that depends on broadcast is DHCP.

For cases where it is undesirable to use dedicated routers it is possible to configure Windows NT to perform a routing function by installing the Microsoft Multi-Protocol Router (MPR) software. MPR can route both IP and IPX and includes a BOOTP Relay Agent for forwarding DHCP broadcasts (DHCP is a development of an existing protocol called BOOTP).

Hubs and Switching

An emerging technology, IP switching offers compatibility with the traditional router based way of building an IP network yet with significantly more flexibility. The concept is based on each computer having a dedicated link to what is effectively a soft configurable patch panel. Under software control in the switch it is possible to group computers into broadcast domains or virtual LANS (VLAN). No routing is necessary for communications within a VLAN. Computers can typically be grouped into VLANs according to MAC address, physical switch port or subnet membership. A powerful capability of the VLAN concept is that computers can be members of more than one VLAN, straddling multiple broadcast domains.

This approach to networking gives us more possibilities than before, allowing us to match the network to the architecture of the software. For example, a DHCP server could be configured as a member of several virtual LANs, each of which contains computers grouped according to the subnet. Thus, the need for BOOTP forwarding or multiple network interface cards is eliminated.

A significant benefit switching brings is higher aggregate bandwidth for a given media type. As each computer has a dedicated link to the switch, it has exclusive use to the bandwidth of that link. Thus, all computers could be transferring data over their network link using 100% of the bandwidth whereas if they were sharing media, the total usable bandwidth would be no more than that of a single switched link.The speed advantage of switching is made possible by using programmable hardware to route packets rather than software as used in more traditional dedicated routers.

Dial-Up Communications

An alternative to a leased line is to use a dial-up connection. In this way costs are reduced by only using a communications link when necessary. Another benefit is that it offers the opportunity to make a network connection over a standard telephone line where a leased line is not available.

The Windows NT implementation of dial-up networking is called RAS (Remote Access Services) which allows clients to connect to a Windows NT server over a dial-up line and operate as if they were directly connected to the corporate network. The communications protocols that support RAS have their roots in the UNIX world.

There are two principle uses for dial-up networking, one is for users to dial-in to an office server allowing them to work from an alternate location. The other is to support general infrastructure and application communications as a substitute for a leased line where the bandwidth limitations can be tolerated, for example:

- Domain synchronization
- WINS synchronization
- Remote resource access

A variation on dial-up communications is Internet tunneling which involves secure communication from one site in the corporation to another via the Internet. Connection at each end is made to a local Internet Service Provider (ISP) with the Internet carrying the traffic between them. This can bring the benefit of low cost as the communications charges are made up from:

- Subscription to each of the ISPs
- Phone charges from each office to the local ISP

These can total less than the cost of a leased line or even ad hoc long distance dial-up between the two offices. The quality of the connection may also be higher using tunneling.

While there are few alternatives to RAS for users to access corporate resources in an ad hoc manner from remote locations, there are established alternatives for temporary inter-site corporate network connections provided by the major network hardware manufacturers.

Multi-homed Systems

Windows NT computers can be configured with multiple network adapter cards, a configuration referred to as multi-homed, to help build a more resilient system, or to handle greater network throughput. Multi-homed computers announce themselves on the network as multi-homed (i.e., several IP addresses with the same computer name) to avert a WINS conclusion that there are several different computers each with the same name.

If, when responding to another computer, a multi-homed system has a choice of more than one network interface it could use, it chooses the one with the optimum path. Note, however, that the server is unaware and unable to take account of certain network and device failure conditions, so it may elect to use an interface that isn't functioning.

Which interface on a multi-homed server a client connects to is a matter that needs consideration. In cases where the IP address is configured on the client using an LMHOSTS file the correct choice can be made for the particular network configuration.

In cases where a multi-homed server's IP address is returned by WINS, the control over which interface a client connects through disappears as there is no way to influence on a per client basis the IP address list returned by WINS for a multi-homed computer. This can lead to a client connecting to a multi-homed server through an entirely inappropriate interface as shown in Figure 9.3.

Figure 9.3 *Client Using WINS to Find Address of Multi-homed Server*

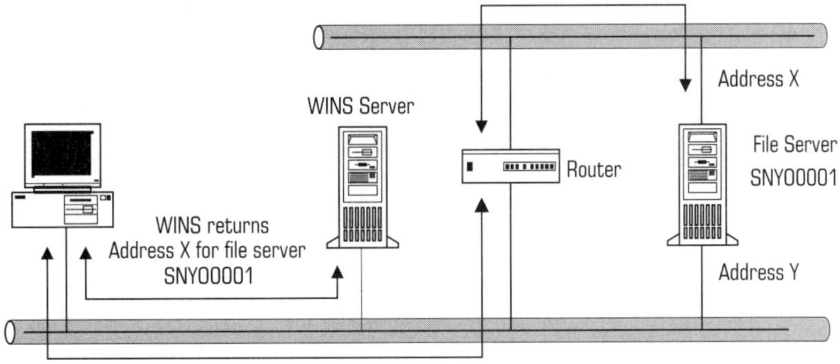

Network Services Design

The focus of this section will be on IP address allocation and its management using the Microsoft DHCP implementation. Dial-up networking will also be covered in as far as it can be influenced by the technical infrastructure design.

Scope of Network Service Design

The scope of a network service design for a Windows NT technical infrastructure must include:

Table 9.2 *Technical Infrastructure Network Design Scope*

Element	Aspect
IP Address Allocation	Server addresses Workstation addresses Other addresses (e.g., printers, routers, etc.)
Hosting the DHCP Service	Which computers run DHCP BOOTP relay agent requirements
DHCP Scopes	Which are allocated by DHCP and what type, leases or reservations Exclusion ranges Lease duration
Scopes Options	Global Options Scope Options
Dial-up Networking	Dial-up WAN connection Dial-up resource access

Requirements on the Design

This section summarizes a small number of requirements that will be used during the case study design. These requirements complement the MBI Business Principles already developed for this case study.

User Requirements

For some users in MBI to be effective in their work they need to be able to connect their laptop computers to the corporate network in any office or dial-in over a phone line from home or a hotel. This type of requirement may come out of the Requirements Gathering activity. It may also be represented by a business principle recognizing the need for a mobile workforce.

Such a business principle would contribute to design decisions concerning:

- The user environment
- IP address management
- The dial-in service

For this case study we shall assume that MBI saw the need for an additional business principle to recognize the importance of user mobility to the bank. The business principle is listed as A-1 in Appendix A.

Common Attributes

All of the common attributes apply to both a DHCP service and a RAS service.

Scalability

One of the most powerful influences on the scalability of the technical infrastructure is the choice of networking protocol. Of the three main choices, NetBEUI will scale the least successfully due to its non-routable nature.

IPX/SPX can be used in a large corporate network, however, it demands measures to ensure its inherent broadcasts don't overwhelm the network. Some large corporations, while using IPX/SPX extensively have partitioned networks that disallow IPX/SPX over certain WAN links. This can clearly cause connectivity problems.

TCP/IP has been designed to scale well in a large environment and has proven itself capable of doing so. For this reason and that it is also a good choice for inter-operation with many different types of platform, this protocol is chosen almost exclusively as the protocol of choice in medium to large Windows NT installations.

DHCP is fundamentally very scalable with no database synchronization needed and minimal load on the server for IP address management. Widespread use of DHCP does, however, depend on ensuring all DHCP clients can successfully reach a DHCP server. Thus, any plans for scalability must include either:

- hosting the DHCP service on a computer per subnet or
- extending the broadcast domain by using BOOTP Relay Agents.

It is therefore unlikely we will ever approach the limiting capacity of a computer operating solely as a DHCP server as network constraints will force the deployment of additional DHCP servers long before that happens.

The main measure of scalability for a RAS service is the number of simultaneous connections that can be established to the corporate network. The number of connections is down to the quantity of hardware installed. If more connections are required, more modems, serial line cards and telephone lines must be installed.

Reliability & Availability

The reliability of a DHCP server is the frequency with which the service becomes unavailable. Its availability can be described in terms of whether a DHCP server can be reached when it is needed by a client.

The DCHP IP address acquisition and renewal mechanism is designed to be resilient to temporary failures of the network or the DHCP server. This is largely through its scheduled retries and the fact that DHCP clients default to continuing to use a leased IP address if, on boot up, they cannot contact the DHCP server.

Thus, a DHCP server could be out of action for days on end without impacting the operation of clients if the lease time was set to long enough and the following *didn't* occur:

- The failure of a network card in a computer holding a DHCP reservation. This will require intervention on the DHCP server to replace the reservation with a new one corresponding to the new MAC address on the replacement network card. Subsequently the client will try to contact the DHCP server for its IP address.
- A mobile user needs to connect a DHCP client laptop to the network, or any other form of initial connection such as the installation of a new computer.

One strategy commonly advocated to cope with possible DHCP server unavailability is to use multiple DHCP servers each with non-overlapping scopes for each subnet. Thus, a client in any subnet could potentially obtain a lease from alternative DHCP servers.

In summary, the DHCP service is capable of tolerating poor levels of reliability in the network or server platform but can still be considered sufficiently available as a result of the repeated retries. DHCP servers can be configured in such a way as to maintain the service should one of them become unavailable.

The reliability of a RAS service is measured by the frequency with which the service is available to a user attempting to dial-in and the frequency with which lines are not dropped and connections not broken. Retries to a RAS service can compensate for unavailability. Reliability is very important if the dial-up link is required for a critical business purpose. The usual way to enhance reliability of the overall service is to use redundant hardware.

Although RAS is a service in its own right, it can play a part in enhancing the availability of the standard network by providing a means of creating an alternative, backup network connection. For example, a leased line may become unavailable so a RAS connection could be created to allow communication to continue. Whether a backup network connection based on RAS would be easier to implement than one using proprietary network hardware is debatable.

Manageability

One of the reasons for deploying DHCP is to ease the management of an IP network. Even if dynamic IP addresses are not in use, its ability to manage reservations and control IP configuration parameters on client computers is valuable. The level of DHCP management is dependent on the level of change in the network topology and the DHCP client population.

The management tools that form part of the DHCP implementation and the RAS implementation both allow the management of remote servers. In addition a monitor installed along with RAS allows operating statistics to be displayed for the local computer. It can sometimes become necessary to force the renewal of a client's IP address, a task that can only be initiated from the client.

The management of a local DHCP service should be integrated with the management of the network and the corporate change management system. The reason for this is that network changes or changes in the DHCP client population will often require an update to the DHCP service. For example, if a computer that uses a DHCP reservation has its network card replaced, the MAC address in the reservation properties on the DHCP server will need to be updated. There is a strong argument for local control of RAS as language, time zone and familiarity with the configuration can aid troubleshooting when it involves telecommunications organizations or Internet service providers local to the RAS server.

Security

The DHCP service creates two security risks. One is the user rights required to configure the DHCP service and the other is the ease with which an undesirable computer may be granted a valid IP address lease on the corporate network.

To administer the Microsoft DHCP service requires a high level of user rights (administrator level). If the DHCP service is running on a computer that also stores sensitive corporate data the DHCP administrator may be able to access that data. One solution is to run the DHCP service on a different computer. In the MBI case study, that computer is the local IT Support domain server.

If dynamic IP addresses are in use there is little to stop any computer configured as a DHCP client from obtaining an IP address lease from a

DHCP server. Use of reservations can ensure that only known and approved computers may obtain an IP address from a DHCP server.

Security is far more of an issue with RAS as by its nature it involves connecting to the corporate network from a publicly available facility such as a hotel telephone socket. Security measures for a RAS service must include not only use of secure technology but equally important, security procedures governing human involvement. Consider that the technology may be watertight but if a hacker calls up the corporate help desk and by impersonating an employee, obtains the dial-up number, a username and a password, all the secure technology will have been wasted.

The job of dial-up security technology is to ensure that those who don't have the right credentials cannot gain access to the corporate network or data. This includes:

- Authenticating a user's credentials before authorizing a dial-in connection.
- Encrypting usernames and passwords used in the initial authentication challenge.
- Encrypting data transferred over the dial-up connection.

Capacity and Performance

The DHCP service involves, in most cases, infrequent amounts of low level communication. For this reason, lack of service capacity is rarely an issue. The nature of DHCP is such that it is not meaningful to talk of its level of performance; it either works or it doesn't.

RAS, on the other hand, has the potential to introduce performance related issues as the dial-up connections created by RAS may have substantially lower bandwidth than a leased line. For this reason caution is needed when designing services to work over such links. In particular, care needs to be taken over the design of the following technical infrastructure services when they are expected to use a RAS link:

- Directory (User account database or SAM) synchronization
- Name resolution (WINS synchronization)
- File and Print

Both directory synchronization and WINS server replication can require significant bandwidth if the complete directory or WINS database is ever transferred. File and print services can call for substantial files to be transferred, potentially tying up a RAS connection for many minutes.

Note that Web based technology will tend to invite substantial transfers of data. This need not be a problem to the individual dial-in user, as they will only impact themselves if a large transfer is initiated. If a temporary dial-up connection is being used as a corporate WAN link then a large data transfer will impact other business users.

IP Address Allocation

The MBI network is divided into subnets each containing a possible 254 usable addresses (0 and 255 have special purposes). In conjunction with the network group the technical infrastructure project team developed a set of rules for the allocation of a subnet's IP addresses to different types of computer.

It had to be accepted from the outset that this recommendation could not be implemented at all locations straight away as there would need to be a planned migration of existing computers to new addresses. The standard IP allocation for an MBI subnet is shown in Table 9.3.

Table 9.3 *Standard IP Address Allocation for an MBI Subnet*

IP Host Type	Quantity	Address Range
Windows NT Servers	19	1–19
Spare addresses	5	20–24
Windows NT Workstations	195	25–219
Other IP Hosts	20	220–239
Printers	10	240–249
Gateways	5	250–254

The spare addresses are required to support the DHCP design addressed later.

While the IP address allocation standard may be applied to all local office subnets, MBI went one step further and specified the standard IP addresses for the computers all offices will operate. The standard computer IP addresses are listed in Table 9.4.

The rationale for allocating fixed addresses to servers is covered in the following section.

Table 9.4 *Standard Computer IP Addresses*

Server	Standard IP Address
Gateways	254, 253, 252 . . .
IT Support BDC	1
Master Domain BDC	2
Resource Domain PDC	3
Resource Domain BDC	4
Resource Servers (File, Print, FAX, etc. . . .)	19, 18, 17 . . .

Deciding to use DHCP

Use of DHCP may bring several advantages to an organization though which ones are the most important will depend on the business needs it is being used to solve. Getting the best out of a DHCP service will therefore rest on a clear understanding of the needs it is being used to satisfy.

The MBI requirements highlight two important needs:

1. The technical infrastructure must support mobile users by allowing their laptop computers to be connected to different points on the corporate network.
2. The other need is to minimize management overhead.

A DHCP service is a good solution to the need of a laptop computer to be able to connect to any part of the corporate network. Properly configured it may also be used to reduce the management overheads associated with a changing workstation population. The decision to deploy DHCP should be recorded as a design principle.

Note that the implication in this design principle alerting us to the fact that if dynamic IP addresses are used then the network monitoring tool currently in use will fail, necessitating an alternative way of monitoring the network. Without Business Principle A-1 supporting this design principle the argument between use of dynamic IP addresses and the needs of the incumbent network monitoring tool would be down to political strength and technical detail. The business principle made it possible to avoid such an argument by setting the business priorities.

Design Principle 9-1—Use of DHCP
DHCP will be used to allocate dynamic IP addresses and IP configuration parameters to all workstations and laptops.
Justification
▪ Allows easier management of mobile users with laptop computers. This supports the Business Principle A-1 requiring that the infrastructure support an increasingly mobile workforce. ▪ DHCP eases the administration of IP configuration details. This supports MBI Business Principle 4, requiring that local management overhead should be minimized. ▪ Flexible use of the address space. ▪ Less administrative overhead than reservations. ▪ Most administration can be done remote from a location and when local co-operation is needed it will usually be to either reboot a computer or renew its IP address lease. ▪ There are many systems already in place with IP addresses in subnets that will in future contain Windows NT computers. The ability to set up exclusions in DHCP scopes will reduce the likelihood of inadvertently giving Windows NT the same IP address as an existing host.
Implications
▪ Need to determine the most appropriate lease duration. ▪ Not all computers are capable of being DHCP clients so their IP configuration details will still have to be managed manually. ▪ Use of DHCP requires that the network supports broadcasts of the BOOTP protocol. A solution to the use of DHCP in a multi-subnet environment will need to be found. ▪ The network monitoring tool currently in use relies on a fixed mapping between network port and IP address. An alternative way of achieving the same network monitoring functionality will need to be found.
Issues
The current DNS implementation at MBI is not dynamic or automatically updated in any way so will be incapable of resolving the IP address of a computer that uses dynamic IP addresses.

The design principle above is confined to mention of workstations and laptops. We should consider the benefit of dynamic IP addresses and automatic configuration of IP parameters for managing servers.

There are two strong arguments for using static IP addresses for servers though the use of DHCP reservations means static IP addresses can be used while retaining the option of configuring the server's IP parameters automatically.

The Microsoft DHCP implementation only allows one scope per subnet per DHCP server, meaning that every computer on the same subnet that has its IP parameters configured automatically by the same DHCP server must receive the same set of parameters. There may be cases where the servers on a subnet need a different IP configuration to the workstations. For example, the MBI WINS design requires that servers use different primary and secondary WINS servers to the workstations. If this can be addressed by locally configured parameters overriding the ones supplied by DHCP then DHCP may still be used. If not there are three solutions:

1. Use multiple DHCP servers to offer multiple scopes per subnet
2. Use an alternative implementation of DHCP that doesn't have this restriction
3. Manually configure server IP parameters

MBI chose to create a design principle that was restricted (Design Principle 9-2) to stating the certain need for static IP addresses on servers while leaving the decision on whether to use DHCP reservations and automatic configuration of IP parameters as a decision to be made on a location by location basis.

The decision to allow certain implementation aspects to be decided on a per location basis may be judged out of keeping with the case study so far. The point to note is that design principles should not be used to restrict a design unnecessarily, just record the key decisions. The document recording the implementation details for each location would specify whether DHCP were used for servers and which IP parameters were configured automatically.

Design Principle 9-2—Use of Static IP Addresses
Static IP Addresses will be used for servers.
Justification
▪ Some servers are explicitly referred to by IP address, for example, WINS and DNS.

continued▸

▪ Some Windows NT servers will need to be accessed by UNIX computers so the DNS entries for the Windows NT servers need to remain fixed because the current DNS implementation does not cope with dynamic IP addresses.
Implications
▪ The need for a static IP address does not rule out the use of DHCP reservations. ▪ IF DHCP reservations are used, IP configuration parameters may be loaded onto servers automatically.
Issues

Hosting the DHCP Service

The MBI server deployment policy developed in Chapter 13 entitled File and Print Services prescribes the use of one or more IT Support Domain servers per location. These servers are intended to host all non-user oriented infrastructure services, including DHCP.

We must decide whether it is necessary to host DHCP on more than one server at each location. Three reasons why this might be desirable along with a brief analysis are presented below:

1. A single computer may not have enough capacity.

   Service capacity is unlikely to ever be a problem, particularly in MBI as the DHCP client population is not large, ensuring a very low level of traffic.

2. A redundant DHCP server configuration may be used to increase service availability.

   The administrative overhead of running more than one DHCP server per location compared to the simplicity of running just one raises the question how critical would it be if the DHCP service was unavailable for a given period of time? If the DHCP service were unavailable two activities would suffer:

   - Addition of a new computer to the network configured to obtain its IP address from a DHCP server.
   - Replacement of a network card on a DHCP client where it uses reservations.

MBI decided that allocation of a small number of IP addresses per subnet as spare to allow manual configuration of IP address and parameters in the event that the DHCP service were unavailable was a lower management overhead than maintaining more than one DHCP server per location.

3. DHCP broadcasts are restricted from passing through routers so a DHCP server is needed for each subnet.

   Using more than one DHCP server is not the only solution to making the DHCP service available in a multi-subnet environment. So, this can be discounted as a reason for multiple DHCP servers.

The three reasons for using multiple DHCP servers have just been dismissed for the case study. So, in summary, each MBI location would employ one DHCP service running on the IT Support Domain Server and a solution will need to be found for forwarding BOOTP broadcasts within the LAN.

Design Principle 9-3—Single DHCP Service
There will be only one DHCP service per location.
Justification
▪ It is not important if the DHCP service is unavailable for brief periods of time so a redundant configuration of two or more DHCP servers will not be required. This depends on the decision to use spare IP addresses in the subnet to allow manual configuration in the rare event that it is necessary at the same time the DHCP service is unavailable. ▪ The processing and storage requirements of an office DHCP service will not approach the limit of a server. ▪ This is the option with the lowest management overhead, supported by MBI Business Principle 4
Implications
▪ This approach minimizes the number of DHCP servers deployed. ▪ Solution will need to be selected for coping with a multi-subnet environment. ▪ Operational procedures should be developed for dealing with DHCP service failure conditions.
Issues

Use of DHCP in a Multi-subnet Office

An implication of Design Principle 9-3 is that a solution needs to be found for ensuring DHCP can be used in a multi-subnet environment. The solution must account for the business requirements as detailed in the business principles for the project which call for scalability and a low management overhead. To scale up from one subnet to many subnets would require one of the following solutions:

1. One of the Windows NT servers forwarding DHCP broadcasts between subnets. This would require the server to be multi-homed.
2. The DHCP server to be connected to all subnets used by DHCP clients.
3. Use of a BOOTP Relay Agent on the routers to propagate the broadcasts to the other subnets.

Option 1 would work as long as we could keep adding network cards to the server to match the number of subnets. The networks group argued that it was not appropriate for general purpose computers to be involved in the forwarding of protocols from one subnet to another. It was a job for a dedicated router.

Option 2 was practical, again as long as sufficient network cards could be connected to the DHCP server. The benefit option 1 and 2 share is that, combined with a router forwarding DHCP broadcasts between subnets, the resilience of the DHCP system may be increased. The networks group were comfortable with option 2.

Option 3 was favored by the networks group as it meant they had full control over the propagation of network protocols. All types of traffic through the routers could be monitored and router configuration controlled using the bundled router management software.

MBI concluded that option 2 or option 3 could be used. In the interests of simplicity, option 3 was chosen, accepting that single-homed computers were more straightforward to configure and the control of network protocol propagation was rightfully with the networks group using dedicated hardware. MBI recorded this design decision as a principle:

Design Principle 9-4—BOOTP Relay Agent
BOOTP (DHCP) broadcasts should be forwarded throughout the office LAN using a Relay Agent on the dedicated router hardware.

continued ▸

Justification
■ Allows use of fewer DHCP servers, leading to less management overhead.
Implications
■ Higher level of broadcast activity throughout LAN (unlikely to cause a problem unless the number of DHCP clients runs into thousands). ■ Need to establish at what point additional DHCP servers are required for an office if commissioning a new subnet no longer requires a new DHCP server. ■ Investigate possibility of using a relay agent that converts the broadcast into a unicast directed at a known DHCP server. This would reduce broadcast traffic significantly.

DHCP Scopes

As the Microsoft DHCP service only allows one scope per subnet, MBI chose to create each scope to encompass the whole set of usable IP addresses in a subnet and to employ exclusions to restrict its use. This way, changes to a scope are possible by modifying exclusions instead of having to delete the scope and create a new one.

Use of DHCP presents the option that Windows NT servers may be configured using DHCP reservations instead of a manual configuration. The main business related influence on such a decision is that of manageability; however, in the case of MBI there is a technical difficulty. As the servers share the same subnet as DHCP configured workstations, they must all share the same scope options. Unfortunately the Naming Service design for MBI calls for the servers to be configured with different primary and secondary WINS servers from the workstations, making the use of the same scope for both impractical. The section, Deciding to Use DHCP, discussed this matter for MBI and decided that the approach should be decided locally. If there were to be a common approach a design principle would be the best way to record it. Thus, we can define the standard scope and its exclusion ranges:

Table 9.5 *Standard Scope Exclusion Ranges*

IP Host Type	Quantity	Exclusion Address Range
Windows NT Servers	19	1–19
Spare addresses (for use in the case of DHCP failure)	5	20–24

Table 9.5 *Standard Scope Exclusion Ranges (continued)*

Other IP Hosts	20	220–239
Printers	10	240–249
Gateways	5	250–254

To complete the basic scope details we should decide on a suitable lease duration. Before making a decision on lease duration we should also consider how often any of the items in the scope options will change, as we would want the DHCP mechanism to automatically update those parameters on the workstations. Of course, if workstations are rebooted on a daily or frequent basis, the scope options will get updated then.

In summary, the lease duration depends on:

- Changes to options
- New computers or replacements
- Replacement NIC

MBI chose to configure a lease period of 90 days for each standard subnet scope. This reflected a recognition that for MBI the primary value of DHCP was not its ability to automatically renew leases but its ability to automatically configure IP settings for a computer population.

Global Options

Of the options that can be set by DHCP, the following apply to all DHCP clients at a location so will be configured as global options using the Microsoft DHCP Manager:

- IP addresses of primary and secondary WINS servers
- IP addresses of primary and secondary DNS servers
- NetBIOS node type (m-node)
- DNS domain

Scope Options

The only option that will vary from subnet to subnet and therefore scope to scope that can be set by DHCP for any MBI location is the value for the primary and secondary gateways. These will be set as scope options using the Microsoft DHCP Manager.

Dial-up Networking

Dial-up technology can be complex as it involves many interdependent factors. It is very important that a design for its use accounts for the following four points:

1. That it is clearly understood what the dial-up link will be used for.
2. Expectations as to what the dial-up link will be used for are compatible with dial-up technology in terms of security, availability, and performance.
3. How and by whom is dial-up networking provided for by the corporation?
4. Specification of all implementation details.

Dial-up networking will be used in two contexts within MBI:

- To support new remote offices on a temporary basis by providing a general purpose dial-up WAN connection
- To support remote users dialing up to access corporate resources

Both are dealt with in the following sections, concentrating on items 1, 2 and 3 from above rather than specification of the implementation details.

Remote Location Configuration

MBI Business Principle 4 states that it should be possible for MBI to rapidly establish itself in new countries. The overall technical infrastructure for MBI has been designed to be scalable, so expansion should not cause any architectural issues. However, establishing an operation in another country can be logistically time consuming and complex. Sometimes it may take many months to procure an international leased line of sufficient capacity to connect the local office to the regional center. Once procured, the cost of the lease can be very high and bandwidth low. In some cases claimed bandwidth is not always achievable as the quality of the line causes a reduction in effective throughput.

The dial-up networking capabilities of Windows NT present two alternatives that do not have the logistical problems of a leased line:

1. Straightforward dial-up
2. Tunneling through the Internet

Another alternative would be to use dedicated hardware for the purpose of establishing a temporary wide area connection. A RAS service has the benefit that it can be co-hosted on an existing computer, making the set up of a new remote office where hardware lead times and skills are in short supply easier. MBI recorded the decision to use RAS as a design principle. An alternative version of this design principle can be seen in Appendix B, Design Principle B-2 (Use of Dedicated Hardware for Dial-up).

Design Principle 9-5—Use of RAS
RAS will be used as a temporary measure when a leased line is required but unavailable.
Justification
▪ Enables the rapid establishment of a new office location. This supports MBI Business Principle 4. ▪ Simple and swift to set up at a new remote location. ▪ Provides a secure mechanism for establishing a temporary wide area connection. ▪ RAS is well integrated with Windows NT. ▪ Does not require the purchase of dedicated hardware.
Implications
▪ The network group will require training in the configuration and use of RAS. ▪ Protocols not supported by RAS cannot be used over the temporary wide area connection.
Issues
Use of public networks for transferring Bank data is currently disallowed by the MBI audit department.

One of the obvious risks with using a dial-up connection is security. The MBI audit department has a rule that Bank data should not be transferred over a public network. This is highlighted as an issue of the design principle that records the choice to use RAS.

Although the technical argument for encryption as a means of securing communications is strong, the strength of MBI Business Principle 4 must be examined to find out what degree of security risk the business will tolerate in order to be able to establish new office locations at short notice.

The way the business principle is worded does not guide us. In practice there will be a level of risk that cannot be tolerated and a description of that risk should be added to the business principle as a qualifier.

The main challenge with seeking guidance from the business on this particular topic will be quantification of the risk associated with different levels of encryption or any other security measure. MBI reached agreement that the encryption capabilities of RAS will ensure the confidentiality of any transferred data. To record this another design principle will be appropriate. The version shown below could be enhanced if it were to specify exactly what type of encryption were to be used.

Design Principle 9-6—Encrypted RAS Communication
Encryption will be used for all RAS connections.
Justification
▪ Enables the rapid, secure establishment of a new office location. This supports MBI Business Principle 4. ▪ The data that may be transferred is commercially sensitive. ▪ Supports the MBI Audit Department security requirements. ▪ If any breach of security were to occur, even if the data was not sensitive, confidence in the Bank would be lost, potentially impacting business.
Implications
▪ Type of encryption needs to be agreed on (potential for another design principle) with the Audit Department. ▪ Ability to use the chosen encryption method in other countries needs to be confirmed.
Issues

MBI decided to define two configurations for supporting a new remote location. One option was to allow extremely swift establishment of an operation and the other to reflect a configuration with more long term potential.

The key characteristics of the two configurations are listed below.

Configuration I

The aim of using this configuration is to establish a presence at a new location in a manner consistent with the rest of the technical infrastructure. That is, it has its own location code and location specific logon script. It functions as a distinct location but is effectively an adjunct to a particular hub site.

- One or more Windows NT workstations at the new remote location dial in to the main regional location, each using their own modem.
- The new remote location is allocated an appropriate three letter code, allowing the use of a location specific logon script.
- Printing is provided by either a locally attached shared printer, or a network printer.
- The logon script assumes one workstation is effectively a server where the group and public shared directories exist.
- The home drives of the users are designated as being on their E:\ partition.
- RAS at the main regional location is hosted on a file and print server. RAS uses the local DHCP server to obtain IP address leases on behalf of the remote workstations.
- The workstations will need to be built from CD-ROM one by one as there is no local IT support domain server to provide a standard MBI build over the LAN from a networked server.

Configuration 2

This configuration is set up when the business confirms the need for a more permanent presence at a location. It is a complete, self-contained installation with the only temporary aspect being the RAS WAN link to the hub location. As soon as a leased line becomes available the RAS link would be decommissioned.

- This configuration has the minimum three servers (file and print, IT support, and master domain BDC) for a complete location. The file and print server operates a RAS connection to a RAS server at the regional hub location. If bandwidth requirements are high the RAS servers can be configured to use multiple modems.
- The logon script for the location will need to be modified to reflect the new shared directories.
- The user's account profiles will need to be modified to reflect their new home drives.
- The DHCP service on the new IT support domain server will be configured with a scope for the new subnet. All workstations will need to release their old IP address lease and acquire a new one.

Moving from configuration 2 to a fully fledged location requires a permanent WAN connection to be set up from a regional hub site to the new location.

MBI Dial-up Networking Review

We shall review the first three design points listed in the preamble to this design section to arrive at a strategy for using dial-up networking in MBI for individual users.

- *What will Dial-Up Networking be used for?*

The principle needs of the mobile MBI user will be to access corporate data and e-mail. Corporate data will be spreadsheets and documents located in various shared directories throughout the corporate network. For the case study we shall assume that regardless of whether the user is dialing up from a workstation or a laptop, all applications are loaded on the local computer so that no remote application access is required.

- *Are expectations compatible with the use of dial-up networking?*

It can be very difficult to answer this question because of the unpredictable nature of the need. For example, a 5MB document could be e-mailed to someone who then attempts to download it over their 33.6kbps dial-up link. It will certainly be possible but whether the user considers it practical is another matter. If the need for a dial-up connection is to allow the user to carry out more routine, predictable tasks then a better judgment may be made. For example, if the need is to submit a management report once a week that is usually around 20kbytes in size, a 33.6kbps dial-up connection should be quite satisfactory. User education through training and experience will bring expectations in line with what is practical.

- *How and by whom is dial-up networking provided?*

Mobile MBI users will be expected to dial up from anywhere in the world to gain access to the corporate network. From some countries good quality international telephone links do not exist so MBI chose to offer a dial-up service at every location. This provided the dial-up user with a choice of connection points with the likelihood being that one would be practical and local enough for a good connection to be made.

Connection to file shares on the corporate network will need to be made manually by the user though if the same set of connections were made regularly a script could be supplied to make those connections automatically.

10

Naming Services

Naming Services occupy an important supporting role in a technical infrastructure. They are relied upon by both applications and other services to provide a convenient way to reference other computers. A naming service needs to be one of the first services implemented in a technical infrastructure.

Naming services were introduced in Chapter 2, Elements of a Technical Infrastructure. They are necessary so that a textual or friendly name humans can understand, can be translated into numbers (address) a computer can understand. In particular, the idea of a set of computers whose task it is to maintain a list of name to address mappings and provide a look up service was used to illustrate a naming service.

The naming services that concern us in a Windows NT based technical infrastructure are the NetBIOS Naming Service implemented by Microsoft called WINS (Windows Internet Naming Service) and DNS (Distributed Naming Service), used in the internet community as a host name service.

Until recently, NetBIOS naming services were confined to a Microsoft environment and DNS to the internet or UNIX based environment. The need to reference resources between the two environments has given rise to the need to integrate the process of name resolution. The Microsoft environment is evolving towards exclusive use of DNS and as it does, reducing its dependence on a NetBIOS naming service. For some time, it will be necessary to provide both services, as well as a level of integration between them.

This chapter provides an overview of both types of name resolution and the integration possible between them, followed by a worked design based on the MBI case study. Because the majority of Windows NT technical infrastructure design projects are faced with the need to accommodate an existing DNS system, it will be assumed that that is the situation with the case study presented here.

Design of the technical infrastructure naming services is part of the design activity shown on the project roadmap Figure 10.1.

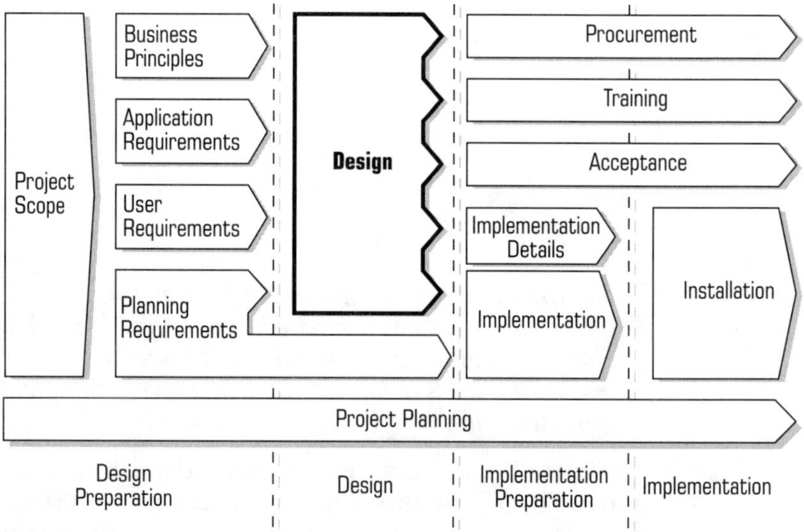

Figure 10.1 *Design Phase of Project*

Structure of Chapter

The chapter is split into two main sections—as shown in Table 10.1.

Table 10.1 *Structure of Chapter 10*

Section	Overview
Technology Review	A review of the basic technologies involved in providing and using naming services used in a Windows NT environment, including: ▪ The management of NetBIOS computer names using Microsoft WINS, an implementation of a NetBIOS naming service. ▪ DNS as the ubiquitous means of implementing a domain naming service. The existing DNS namespace employed at MBI is used as an illustration. ▪ The integration possible between the two naming service implementations is examined for the benefits it brings. ▪ Naming services and Windows NT 5.
Naming Service Design	A WINS based naming service is designed for the MBI case study in four phases: ▪ Choose the most appropriate WINS replication architecture for the needs of the corporation. ▪ Map the replication architecture onto the physical network accounting for the WAN topology. ▪ Size the WINS server and network capacity. ▪ Integrate with DNS. ▪ Specification of the client configuration details. Finally, migration to a Windows NT 5 environment is considered.

Technology Review

Both WINS and DNS return an IP address to a name resolution inquiry. That is about the only thing they have in common. The following sections describe enough of each for the reader to be able to understand the key design issues involved in the deployment of WINS and its integration with DNS. We begin first with some background on NetBIOS name resolution before introducing WINS.

NetBIOS Name Resolution

NetBIOS names are used by Windows NT and other LAN Manager based network operating systems for communications. They are "friendly" names that allow one computer to reference another. In an IP network, a NetBIOS name needs to be converted to an IP address for the network layers to be able to identify and locate the target computer. Figure 10.2 shows the architecture for how applications using the NetBIOS network interface are layered on the TCP/IP protocol stack. NetBIOS name resolution is a function required by Microsoft network aware utilities and operating system components that access the network through the NetBIOS interface. The Windows Sockets interface is used by utilities that have their heritage in the world of UNIX.

Name Resolution

There are three principle methods of resolving a NetBIOS name in a TCP/IP network.

1. Reference to a text file (lmhosts) containing name to address mappings.

   The lmhosts file may reside on the local computer requiring the name resolution or be accessed from a shared network location. Use of the latter allows easier maintenance of the mappings in the file.

2. A network broadcast asking the target computer to respond with its IP address.

   The name resolution is carried out by the target computer itself.

3. Use of a NetBIOS name resolution service such as WINS.

   WINS name resolution is carried out on the server running the WINS service.

Complementing these is a NetBIOS name cache resident on the local computer which is populated by:

- Successful name resolutions using any of the three methods listed above.
- Tagged entries found in the lmhosts file at boot up time.

Cache entries loaded at boot up from the lmhosts file will remain in the cache until shut down. Entries discovered through other methods will expire after five minutes.

Figure 10.2 *Windows NT NetBIOS over TCP/IP Architecture*

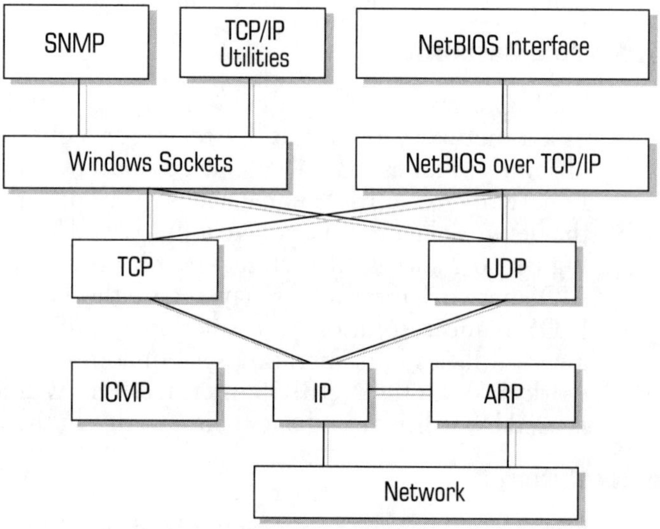

LMHOSTS

Windows NT and other Microsoft network operating systems allow a text file called LMHOSTS to be used for NetBIOS name resolution. The format used is as shown in Figure 10.3

Figure 10.3 *Example LMHOSTS File*

```
#
16.36.144.48     SLDN0001   #PRE  #DOM:Europe
16.36.144.49     SPRS0001   #PRE
16.36.32.13      SPRS0002   #PRE
16.182.32.229    SMLN0001   #PRE
16.182.32.39     SLND0002   #PRE
BEGIN_ALTERNATE
INCLUDE \\SMLN0001\public\lmhosts
INCLUDE \\SLDN0002\public\lmhosts
END_ALTERNATE
```

There are some important things to note about the LMHOSTS file and how it can be used.

The #PRE directive causes the entry to be put in the computer's NetBIOS name cache.

The #DOM directive identifies mappings for domain controllers. This is used by Windows NT domain related functions that require communication with a domain controller.

The BEGIN_ALTERNATE and END_ALTERNATE statements allow alternative remote lmhosts files to be parsed should one be unavailable for any reason. The list of files between the two statements are tried in the sequence they occur.

The INCLUDE statement allows additional remote files to be parsed as if they are local. This is useful because it allows a small number of common lmhosts files to be maintained on selected servers, eliminating the problem of having to maintain full lmhosts files an all systems. Clearly the computer name referenced in the INCLUDE statement should be the subject of a mapping earlier in the file (the entry for this computer should also be the subject of a #PRE directive).

Using a text file for mappings has some problems, one is that it has to be kept up to date manually and without errors and the other is that it either has to be accessible over the network or possibly distributed to every computer on a regular basis. In large networks, the file can also grow to a substantial size, making name resolution slow with the possibility of timeouts before it is completely searched.

Exclusive use of a static NetBIOS name resolution method like lmhosts when an automatic method of allocating dynamic IP addresses to computer names such as Dynamic Host Configuration Protocol (DHCP) is used becomes impossible. The reason is that the lmhosts file gets out of date rapidly as the IP address to computer name mappings change under automatic control of DHCP. If dynamic IP addresses are used, WINS is essential to ensure correct and up to date mappings.

Broadcast

By broadcasting a message to all other computers on the network, requesting the computer with the NetBIOS name matching that in the message to return its IP address, name resolution can be accomplished without reference to text files. There are two main problems with broadcasts as a method of name resolution.

1. The more computers there are on the network, the more broadcasts there tend to be. With thousands of computers on a network, the level of broadcasts can use up a substantial portion of

available network bandwidth potentially impacting application performance.

2. The second problem is brought about by trying to reduce the quantity of broadcasts by blocking broadcast traffic at certain network devices such as routers. Thus, only computers on the same network segment as the inquiring computer will respond to name resolution broadcasts.

These two drawbacks mean that broadcasts should not be used as the only name resolution method if using a routed network where broadcasts are not forwarded. The broadcast method does have the advantage that it is very fast and if circumstances permit, may be considered.

NetBIOS Name Server (WINS)

An alternative to both text files and broadcasts is a network based service for returning IP addresses in response to name resolution queries. Generically titled a NetBIOS Name Server, the implementation we will cover here is called the Microsoft Windows Internet Name Server (WINS).

The most significant benefit of WINS is that it is a dynamic name service, automatically updating its name to address database as computers appear and disappear on the network. This ensures minimum administrative effort and a name service that is synchronized with the computer population.

Consider a file server and workstation each running Windows NT and connected together over an internet network. Both systems are only running TCP/IP, so the mechanism for connecting to a remote file share is to use the NetBIOS protocol over the TCP/IP transport. The workstation may resolve the computer name in the

```
net use ?:  \\smln0001\apps$
```

command to an IP address by directing an inquiry to a designated WINS server.

WINS offers more that just name resolution. Network addresses must be unique within a defined network and every NetBIOS computer name must be unique. Ensuring unique NetBIOS names on a network is the other main task accomplished by WINS. The mechanism for this is covered in the section Name Registration/Release on page 259.

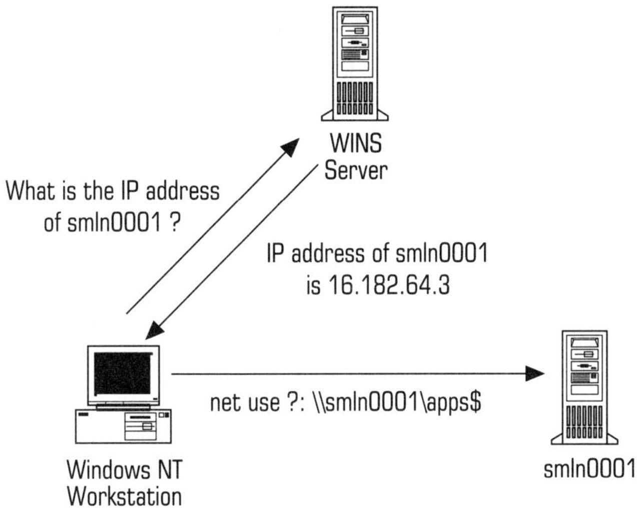

Figure 10.4
WINS Name Resolution

WINS also implements an equivalent function to the LMHOSTS #DOM directive by tagging the entries in its database to identify domain controllers and which domain they belong to. Thus, to locate a domain controller for a given domain, a client can query WINS for a list of the addresses of domain controllers in that domain.

Configuring servers to resolve names requires that thought be given to a number of the common attributes such as scalability, performance and resilience. These issues will be examined in more detail later in the chapter.

Node Type

So far we have mentioned three main methods of NetBIOS name resolution. They are summarized in Table 10.2.

All of these methods have contrasting characteristics and lend themselves naturally to different network configurations and usage patterns. In many cases use of just one of the methods will not suffice, two, or more, must be used.

Table 10.2 *NetBIOS Name Resolution Methods*

NetBIOS Name resolution method	Summary
lmhosts	A text file containing NetBIOS name to IP address mappings that is resident either on the computer requiring a name to be resolved or from a server
NetBIOS Name Server (NBNS) (e.g., WINS)	A network service using servers to maintain a dynamic list of NetBIOS name to IP address mappings
Broadcast	A broadcast requesting the target computer to respond with its IP address

The question now is, which method or methods are used by a computer needing to resolve a computer name? A way of expressing the answer lies with Internet RFCs[1] 1001 and 1002, where four types of node are identified, governing which name resolution methods are used and in what order they are invoked. A Windows NT computer will be configured by the administrator as one or other of these node types, providing flexibility for coping with different network configurations.

Table 10.3 *NetBIOS Node Types*

Node Type	Resolution Method
B-node	Broadcast only
P-node	NetBIOS name server only, such as WINS
M-node	B-node method followed by P-node method
H-node	P-node method followed by B-node method

Microsoft has enhanced the B-node behavior by allowing use of an lmhosts file if the broadcast failed to resolve the name. The NetBIOS name cache is always checked prior to the use of any other name resolution method. It is important to be aware of the different node types as they have a bearing on the scalability and performance of the name resolution process as implemented in a complex corporate network.

[1] An Internet RFC is a Request For Comment issued by the Internet governing body. It is the vehicle for defining Internet related technologies.

Non NetBIOS Name Service Capable Clients

Not all computers that use NetBIOS computer names are capable of being WINS clients. They can only use broadcast or an lmhosts file. These are computers whose operating systems were designed before WINS was introduced and include Windows 3.1 and Windows for Workgroups. In a network where many other computers use WINS the need to maintain lmhosts files for the non-WINS clients can be a burden and broadcasts are likely to be blocked by the routers. One way of solving this is to use a WINS proxy agent on the subnet.

Figure 10.5
WINS Proxy Agent

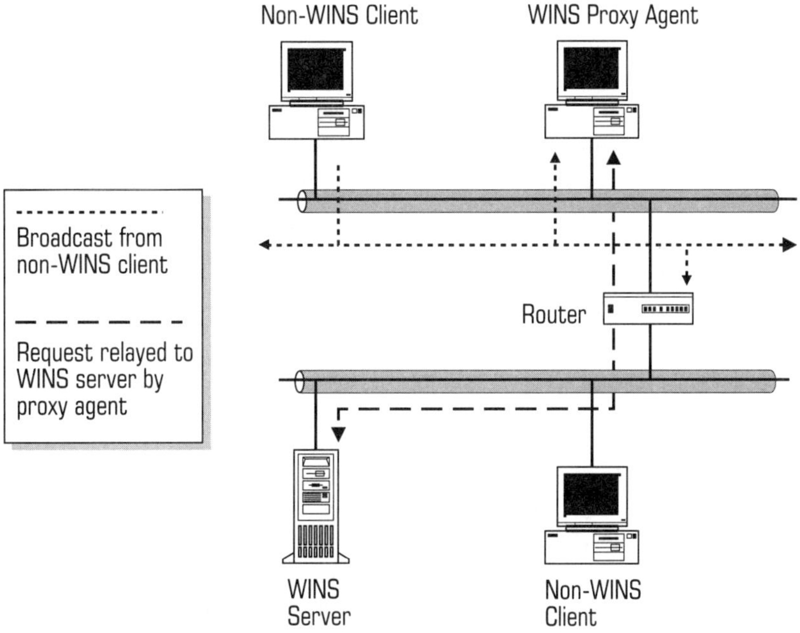

A WINS proxy agent intercepts the NetBIOS name resolution broadcasts emitted by a non-WINS client by listening for this type of broadcast and forwards the request to a WINS server. The proxy agent then relays the response from the WINS server back onto the local network for the non-WINS client to use.

Name Registration/Release

The name registration and release process is designed to ensure that no two computers use the same NetBIOS computer name on the Internet. If this mechanism wasn't present, the existence of computers sharing NetBIOS names but having different IP addresses would cause failed and inconsistent communications if they were referred to using the computer name. They would still have a separate identity with respect to their IP addresses.

In the absence of a NetBIOS name service a new computer on the network would broadcast a NetBIOS name registration request and proceed to use that name if no challenge (negative name registration response) was received from a computer already using that name. Names are released by the computer ceasing to reply to broadcast name registration requests.

WINS solves this problem by letting name registration requests be directed at a WINS server. The WINS server then ascertains whether the name is already in use by interrogating its own database. It is therefore important for the database at the target WINS server to be complete. If it were to contain only a subset of the NetBIOS computer names in use on the network it could not guarantee to determine whether a duplicate existed.

Name release using WINS is triggered by a client sending a message to WINS releasing its name when it shuts down. Non-WINS clients will need to have their names and addresses added to the WINS database as static entries. This ensures that WINS can resolve name requests for non-WINS clients.

Name Renewal

Name renewal is the process by which name to address mapping entries are perpetuated in the WINS database. If names aren't renewed they are eventually removed from the database. They will fail to be renewed if the computer whose name was registered has been switched off (rather than shut down). Or, perhaps, there is no longer a network link between the WINS server and a registered computer. Normally we would expect to see names being released in an orderly fashion. If a name is either released or has failed to be renewed, the entry is eventually removed from the database using a timeout mechanism.

WINS Database Replication

WINS lets us use multiple name servers in a network to provide redundancy and to ensure reasonable name resolution performance for all computers in a WAN. Each computer acting as a WINS client can be configured to use two WINS servers—one as a primary, used by default, and the other as a secondary, used if the primary is unavailable.

To work, this system needs all WINS servers to contain the same information in their databases. As only one WINS server will be contacted by a client to change the database, they must all exchange information with each other about which computer names are in use and which IP addresses they map to. The process that supports this sharing of name to address mapping information is called replication.

Which servers replicate with which other servers, how frequently, and under what conditions has to be planned by the system architect and configured into WINS. Servers are configured as push and/or pull partners with one or more other servers. The overall set of push and pull relationships should ensure that all servers get all information.

Table 10.4 *WINS Push/Pull Relationship*

Role	Explanation
Push Partner	Push partners send a message to pull partners informing them when the threshold of database changes has been reached (minimum of 20). Pull partners respond with a replication request to the push partner, upon which they receive database updates from it.
Pull Partner	Pull partners request updates from push partners at set time intervals.

Thus, database updates are always pulled. The trigger for the operation can be either that a regular time interval has expired on the pull partner or a minimum number of database changes or registrations have occurred on the push partner. The direction of the update is defined by the designation of the pull partner as the server receiving the updates and the push partner as the server sending the updates.

WINS servers can have multiple push/pull partners and can be a push and pull partner with the same server if necessary, ensuring a regular exchange of database information keeping both servers up to date. Because of the fact that it takes time for either trigger condition to cause a database update there will be a delay before all WINS servers are updated with name registrations or changes registered on any particular server. In cases where it is essential for updated WINS database entries on one server to be replicated to other WINS servers it is possible to trigger an update through manual intervention.

The diagram following illustrates a basic replication relationship between two WINS servers. They are configured as full replication partners meaning each is a push and pull partner with the other.

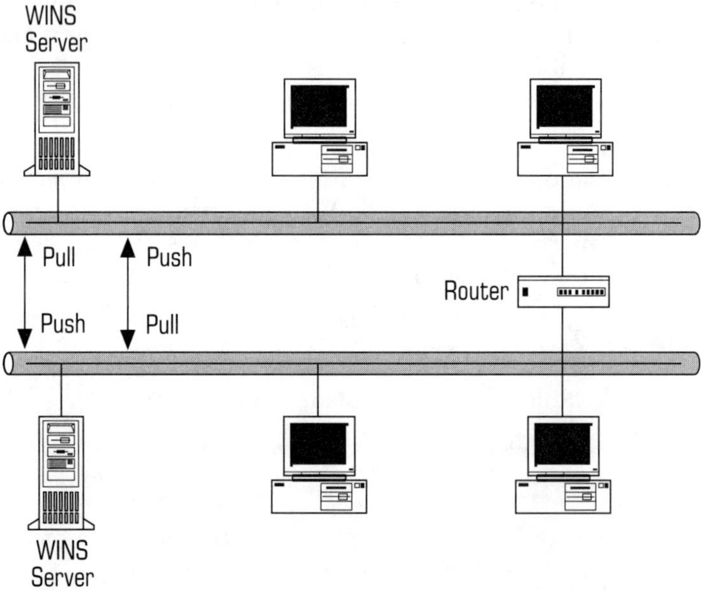

Figure 10.6 *Multiple WINS Hub Configuration*

A WINS server may be configured to replicate with several other WINS servers, potentially leading to complex replication relationships. A series of WINS servers configured such that server A replicates with server B which replicates with server C and so on is referred to as a replication chain.

DNS

DNS was developed to solve a weakness in the original Internet name resolution mechanism where Internet based systems used a text file to map names to IP addresses. On UNIX systems this file was the /etc/hosts file. While appealingly simple in a small network, use of a text file demonstrated a number of problems when the network grew. The basic problem was rooted in the impracticality of maintaining access to up to date /etc/hosts files in a large and changing network. DNS solved this by introducing a scaleable network service where changes can be made in a controlled manner.

DNS predates WINS and is in wide use throughout the Internet, academia, government and corporations. Many corporations undertaking the design of a Windows NT based technical infrastructure will find there are existing DNS systems in use. All examples in this section are based on the existing MBI DNS system.

DNS Name Space

The architecture of DNS is geared around the structure of a DNS name, so we shall begin with a description of DNS names. The DNS name space is hierarchical and in diagrammatic form resembles an inverted tree. Each point on the tree represents a *node* and a complete *domain name* is built up from the chain of node names starting with the particular node and working up to the root, as shown in the diagram below. The root domain is represented by a single dot.

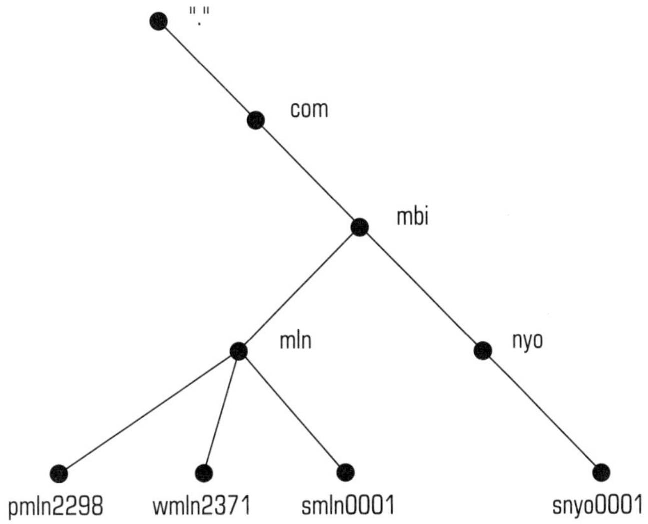

Figure 10.7 *MBI Domain Name Space*

Working up the hierarchy shown in Figure 10.7 we see that individual computers have host names such as smln0001 and snyo0001. Each of these hosts is part of a domain aligned to location. New York is represented by nyo.mbi.com and Milan, mln.mbi.com (shown in Figure 10.8). Each location aligned domain is part of a domain aligned to MBI called mbi.com. The com part of the name shows that MBI is a commercial organization.

Domain names can be specified as a shortened sequence of node names and used to define the domain's relative position in the name space. A domain name that includes all domains up to the root is called a Fully Qualified Domain Name or FQDN and is effectively an absolute reference. Portions of the name space beginning at a node and including all associated sub-nodes are called *domains*.

Figure 10.8
DNS Domains

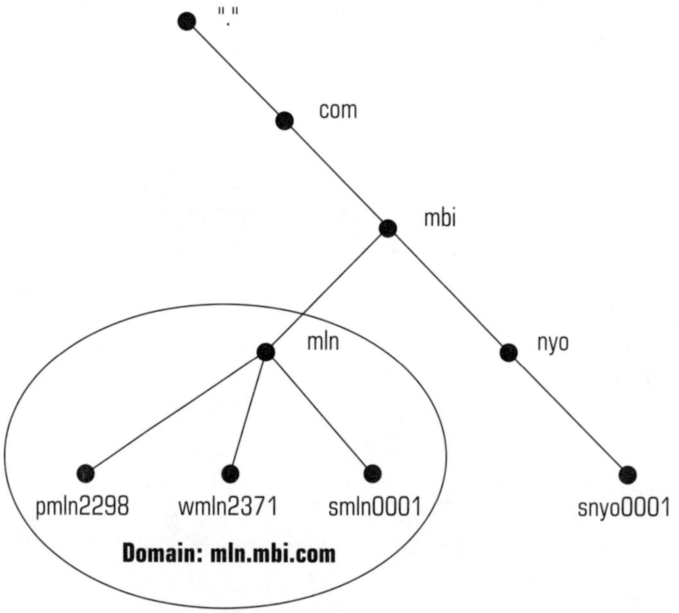

Node names need not be unique in the overall name space but they must be unique among their peers in a domain. Thus the following is fine because the hosts umberto are each parented in different domains:

```
umberto.mln.mbi.com
umberto.nyo.mbi.com
```

To someone unacquainted with DNS, its relationship to the way IP addresses are written can be open to misinterpretation due to the fact that they both use the period character to delimit fields. The only relationship between DNS and IP addresses is that the DNS entries map a DNS name to an IP address. There is no automatic translation of domain names into IP address octets[2] as might be assumed. However, it may be that through planning, an organization has subnetted their IP address space on octet boundaries and allocated a single different DNS domain per IP subnet. This would produce a situation where there was a coincidental apparent mapping:

```
umberto.mln.mbi.com        132.182.32.2
```

[2] An octet is an eight bit binary value. Splitting binary numbers at octet boundaries makes them easier to write down and manipulate. IP addresses consist of 32 bits, which conveniently breaks down into four octets. The period is just a delimiter.

The DNS database can be distributed amongst several DNS servers, each holding a portion of the whole database. To be able to map any name to an address the DNS servers need to communicate amongst themselves as it is possible that a DNS server is queried for a host name it does not have in its portion of the database.

DNS Processes

DNS operates using a client/server process. The client portion makes a name inquiry and the DNS server returns the IP address for that name.

To make the inquiry, the client builds a request ready for sending to a designated DNS server. If use of a hosts file is enabled and the name can be resolved through an entry in this file then the request need not be sent. The part that builds the request is called the resolver and is usually implemented as code routines that are compiled into an application. For example, FTP (a file transfer utility with its roots in the UNIX operating system and available on Windows NT) will have resolver code built into it to be able to make a connection to a host computer referenced by its host name.

If the name can't be resolved by a hosts file, the resolver sends the request to a DNS server which then attempts to map it to an IP address. When it has done so it returns the information to the resolver code embedded in the application. The process of mapping an address is transparent to the client but may involve a sequence of activities at the designated DNS server if it concludes that the mapping must reside on another DNS server.

The hierarchical nature of DNS makes it easy to allocate responsibility for managing different portions of the namespace to different organizations. For instance, MBI manages the domain mbi.com which includes many thousands of IP hosts. DNS has proven to be inherently scalable providing an efficient service in a namespace consisting of millions of names.

WINS/DNS Integration

It is common to find DNS is in use in many places where WINS is being introduced. There is a natural urge to combine the two services as, after all, they do map syntactically different names to exactly the same type of information. The unfortunate fact is that they were never designed to work together and so pain is felt by those needing to deploy both.

Microsoft has made moves to address this incompatibility by

1. Allowing traditional NetBIOS utilities such as the `net use` command, used for connecting to shared resources, to employ domain names instead of NetBIOS computer names. For example:

```
net use ?: \\smln0001.mln.mbi.com\apps$
```

could be used as an alternative to

```
net use ?: \\smln0001\apps$
```

If the syntax is that of a domain name then DNS is used for name resolution. If the syntax is that of a single host or computer name it is assumed to be a computer name causing a NetBIOS name resolution method to be used.

2. Allow their DNS implementation to resolve the host portion of a domain name using WINS if that host name cannot be found in the DNS database. The computer using the NetBIOS name would still need to register its name in the usual way on boot up and the NetBIOS naming service would ensure the name being registered was unique in its database. This mechanism is explained in more detail below.

To illustrate the use by DNS of a WINS server to assist name resolution we shall take an example based on the MBI DNS name space. We assume:

- The computer whose name we are attempting to resolve to an IP address, smln0001 is a Windows NT server that has no entry in the DNS system.
- smln0001 has successfully registered its NetBIOS computer name with WINS.
- The DNS servers in use are hosted by Windows NT server running Microsoft DNS.

  Note that while Microsoft DNS is completely compatible with other standard implementations it is the only one that offers the added functionality we are describing here.
- The DNS servers are configured to reference a WINS server if the host name portion of the domain name cannot be resolved from the DNS database.

Table 10.5 shows the basic steps involved when Microsoft DNS resolves a DNS domain name using WINS. Figure 10.9 shows the relationship between the computers involved in the name registration and resolution.

Table 10.5 *Resolving a NetBIOS Name using DNS*

Step	Action
1.	A workstation requests that DNS resolve the name smln0001.mln.mbi.com
2.	The DNS lookup process locates the DNS server that is authoritative for the mln.mbi.com domain
3.	The authoritative DNS server cannot find the host name smln0001 in its database
4.	The authoritative DNS server strips all domain names from smln0001.mln.mbi.com, leaving only smln0001, then passes this as a NetBIOS name resolution query to a WINS server
5.	If the WINS server contains the NetBIOS name to IP address mapping for smln0001 it passes the IP address of that computer back to the authoritative DNS server
6.	The resolved IP address is then passed back to the requesting workstation

Figure 10.9 *Using DNS to Resolve NetBIOS Names*

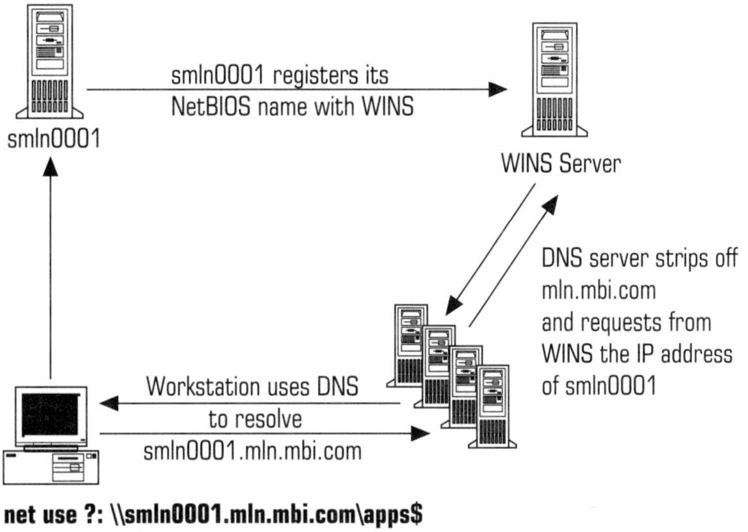
smln0001 registers its
NetBIOS name with WINS
smln0001
WINS Server
DNS server strips off
mln.mbi.com
and requests from
WINS the IP address
of smln0001
Workstation uses DNS
to resolve
smln0001.mln.mbi.com
net use ?: \\smln0001.mln.mbi.com\apps$

Moving to Windows NT 5 Active Directory

With Active Directory, use of DNS becomes critical as:

- Each Windows NT 5 Active Directory name is a DNS domain name

- DNS is used as the Windows NT 5 locator (name resolution) service

Several key aspects of the Windows NT 5 dependency on DNS need to be noted:

- As DNS is the locator service for Windows NT 5, all computers must be registered in DNS. For this reason a Windows NT 5 implementation is made considerably easier if the DNS servers used allow dynamic updates. This is because the Windows NT 5 domains, clients and servers are able to register themselves with a DNS server automatically. It is possible to use nondynamic DNS servers, however, the Windows NT 5 configuration will need to be entered into DNS manually. This would be a complex and error prone operation.

  Dynamic DNS is a proposed standard specified in RFC 2136.
- The complete DNS namespace used by the Active Directory need not be contiguous. This lead to the concept of a Forest and Trees introduced by Microsoft to cope with non-contiguous namespaces.
  - A *Tree* is a contiguous section of the namespace likely to comprise several domains.
  - A *Forest* is a collection of Trees. Trusts may be set up between the domains in different trees to allow company wide resource access and control.
- Member computers of a Windows NT 5 domain need not be DNS sub-domains of the DNS domain. So, for example, if a domain was called europe.mbi.com, computers in that domain do not need to be called computer_name.europe.mbi.com
- Computers locate domain controllers by querying a DNS server for a list of domain controllers for a particular domain.

There is nothing in Windows NT 5 that mandates use of NetBIOS names so a Windows NT 5 based technical infrastructure does not depend on a NetBIOS name resolution service such as WINS. It is likely, however, that there will be several other components such as applications and third party utilities that will continue to depend on NetBIOS names and so it will be impractical to decommission NetBIOS name resolution methods until they can be removed from the system.

Naming Service Design

In this section we start the process of name service design using the MBI case study as a basis for examining the many configuration options available. First, the scope of the design is specified, followed by an examination of the factors affecting the attributes of a name service design. Finally, design for MBI is produced in four phases using several design principles.

The design will assume a basic DNS system is already in use in MBI and focus on the design of a NetBIOS naming service and its integration with DNS. There is an important point to note about the following case study design. The computer naming standard used by MBI (Chapter 16, Naming Standards) ensures each computer has a unique name within the organization. This will not always be the case in a real company so the case study makes the assumption that the NetBIOS name registration mechanism is the only means of ensuring no two computers with the same name are registered on the network.

Scope of Naming Services Design

The design of a WINS naming service must include:

Element	Aspect
Name Servers	▪ Replication architecture ▪ Replication settings ▪ Location of servers on network ▪ WINS server sizing ▪ Network capacity required ▪ Integration with other name services
Name Service Clients	▪ Primary and secondary WINS server setting ▪ Primary and secondary DNS server setting ▪ DNS domain setting ▪ NetBIOS node types ▪ Use of lmhosts and hosts files

Requirements on the Design

This section summarizes a small number of requirements that will be used during the case study design. These requirements complement the business principles already developed for this case study.

- For the new settlements application to be able to communicate from any office to any other office in the corporation it must be possible for a computer in one part of the network to resolve the IP address of any other computer on the network. This is noted as an implication of MBI Business Principle 1.
- MBI currently use DNS for host name resolution amongst its Unix computer population. DNS host names are increasingly being used on the Windows NT platform so there is a requirement for the naming service to be able to resolve IP addresses for the host names of Windows NT computers.

Common Attributes

The common attributes all apply to naming services, indicating that there are several important aspects to consider when designing this service.

Scalability

The scalability of a naming service can be measured by the increase in workload it can accommodate at a given site, or the number of additional sites that can be supported, without breaking the original architecture. Increase in name resolution workload at a site can usually be accommodated by using a higher capacity name server. It would be rare to need to use more than one name server simply to cope with volume. Increasing the number of sites supported will usually lead to use of additional name servers.

The scalability of a WINS system will depend to an extent on the WINS replication architecture. A common type of scalable replication architecture is where several WINS servers replicate to and from a central WINS server. Replication architectures based on this unit are described in more detail in section Phase 1: Choice of WINS Replication Architecture.

For each additional WINS server a decision must be made as to what role in the replication architecture it is going to perform. Different roles will impact the overall system in different ways. For example, adding another server in a chain of WINS servers would lengthen the propagation delay for WINS database changes.

Reliability

A reliable naming service is one that is able to return the correct name/address mapping when requested. Incorrect data could be returned if:

- The correct data had not propagated to the server.

- Manual data entered into the name service could be out of date or entered inaccurately.
- The name server could be unavailable.

Designing for reliability involves ensuring the name service is available and that the databases on each name server are completely accurate.

Availability

The name service is likely to be critical to the successful functioning of several applications and services in a corporation. Its availability is therefore very important. The service may become unavailable either through failure or planned downtime with failure being the most likely. Strategies for minimizing the impact of name service failure should be employed, such as falling back on use of broadcasts for name resolution. IT support should also plan to be able to recover from a name server failure in a timely fashion to minimize outage.

Manageability

The manageability of a naming service can be considered as the level of pro-active and remedial effort required to keep it functioning satisfactorily. At a minimum the service should offer the following capabilities:

- Remote management of name servers
- Notification of a malfunctioning name server
- Straightforward resolution of problems without affecting the availability of the service

For most name services it is difficult to enhance any of these capabilities through configuration, the only solution being to rely on built-in features.

Security

As a name service simply provides a mapping from the public computer or host namespace to a network address, it has no role in restricting access. That is either done at a lower level with a firewall or at a higher level with operating system or application security.

Security does need to be considered as far as management of the naming service is concerned as unauthorized access to the management interface of the naming service can lead to accidental or deliberate damage. Ideally, the naming service computers should be locked in a computer room to prevent physical access and only those with the necessary permissions able to manage the service.

Capacity

Name service capacity can be seen from two angles. One is the capacity to manage a given quantity of name to address mappings in the name server database and the other is the rate of name service requests (registrations, resolutions and renewals) that can be sustained. The former measure is unlikely to be a significant concern with either WINS or DNS. However, the rate of name service requests may be. If it is, the preferred solution is to increase the capacity of the name server computer as this does not affect the integrity of the name service architecture. Increasing the number of name servers to cope with an increase in name service request activity may bring with it management overhead and a small amount of overall name service degradation.

Performance

Name service functions tend not to be very demanding on a computer and hence name service performance is not usually an issue. The main method of improving name resolution performance is to combine use of a name service with a name cache on the name service client computer. The measure of name service performance would be the speed with which it carried out its functions. When performance degrades, if things get to that stage, then it is time to increase name server capacity.

Specific Attributes

There are no specific attributes considered for naming services.

Design Phases

We will develop the design of a naming service for MBI in four phases:

Phase 1: Choice of Replication Architecture
Phase 2: Mapping onto Physical Network
Phase 3: Sizing and Capacity Calculations
Phase 4: Integration with other Naming Services (DNS)

None of these four phases is entirely self-contained. We should expect, for example, that the replication architecture we arrive at in Phase 1 will need modification in Phase 2 when the network topology is considered.

Phase I: Choice of WINS Replication Architecture

This section will consider five basic WINS replication architectures and examine their benefits and drawbacks with respect to MBI. It will be useful to define some terms:

WINS Replication Architecture	The set of replication partnerships among a population of WINS servers.
Hub	A WINS server that replicates with more than one other WINS server.
Spoke	A WINS server that replicates with just one other WINS server.
Up	Replication from spoke to hub.
Down	Replication from hub to spoke.
Stage	A replication link between two WINS servers is referred to as a stage when it is necessary to describe the number of replication links an entry has to be propagated over. For example, a two stage propagation would involve three WINS servers configured so that one replicates with another which replicates with the third.
Local resource server	A computer hosting file or print services accessed primarily by workstations at the same location.
Global resource server	A computer hosting file or print services accessed primarily by workstations from other locations.

The five WINS replication architectures discussed are all variations on the hub and spoke model.

- Multiple Hub
- Multiple Hub/Single Down Spoke
- Multiple Hub/Single Up Spoke
- Multiple Hub/Single Spoke
- Multiple Hub/Dual Spoke

Note that there are many other possible architectures that could be examined for suitability. For each of the five examined here there may be variations not mentioned that overcome some of their drawbacks. As with all the other worked examples it is the approach that is important, not the detail.

To start, it is worth studying the business principles and design inputs for any obvious statements that have a bearing on the replication architecture as this could help us to swiftly narrow down the possibilities we examine.

The business principle stating that there should be no duplicated systems within the MBI group is directly equivalent to saying that there should only be a single WINS replication architecture for MBI. We should therefore capture this as a design principle:

Design Principle 10-1—Single WINS Replication Architecture
There will be a single WINS replication architecture.
Justification
▪ No duplicated systems within the MBI group (MBI Business Principle 3) ▪ Duplicate WINS replication architectures will never be able to guarantee uniqueness among NetBIOS computer names. ▪ Easier to manage.
Implications
▪ Subsidiaries within MBI will not be allowed to maintain separate WINS replication architectures. ▪ Will benefit from being managed by a single support group.
Issues
▪ May require some migration towards the new replication architecture where WINS is already in use.

This principle is important for our design because it means we can resist any suggestions that parts of the organization have special requirements that can only be met with a separate WINS replication architecture.

MBI Business Principle 2 suggesting the technical infrastructure may be phased in means we can state another principle of design for the naming service:

Design Principle 10-2—Phase in the Naming Service
The naming service will be designed so it may be implemented in a phased manner.
Justification
▪ Support the business principle stating that the new Settlement System will be phased in, potentially leading to a similar phasing in of the technical infrastructure (MBI Business Principle 2). ▪ Allows an orderly cleaning of the name space in advance of using WINS. This would be done to avoid duplicate NetBIOS node names.

Implications
▪ Phasing in use of a WINS service is easier if the WINS servers are in place and replicating correctly in advance of name service clients requiring them. It would be awkward to have to use temporary WINS servers. ▪ To adhere to the design principle stating the need for each WINS server to contain the complete NetBIOS name space (Design Principle 10-3) it will be necessary to grow the WINS service from a single configuration. It will not be practical to grow it as two configurations and then to join them. ▪ The business principle stating that there should be no duplicated systems supports the second implication (MBI Business Principle 3). At any stage the WINS configuration must be complete as far as the section of the organization it is designed to service is concerned.
Issues

Multiple Hub

The first configuration we shall look at is the multiple hub, a version of which is illustrated in Figure 10.10. This consists of a number of WINS servers configured in a chain as full replication partners, that is, they are all push and pull partners with the adjacent members of the chain. All other computers on the network use one as their primary WINS server and another as their secondary WINS server.

- *Advantages*

  The benefits of this configuration are that each WINS server has a full copy of the database containing entries for all of the corporation's NetBIOS computers. This configuration will work well in a modest sized organization where the WINS servers can be accessed easily by the complete computer population.

- *Disadvantages*

  This configuration does not cope well with a highly dispersed computer population connected by many slow network links. For example, consider a system using two WINS servers with one located in New York and the other in London. To locate a local Hong Kong server using WINS a local Hong Kong client would need to query a remote WINS server in New York or London. The only way of providing WINS servers nearer to the naming service clients yet retaining this multiple hub configuration is to increase the number of replication stages. This increases the propagation delay and the management overhead.

- *Suitability for MBI*

This replication architecture meets the functionality needs of MBI because we know that the new Settlement System requires that it be possible to connect from any workstation to any server in the network. MBI does have a dispersed computer population and would definitely benefit from the use of WINS servers on the same local network as the naming service clients, which this configuration does not provide. The above example illustrates the constant challenge with using a NetBIOS name resolution service such as WINS, which is to provide the minimum number of local servers to minimize replication and management, while maximizing the performance of name resolution.

Figure 10.10 *Multiple Hub WINS Configuration*

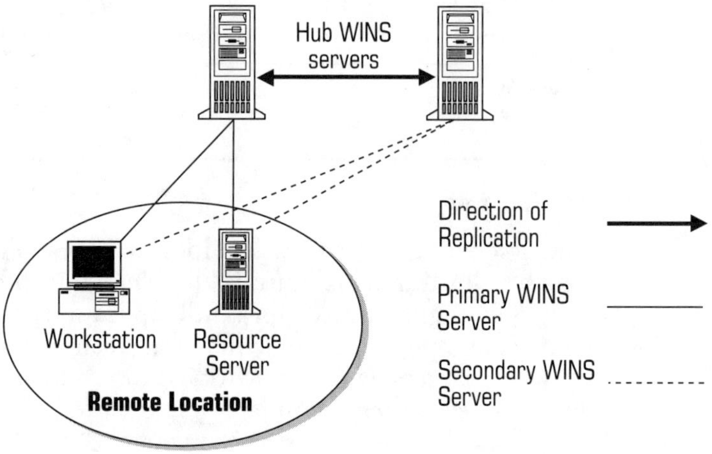

Multiple Hub/Single Down Spoke

This configuration is a development of the multiple hub that is designed to work better with a more dispersed computer population. Its chief modification is the use of local spoke WINS servers that are replicated to from the hub servers. The direction of the replication is from hub to spoke.

Resource servers that need to be accessed from anywhere on the network should use two hub servers as their primary and secondary WINS servers, ensuring every WINS server in the replication architecture will have an entry for them. Resource servers that don't need to be accessed from anywhere in the network, only locally, should use their local WINS server as their primary and use one of the WINS hub servers as their secondary.

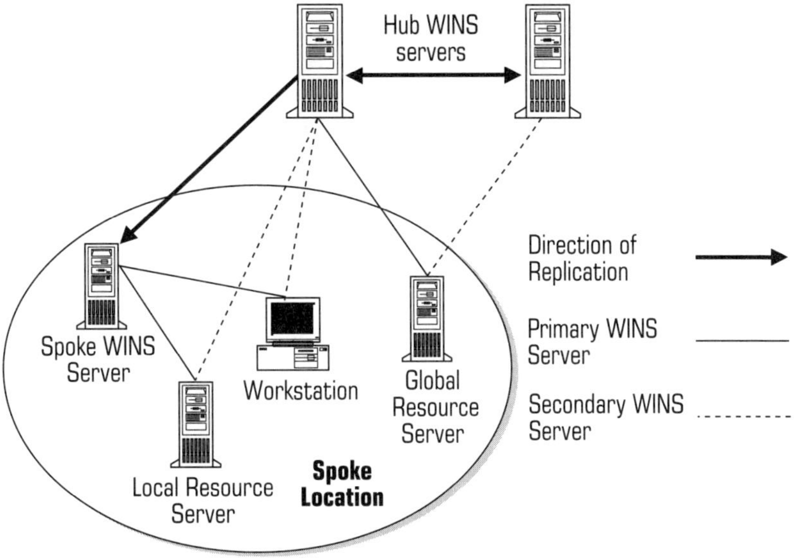

Figure 10.11 *Multiple Hub/Single Down Spoke WINS Configuration*

- *Advantages*

  In the majority of cases WINS name resolution is now local, which means a WAN connection does not need to be used for this purpose. This is a benefit in cases where WAN bandwidth is scarce and it also removes a dependency on the network which could impact reliability.

- *Drawbacks*

  There are three major drawbacks to this system.

  1. It allows duplicate NetBIOS computer names to be registered at different local sites as the local WINS databases are not replicated to the WINS hub servers.
  2. Should a local WINS server fail, computers at that site would begin to use their secondary WINS server (one of the WINS hub servers), which would not have any entries in its database for the systems at the local site unless they happen to be global resources. In this case local site communication, unless to global resources exclusively, could break down temporarily. This situation would not last forever as the process of NetBIOS name renewal would cause the secondary WINS server to become populated eventually.
  3. If a computer is offering local resources then it will be impossible to manage them from a computer that uses a different WINS server because the name of the local resource server won't be in

any other WINS server's database. There are, however, important reasons why we would want to be able to resolve local names. For example, the Microsoft SMS help desk functionality that allows help desk staff take control of a computer remotely would need to resolve the computer name to an IP address. In most situations this would not work using the Multiple Single Down Spoke WINS configuration.

We need a design principle which will move us away from problems like this. Knowing the requirement that every computer be resolvable from everywhere and knowing a rule by which we could achieve that we can write down a design principle:

Design Principle 10-3—Complete NetBIOS Name Space
Each WINS server will contain the complete NetBIOS name space.
Justification
▪ The implication of MBI Business Principle 1, requiring the infrastructure to support global communication between applications, is facilitated by each WINS server containing the complete NetBIOS name space. ▪ If all WINS servers contain the complete NetBIOS name space then failure of a WINS server used by a naming service client as a primary will not cause any loss of functionality as the WINS server used as a secondary will still be able to resolve the name to an address. ▪ To avoid duplicate NetBIOS computer names on the network. ▪ Some management services will need to make connections to remote computers using the NetBIOS name. If that name can't be resolved, the computer can't be managed (MBI Business Principle 5).
Implications
▪ More replication traffic than would be necessary under some other circumstances. ▪ Each WINS server will contain many entries that will never be used.
Issues

- *Suitability for MBI*

In summary, this design seems to have too many drawbacks to be useful. It is true that it keeps replication traffic to an absolute minimum but at the expense of functionality. It does not conform to the MBI need for every WINS server to contain the complete namespace so we should reject this model for MBI.

Multiple Hub/Single Up Spoke

This is a modification of the previous model with the direction of the hub/spoke replication being reversed so that the spokes update the hubs. All systems would use the local WINS server as their primary and a hub server as their secondary.

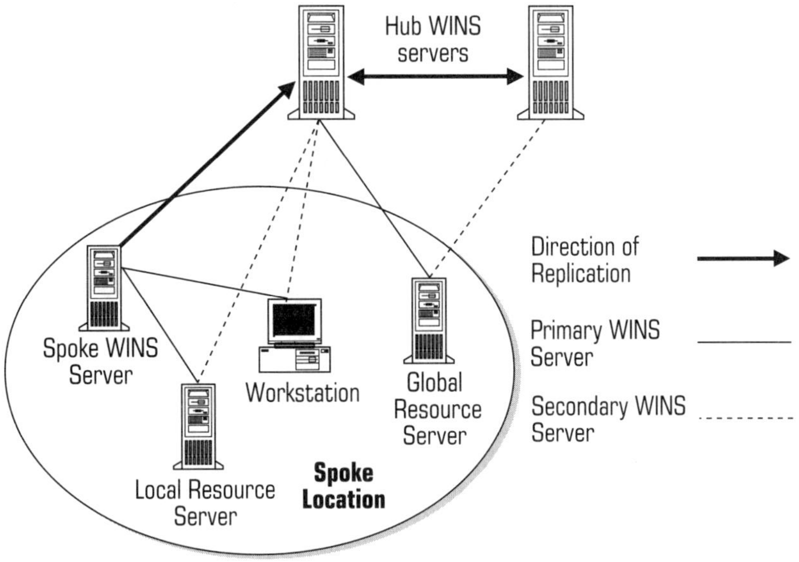

Figure 10.12 *Multiple Hub/Single Up Spoke WINS Configuration*

- *Advantages*

  This configuration has the advantage of keeping name resolutions local for local resources. This model overcomes the significant problem with the previous configuration in that it is now possible to resolve the names of all the computers in the network as the hub servers will contain the complete set of computer names.

- *Disadvantages*

  The up replication means that all changes to the database on the spoke WINS server are replicated to a hub server even through the majority will rarely be used. It is still possible for duplicate NetBIOS computer names to be registered at different local sites as the local WINS servers do not contain the full namespace.

- *Suitability for MBI*

  As a configuration for MBI it is not satisfactory because it doesn't conform to the design principle requiring each WINS server to contain the complete namespace. The possibility of having duplicate computer names registered will admittedly be low considering that MBI has chosen a computer naming convention that guarantees uniqueness.

Multiple Hub/Single Spoke

This configuration is still based around the multiple hub configuration but instead of replicating in only one direction between hub and spoke, this configuration does full replication. Local clients and local resource servers would use the local WINS server as their primary and a hub server as their secondary. To speed the propagation of name/address information to all WINS servers, global resource servers should use one of the hub WINS servers as a primary and either another hub or a local WINS server as a secondary.

Figure 10.13 *Multiple Hub/Single Spoke WINS Configuration*

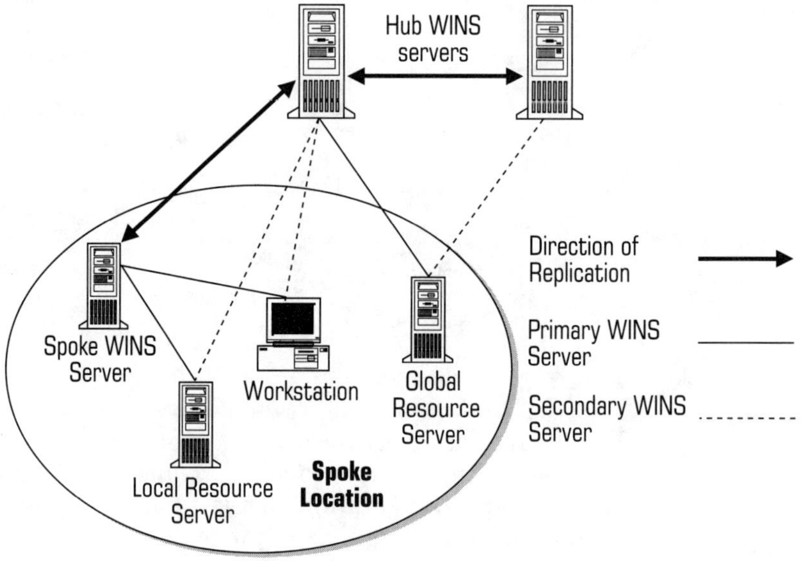

- *Advantages*

  There are three strong advantages to this configuration:

  1. The configuration offers a guarantee of NetBIOS name uniqueness as every WINS server contains the complete set of NetBIOS names.
  2. Performance is likely to be good, with all name resolution requests going to a local WINS server.
  3. This configuration is easily scalable by adding spoke WINS servers as full replication partners of either hub.

- *Disadvantages*

  There is an important aspect to this configuration that will be disadvantageous if any of the WAN links between replicating WINS servers are poor. The effect of full replication is to cause all WINS database changes that occur anywhere in the network to be propagated to every other WINS server. Thus, a WINS server in Milan will be sent changes caused by, for example, a laptop computer being connected to the network in Tokyo.

- *Suitability for MBI*

  This configuration meets the requirements of MBI from a functionality perspective. It also has the benefit of offering complete name service functionality should one of the WINS servers become unavailable for a period of time. The level of replication traffic to the spokes should be something that needs to be evaluated on a WAN link by WAN link basis to ensure it will not cause problems.

Multiple Hub/Dual Spoke

The difference between this configuration and the last one is the dual spoke WINS server configuration at each site.

Figure 10.14 *Multiple Hub/Dual Spoke WINS Configuration*

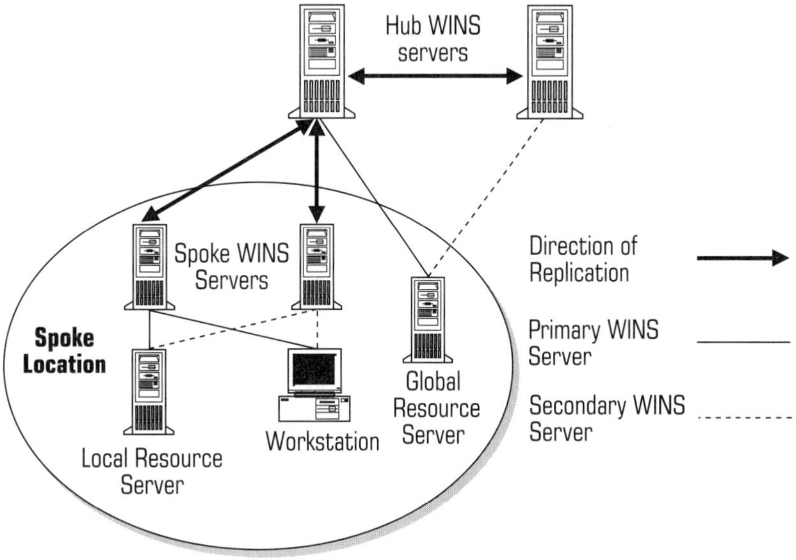

We can now have the clients and local resource servers using the local spoke WINS servers as primary and secondary servers, leaving the global resource servers to continue using the hub WINS servers as their primary and secondary servers.

- *Advantages*

  This configuration offers the same benefit as the previous configuration by ensuring a complete WINS database at each WINS server, enabling all WINS servers to guarantee the uniqueness of registered names. This configuration is more resilient than the single spoke version as failure of a local WINS server would not impact name resolution because an alternative is available. An additional advantage is that the load can be split between the WINS servers at each location with 50% of the computers designating one as their primary and 50% the other. Management of the load balancing strategy would be determined by the system administrator as there is no automatic mechanism available to do this.

  This configuration might be chosen if there was an excessive load on the WINS servers and using two computers was the only way of meeting the need. It may also be chosen as a solution that avoids the use of the WAN for accessing a WINS server if one of the local servers fails.

- *Disadvantages*

  The main drawback of this configuration is the potentially heavy use of the network between the hub site and the local site. Consider that it is directly equivalent to running two sites with the same computer population at each, over the same WAN link. Thus, an update registered on one local server will get replicated to the hub and then replicated to the other local server, so every update travels across the same WAN link twice. The same is true for updates initiated by WINS servers at other sites.

- *Suitability for MBI*

  Although the calculations have not yet been done to determine whether any of the MBI locations will need two WINS servers for capacity reasons, it seems unlikely given that the maximum population at any location is a few thousand. The extra resilience gained from using two local WINS servers is welcome, however that would have to be analyzed in detail to quantify the exact benefit.

  The increased WAN bandwidth caused by using two local spoke WINS servers should be taken seriously if there is the possibility that the WINS replication traffic could impact business traffic. If business traffic were affected one solution would be to make a decision trading off the impact of that on the business against the extra resilience achieved by using two spoke WINS servers. An alternative solution would be to recommend greater network bandwidth be provided.

This is clearly an area where the business priorities need to be established. The five business principles created for MBI do not say enough to be able to resolve this issue so the business representatives were consulted. The new business principle MBI arrived at stated that application traffic must have priority over infrastructure service traffic. This is listed as Business Principle A-2 in Appendix A.

Summary MBI Replication Architecture

We have examined several replication architectures and shown that one, the multiple hub/single spoke, matches our functionality requirements and looks likely to be efficient in the MBI environment. We need to confirm, by studying the WAN topology and doing some sizing and capacity calculations, whether this is the case. Although we have chosen an architecture we still need to determine how many hubs to use.

WINS Name Renewal Parameters

An aspect of reliability, noted in the discussion of how a naming service may be characterized in terms of the common attributes, is accuracy of name resolution. To ensure the data is accurate in the WINS database obsolete entries should be removed so an invalid name to address mapping is not returned. On the other hand, entries should not be removed too swiftly from the database or they will cause an increased level of WINS synchronization traffic as the changes are propagated throughout the set of WINS servers. The goal, therefore, is to make sure the parameters for a WINS server are tuned to the behavior of the NetBIOS name service client population. The MBI client population generates little change. However, to minimize what change there is, it was decided to configure the WINS parameters so that a week long vacation, during which the workstation was switched off, was not quite long enough to cause the entry to be removed from the primary WINS server.

Design Principle 10-4—WINS Name Renewal Settings
▪ WINS timers should be set so that a ten day break does not cause a released name to become extinct triggering replication traffic as its removal from the WINS server is replicated throughout the rest of the WINS system.
Justification
▪ Minimizes non-application bandwidth usage (Business Principle A-2) because minimizing changes to WINS has the effect of minimizing the replication traffic. ▪ A week's vacation comprises five working days and two weekends—making nine days. Thus there is a ten-day gap between Friday and a week on Monday.

continued▸

continued

Implications
▪ Nondefault WINS settings. ▪ Administrators used to supporting systems with default settings will require familiarization to come to terms with the slightly different behavior of a customized system.
Issues

Table 10.6 *WINS Name Renewal Parameters for MBI*

Parameter	Value	Explanation
Renewal	6 days	This sets client systems to renew their name with the WINS server once every 48 hours (half 96 hours).
Extinction	10 days	If a name is released, it will stay in the WINS database this period of time until marked extinct. This is set to be the length of time necessary to cope with a one week vacation.
Extinction Timeout	6 days	This sets the time before a name marked extinct (extinction interval expired) is purged from the WINS database. This is set at the default of 6 days.
Verify	24 days	The time interval between verifications with a remote WINS server that a name not local to the database is still valid. This is left at the default of 24 days.

Note that it would be rare to need to change the WINS renewal parameters. As can be seen from the MBI case, the reduction in replication traffic caused by this change is likely to be vanishingly small.

Phase 2: Mapping WINS on to a Physical Network

So far we have discussed various WINS architectures without considering the topology of the network we will be using. This can be an important factor as we may find that a WINS architecture that looks appropriate from a geographic point of view is not suited to the underlying WAN.

Why consider the WAN at all? The basic reason is that WAN links tend to be much slower than LAN links and so we need to be more careful about how we utilize WAN bandwidth. We shouldn't forget that the purpose of the WAN is to serve a business purpose, it isn't put there for WINS servers to chatter to each other.

Usually we will want to minimize the replication traffic on a particular WAN link, not least because it is a waste of resources to use more than is necessary, but excessive WINS traffic may incur performance problems for traffic over the link. This argument leads to a design principle that is applicable in most situations.

Design Principle 10-5—Replication over the same WAN Link
The same replication data should not travel across the same WAN link more than once.
Justification
▪ Supports the business principle stating that application traffic must have priority over infrastructure service traffic (Business Principle A-2). ▪ WAN bandwidth is scarce.
Implications
▪ This may lead to longer chains of replicating WINS servers.
Issues
▪ This may be difficult to achieve without installing new network links.

Let us illustrate the implication recorded in the design principle with an example. Suppose the organization for which we are planning a WINS configuration has three regional head offices and several local offices throughout the rest of the country. The regional offices are spread out, located in Philadelphia, Seattle and Los Angeles and the local offices are geographically dispersed. From a geographic point of view we might be tempted to put a hub WINS server in each of the regional offices and configure them in a push/pull configuration. Local offices would each have a WINS server as a full replication partner to a single nearest hub server.

Thus, we may have a WINS hub in Seattle with a full replication relationship with a WINS hub in Philadelphia which in turn has a full replication relationship with a WINS hub in Los Angeles.

A look at the WAN topology shown in Figure 10.15 might mitigate against this. Consider that the WAN treats Philadelphia and Miami as the network hubs and all other offices as network satellites. So a replication between the Seattle WINS hub and the Austin WINS spoke would go via Philadelphia, passing the same information down the

Philadelphia to Miami link as a replication between the Philadelphia WINS hub and the Mexico WINS spoke.

Examination of Figure 10.15 shows that it would be more sensible to designate Philadelphia and Miami as the locations for WINS hubs.

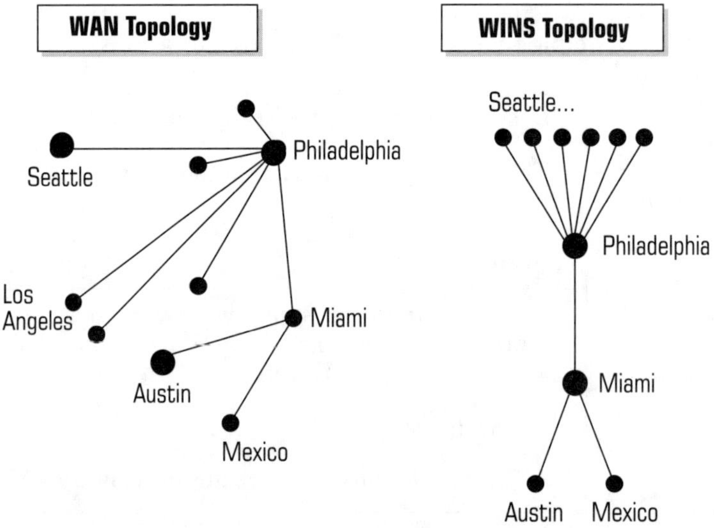

Figure 10.15 *WINS Topology Influenced by WAN*

Let us look at the WAN topology in MBI and how that might influence number and placement of WINS servers. Figure 10.16, MBI WAN Topology, shows that MBI has four principle network hubs, New York, London, Paris and Singapore. Notice that whereas New York, London and Singapore each have a direct WAN link to each other, Paris connects to the other hubs via London. In addition, London has a direct link to all the same locations as Paris. To minimize the WINS replication chain for Zurich (which is the only candidate for being a spoke of Paris) we should make it a spoke of the London hub, reducing Paris to a spoke of London as well, on the basis that no other locations replicate with Paris.

Thus, to minimize the number of hubs and yet reflect the WAN topology we should choose three WINS hub locations, one at each network hub except Paris.

In some organizations there can be political pressure to place what are seen as key servers in certain locations. In MBI, Tokyo management is lobbying for the regional WINS hub server to be located in Tokyo. Use of Tokyo as a WINS hub site over the current WAN topology would not comply with Design Principle 10-5 demanding that the same replication traffic should not travel over the same WAN link more than once. This design principle is supported by Business Principle A-2 stating that application traffic should take priority over infrastructure service traffic, therefore sealing a strong business driven argument for staying with the configuration arrived at above.

Figure 10.16
MBI WAN Topology

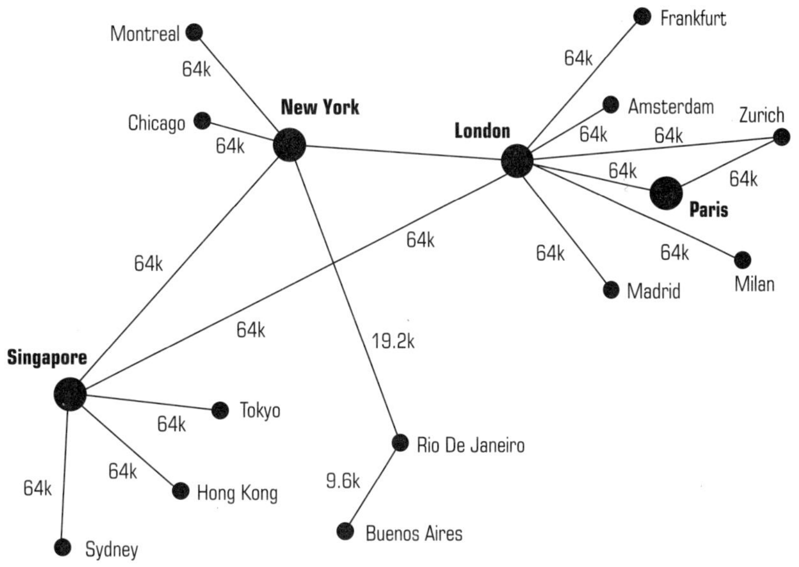

Another aspect that should be considered when mapping the architecture onto the physical network is the length of the replication chain. In general the less WINS servers in this chain the better as it will ensure the speediest propagation of name server entry changes. In the case where there is pressure to deploy greater numbers of WINS servers than might be technically necessary a design principle should be developed to clarify the policy. Such a design principle will not need to be invoked for MBI, though an example is shown in Appendix B, Design Principles (B-12).

We also need to consider very carefully how we address the needs of non-hub sites. This is very straightforward where there is a single WAN hop from a hub site to a spoke site. The configuration is more difficult to address if there is more than one hop, as is the case with the link from New York to Buenos Aires in the MBI case study. Although recommendations can be made based on good WINS architecture practices, decisions regarding multi-hop links are best taken with a full understanding of the network bandwidth implications for each option. Phase 3 of the WINS design deals with determining the network bandwidth requirements so it is there we will resolve the issue of how to make the NetBIOS name resolution service available to systems in Buenos Aires.

Figure 10.17 shows the WINS design for MBI so far.

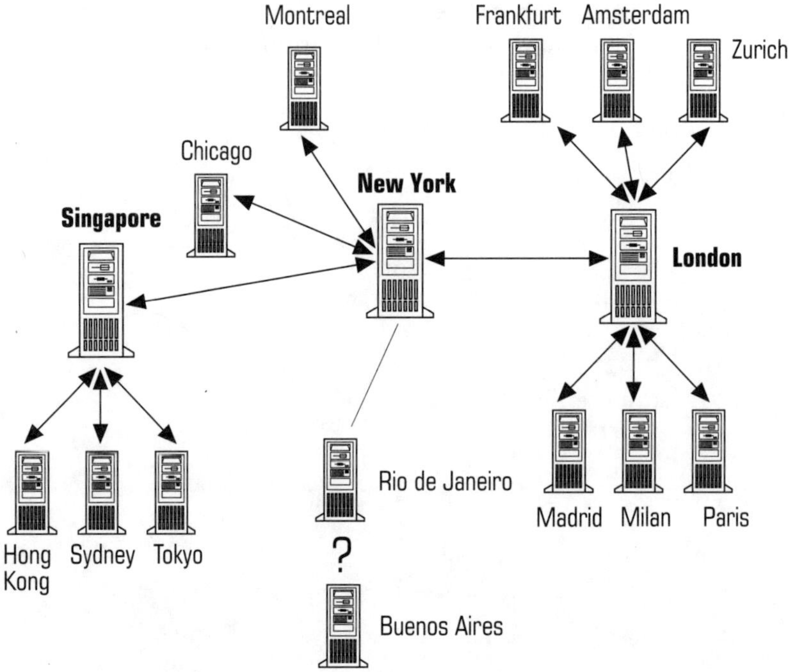

Figure 10.17 *MBI WINS Architecture*

The basic architecture chosen is that of multiple hubs with single spokes. All replication relationships are bi-directional. This ensures that each WINS server has a complete copy of the NetBIOS name space. The diagram is incomplete for Buenos Aires as we are currently undecided as to how to configure it into the WINS system.

Phase 3: WINS Sizing and Capacity Calculations

We now have a preferred replication architecture and a mapping of that architecture onto the corporate WAN in a way that meets our functional needs. We must now consider what is required of the network and the computers for that functionality to be delivered in a manner that meets the performance needs.

A WINS design should be able to state requirements in the following two areas:

- Network bandwidth
- Computer capacity

So far we have discussed network bandwidth requirements in relative terms and hardly mentioned computer capacity at all, though assuming both will be available in ample quantity. Unfortunately this will not always be the case, constraining our design. In other more fortunate circumstances we may be in a position to request the necessary capacities. In both cases we will still need to know how much network activity our design will incur and what computer capacity it will consume.

Our requirements are derived from the following:

- WINS replication architecture
- WINS partner replication data volume
- WINS client induced registration, renewal, release and resolution activity

For a given WINS replication architecture, unless we have some data from a comparable environment, we will need to estimate the partner replication data volume and the registration, renewal, release and resolution activity. The estimates will need to be based on a variety of assumptions such as the average level of NetBIOS name cache validity.

The calculation to arrive at an estimate of bandwidth usage is quite detailed, particularly for a configuration such as the one MBI is working towards. To simplify things an artificial example is chosen so that the details of the configuration don't obscure the assumptions and the calculations. We will assume for the sake of the MBI case study that the bandwidths available are sufficient for the estimated WINS traffic.

Note that for some networks where bandwidth is abundant these calculations may seem a waste of time. Whether this is true or not, it should be considered good design discipline to develop an understanding of the demands a service is going to place on any other part of the infrastructure as this will avoid design discussions based on unsubstantiated assumptions. For example, you may need to prove just how little bandwidth will be required to be able to convince the networks division to allow the service to be set up. Another point to note is that not all countries are in a position to offer good quality, cheap bandwidth. In such cases these calculations become very important.

An Example Calculation

The WINS replication architecture we will use for the example is shown in the diagram below and consists of a hub and three spokes. We can assume this is a good match to the WAN topology. At each of the four sites there are 10,000 workstation WINS clients and 100 application servers, also WINS clients. The servers are accessed frequently from any site so the decision has been made to designate the hub WINS server as the primary WINS server for the application server computers, thus shortening the propagation time to all spokes for server name/address changes. The servers designate their local WINS server as their secondary.

All the workstations designate the local WINS server as their primary server and the hub server as their secondary. All computers are configured as h-nodes meaning they will use WINS first and broadcast second.

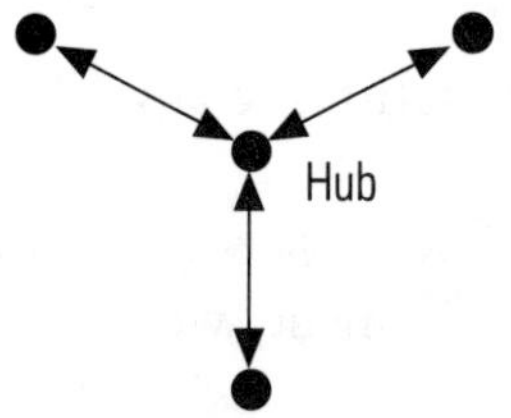

Hub
10,000 Workstations at each location with local WINS server as primary and hub WINS server as secondary. 100 Servers at each location with hub WINS server as primary and local WINS server as secondary.

Figure 10.18 *Example Bandwith Requirements Calculations*

Network Traffic

The figures for network traffic below are accurate enough for the purposes of the example though when performing the name resolution traffic calculations for your design be sure to consult the latest Microsoft literature to get more accurate values.

Assumptions:

Symbol	Name	Value	Symbol	Name	Value
N	Number of sites	4	Rs	Resolutions per day per server	10
Tr	Registration traffic	200 bytes	Cw	Cache hit rate on workstation	Assume = 90%
Tn	Renewal traffic	200 bytes	Cs	Cache hit rate on server	Assume = 50%
Tl	Release traffic	200 bytes	Il	Name renewal interval	48 hours
Tn	Resolution traffic	200 bytes	Ir	Replication interval	24 hours
W	Workstations per site	10000	Nw	Number of NetBIOS names registered by a workstation with WINS	3

Symbol	Name	Value	Symbol	Name	Value
S	Servers per site	100	Ns	Number of NetBIOS names registered by a server with WINS	7
Rw	Resolutions per day per workstation	10	We	Average WINS entry size	80 bytes

1. All servers are left running continuously so they don't register routinely. All workstations are switched on each day.
2. Steady state (i.e., no new registrations).
3. 1% computers change name to address relationship per day or fail to renew for some reason.
4. The cache hit rate is the percentage of name resolution attempts that can be satisfied by the NetBIOS name cache on the computer. This cache may be loaded from entries in the lmhosts file or previous successful name resolutions.

The following table shows how the bandwidth needs can be calculated. First we will study a spoke site:

Activity	Local Traffic	Remote Traffic
Registration	$W \times Tr = 2MB$	—
Renewal	—	$\frac{S}{I1} \times Tn = 10k$
Release	$W \times T1 = 2MB$	—
Resolves	$(100 - Cw)\%$ of $Tn \times W \times Rw = 2MB$	$(100 - Cs)\%$ of $Tn \times S \times Rs = 100KB$
Replication from each spoke site to the hub	—	1% of $W \times We \times Nw = 24k$
Replication to spoke from hub caused by server registrations	—	1% of $N \times S \times We \times Ns = 2.2k$
Replication to spoke from hub caused by workstation registrations	—	1% of $(N - 1) \times W \times We \times Nw = 72k$
Totals / day:	6MB	208KB

The above calculations depend on the fact that WINS optimizes replication traffic by not propagating an entry when a name is re-registered with the same address.

Note that the name resolution traffic that travels over the WAN is about the same volume as the replication traffic. This should emphasize the need to include all WINS related traffic when considering a design, not just the replication traffic which is frequently the focus of attention.

We should be careful not to read too much into this table as it rests precariously on some assumptions such as the number of workstations changing their name/address mapping per day and the NetBIOS name cache hit ratio. In practice it is very difficult to make anything other than assumptions with a large error factor though a more detailed analysis would include estimates for the errors.

For example, we could say that we are sufficiently uncertain of the cache hit ratio for the servers that it could be anything from 10% to 50%. This means the resolution traffic generated by the servers and resolved remotely is between 180 KB and 100 KB, nearly a factor of two difference. Having examined the relative sizes of the WINS traffic, let's look at the absolute size in comparison to the bandwidth of a network.

An Ethernet LAN will manage 10 MBits/sec maximum, though could do a lot better with emerging technologies such as Fast Ethernet at 100 MBits/sec, ATM and switched networks. The WAN on the other hand can vary tremendously from 9.6 k baud (9,600 bits per second) to megastream or T3 links offering millions of bits per second. We should always remember we are dealing with bits for capacity and bytes for data. Thus, a 9.6k baud line has a bandwidth of about 1 kBytes/sec. A 64k line has a bandwidth of about 6kBytes/sec. Before starting to estimate the time it would take for a particular operation, check whether all the bandwidth is available for data. Sometimes a portion of the bandwidth is dedicated to voice.

The analysis of how a configuration performs with a particular network can only really be enhanced by use of measured, real life data from a similar configuration.

Detailed Lab Testing

In some cases the arguments for a WINS environment with particular characteristics will demand that the network be upgraded. In others, the WINS design will need to be modified as the cost of a network link upgrade cannot be justified. The answer lies with determining what the business priority is. If, at the early stages of technical infrastructure analysis it can be foreseen that the likely WINS design, or any aspect of the technical infrastructure design, will demand a network upgrade then a business principle should be established to settle the decision.

Resolving Multi-hop Network Links

The calculation in the preceding section illustrated that, in the example at least, WINS replication is much less demanding on the network than a high level of remote name resolutions. If we assume the example to be representative of the situation at MBI then we can deduce that it would be preferable to place a spoke WINS server at Buenos Aires and treat Rio De Janeiro as a hub. This would be consistent with Design Principle 10-5 of demanding that the same WINS replication data should not travel across the same WAN link more than once. If both the South America sites had been configured as spokes to New York, twice as much replication traffic would pass across the New York to Rio de Janeiro link as would be the case with the proposed configuration. The drawback to using Rio De Janeiro as a WINS hub is that there is a greater propagation delay in getting updates to and from the Buenos Aires WINS server.

The problems posed by multi-hop links should be borne in mind when considering how to incorporate a new location into the infrastructure. This is something we are told to prepare for in MBI Business Principle 4 so we should be clear how the design we are developing can be scaled. The WINS replication architecture chosen is very scalable if we are adding spoke sites but not very scalable if we are adding hub sites. In actual fact, with this replication architecture a spoke site turns into a hub site as soon as it is configured to replicate with another non-hub site. The solution therefore is to require that any new location has a direct network link to one of the existing hub sites, making it practical to add it as a spoke in the WINS replication architecture. The scope of a technical infrastructure project may or may not encompass the network infrastructure, however the solution is best represented as a principle of network design.

Design Principle 10-6—Scaling to Support New Locations
A new location should be given a direct network link to a hub site.
Justification
▪ Supports the MBI Business Principle 4 demand for infrastructure scalability by allowing the WINS replication architecture to scale by the addition of a spoke site. ▪ Doesn't place any extra burden on an existing network link.

continued ▸

continued

Implications
▪ This solution may cost more in line rental than had the new site been connected to the nearest MBI site.
Issues

Replication Settings

MBI has set the replication settings to minimize the impact on the WAN links during the working day. The settings are shown in Table 10.7. The Update Interval is the time between requests from a WINS server to its replication partner asking for all updates to be sent. The Update Count is the threshold of changes at which a WINS server notifies its replication partner updates should be requested from it. The number is expressed as a percentage of the total number of entries in the WINS database corresponding to systems at that spoke location. Although an actual figure, not a percentage, needs to be configured in WINS it avoids having to list the actual value for each spoke location. As an example, if the number of entries in the WINS database generated by a location was 1650 the setting on the corresponding spoke WINS server would be 165. Thus, 165 changes need to occur at that WINS server before it notifies the hub WINS server of the need to replicate.

Table 10.7 *WINS Replication Settings for MBI*

Site	Interval/Count	To Hub	To Spoke
From Hub	Update Interval (Pull)	Every 24 Hours Start = midnight hub time	4 Hours Start = midnight spoke time
	Update Count (Push)	10%	10%
From Spoke	Update Interval (Pull)	Every 4 Hours Start = 2am spoke time	N/A (spokes do not replicate with other spokes, only hubs)
	Update Count (Push)	10%	N/A (spokes do not replicate with other spokes, only hubs)

The replication timings have been chosen to avoid any WINS server carrying out too many replications at any one time.

The replication parameters specified above will in some cases cause a significant propagation delay before a name is registered in all WINS servers.

Table 10.8 *WINS Propagation Delays for MBI*

From	To	Time
Spoke	Hub	4 Hours
Hub	Hub	24 Hours
Hub	Spoke	4 Hours

If this is likely to cause a problem in a specific case where perhaps an important server is added to the network and it has to be resolvable world-wide within minutes, a forced replication of the necessary WINS servers can be initiated by an operator with sufficient system rights.

There are several other WINS settings that should be specified for a complete design, even if they are left at their defaults. By writing them down in the design it discourages local initiative when setting the systems up.

Computer Capacity

Name resolution is not real business work so it should be transparent to the user. If computers are slow to boot up because they are waiting on the WINS server to get through a backlog of name registration requests the naming service will not be transparent and users of what might be modern, high speed computers connected to a state of the art network will get frustrated. Correctly sizing the computers hosting the naming service is an important element of a successful design.

The chapter on Implementation Preparation describes the process of sizing a system correctly. Here we will highlight some of the specific factors affecting the sizing of a WINS service.

- *Name Registration*

  Caused by computers being switched on or new computers being added to the network, we would expect this to peak in the morning as staff arrive at work. Develop a clear understanding of the "switch on" profile over time to understand the peak rate of registrations the WINS server is going to need to be sized to handle.

- *Name Resolution*

  It is reasonable to assume that name resolution requests are fairly well spread out throughout the day though the effect of an empty name cache on a recently powered up workstation will mean that there could be a rash of WINS lookups at the beginning of the day.

- *Published Performance Data*

  Finally, use any published sizing data as a crude starting point only. The best policy is to gather some real data from which to extrapolate and interpret for your new environment. You can either gather this data as part of a pilot or from other friendly corporations. The Implementation Preparation chapter offers some additional pointers to getting this right.

- *Co-Hosting WINS with Other Services*

  It is common to find infrastructure servers handling multiple services such as file, print, DHCP, and WINS. Thought needs to be given to how each service impacts others. For example, a WINS service hosted on a computer running a print service may well be slow to register a name if the same computer is handling several large print jobs.

- *Capacity in Event of a WINS Server Failure*

  Although it is noted elsewhere that WINS replication architectures generally benefit from employing the minimum number of WINS servers it is wise to balance this with a consideration of what happens when a WINS server fails or is unavailable. The design will be a trade-off between the importance of continued name resolution at the required level of performance against cost and manageability. This again is a situation where a business principle should set the priority.

Phase 4: WINS/DNS Integration

The purpose of integrating WINS and DNS is to allow the names of computers that register NetBIOS names with WINS to be resolved to IP addresses by a query to a DNS server. The reason this may be important is to support programs that refer to Windows NT computers using DNS domain names. An example could be where a Windows NT server is used as a Web server.

Figure 10.19
MBI WINS/DNS Service Integration

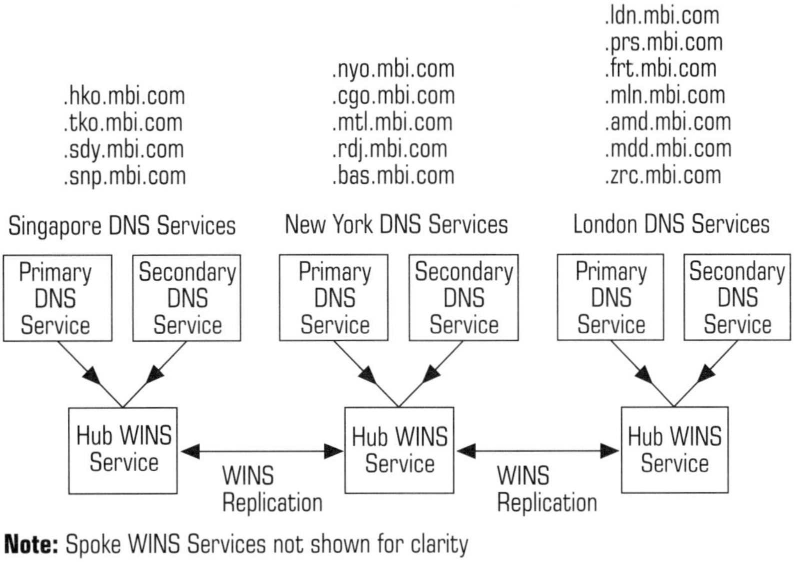

MBI presents us with a straightforward example. Currently MBI operate six Unix hosted DNS servers, with each of three hub sites containing two, one configured as a primary DNS server and the other a secondary. Each pair of DNS servers is responsible for the domains in its region. Thus, the DNS servers in London can resolve domains in London, Paris, Milan, etc.

For this example we will assume the use of Microsoft DNS to provide the solution for WINS/DNS integration. On this basis the Unix hosted DNS service at MBI will have to be migrated to a Windows NT hosted Microsoft DNS service. Each of the Microsoft DNS primary and secondary server pairs at a site would be configured to use the local WINS hub server for resolving NetBIOS names that had been expressed in DNS domain name form and submitted to a DNS server for resolution. Figure 10.19 shows the new Windows NT based solution using dedicated computers for the Microsoft DNS service.

The Microsoft DNS service should be hosted on computers that are members of the MBI IT Support domain (introduced in Chapter 11, Windows NT Domain Design) in keeping with the MBI strategy of using computers in this domain to host the non-user oriented infrastructure services. If the sizing calculations allow it, the primary Microsoft DNS service should be co-hosted with WINS providing the benefit of speedy lookup from DNS to WINS. Co-hosting also reduces network bandwidth as a reference to WINS from DNS is local to the host computer. MBI chose to make this a Design Principle, 10-7.

Design Principle 10-7—Use of the Integrated Naming Service
The Microsoft DNS service should be co-hosted with WINS.
Justification
■ Minimizes non-application use of network bandwidth (Business Principle A-2). ■ Supports the need to be able to phase in the new technical infrastructure (MBI Business Principle 2). ■ Optimum performance.
Implications
■ Each Microsoft DNS server must be configured to reference a WINS server that has the correct set of computer name to address entries. (This is simple with the MBI design as each WINS server has the complete set of NetBIOS computer names).
Issues
■ Sizing calculations may show that the computer being proposed for hosting the naming services does not have sufficient capacity to run both DNS and WINS.

Name Service Client Configuration

Once the name service architecture and server placement is known, most of the information needed to specify the name service client settings should be available. This section shows how these details were specified for the Chicago office of MBI. The design tells us which WINS servers to use for workstations, but there is still a decision to make about servers. The multiple hub/single spoke architecture offers the choice of using one or two hub servers and one spoke server as primary and secondary WINS for the server systems. MBI chose to use the hub server as the primary and the local server as the secondary. This way the presence of a server is propagated throughout the WINS system more speedily and if the WAN link fails the server can still access a local WINS server.

The MBI DNS system (described in the section Phase 4: WINS/DNS Integration) uses primary and secondary DNS servers installed at each of the three WINS hub sites. The Microsoft implementation of DNS software is used with the primary DNS server co-hosted with WINS on the IT support domain server. The MBI policy of allocating file and print servers along with any other office servers to the same subnets as the client systems that use them means that clients will be able to resolve most commonly needed NetBIOS names using a broadcast on the local subnet. The client workstations will therefore be configured as m-node. Most of the references a server will need to make will be off the local subnet so it makes sense to configure servers as h-nodes. Chapter 13, File and Print Services, defines the server to subnet allocation policy.

Table 10.9 *Name Service Client Settings for MBI Chicago Office*

Setting	Value	
	Workstation	*Server*
Primary WINS server	SCGO9999	SNYO9999
Secondary WINS server	SNYO9999	SCGO9999
Primary DNS server	SNYO9999	SNYO9999
Secondary DNS server	SNYO9998	SNYO9998
Node type	m-node	h-node
Use of lmhosts	no	no
Use of hosts	no	no
DNS Domain	cgo.mbi.com	cgo.mbi.com

Summary MBI WINS design

As the path to a naming service design for MBI has been long, we shall summarize the design that has been arrived at here:

1. The architecture is based on a multiple hub/spoke model
2. There are four WINS hubs, Rio de Janeiro, New York, London, and Singapore, connected together in that sequence
3. All other locations have a WINS server that does two way replication with the topologically nearest hub server
4. The DNS service will be implemented using Microsoft DNS
5. There will be a primary and a secondary DNS server at all of the main hub locations excluding Rio de Janeiro
6. The primary DNS server will be co-hosted with the hub WINS server (member of the IT support domain)
7. Workstations will be configured as m-nodes as most name resolutions can be satisfied with a broadcast

8. Servers will be configured as h-node as most name resolutions they make will be remote

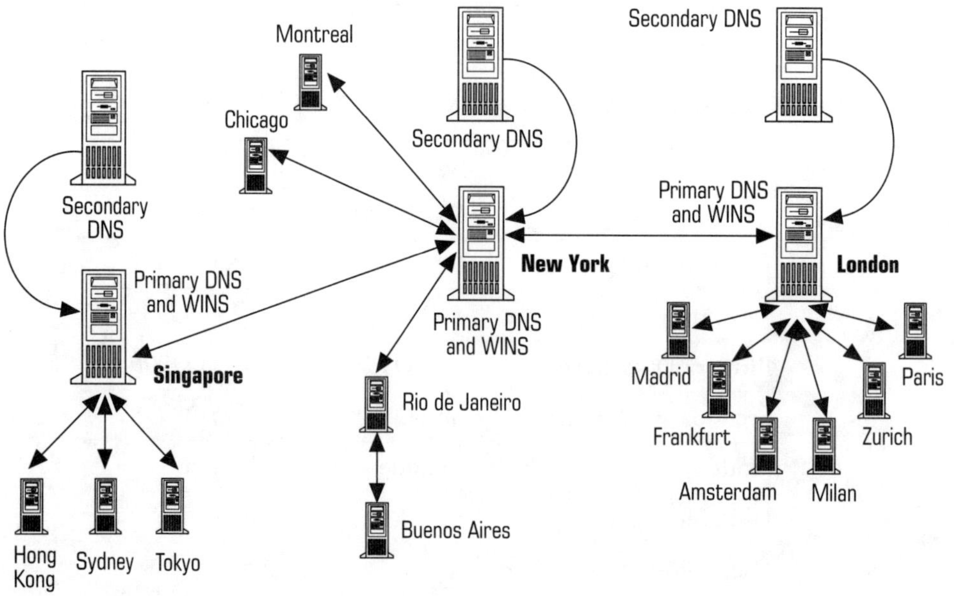

Figure 10.20 *Summary MBI Naming Service Configuration*

Migrating to Active Directory

As with any migration there needs to be both a target design and a migration plan to get to it. The following two sections consider a target design and migration plan for the MBI naming services to support an upgrade to Windows NT 5. Note that the design of a Windows NT 5 domain and associated DNS namespace would ideally be taken as aspects of the same exercise as they are so closely related. Their treatment has been split between the domain design chapter and this one because the chapter structure used in this book was chosen to suit a Windows NT 4 technical infrastructure design.

Draft Name Service Design to Support Windows NT 5

We shall assume that the MBI requirements specification for the technical infrastructure states a continuing need for a NetBIOS name resolution service so we can safely leave the current design alone. Instead, we shall examine the existing MBI DNS namespace and implementation in the context of the proposed Windows NT 5 domain design (shown in the chapter on Domain Design).

The domain design chapter develops a Windows NT 5 domain structure that has the following DNS namespace:

Tier 1	mbi.com
Tier 2	<Regional_Domain>.mbi.com
Tier 3	<Local_Domain>.<Regional_Domain>.mbi.com

Additional tiers may be added below tier 3. An example local domain name would be nyo.northamerica.mbi.com

Notice that the regional domain level, introduced to satisfy the regional organizational structures of MBI, is absent in the original inherited DNS namespace shown in Figure 10.19. This means that many existing computers will have DNS domain names that are not subdomains of the corresponding Windows NT 5 domain to which they belong. Although MBI will be making no changes to existing DNS domain names (as recorded in a design principle in the Migration Strategy section following) our design for Windows NT 5 should state how DNS domain names are to be allocated in the future to enable consistent name allocation leading towards an organized name space.

It is recommended that any existing DNS implementation be thoroughly reviewed before depending on it to support a Windows NT 5 based infrastructure. In particular the following aspects should be examined:

- DNS server deployment—are the servers in the right places in the organization?
- DNS server software suitability, e.g., dynamic update capability, manageability.
- DNS server capacity—is the capacity sufficient and available where it is needed?
- Allocation of domains to zones and overall administrative responsibilities.

Migration Strategy

Use of DNS is so prevalent that it would be unusual to find an organization that did not use it. On the other hand it is quite common to find that the use of DNS does not completely pervade an organization and in cases where organizations have merged, there may be more than one DNS namespace in use. Thus, while it might be desirable to determine the DNS namespace based on a Windows NT 5 Active Directory design it will not always be practical as the magnitude of the changes required to the existing namespace may be prohibitive.

For this reason, one of the first questions to resolve is whether the existing DNS namespace will be used without change for the new Windows NT 5 Active Directory configuration or whether a new namespace should be designed. The answer to this question should be recorded as a design principle. MBI chose to retain their existing DNS namespace unchanged and to simply add domains where necessary to accommodate the Windows NT 5 Active Directory domain design. The design principle below shows how they recorded the decision.

Design Principle 10-8—Retention of Existing DNS Namespace
The existing DNS namespace and its usage will not be changed to accommodate Windows NT 5 Active Directory.
Justification
▪ Suitable Windows NT 5 DNS domain names can be constructed within the existing DNS namespace. ▪ Windows NT 5 domains can accommodate member computers that are not DNS sub-domains of the Windows NT 5 domain to which they belong.
Implications
▪ It will not be possible to tell by looking at a computer's DNS domain name which Windows NT 5 domain it belongs to. ▪ The DNS zone allocation needs to be reviewed to ensure it is consistent with the introduction of Windows NT 5 domains.
Issues

11

Windows NT Domain Design

Domains are the entities from which a Windows NT technical infrastructure is built to meet the security and technology management needs of an organization. Specifically, users should be able to access the applications and data they need from wherever they are working and the whole infrastructure should be manageable from wherever the expertise resides. To create such an infrastructure mandates a complete understanding of the needs of users and IT Support.

Windows NT is designed around a client-server architecture, rendering the network transparent to administrative tools and system components. Thus, the same tool can be used to manage resources on a local computer as on a remote computer. The flexibility is immense. However, to exploit it in a business critical distributed environment requires two key services to be in place:

- Security
- Management

Security is needed so there can be sensible restrictions and permissions associated with intra- and inter-computer resource access. Efficient management of the distributed systems from a chosen point in the network is essential if the operational overheads are not to outweigh the benefits of distributed computing.

The Windows NT Domain is a concept used by Microsoft to allow the secure management of a set of users and their resources.

Considerations for Windows NT Domain Design

Windows NT domains offer a wealth of configuration options, so we need to make some choices if we are going to get the right one for a particular situation. Because the two principle reasons for having a domain are security and management, the two factors driving the choice of a domain architecture for a particular organization are:

- the organizational structure of a business
- the structure of its IT Support organization

For a domain to function, member computers need to be able to communicate with other member computers, so the design of a domain structure will also need to take into account where different parts of the organization are located along with the nature of the underlying communications infrastructure in between. Each case will be different and so demand a unique configuration.

To be able to complete the design by determining the capacity and placement of the domain's computers we therefore need to consider two additional factors:

- the geographic distribution of the organization
- the communications infrastructure

The four factors just identified are dealt with as the specific attributes of a Windows NT domain design later in the chapter. Domain design is a design activity and its position in the overall project roadmap is shown in Figure 11.1.

Figure 11.1 *Design Topic (highlighted)*

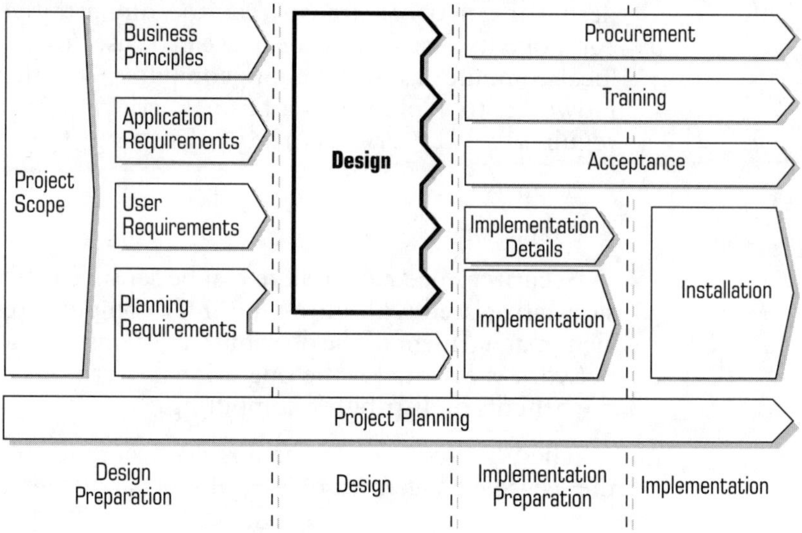

Chapter Structure

Table 11.1 shows the structure of this chapter.

Table 11.1 *The Structure of Chapter 11*

Topic	Contents
Review of Windows NT domain structures	■ A Windows NT domain ■ Linking domains together using trust relationships ■ Standard domain models ■ Advanced domain models ■ Moving to Windows NT 5 Directory Services
Review of Windows NT domain processes	■ Account database synchronization ■ Authentication and validation
Designing a domain structure	■ Choice of architecture ■ Implementation details
Planning for Windows NT 5 ActiveX Directory Services	■ Developing a plan to migrate to a Windows NT 5 Directory Services version of the case study domain structure

Technology Review

In the case of a single, stand alone Windows NT computer, a user has to logon on by supplying a valid account name and password combination before they can gain access to any of its resources, a process known as *authentication*. A Windows NT domain extends that concept to a collection of computers that share the same account database. Thus, users logon to the *domain* using an account name and password combination which is authenticated against the domain's shared account database. Once logged on to a domain, given sufficient permission, a user may access resources on any of the computers within that domain. A Windows NT account database is frequently referred to as the Security Account Manager or SAM.

The account database in a domain is held on a computer designated as the Primary Domain Controller or PDC. Updates to this database such as password changes are then replicated on a periodic basis to one or more Backup Domain Controllers (BDCs) in the same domain. BDCs are also capable of authenticating users and can be located around a corporation to provide performance and availability benefits.

Domains can be linked using *trust relationships* to create super security and administrative groupings.

Linking Domains with Trusts

Trusts are a mechanism for combining domains for:

- Administration of users and resources

- Controlling access to resources

A one way trust will allow a user with an account in Domain A to have the potential to access resources in Domain B. Domain B *trusts* Domain A to authenticate the user. This is only meaningful if the *trusted* domain (Domain A in the illustration) holds the particular user's or set of users' accounts. A one way trust relationship is illustrated in Figure 11.2.

Figure 11.2 *One Way Trust Relationship*

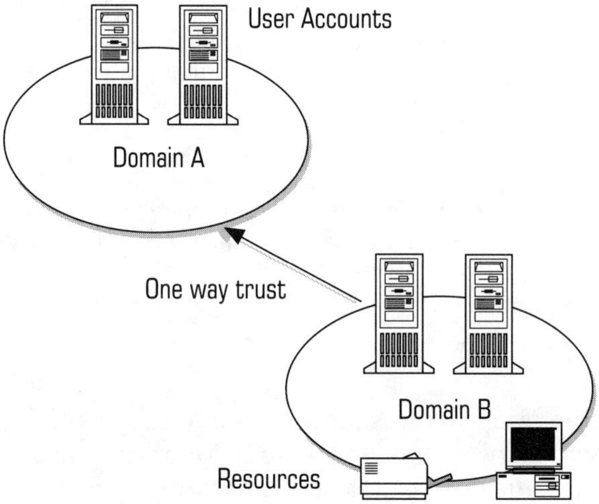

If both domains have users defined in their user account database and there is a need to give users in each domain access to resources in the other domain a two way trust relationship can be set up. This is no more than two one way trusts. This is illustrated in Figure 11.3.

Figure 11.3 *Two Way Trust Relationship*

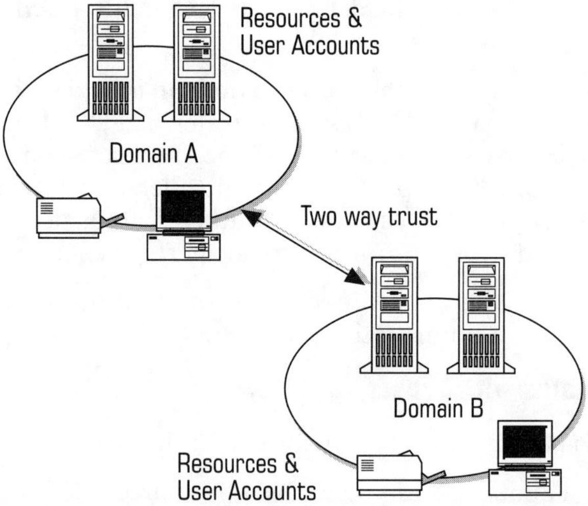

Trusts will also allow a user to logon at a computer in any domain that trusts the domain that contains the user's account. In multi-domain structures this capability is typically used to allow mobile users to logon at different parts of the organization.

Domain Models

There are four principle domain models: single, master, multiple master and complete trust. They are each characterized by the location of the account database or databases and the associated trust relationships. In the following models a *resource domain* is one that contains no user accounts, only user's resources, for example, a file server. An *account domain* is one that contains only user accounts. An authentication domain is frequently referred to as a *master domain*.

Note that Windows NT Groups play no part in differentiating the models although they are an important means of managing users that can be tailored to a particular domain structure. The four models are described in the following sections.

Single

The single domain model is the most basic configuration and has both user accounts and resources share a single domain.

Figure 11.4 *Single Domain Model*

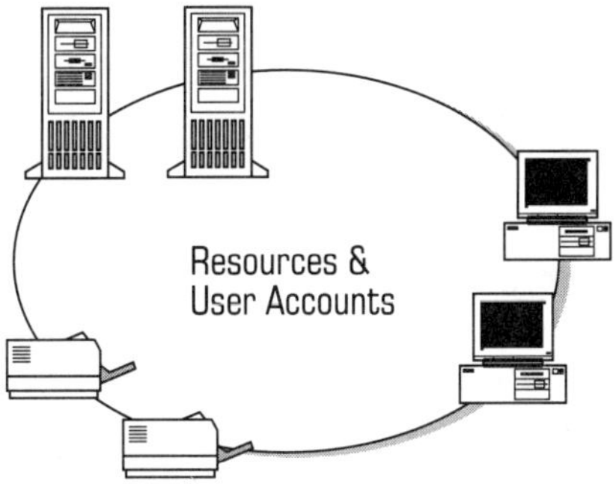

- ***When to use***
  - Single or well integrated user population
  - Single or well integrated management and operations organization
  - Requirement to manage users and resources together
  - For ease of administration
- ***When not to use***
  - Highly geographically dispersed organization

- High degree of security needed between different organizational groups (unless the solution is to use several distinct Single Domain Models)
- When the number of SAM entries approach the NT architectural limit for a single domain

Master

The master domain model consists of a single master domain, and one or more resource domains. Each resource domain trusts the master domain but the master domain does not trust the resource domains.

Figure 11.5 *Master Domain Model*

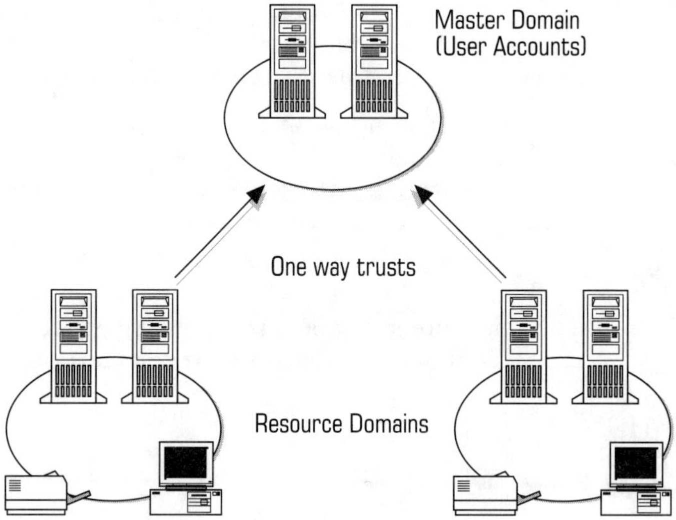

The master domain model splits out resources into separate domains. This allows easy alignment of resource management responsibility to resource domains, while retaining a single SAM for the complete model. This model offers a higher degree of scalability than the single domain model as additional resource domains may be added to cope with growth. The single master domain model is discussed further in the section Adapting Domain Models, later in this chapter.

- ***When to use***
  - When local resource management is required
  - When centralized account management is required
- ***When not to use***
  - When the number of users causes the SAM to approach the NT architectural limit for a single domain

- When it is necessary to use multiple SAMs to split the responsibility for the management of the user population
- Highly geographically dispersed organization

Multiple Master

The multiple master domain model consists of two or more master domains and one or more resource domains. Each resource domain trusts each master domain ensuring that no matter in which master domain users have their account, they can logon at a computer in any of the resource domains.

Primarily for management purposes each master domain trusts the other master domains ensuring an administrator or operator may logon at a computer in any domain regardless of which master domain their account is in. The multiple master domain model is discussed further in the section Adapting the Domain Models.

Figure 11.6 *Multiple Master Domain Model*

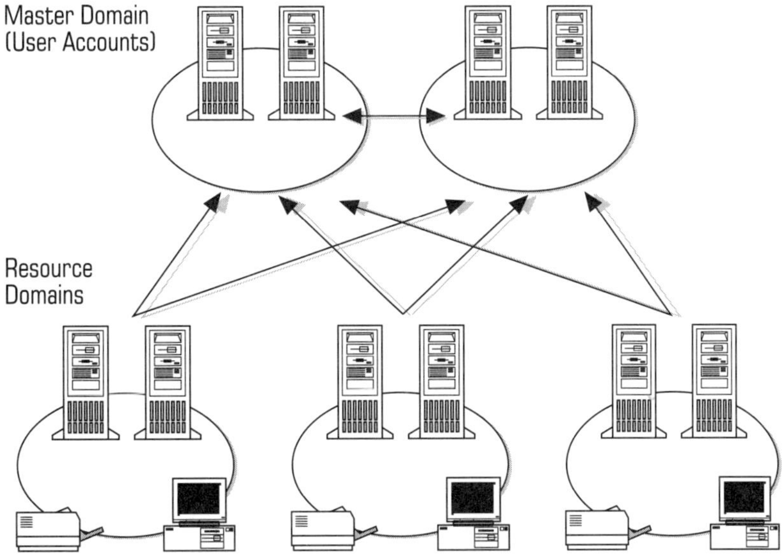

This model is highly scalable, both in terms of user accounts and resources.

- ***When to use***
  - When the SAM needs to be split:
    - for better overall availability (the unavailability of one master domain does not disable the entire user population from logging on and accessing resources)

- because there is a need to partition the SAM for management purposes (a part of the organization requires management control over only their user accounts)
- or the total number of entries exceeds the maximum size allowed for a SAM

- When a highly scaleable architecture is needed

- *When not to use*
  - When there is a need for central resource management (the multiple master model doesn't preclude central resource management but there may be better options)
  - The management overhead of all the trusts cannot be justified. The overhead is caused by the need to manage user access to resources across a number of trust relationships

Complete Trust

The complete trust model is one where every domain trusts every other domain, ensuring there is a two way trust between any two domains. It is customary for each domain to contain both resources and accounts.

Figure 11.7
Complete Trust Domain Model

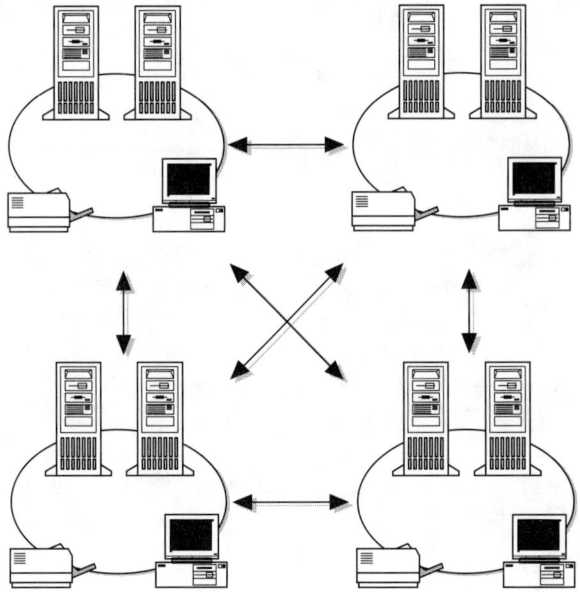

- *When to use*
  - When there is a strong need for local control of both accounts and resources
  - When the number of domains is not too large (a realistic maximum would be in the region of 15) or the overhead in managing the cross-domain group memberships will be excessive
  - As a target model for bringing together an inherited collection of unplanned domains
- *When not to use*
  - When there is a need for central control of user accounts
  - When implementing a scalable architecture is not necessary

Adapting the Domain Models

The four standard domain models just introduced usually suffice as the starting point for an implementation. In practice, organizational and geographic considerations can lead to the initial choice of model being developed into a new configuration, customized to better meet the needs of a business.

This section describes five scenarios that show the master and multiple master domain models adapted to common practical situations. The first two adaptations introduce the *partitioned master*, which is a multiple master model with less than the full set of trusts, and the *management master*, a model built from several single master domains using a dedicated master domain for administrative staff.

The third and fourth scenarios examine the implications of using the multiple master model in two different ways, one aligned with geography and the other with organization. The fifth scenario discusses the benefits of putting non-customer oriented services (e.g., DHCP) on computers in a distinct resource domain, to be referred to as the IT Support Domain.

Following discussion of these adaptations a brief look is taken at the issues involved with migrating from an existing ad hoc domain structure to one of these more formal models. Finally, before embarking on the design, consideration is given to how the introduction of Windows NT 5 Directory Services might influence our design decisions so that upgrading from Windows NT 4 is non-disruptive.

Partitioned Master

There are many business situations where it is desirable to keep organizational entities separate by imposing restrictions on transfer of data, people or access to applications. Some examples might be:

- Payroll department from rest of organization
- Students from administration in a university
- Corporate finance from trading

One way of achieving such partitioning is to organize users into appropriate groups and apply permissions on the resources for the groups. A single or multiple master model is the ideal starting point, particularly as resource domains can be allocated to the different parts of the organization that need to be kept separate.

There are cases when implementing cross organizational restrictions through use of groups and permissions alone is not enough to satisfy internal audit or regulatory requirements. In such instances something stronger is needed; fortunately, it is not always necessary to go to the extreme of physical separation. Ideally, we would like the ability to administer the complete system from a limited number of points, while imposing a higher degree of restriction on the user population. Trust relationships, or lack of them, allow us to reach this compromise.

Figure 11.8 *Partitioned Multiple Master Domain*

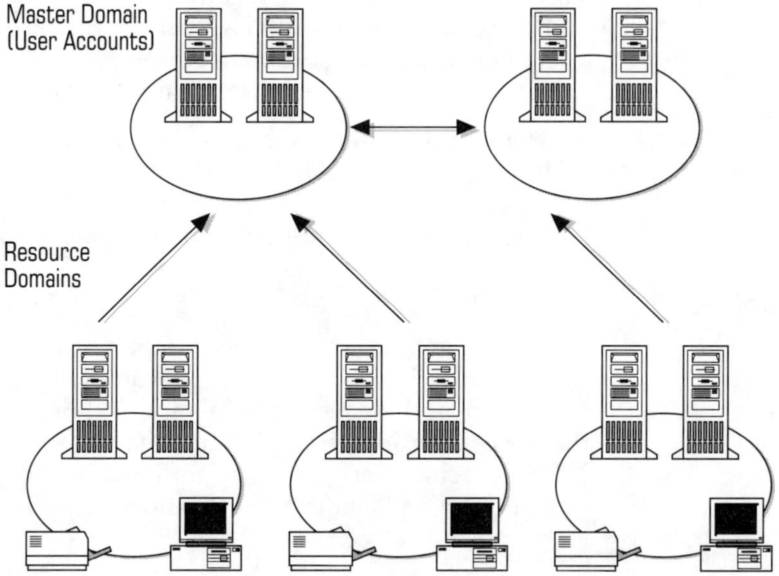

The partitioned multiple master domain is a version of the multiple master domain but with each resource domain only trusting one master domain. In the scenario we are describing, all domains would be set up to map onto organizational units. Another way of looking at this model is as a collection of single master domains linked with two way trusts between the master domains.

This configuration serves our purpose because it is now even more difficult to accidentally or maliciously grant users access to resources they should be restricted from. The drawback is that a user cannot log in from their master domain at just any computer because trusts are non-transitive. They are confined to those computers in resource domains that trust the master they have an account in.

The two way trusts between the master domains are there for management and administration. We are making the assumption that the operations and management staff will still be given the responsibility to be able to logon from any master domain and manage all resources in the entire domain structure.

Note that unless key operational staff are given accounts in each of the master domains, they too won't be able to log in at just any computer. This point should be considered very carefully, though in such a partitioned organization it is common to find the IT Support organization partitioned as well, reducing the need for cross organization administrative access.

Management Master

By adding a master domain dedicated to operations and administration staff we can take the partitioned master one stage further to arrive at a model called the Management Master.

The management master domain is set up so that every domain trusts a single management domain. The management domain only contains the accounts for the operations staff, no users logon from this domain.

This configuration allows operational staff to logon from the management domain at any computer in the entire domain structure but ensures there need be no trusts between the user master domains or between a resource domain and any additional user master domains. The diagram shows two single master domain models in the management master configuration. In practice there could be a mixture of independent single master and multiple master domain models linked together in this manner. This model is particularly suitable where there is a single support organization but the business consists of a number of major organizational or geographic entities which would normally demand a separate single master or multiple models.

Figure 11.9 *Management Master Domain*

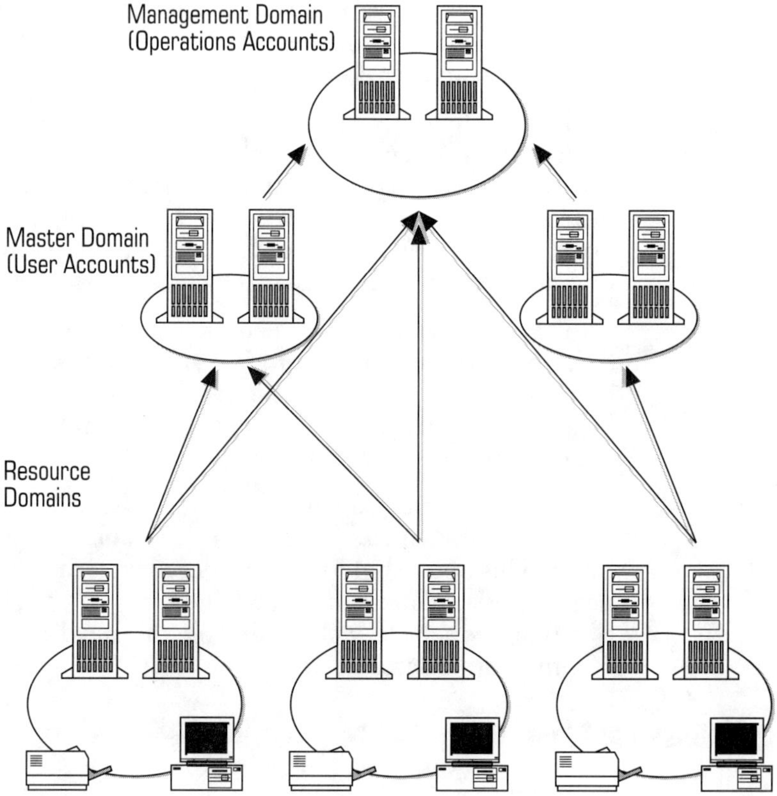

Geographic Master

This application of the multiple master domain model is based on organizing the master domains along geographic lines. The associated resource domains may be based on geography or organization. The diagram on the next page illustrates an example.

The implication of this way of applying the multiple master domain model is that all user accounts for a region, which usually incorporates several resource domains each aligned to business or location, are kept in one account database. This is fine as long as there is cross organizational account management.

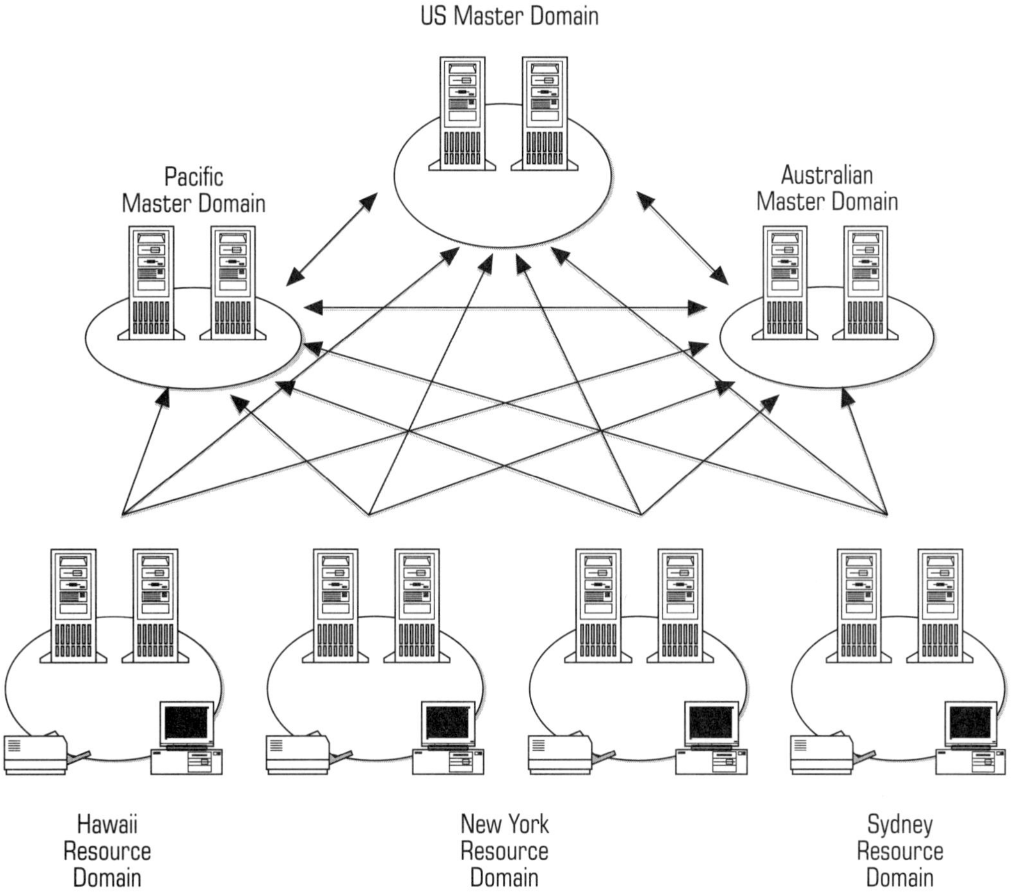

Figure 11.10 *Geographic Multiple Master Domain*

If resource domains are organized on a geographic basis there only needs to be one resource domain per location. In practice a single resource domain can span multiple locations. The principle advantage of the geographic master domain is that for organizations with multiple lines of business in each location, there still only needs to be one (possibly two for resilience) backup domain controller from the master domain in the location of the resource domain to speed logons and resource access.

Organizational Master

This domain model is the application of the single, single master and multiple master domain models to a company with multiple distinct organizations within it.

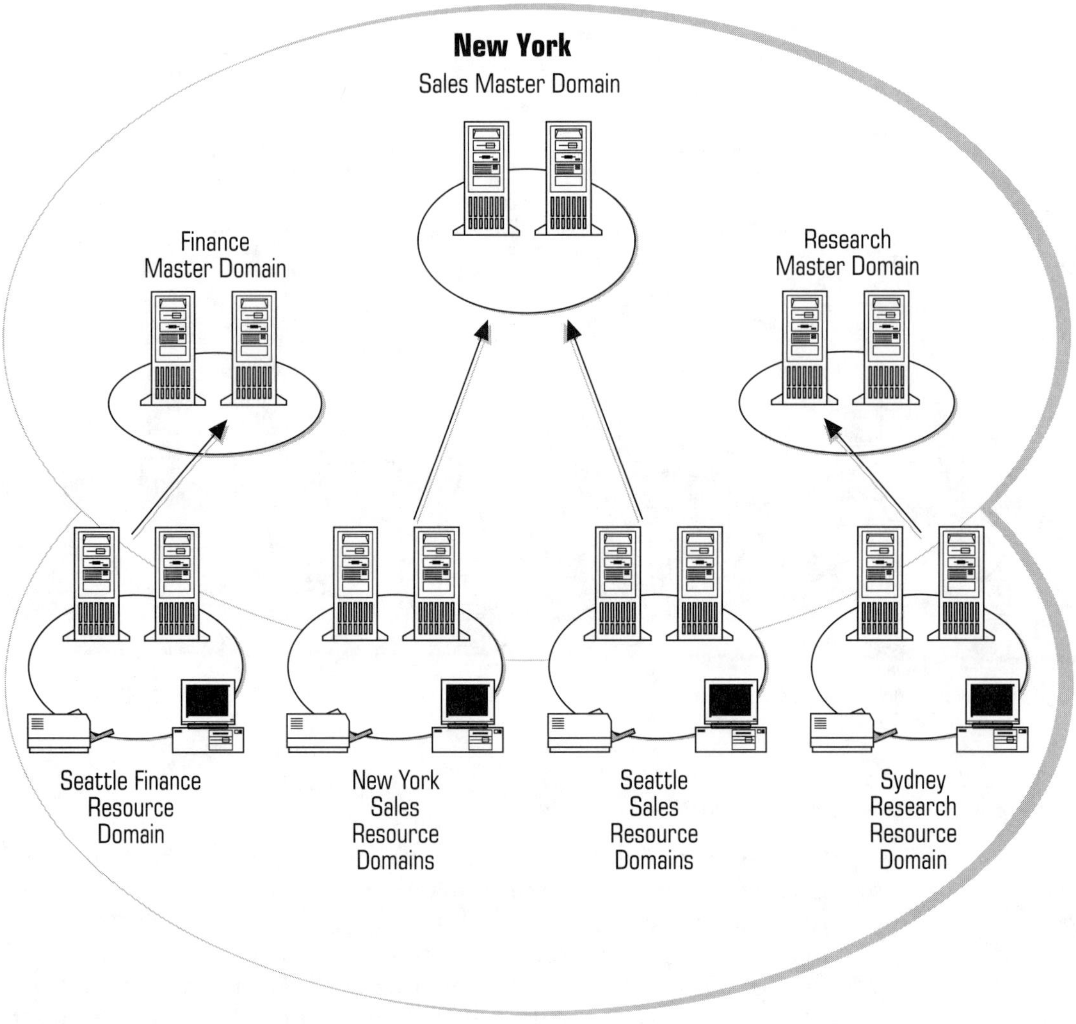

Figure 11.11 *Organizational Master Domain Model*

Conceptually it is a set of domain models in parallel, each aligned to an organization within the corporation. (Figure 11.11 only shows parallel single master domains, however it is equally valid with single and multiple master models).

Whether the separate domain structures acquire additional trusts between them and develop into a partitioned multiple master or full multiple master model is dependent on the degree to which there is a need to:

- Share data between organizations.
- Allow users to logon from their usual master domain at a computer in another organization's resource domain.
- Access an application or data in another resource domain.

The master domains need not share the same location but for our example in Figure 11.11 they do.

The thing to be cautious about with this model is the possible need for a BDC from each master domain at any location, potentially running the cost up. Note that the organizational master domain model lends itself to the addition of a management master domain if there happens to be a single support organization.

IT Support Domain

Many services may be hosted on Windows NT servers including file services, print services, naming services, DHCP, DNS, Backup, e-mail, enterprise applications, computer monitoring, network monitoring and user authentication (domain controller). Some of these services are directed specifically at users and others should be transparent to all except the IT Support personnel. Further, any routine or abnormal occurrences relating to the non-user services should not impact the work of users.

Unfortunately it is sometimes necessary to either reboot a server or for it to consume great CPU or IO resource, which would certainly impact a user if that same server was used for file, print, FAX, or some other service. Additionally, the level of user rights necessary to fully operate some of the "internal" services can exceed those necessary to administer file and print services. For these reasons it can be beneficial to host these services on separate computers running in a new, dedicated domain. Thus, users can be protected from service interruptions and the need for over-privileged administrators on the user oriented servers is removed.

The new domain is referred to as an *IT Support Domain* and can be implemented as another resource domain in a multiple or single master model, or even a complete trust model. In ideal circumstances, each location would have one or more servers hosting the support functions and being members of the IT Support Domain. In some cases this will call for more hardware than would otherwise have been deployed so its benefit has to be weighed against its additional cost.

One of the benefits of using an IT Support Domain is that it provides a single security environment for those services that need to communicate with one another. Among the services that benefit from the simplicity of working within a single domain are Microsoft SMS and Microsoft Exchange.

Non-conforming Domain Models

Windows NT has been in existence for a number of years now and it is rare for an organization not to have experimented with Windows NT domains. Indeed, the ease with which a domain can be created, regardless of how appropriate it is in the overall picture, coupled with the inertia of IT departments, has led many organizations to suffer from poorly planned domains. This naturally leads to complications when the corporation decides to rationalize domain deployment on a company-wide or even organization-wide basis.

The solution has to be a combination of political will and technology. At a high level, the options are:

1. Create a completely new domain architecture and migrate the users of existing domains to the new domains.
2. Build on the existing domains.
3. A combination of the previous two options.

Option one will lead to an optimum design though there will be pain along the way as users have to get accustomed to logging in from a different domain and a new set of (probably more severe) restrictions on what they can do. The support organizations running the original domains may feel hard done by to start with as some of their work is undone and power reduced, though they may feel relieved that things are being sorted out. The technical issues with migrating are largely logistical, particularly if the same hardware is to be used for servers and domain controllers in the new domains. User data will need to be transferred and its file ownership set to the new user account to ensure users can still access their files after logging on from the new domain. Tools are available for transferring users from one domain to another.

The second option calls for a compromise based on the existing domain structure. This option should only be chosen if the existing structure is practical to build on or the political strength of the parts of the organization operating these domains is such that change is resisted. Building on what is an ad hoc domain structure will inevitably lead to a sub-optimal domain architecture, containing too many domains, too many trusts and a mixing of user account domains with resource domains.

If option two really is unavoidable then the following rules of thumb should be followed:

- Minimize the number of trust relationships. This helps ensure the security regime does not become too complicated and hence prone to inadvertent abuse.
- Maintain a split between master domains and resource domains. This placates a business group's desire to control their own resources but effectively moves the security veto (through account rights) to a central administrative group.
- Minimize the number of domains. Again this will help reduce the number of trusts required and hence the complexity of the architecture. Keeping complexity down will reduce human error.
- Aim for a multiple master model. To some extent, the above guidelines point to this objective. By using a standard (albeit with some variations) Microsoft model, administrators recruited to the organization will have an instant familiarity with the model in use. If this weren't the case, new recruits could easily misinterpret conventions and compromise the integrity of the model by putting users or trusts in the wrong place although operational procedures should guard against this.

The options will involve a careful analysis of the capabilities of the current domain structure that users depend on, so they can be replicated in the new structure.

Domain Processes

There are three key processes that take place within a domain, all implemented by the Windows NT NetLogon service:

- Account database synchronization from PDC to BDC
- User logon authentication
- User validation (when attempting to access a resource)

Each is important because the way they operate on the network will need to be considered for us to be able to design the optimum domain structure. We will see that a configuration that works well for one process may have adverse implications for one of the others. The design challenge involves using knowledge of the domain processes, the network, and user needs to optimize the combined configuration of the three processes. In this section we analyze the three processes to determine the network traffic they generate for certain configurations.

It should be borne in mind throughout this section that any figures used or calculations are to show general guidance on the method of determining traffic volumes. As Windows NT is updated, the quantities of data involved in some of these transactions are likely to change. Indeed, the transactions themselves will change.

The natural desire to determine an accurate traffic volume figure for the various processes should be curtailed and put in the context of the following two observations. Even if we obtained an accurate figure for domain process traffic volume we would need accurate figures for all other network traffic to calculate equally accurate figures for domain process throughput rates. For example, suppose we knew that the account database synchronization process needed to transfer 34520 bytes over a 9.6k line. It is easy to calculate how long it would take if nothing else was using the line but if there was random business traffic causing periods of 100% utilization lasting many minutes then it is very difficult to predict accurately how long the synchronization transfer will take.

User behavior can influence the level of infrastructure process traffic significantly. User behavior is notoriously difficult to predict particularly in the case where a new system is being developed and there are no benchmarks to provide a reference.

The recommendation is that domain process traffic volumes are calculated to increase general understanding of how a particular configuration will operate on a given network. Potential error factors should always be borne in mind. Each of the three domain processes are examined in more detail in the following sections.

Account Database Synchronization Process

The concept of multiple backup domain controllers in a domain has already been introduced. Each domain controller holds a copy of the entire account database for the domain in which it is a member. The reasons for having the account database replicated across several machines are:

- Availability of the domain authentication and authorization service. If one domain controller should fail, others would be available for use.
- To ensure authentication and authorization can happen speedily by placing a domain controller local to a user population to avoid slow WAN links.

- Multiple domain controllers can cope with a larger authentication and authorization workload.

To carry out the synchronization, updates to the account database on the primary domain controller are periodically copied to the backup domain controllers. This process will use bandwidth that in some cases will impact performance of applications. To understand how synchronization affects application performance we need to calculate the volume of traffic generated and the frequency with which it is sent.

Synchronization Traffic

To calculate the synchronization traffic we need to know:

1. Number of bytes to be sent across the network to synchronize a remote BDC for each type of SAM change.
2. The frequency and type of changes made to the SAM over a given period of time.

Figure 11.12 *Account Database Synchronization in a Domain*

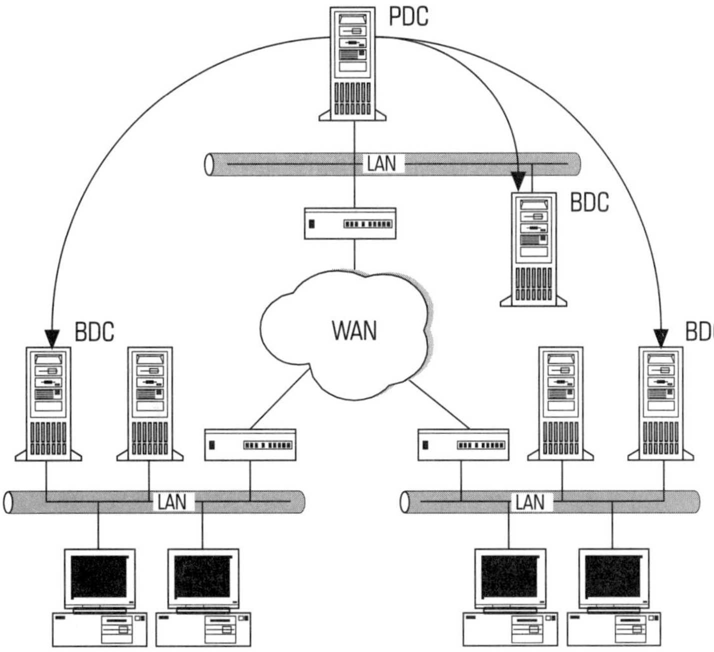

An example is shown in the section Domain Process Traffic later in this chapter using the information from Table 11.5, Account Database Entry Sizes, plus estimates for the frequency with which SAM data changes.

Synchronization Frequency

The frequency with which account database changes are synchronized with the backup domain controllers is controlled by a set of entries in the registries of the domain controllers. The primary domain controller registry entries control the frequency at which backup domain controllers are notified (pulsed) of the need to synchronize. The backup domain controllers use the value of a registry entry to govern the rate at which synchronization data is requested from the primary domain controller.

Tuning this mechanism over slow connections is essential if SAM synchronization is not to have an adverse impact on other applications communicating over the same WAN link.

Logon Process

Logon to a domain by a user at a computer will generate network traffic as the logon request is validated by a domain controller in the logon domain. The speed with which a user gets logged on is frequently a significant factor in their perception of the overall system performance so it is wise to consider this when deciding on the location of the domain controllers with respect to the network topology as WAN conversations are where the network can introduce delays.

Illustrated below are three typical logon scenarios, all based on NetBIOS over a subnetted IP network, showing the summary LAN/WAN connections necessary for a logon. For more information on the name resolution methods mentioned refer to Chapter 10, Naming Services.

Figure 11.13 *Logon Over WAN*

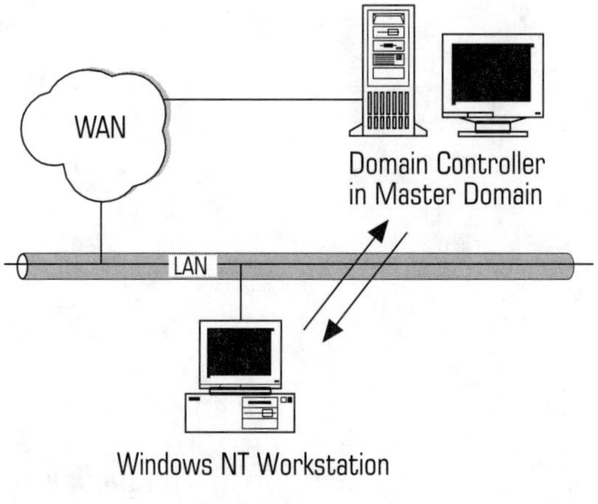

In Figure 11.13, Logon Over WAN, the workstation must have used either an lmhosts file with a #DOM entry or WINS to locate the remote domain controller.

Figure 11.14
Logon Using BDC on Local LAN

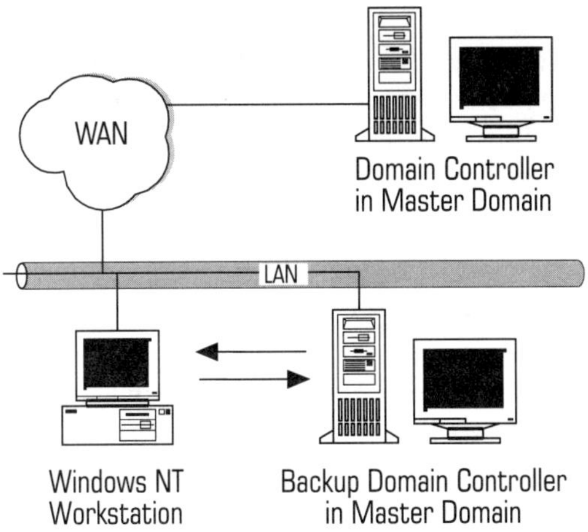

In Figure 11.14, Logon Using BDC on Local LAN, no WAN communication is necessary for the logon authentication process to complete. If the workstation and the BDC were on the same LAN segment a broadcast would have sufficed for the workstation to locate a domain controller from the correct domain. If the two computers were separated by a router lmhosts with a #DOM directive or WINS could have been used by the workstation to locate the local BDC.

Figure 11.15
Pass Through Authentication

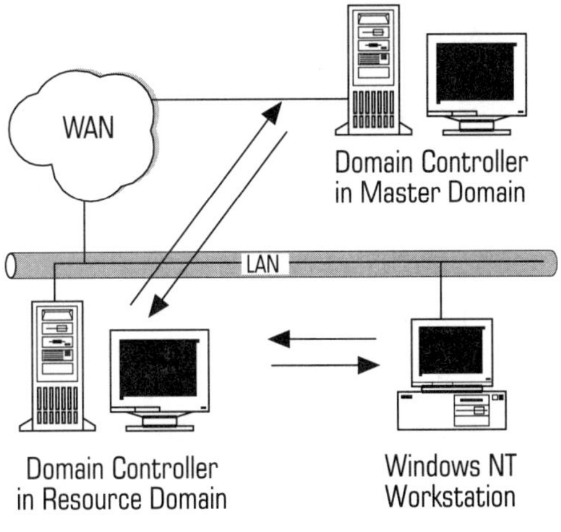

Figure 11.15 shows how a domain controller from a domain that trusts the master domain the user is attempting to logon from facilitates the authentication process by passing the logon request through to a master domain controller.

Logon Traffic Volume

The amount of traffic generated by the logon process will vary considerably depending upon the services and protocols used. An estimate based on published information:

4KB < traffic per logon < 20KB

Among the causes of this traffic are:

- Obtaining the trusted domain list from a resource domain controller
- Creation of secure channel between workstation and resource domain controller
- NetLogon, workstation to resource domain controller
- NetLogon, resource domain controller to account domain controller

User Validation Process

The request to use a particular network resource for the first time causes a process called user validation (authorization) to take place. The resource connection request, for example:

```
NET USE H: \\SERVER\Share
```

is accompanied by the client's username, password, security token, and logon domain name. The server checks to see if the username and password elements match a user account on that server, if they do access is granted. If not, the server uses the logon domain name to attempt to validate the user with the domain the user claims to have logged onto. For this to work, the server must be in a domain that trusts the user's logon domain.

The following diagram illustrates the basic user validation process in terms of network communications. Again the example is based on the NetBIOS over TCP/IP (NBT) protocol combination.

As WAN connections are generally slower than LAN connections, the quantity of WAN traffic has an impact on the performance of this process. As a worst case scenario, the resource server would be remote from the workstation and the domain controller remote from the resource server, causing two WAN conversations. Placing the resource server on the same WAN as the workstation or the domain controller would reduce WAN conversations to one. The ideal case is where the resource server, the workstation and a domain controller from the relevant master domain are all present on the same LAN, eliminating the need for a WAN conversation in order to gain access to resources.

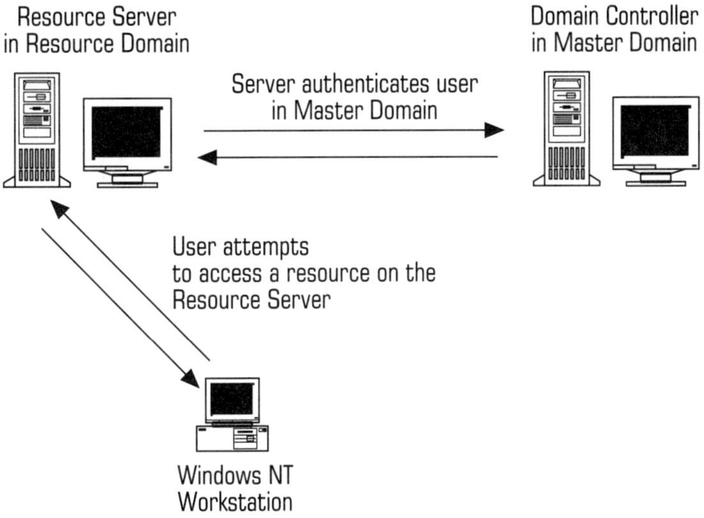

Figure 11.16
User Validation

Moving to Active Directory

The next major version of Windows NT will bring with it a radically new approach to creating a domain structure. Based around Active Directory, a distributed repository containing information about all NT objects, many of the restrictions associated with domains in NT 4 will be lifted. Table 11.2 summarizes the key differences.

Table 11.2 *Differences Between Windows NT 4 and Windows NT 5 Active Directory*

Windows NT 4	Windows NT 5 Active Directory
Trusts are non-transitive, effectively restricting a domain hierarchy to two tiers.	An unlimited hierarchy of domains may be constructed with an implicit two way trust being possible from any domain to any other domain in the tree.
The domain is the finest level of granularity for aligning with organizational (user and administrative) entities.	Arbitrary sets of resources can be grouped and defined as Organizational Units (OUs) within a domain for the purpose of applying administrative control and access rights. OUs can be linked in a hierarchy with access rights inherited downwards.

Table 11.2 *Differences Between Windows NT 4 and Windows NT 5 Active Directory (continued)*

Windows NT 4	Windows NT 5 Active Directory
Master domains are used to group user accounts for the purposes of account administration and to allow logon at a computer from any number of trusting resource domains.	The need to use a convention to distinguish domains according to whether they have resources or user accounts is no longer necessary. Domains will commonly contain both user accounts and resources.
The name of a Windows NT 4 domain is purely arbitrary.	Active Directory domain names are also arbitrary, however, they are DNS domain names, forming part of the corporate DNS namespace.

The possibility of a complete set of trust relationships makes it practical, with appropriate permissions, for a user to logon at a workstation or access resources in any domain regardless of which domain their account is held in. The convention of using account domains distinct from and trusted by resource domains is no longer relevant, as the best place now for a user account is in the user's local domain along with the resources they commonly use.

Active Directory has been designed to map efficiently onto the typical WAN/LAN network topology found in most large organizations by using two replication mechanisms:

1. To keep all copies of the directory in a domain in synchronization, the Active Directory uses what Microsoft calls multi-master replication, which means that a change made to any domain controller will be replicated in full to all other domain controllers in the same domain. Thus, the distinction between BDCs and PDCs disappears and updates to the directory, for example adding a user, can be carried out using any domain controller in the relevant domain.
2. A *subset* of a domain's directory is replicated to *catalog servers* in other domains throughout the network. Catalog servers are computers that maintain summary directory information from other domains and provide a mechanism for resources to be located efficiently anywhere in the domain hierarchy without the need to replicate whole directories around the WAN.

Thus, a domain naturally maps itself to a region of high connectivity, typically a LAN and the directory subset replication among catalog servers, involving less transfer of data, naturally maps onto the WAN links between domains. This is more sympathetic to a typical corporate network as it allows the majority of logons to be authenticated locally without the common Windows NT4 drawback of having to replicate an entire directory (SAM) across a WAN link.

Use of the Organizational Unit concept allows the access to and control of resources to be aligned closely to the hierarchical organizational structure likely to be found in any corporation. Organizational Units (OUs) do not have to be aligned to organizations within a corporation, they could be mapped to geography at one level and organization at another.

Examples of where OUs may be appropriate:

- An OU may be created for each floor of an office block and OUs below that created for different organizational groupings on each floor.
- OUs may be used to reflect the needs of different groups of users and resources within a single business unit.

The domain structures available in Windows NT 4 are at best a subset of what is possible in the Active Directory therefore it is improbable that there is anything that could be done with Windows NT 4 that can't be done with Windows NT 5 Active Directory.

The Active Directory lets a secure user and resource management environment be created that maps more effectively onto a corporation's organizational structure than NT 4 domains are able to. The key to a successful Active Directory implementation will be a thorough understanding of that organizational structure and how the users within it utilize infrastructure resources. If the transition to Active Directory from a Windows NT 4 domain structure is to involve the least disruption, the Windows NT 4 domain structure should be designed with the needs of the organization uppermost in consideration. The domain structure developed for MBI in the following sections does just that. A section at the end of the design shows how the Windows NT 4 domain structure for MBI might be migrated to Active Directory.

Domain Design

We will now take what we know about Windows NT domains and create a design for our case study, the Midas Bank International. We will do the design in two stages:

Stage 1. Determine the most appropriate domain architecture.

Stage 2. Work out where the domain controllers should be located, their required capacity and their configuration details.

Design principles are used throughout both stages to capture the key design decisions.

Before starting stage one, we will:

1. Define scope of a Windows NT domain design
2. Review the requirements on the design
3. Analyze the factors affecting our choices in terms of the common attributes

The specific attributes for domain design, listed in the introduction to this chapter have a direct bearing on stage one of the design and so will be discussed in that section.

Scope of a Windows NT Domain Design

A Windows NT domain design includes the following elements:

Table 11.3 *Windows NT Design Scope*

Topic	Elements
Domain Architecture	Logical domain structure showing: ▪ Master domains, resource domains and trusts ▪ How the architecture maps onto the corporate organizational structure ▪ How the architecture maps onto the corporate network ▪ Strategy for administration of user accounts and system resources
Implementation Guidelines	▪ Location, number and capacity of domain controllers ▪ Domain process settings
Domain Names	▪ Domain naming conventions (these are covered in Chapter 16, Naming Standards)
Migration Plan for getting to Windows NT 5 Active Directory	▪ Draft Active Directory based domain architecture ▪ Migration strategy

The last section of the design, the plan for getting to Active Directory, is particularly important if the design is going to position the organization well for the future.

Two topics intimately linked to the domain design are domain naming standards and how users are organized into Windows NT groups. For clarity they are each covered in separate chapters (16 and 12, respectively).

Requirements on the Design

For purpose of this case study we will draw on the business principles developed for MBI in Chapter 5 for most of our requirements, as it is their role in the design process we want to illustrate. The user requirements and application requirements listed below have been created for the purpose of this exercise.

User Requirements

Must offer a high degree of availability.

Application Requirements

For the new settlements application to be able to communicate from any office to any other office in the corporation there must be a single security environment. This is noted as an implication of MBI Business Principle 1.

Common Attributes

In the following sub-sections we discuss the way the common attributes influence the design of a domain structure.

Scalability

It is useful to define the distinction between two important attributes in the context of a domain design:

1. Capacity
2. Scalability

Capacity is the measure of how many users and resources can be added to the system before additional computers or domain entities (domains, domain controllers and trusts) are added. Scalability is the extent to which computers and domains can be added without breaking the original domain design. Indeed, we can tighten this definition further by demanding that the incremental impact of any additions to the structure is less than the impact from earlier additions. We could measure that impact in terms of domain process traffic or administrative overhead.

So, for example, as additional domain controllers are added, the design not only stays true to the original philosophy but administrative overhead grows in steadily decreasing amounts.

The best strategy for ensuring a scalable design is to envision a set of likely scenarios where the system capacity needs to be increased and to confirm that scaling is possible without negative consequences. Typical scenarios might include:

- Increase in user population at a particular location
- Addition of a new office location
- Addition of a new business unit—possibly through acquisition
- Expansion into a new geographic region

Each scalability scenario should be distilled into what it means in terms of the addition of:

- Domain controllers
- Resource domains
- Master domains

Worth noting at this juncture is that using this definition of scalability, the complete trust model fares badly due to its non-linear relationship between number of domains and complexity. The master domain models scale best with the single domain model coping reasonably well until its architectural limits are reached.

Reliability and Availability

The reliability and availability of a domain is effectively that of the service that performs SAM synchronization and authentication. This sevice is designed to continue functioning in the face of a degree of underlying computer and network infrastructure failure through use of multiple distributed computers, or domain controllers. Thus, a domain can offer a relatively high degree of availability by allowing authentication to take place using any of the backup domain controllers in a domain, eliminating dependence on any one computer and in some cases network link (network topology dependent).

By using several domain controllers, the domain effectively maintains several copies of the SAM, so corruption of one copy need not have devastating consequences, though repair would require manual intervention.

Manageability

Those who supervise the management and operation of a domain structure, while using privileged accounts, are still subject to the same restrictions imposed by the location of their account and the domain trust relationships. For that reason, the structure of the support organization should be considered alongside the structure of the business when choosing the domain architecture. Accommodation of management and operations requirements can lead to additional trust relationships being implemented in order to avoid the need for multiple accounts per administrator.

One of the most significant challenges in planning a domain architecture for manageability is how to plan for the administration of the user population. In master and multiple master domain configurations, where there are more resource domains than master domains, the common dilemma is whether to give an administrator from one of the resource domains rights to administrate accounts in the corresponding master domain.

The issue being that were they granted this right, they would automatically be able to administer the accounts of users associated with other resource domains. This may be considered a business risk if unauthorized interference with the account details of a user were to stop that user carrying out their job.

The decision on which technical option to choose has to be political and is related to the security of the domain structure. The technical options are as follows:

- If an administrator from a resource domain needs to be able to administer the user accounts of people using that domain but mustn't be given the ability to manage the accounts of users accessing other resource domains, then a new master domain could be created. This would have the drawback of introducing new trusts and will cause difficulties if BDCs are required in several offices to speed logon.
- Convert the resource domain to a combined master and resource domain. The result of this might be the introduction of several trusts to the new domain from other resource domains. This is the recommended option as it positions the structure well for migration to Windows NT 5 Active Directory.
- Wait until Windows NT 5 Active Directory where the granularity of control over user accounts is far greater than in Windows NT 4.
- Use a third party tool for "partitioning" the SAM so portions can be managed securely and independently.

If addressing this issue is likely to be contentious then a business principle should be sought and agreed upon, stating the level of administrative access different types of administrator should have over both resources and user accounts.

Security

A domain architecture provides the basic structure upon which a security plan can be implemented. While domains offer natural security boundaries and a well planned design can block access to resources by all but designated individuals, it is important to note that the default rights of administrators are sufficient to circumvent most security measures. It is therefore important that the domain design should be chosen to reinforce and complement other means of achieving the desired security arrangements, such as Windows NT groups and not be seen as the complete solution.

Capacity and Performance

Assuming unlimited network bandwidth, the capacity and performance of a windows NT domain structure is entirely dependent on the ability of the constituent domain controllers to replicate the SAM and process authentication requests. The level of system load this generates can be measured or calculated based on usage estimates. Published guidelines are available for system sizing (shown elsewhere in this chapter), though first hand experience of system performance in the environment you are planning for is more valuable. Unfortunately, we can never assume unlimited network bandwidth, in which case capacity and performance calculations become more complicated as we factor in the effect of limited capacity and potentially unreliable network links on the domain processes.

Note that although the domain controllers are sized appropriately, poor WAN connections will introduce bandwidth limitations and latency, both of which will contribute to poor domain performance. The main strategies for overcoming this are as follows:

- Minimize the number of replications occurring over the same WAN link. Another way of putting this is to ensure that the PDC for a domain is at the physical topological center of the section of network covered by that domain.
- Place backup domain controllers at appropriate positions on the network to maximize local authentication performance. Increasing the number of BDCs will cost more money and ultimately consume more bandwidth as replication traffic increases.
- Partition the account database into several master domains to reduce replication traffic involved with each domain. This will increase the number of trust relationships making the whole structure more complex to manage.
- Upgrade the WAN links.

Stage I: Choice of Architecture

In the introduction to this chapter we saw that four specific attributes were important in determining a domain design. We will now consider them in turn, analyzing how each affects the possible design. As a reminder, they are listed here with an overview of how they will be used to guide our choice of domain architecture:

- **Organization**—Using our knowledge of the corporation's organization structure we identify the most suitable domain architecture. This is done first so we stand the best chance of getting an architecture that matches the business.
- **Administration**—The needs of the IT Support organization are then considered, potentially modifying the working architecture.
- **Geography and Communications**—Physical constraints are then taken into account to end up with a proposed architecture that can be used in stage 2 (Implementation Guidelines) of the design.

A word of caution: while the following domain design exercise is presented as a sequential process, in practice it isn't as there are many interdependent factors involved. Constructing a domain design should be done in an iterative way, revisiting most aspects of design more than once.

Organization

An organization is a political structure, at the root of which is power over people and resources. The nature of organizational politics is that there is constant conflict and change. Thus, as we consider mapping a domain structure onto an organization we should expect the target to move and for arguments to ensue. Power usually increases as you go up an organization and for that reason it is vitally important that the business principles influencing domain design are created and sponsored by the highest authority if you are to stand a chance of getting a design decision to stick.

High Level Organizational Considerations

The organization of MBI is very fragmented culturally though there are reporting lines from the subsidiary head offices to the corporate head office (see Figure 11.17 for an abbreviated view of the organizational structure). Even if we ignore any potential organizational changes associated with the introduction of the new settlements application and the Windows NT infrastructure we must recognize that there will be a strong desire for the subsidiary head offices to maintain authority over their respective regional offices. We can say this because we know banks tend towards a very rigid hierarchical culture; other businesses will be different. This would suggest we should concentrate on the domain models offering a two tiered architecture, the single master and the multiple master.

There are four separate organizations within MBI so we have the following two options:

- four independent single master domain structures with the master domains being aligned to subsidiary and a resource domain allocated to each subsidiary office.
- an organizational multiple master model still with master domains aligned to subsidiary and a single resource domain per subsidiary business line.

Each of the subsidiaries is known to support one or other of these options as a way of supporting organizational independence.

On the other hand we know from MBI Business Principle 3, the intention of MBI management is to treat the corporation as a single organization and to avoid duplication of structures, which would suggest a more organizationally integrated model such as one based on a single master or geographic multiple master.

This is a classic case of conflicting priorities with the leadership stating how the organization should be treated, encouraging integration to achieve business goals, at odds with sections of the organization interested in maintaining organizational divisions.

To resolve this conflict we should refer to the business principles.

None of the MBI Business Principles support the long term maintenance of a divided organization. Instead, they recognize the corporate goal of an integrated organization (MBI Business Principle 3), though pointing out the need to recognize the authority of the subsidiaries during the transition (MBI Business Principle 5). MBI Business Principles can be found in Chapter 5.

Knowing that a domain structure is very hard to change once implemented, we should aim for a model that reflects the future state rather than the current or short term state. Thus, we should go with a domain model that brings the organization together. By anticipating this potential political conflict at the business principle creation stage of the project the MBI technical architect was able to encourage the development of business principles that would resolve the conflict when it arose.

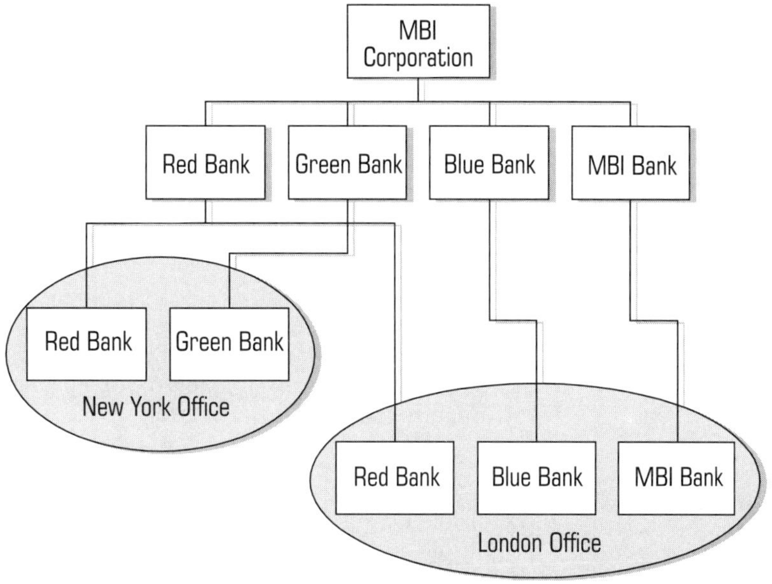

Figure 11.17 *Abbreviated Organizational Structure of MBI*

We must now decide between a single master or a geographic multiple master. The decision needs to take into account the following two factors:

1. Whether the organization has a small number of natural top level geographically aligned organizational units.
2. Whether the network discourages a single master through bandwidth limitations or size of SAM.

We will consider the second factor later in the chapter. Dealing with the first factor is not usually difficult, though in the case of MBI the corporation is about to undergo a major organizational change so the question is harder to answer. We shall assume for the purpose of the case study that MBI plans to introduce a high level regional reporting structure so we should feel comfortable going with a geographic multiple master at this stage.

It is important to note that due to the lack of ability to organize hierarchical control of resources and users in NT 4 domains, the benefit of aligning master domains to geographic reporting entities is limited. However, it does make sense from a broad organizational ownership perspective. Clearly consultation with MBI management is essential here if we are to use the correct geographic regions. See the earlier section entitled Geographic Master in this chapter for a general description of the basic model identified by this design principle.

Design Principle 11-1—Geographic Multiple Master Domain Model
MBI will use a Geographic Multiple Master Domain model.
Justification
▪ Master domains can be aligned to the regional reporting centers for the purpose of administrative control. ▪ Use of multiple master domains ensures that in the unlikely event one suffers a problem such as the PDC failing, only a fraction of the workforce faces the higher risk of service interruption. ▪ MBI is already a global organization and this is unlikely to change suggesting that this choice will lead to a stable design. A domain model based on aligning master domains to organization may suffer change as the organization changes structure.
Implications
▪ A multiple master model leads to many trust relationships. ▪ A multiple master model leads to many groups and group memberships. ▪ A group usage policy should be created to ensure that confusion and mistakes do not arise through administration of groups. ▪ A plan for migrating this domain model to Microsoft Windows NT 5 Active Directory should be drawn up to confirm that the migration may happen smoothly.
Issues

Authority Over User Accounts

To confirm that the geographic multiple master is going to be satisfactory, we need to consider how we are going to allow the subsidiaries, for the limited time that they will exist, the level of control over user accounts they have been denied through the choice of this domain model. Giving an organizational unit direct control over its own user accounts can be done in two ways.

1. First, put the user accounts in the local domain.

   This option potentially breaks the domain model and requires additional trusts to be set up if it is necessary to allow users to logon at workstations in other domains and to share resources across domains.

2. Give local administrators the rights to administer the account database on the appropriate master domain.

The second option will give an administrator from a local resource domain control over *all* the accounts in a master domain SAM even though the intention is to give them control over a subset of those accounts. This is because access to the SAM in a domain cannot be partitioned. Note that there are third party tools available for allowing administrators to be given access to portions of the SAM to solve this exact issue.

MBI chose to reject both these options and settle for the compromise of placing the direct administration of users' accounts in the hands of the emerging unified IT Support. They also began a procedure for local offices to exercise *indirect control* over their users' accounts by formally requesting actions of the IT Support group. The decision to adopt this approach was taken after recognizing that giving organizational units direct control of their users' accounts would end up duplicating systems and processes, going against one of the business principles and working against the integration of the organization.

The reader might like to review the two business principles referred to in this design element and reflect on the need for careful wording to convey the required intentions and priorities. Note the phrasing in implications 1 and 2, Business Principle 5 where they say "or a suitable administrative procedure to do so." Without these clauses we would not be able to resolve the design decision in business terms using the existing business principles.

Authority Over Resources

Having confirmed the Geographic Multiple Master as a starting point, we can now look at how the resource domains should be allocated by studying the authority desired by organizational units over their resources.

The main influences on the allocation of resource domains in this case study are two business principles:

- MBI Business Principle 5 points to the need to continue to recognize the authority of subsidiaries and regional offices over their own user accounts and resources.
- MBI Business Principle 3 encourages the treatment of MBI as a single integrated organization with no duplicated systems.

Although in the preceding section we spoke of subsidiary offices and their need to control user accounts, we have not committed ourselves to aligning a resource domain with a subsidiary office. We are therefore free to determine how to align resource domains according to the needs of an organizational unit to control its own resources.

To get a clearer idea of what we are dealing with let us remind ourselves of what we know:

- In many cities around the world MBI maintains more than one subsidiary office.
- Consistent with the MBI Business Principles, we also know that in cities where there is more than one subsidiary office, there are plans to integrate them into one single MBI office, dissolving the identity and organization structure of the subsidiaries.
- Until the organizational integration takes place, it must be possible to recognize the authority of a subsidiary over its resources.
- Although we are dealing with an organization in transition from one structure to another, domains are relatively inflexible structures.

The last point is critically important and is the same one that led us to choose a geographic multiple master model instead of an organizational multiple master. We took guidance from the MBI Business Principles and chose an architecture for the future, adopting a strategy of accepting some short term pain for a longer term gain. We must therefore do the same again here. We should not default to aligning resource domains with subsidiary offices simply because it may be the best option at the present. We should look to what is the best option for the future. With that in mind, let us now try to define what an organizational unit will be in the future. Several options present themselves:

1. A continent or region
2. A country
3. A city
4. A subsidiary office

There is no simple formula for choosing between these options as the choice is intimately tied to the organization the domain structure is there to serve. Each option is examined for its relevance to MBI.

If we went with the first option, the resource domains would effectively be aligned one to one with the master domains. This would not be an unreasonable approach, but it may not be the best solution for MBI as we would be ignoring the opportunity to exploit the greater granularity presented by resource domains.

For MBI a country is synonymous with city except in the U.S.A. So, we may as well consider the second and third options as equivalent. With the merger of the offices in each city, MBI intend to have each city report to the geographic head office. Thus, a city will become a well defined organizational unit. Until the office mergers, however, some resource domains will need to span the offices of several subsidiaries. The communications implications of this are discussed later in the chapter.

If resource domains are allocated to existing offices as suggested in the fourth option we will be presented with a migration exercise when MBI merges them into single offices. Another downside would be that a far greater number of trusts would have to be set up to connect the greater number of resource domains.

Overall the third option appears the best fit so we can complement the previous design principle:

Design Principle 11-2—Allocation of Resource Domains
There will be one resource domain per city.
Justification
▪ A city will become a well defined organizational unit after the MBI organizational integration. ▪ Although a single resource domain may be shared by several subsidiaries, control over their own resources may be granted to them using Windows NT groups.
Implications
▪ Dedicating a resource domain to a city that has very few MBI employees would be relatively costly.
Issues

How are we going to address the interim need for subsidiary offices to exert some sort of control over their own resources? The answer lies with the use of Windows NT groups to govern access to resources. Groups are far more simple to create, delete, or change membership of than domains are to change. So, providing groups meet the need, they can compensate for the domain design in the short term.

Refer to Chapter 12, Windows NT Groups, to see how this has been done for MBI.

What Other Domain Architecture Could We Have Chosen?

The management of MBI has decided to combine their diverse organizations into one. This will of course take time though it is clear that we should put in a domain architecture to support this intention. So what other choices were there?

Single Domain

For

- This would have been the simplest option conceptually, although the same amount of consideration would be needed to plan resource and user account administration as for any other domain model.
- There will be none of the complexities of managing the implications of trust relationships such as cross domain group memberships.

Against

- The use of a single SAM for an organization this size (see Table 11.3 for population) would risk constraining business expansion by reaching physical SAM size limitations.
- We should also note that as MBI is a highly dispersed organization, using just one account domain would be the worst option in terms of SAM replication traffic over the WAN.

Single Master

For

- Even though it is aiming to be a single, integrated organization, MBI will remain hierarchical, treating cities as its highest level organizational unit. As we saw in the preceding arguments, resource domains were judged appropriate for devolving responsibility for the management of local resources to the city based organizational units, making the single master domain model preferable to the single domain model.

Against

- This model suffers the same drawbacks of using a single SAM as the single domain model.

Complete Trust

For

- A complete trust model would have given organizational units complete control over their own resources and user accounts.

Against

- If any domain model is designed to support divisions within a business, this is it. It would probably have been supported by some of the MBI subsidiary offices but it doesn't help achieve the goals of the business or support the MBI Business Principles.

Organization and Active Directory

The discussion above illustrates a fundamental conflict that is common in many organizations. The top down view of the organization presented by its leaders tends to want to suppress the natural inclination for independence among the constituent business groupings. The argument reveals itself when an attempt is made to align with the organization the instrument of power, the domain. While Windows NT 4 based domains present restrictions on what can be implemented (mainly to do with its limit of a two level domain hierarchy), they are largely in the area of administration. The issue we are dealing with here is a fundamentally political one that does not go away with Active Directory domains.

The way forward is to develop a clear view of an organization to start with. Windows NT 4 domains should be aligned with this view as best possible and subsequent migration to Active Directory will improve the alignment by offering a greater level of domain hierarchy.

Administration

What we are interested in here is how the structure of a corporation's IT Support organization places demands on the domain architecture. This is closely related to the previous section again because we are considering the way an organization influences the domain architecture but we need to consider the topic separately as it is not uncommon for the IT Support organization to be distinct from or poorly aligned to business groups. We shall consider the responsibilities of the IT Support function as user account management, resource management, systems management and support services.

The MBI Business Principles say nothing specific about administration of the technical infrastructure and only a little about support so we shall examine what little we do know. We know that in the current state of MBI, there are separate IT Support organizations, one for each subsidiary bank. We also know, based on the implications of MBI Business Principles 2 and 3, that the IT Support organization will have to become more of an integrated service to cope with the new technical infrastructure.

The model favored after considering the business organization was one based on a geographic multiple master, which would suit an IT Support organization split along geographic lines. As the intention is to draw the support organizations together into one, it is doubtful then whether the geographic multiple master is the optimum target architecture from the IT Support perspective. If we wish to design a system that allows the support infrastructure to grow into one cohesive unit we might look at adopting the management master domain model, bringing together all support staff under one domain. This model would make it easier to control who gets rights to administer what.

Having argued thus far, we could make a recommendation as to which approach to take, but we should be ready to admit that we really need more guidance in terms of how the business wants to run its IT Support organization. This is an important admission and it should force us to go back to the relevant business leaders and enlist their assistance in completing our design. We should conclude from this that our set of business principles is incomplete. With hindsight, we should have encouraged the development of a business principle on the subject of the support organization. Indeed, we should have ensured that support was adequately identified as within the scope of the project.

The table offering suggested topics for project scope areas and business principles contained in Chapter 7, Developing Principles, can of course be used to help avoid omissions such as this. The other way of increasing the chances of a complete set of principles first time around is to have already thought through the design process some of the way. By doing that, questions arise that should be pointers to the need for appropriate business principles.

Assuming the Management Master Domain is appropriate we can assert the following design principle.

Design Principle 11-3—Use of a Management Master Domain
▪ The accounts for all administrative staff will be created in a dedicated master domain.
Justification
▪ Although MBI has three regional reporting centers, each needing control over the resources of its region, MBI plans to have a single global support organization. By grouping the administrative users' accounts in one domain greater control is possible.
Implications
▪ An additional master domain will mean more trust relationships. ▪ High degree of dependence on the continued functioning of this domain for administrative users to be able to carry out their jobs. ▪ The group usage policy should include groups in the management master domain.
Issues

We're making progress but we still don't know:

- How many master domains we are going to have, or where they will be located.
- Whether there will be a role for an IT Support Resource Domain.
- Any computer configuration details.

Geography and Communications

So far we have concentrated on choosing a domain architecture that was right for the structure of the business and its IT Support organization. We now need to begin considering the effect the geographic distribution and communication links have on this proposed architecture.

When organizations are split geographically it is usual to find that along with the split goes a division of autonomy such that there is overlap in infrastructure functions from one site to the next. The fundamental reasons for this are communications and the need for human intervention on a local scale (e.g., to do things such as move computers around).

It is clear that the geographic distribution of an organization and its communications infrastructure are inextricably linked, hence their treatment together here. We will also see that while geography and communications influence domain architecture they also heavily influence the detailed domain design that follows.

Existing and Planned Communications Infrastructure

MBI currently has a far from optimal network, based as it is on what it inherited from its subsidiaries. Figure 11.18, Planned MBI WAN Design, shows the network topology recommended by a team of external consultants. Key aspects are a rationalization into four principle hubs, one for the USA, one for Asia and two for Europe. Also important to note are the dual routes between three of the four hubs.

Based on the domain architecture developed in the preceding sections the master domain or domains should be allocated on a geographic basis. This means we have the immediate possibility that we could choose to go with four regional master domains plus a management master domain:

- New York
- London
- Paris
- Singapore
- Management (location to be determined)

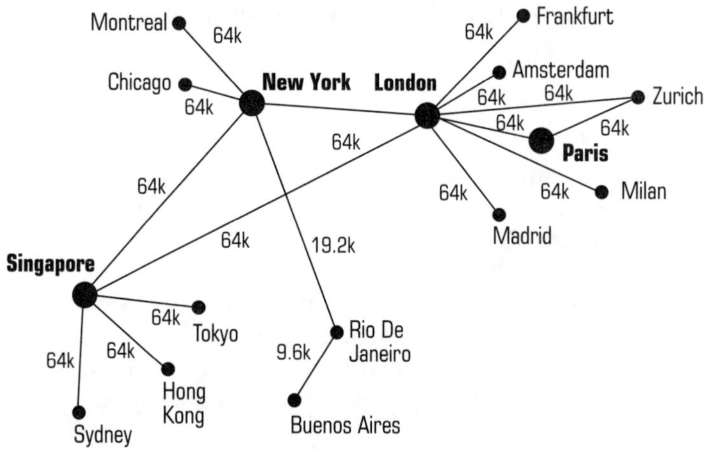

Figure 11.18 *Planned MBI WAN Design*

Confirmation would be needed that the location of these network hubs reflected the location of the planned regional administrative centers. One problem remains however. There is political lobbying to have the Asian master domain located in Tokyo rather than Singapore.

From the diagram we can see that Tokyo is not one of the network hubs and on our evidence is not even a regional administrative site. While our immediate reaction might be to dismiss this on technical grounds we should look at the implications of this suggestion and be prepared to make a recommendation where the regional master domain should be located, based on technical criteria. We should be clear where our responsibilities lie as technical architects. They don't usually extend to resolving political issues like this. The evidence to support a recommendation for where the Asian master domain will be located will be found when we work through stage 2 of the domain design process.

Application Requirements

MBI Business Principle 4 states the requirement for the proposed applications to allow swift movement into new markets wherever they emerge. The business analysts have deduced that for an application to achieve this, the technical infrastructure must provide support by allowing a user access from any workstation to any other application server or database on the network. This directly translates into ensuring every resource domain trusts every master domain. This should be captured in a design principle as shown below to guard against any urge to omit trusts.

Design Principle 11-4—Trust Relationships
All resource domains will trust all master domains.
Justification
▪ They are required to allow users to move from one office to another and still be able to logon and access their home information. ▪ They are required to allow full resource sharing across resource domains should the permissions be granted.
Implications
▪ No opportunity to partition model using trusts to enhance security. ▪ This is a consistent design. The simplicity this gives will help reduce the likelihood of errors.
Issues
▪ Need to ensure there are no security issues imposed by regulatory requirements or commercial secrecy.

Summary of the Proposed Domain Architecture (Stage I)

The existing infrastructure in MBI has not placed any significant constraint on our domain architecture.

The current organizational structure threatened to influence our design significantly. However, the existence of MBI Business Principles supporting a more integrated organization allowed us to design for the future without ignoring the existing state. Planning for the merger of the various distinct IT Support groups into one cohesive global organization was accounted for by including a single, world-wide dedicated master domain.

The geographic structure of MBI encouraged a multiple master model, with resource domains mapping onto a location, or city, ensuring local control of resources directly and control of user accounts through administrative procedures. Recognition of the need by subsidiary offices to control their own resources in the interim before corporate integration will be done using groups.

The requirement that the new application be global has been translated in its analysis and design, to a requirement that resources anywhere in the infrastructure should be accessible from anywhere else. This requirement has determined that no trusts be omitted from the multiple master domain model.

Note, the management master domain is called Admin according to the domain naming standard developed for MBI in Chapter 16.

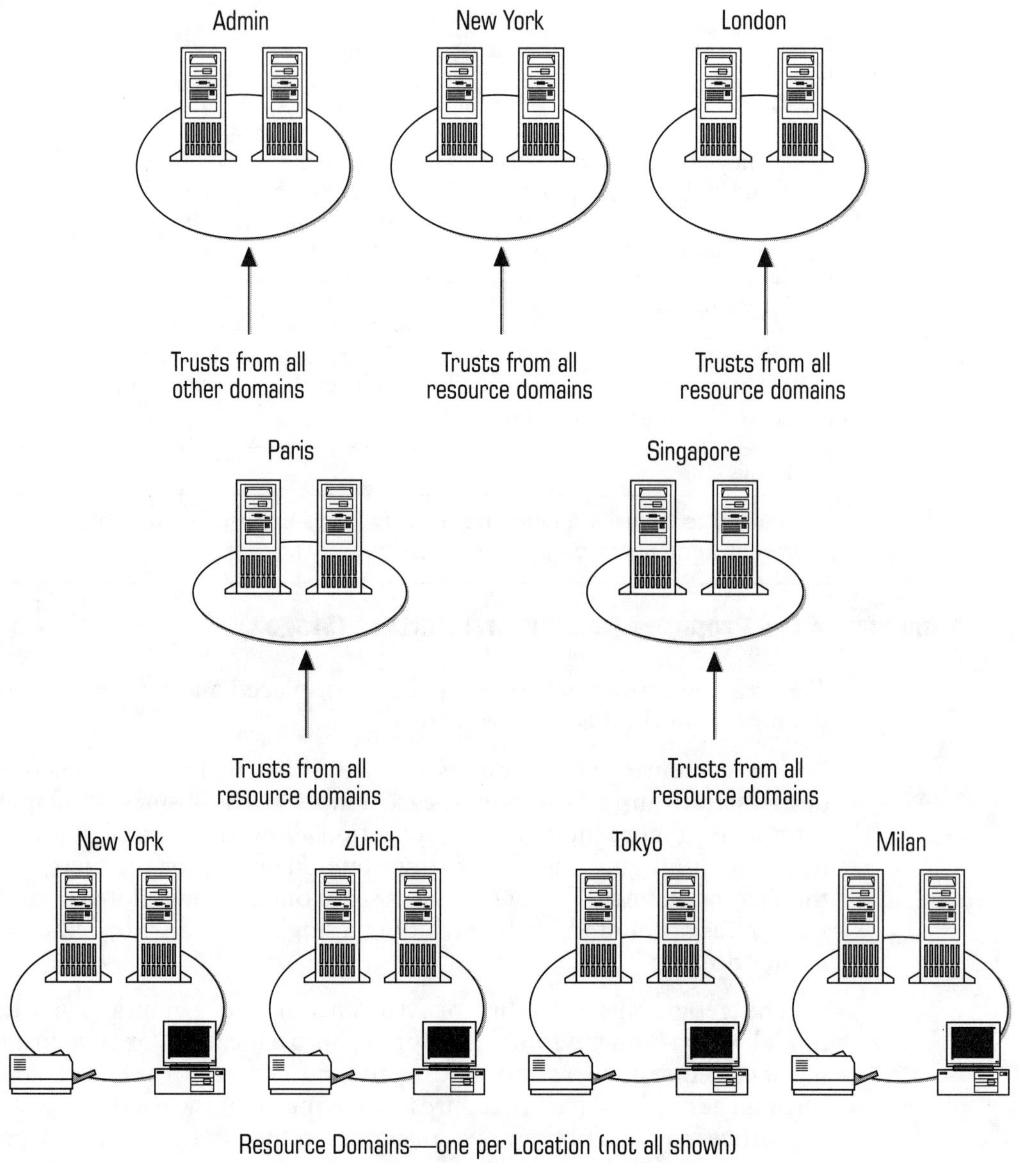

Figure 11.19 *Proposed MBI Domain Architecture from Stage 1*

Stage 2: Implementation Guidelines

At this point we have a proposed domain architecture that is a geographic multiple master with four master domains plus another master domain for hosting the accounts of the IT Support staff to reflect the plans to combine the support organizations throughout the bank. What we need to work out now is the physical implementation details of this domain architecture. We will do this in the following way:

1. Determine domain controller locations
2. Calculate resulting domain process traffic
3. Calculate computer capacity required
4. Decide any special domain process settings

Throughout this process we need to be confirming whether the domain architecture proposed in stage 1 of the design process is suitable for the physical characteristics of the deployment environment. The principle considerations on this point are the WAN bandwidth and topology. The use of an IT Support resource domain needs to be considered and lastly, for the purpose of the example, we need to study the request to have the regional master domain for Asia located in Tokyo.

Domain Controller Locations

The recommended way to decide PDC and BDC locations is by starting with what we are most certain of and working through the design. This way, as we make decisions we narrow down the options in front of us, simplifying the job.

Co-locating a BDC with a PDC

We can start with the obvious need to put a master domain primary domain controller in each of the master domain locations. The need for a backup domain controller located next to each primary domain controller is a trade-off of cost against availability. This is a business decision so we should look either to the business principles or a statement on availability based on the needs of the administrative function.

If a master domain has several backup domain controllers deployed, one per city to allow for higher performance, local authentication, and authorization then the need for a backup domain controller co-located with the primary domain controller for availability is reduced. However, should a primary domain controller fail and the recovery strategy is to promote a backup domain controller, the master domain could effectively "move" to another location which may be less suitable for communications related reasons. A co-located BDC would allow that computer to be promoted to a PDC without disturbing the way the domain processes map onto the network.

None of the MBI business principles say anything about availability. However, one of the requirements highlighted for the purpose of the case study states a need for it.

Design Principle 11-5—The need for a co-located BDC
A master domain PDC will have a co-located BDC.
Justification
▪ The BDC can be promoted to a PDC should the PDC ever be out of action for an extended period of time.
Implications
▪ A procedure needs to be established for dealing with the failure of the PDC and just as importantly, its subsequent recovery.
Issues

For many business situations we would expect to see a business principle making a statement about availability.

Master Domain BDCs Deployed at Each Location

We could consider placing a BDC from each of the four master domains in each location or city. We would do this if we thought there would be a high degree of cross master domain resource access or many users traveling to and logging on in offices aligned to other master domains. No statement of such a requirement has been made during the MBI data gathering exercise so the bank chose not to go for this costly option.

Design Principle 11-6—Location of Master Domain BDCs
▪ There will be a single BDC from the regional master domain per location.
Justification
▪ Minimizes logon time. ▪ Minimizes dependence on the WAN link for logon authentication. ▪ BDCs from other master domains would rarely get used, making their deployment uneconomical.

continued▸

continued

Implications
■ A visitor from another region will probably experience slower logon than someone who has their account in the local regional master domain.
Issues
■ Small sites may find it difficult to provide a secure environment for the BDC.

No functionality is lost with this decision, it just affects the degree to which user mobility can be supported easily.

Resource Domain Controllers

Each resource domain will need a PDC but we need to determine whether BDCs are required. In the case of MBI, as with many other organizations, there will be a number of file, print, and application servers at each office, any of which could carry out the role of resource domain BDC. Thus, we can easily require that there be one computer adopting the role of resource domain BDC in each office.

Design Principle 11-7—Domain Controller Locations
There will be a single non-dedicated BDC for the local resource domain co-located with the PDC.
Justification
■ To enhance overall availability. ■ There is no extra cost as the resource domain BDC may be used for general resource serving.
Implications
■ A procedure needs to be established for dealing with the failure of the PDC and just as importantly, its subsequent recovery.
Issues

Physically Housing the Domain Controllers

Given our need for high availability we should ensure that all domain controllers are secure from any physical tampering, deliberate or accidental, which might cause a malfunction.

Design Principle 11-8—Use of secure computer rooms
Domain controllers will be located in a secure computer room.
Justification
■ More secure from physical tampering or console access.
Implications
■ Access to the secure computer room will need to be provided to those whose task it would be to recover a domain controller from a failure.
Issues

MBI has chosen to implement a master domain for the IT Support group user accounts, so must identify a location for the PDC. New York appears central from the point of view of the network topology so that is where the PDC will go. The location of BDCs for this domain depends on where the IT Support staff will be working.

MBI plans to have IT Support teams located at each master domain site to better address the need to local language capability and the different time zones, so there should be BDCs in New York, London, Paris and Singapore.

Domain Process Traffic

We should treat this part of the design process as an exercise in confirming the proposed domain controller deployment developed in the preceding section. In this example we have chosen to compare the domain process traffic associated with two alternate scenarios to illustrate the impact of different deployment strategies. However, in practice, it is usually sufficient to calculate the traffic associated with just the proposed scenario.

The two scenarios are:

1. Assuming there are no local master domain BDCs:

This will involve calculation of the remote logon and resource authorization traffic.

2. Assuming there is a local master domain BDC:

   This will involve calculation of the SAM replication traffic to the local BDC.

Lastly we look at the figures we have and try to apply them as realistically as possible. Cost of computer and cost of network will be the financial trade-off for a given level of performance.

For both calculations we will need to know the user populations at each site. Table 11.4 summarizes the population information.

Table 11.4 *Population Distribution of MBI*

Location	Population	Location	Population
London	1740	Singapore	370
New York	2880	Tokyo	90
Paris	550	Hong Kong	175
Frankfurt	540	Sydney	50
Milan	50	Chicago	200
Amsterdam	75	Montreal	440
Madrid	350	Rio De Janeiro	200
Zurich	550	Buenos Aires	5

High quality low cost network bandwidth is becoming easier to obtain throughout the world, with the USA and Europe leading the way. In some parts of the world, however, it is still difficult to obtain leased lines or phone lines of sufficient quality to deliver a reasonable fraction of the bandwidth of what is considered normal on these two continents. The calculation we are about to perform is therefore much more relevant when we are dealing with regions of poor WAN connectivity. Note also that in some cases the leased lines to regions of poor connectivity carry both voice and data, reducing the bandwidth available for data traffic further.

It is worth recognizing that the increasing availability of high speed communications lines is being matched by the demands of the software organizations are beginning to use, Web technology being the most notable. Thus, even if there is a good network link, the bandwidth available for non-application traffic such as domain controller replication may still be low.

The following example assumes the full bandwidth is available to domain traffic. In practice we could be dealing with as low as 25% of the total bandwidth.

Assuming no Local BDCs

We should do this calculation for each site, however for brevity will concentrate on just one, Rio de Janeiro. The PDC for Rio de Janeiro's regional master domain is in New York and the two sites are linked by a 19.2kbps line.

Assumptions: 10kb / logon
10kb / share or printer connection
Each person makes C connections / day
Each person makes one logon / day

Note: The assumptions for logon and share connection are made for illustration only. As Windows NT is enhanced values for these mechanisms may change. Always consult the latest Microsoft reference material.

To generalize, if the number of people at a site is P, then the daily domain process traffic is:

$$10 \times P + 10 \times (P \times C)\text{kbytes or } 10 \times P \times (C + 1) \text{ kbytes}$$

If we say P is 200 for Rio de Janeiro and C is 3 we get a figure of 8MB.

The 19.2kbps line has a bandwidth of roughly 2kbytes/sec (if we're lucky) which would take 8MB/2kb = 4000 seconds or approximately just over one hour. Consider that in the region of 50% of logon activity takes place between 8:30 and 9:30 and if all three network connections were to different servers and all set up in the logon script then we are likely to have a problem with logon performance.

Note that if a user who normally works in one office, logs on from another office it is possible that their profile will be downloaded from a remote server as part of the logon process. User profiles can grow to a significant size with up to 1MB being possible though between 100kbytes and 300kbytes would be more common, so careful planning should be carried out to ensure files of this size are not sent across a slow network link. Note that we are assuming user profiles are stored locally for this example.

The problem would be even worse if applications needed to use the communications line as well. It is worth considering what bandwidth we might require if we were determined not to use a local BDC. If we set a target of a maximum of 30% utilization for the network link (to ensure reasonable response times) and estimate that application related data traffic uses about 20% of the total bandwidth then we are looking at a network link with ten times the capacity of the one in our example, or 200kb/sec.

Assuming Local BDCs

Continuing with the Rio de Janeiro example, let us now assume we have a BDC from the New York regional master domain located in the Rio de Janeiro office. This machine can now authenticate users and authorize access to resources. The issue now becomes one of how much traffic is generated by SAM replication.

The replication traffic crossing the Rio de Janeiro/New York link will be made up of the aggregate account changes for the entire North America master domain, which numbers 3745 users. We need an estimate for how frequently account details change. Let us say that we can ignore anything other than routine forced password changes, so assuming a password lifetime of 20 days there will be approximately 3745/20 = 187 changes per day. We shall estimate the number of NT Group changes at 10 per day.

Table 11.5 *Account Database Entry Sizes*

Element	Account Database Entry Size
User	1kb
Global group	512 bytes + 12 bytes per user
Local group	512 bytes + 36 bytes per user
Computer	512 bytes

Assuming each user record represents about 1kb in the SAM (from Table 11.5) the replication will involve 187kb of data, add to this the group changes at 4kb each the total is approximately 230kb/day. This is substantially smaller than the volumes estimated for using a remote BDC and is therefore more practical over such a low speed line, particularly as we can schedule the synchronization to a time of day when the network is not likely to be heavily used.

Remember that when a BDC is set up for the first time the whole SAM will be sent from the PDC with potentially serious network consequences over slow WAN links.

Deciding BDC Locations

The case for a master domain BDC at the Rio de Janeiro site is convincing. For the sake of the case study we shall assume that there will be similarly convincing arguments for all the other sites except Buenos Aires, which is connected to New York via Rio De Janeiro. Let us look at Buenos Aires in more detail. Refer to Figure 11.18, Planned MBI WAN, to see the planned network topology.

Assuming Rio De Janeiro has a BDC we are left with several options:

1. **Use the Rio De Janeiro master domain BDC**—Logging on at Buenos Aires using the Rio BDC will generate about 2.5% (as the population at Buenos Aires is 2.5% that of Rio De Janeiro—5×100/200) of the traffic (200kb) estimated for Chicago to be carried over a link with 50% the capacity. The total transfer time would amount to about three minutes.
2. **Put a master domain BDC in Buenos Aires**—The 230kb synchronization traffic from the New York PDC would need to travel twice over the New York to Rio link and once over the Rio to Buenos Aires link. The transfer would take in the region of four minutes on the Rio to Buenos Aires WAN link.
3. **Not be part of the domain structure**—For such a small office not accustomed to the features of a domain it may be debatable whether being part of one is beneficial. The need would be driven by the requirements of an application such as the new settlements system or e-mail. If there weren't a compelling need for a permanent connection to the domain structure then Buenos Aires could be set up as a workgroup with a system of dial-up access to the rest of the infrastructure that can be used when connectivity is required.

The MBI Business Principle identified in the Naming Services chapter stating that application traffic must have priority over infrastructure traffic led to a design principle in that chapter which said that WINS replication traffic should not travel over the same network link more than once. If MBI were to apply the same type of principles to domain synchronization traffic then on that basis option 2 must be rejected.

We should also consider the nature of the network traffic and the impact on the user. In particular, the logon traffic for each user, about 40kb (using the formula above and assuming three network and printer connections set up upon logon), will take about 40 seconds over the 9.6 kb line making logon an impractically slow process. In an artificial worst case scenario if only 25% of the bandwidth were available for logon traffic and all five people were logging on simultaneously the time to logon would stretch out to 40 × 4 × 5 = 800 seconds or 13 minutes for each user. This is compared to what might be two or three seconds if carried out with a local BDC.

Thus, options 1 and 2 may not be suitable, each for a different reason, leaving option 3 as looking like the only alternative. Before reaching this conclusion we should check whether treating Buenos Aires as a workgroup is going to go against any requirements or MBI Business Principles. Indeed, the application requirement, captured in an implication of MBI Business Principle 1, that all locations must be effectively in a single security environment means that Buenos Aires must be a domain or be part of the Rio domain trusting the other master domains. The only course of action therefore is to recommend the installation of a suitable high speed communications link between Buenos Aires and New York.

This type of conclusion is a good candidate for a design principle stating the minimum network bandwidth that must be available, after business traffic has been discounted, for a location to be a part of the corporate security environment. An example design principle (B-20) is shown in Appendix B. This way we can set out a rule, supported by an argument rooted in the business priorities.

Computer Capacities

Now we know where all the domain controllers will be located we can calculate the capacity of each computer based on the size of the SAM it holds. The size of the SAM can be calculated using the information in Table 11.6 for the corporate population distribution and the information in Table 11.5 for SAM record sizes. Once the SAM size is known the recommended computer configuration can be found in Table 11.6.

Table 11.6 *Server Recommendation for a Given SAM Size*

SAM (MB)	User Accounts	CPU	Memory (MB)
5	3000	486DX/33	32
10	7,500	486DX/66	32
15	10,000	Alpha, MIPS, Pentium	48
20	15,000	Alpha, MIPS, Pentium	64
30	20,000-30,000	Alpha, MIPS, Pentium	96
40	30,000-40,000	Alpha, MIPS, Pentium	128

This table lists the Microsoft guidelines. An important consideration when sizing computers is the amount of capacity left for expansion. MBI chose to allow for a 100% increase in usage and recorded the guideline as a design principle (B-18), shown in Appendix B.

Domain Process Settings

The previous section involved some rough calculations of domain process data transfer requirements over a WAN connection. One of the main unstated assumptions was that the data would be transferred continuously using the full network bandwidth until it was complete. While Windows NT Server will attempt to do this by default, this is not very desirable as the network will be being used for other purposes, not least of which will be real work. Thus, the domain synchronization data transfer will take longer than estimated and in all likelihood adversely affect the performance of other applications.

We can reduce its impact by tuning the computer settings controlling the synchronization process. This is referred to as *governing* the transfer. Care must be taken to ensure that synchronization occurs faster than SAM updates otherwise the BDCs will lag the PDC. This will eventually lead to the SAM change log filling up on the PDC triggering a full SAM replication. Over a slow WAN connection this would be undesirable.

Let us consider governing the SAM synchronization over the New York to Buenos Aires WAN connection. Assuming the quantity of data to transfer is 256kb per day (slightly more than the 230kb in the example above), with no governing the domain controllers would attempt to transfer the data over the 9.6kb line in 128kb chunks as fast as possible!

Setting the governor to 50% would mean that the buffer would be reduced to 64kb and there would be an outstanding request on the network 50% of the time. This is still too dramatic, the following table shows how throttling the process further might help:

Table 11.7 *Governing SAM Synchronization for Buenos Aires (9.6 line)*

Governor %	Buffer Size	Time per Buffer	Total Time
100	128kb	~128 secs	~256 secs
50	64kb	~64 secs	~512 secs
25	32kb	~32 secs	~1024 secs
12	16kb	~16 secs	~2048 secs
6	8kb	~8 secs	~4096 secs

For such a low speed connection we should be aiming to minimize the impact of SAM synchronization. On the evidence in Table 11.7 we should set the governor at a low value to smooth out the data transfer.

Tidying up the Design

It would be unusual to arrive at the end of stage 2 with a complete design and no loose ends to tidy up. Let us take stock of the MBI design to see where we need to apply a bit more effort to conclude our work. We will study:

- The desire for the Tokyo office to host the regional master domain PDC.
- The optimum number of regional master domains required.
- The need for an IT Support Domain.

Locating Master Domain PDC in Tokyo

We know that Tokyo wants to host the regional master domain PDC, however we went ahead and specified it should be located in Singapore based on the WAN topology in the region. We should analyze this issue further to help the business understand the implications of using Tokyo as the alternate PDC location. If the regional master domain PDC were located in Tokyo and the WAN topology remained the same the following would be true:

- Loss of the Singapore to Tokyo network link would mean the SAM could not be updated in any way from Singapore, Sydney, or Hong Kong.
- SAM synchronization traffic to Hong Kong, Sydney and Singapore each has to travel down the Tokyo to Singapore network link, effectively tripling the synchronization traffic compared to siting the master domain PDC in Singapore.
- If the support group administering the master domain were located in Singapore, then all domain related admin traffic would have to take place over the WAN.

The above points should be supported by a quantitative analysis of the likely WAN traffic. The recommendation is that the regional master domain PDC be located in Singapore all the time the WAN topology is as planned in Figure 11.18, Planned MBI WAN Design. If the PDC needs to be located in Tokyo then the backbone WAN links from New York and London to Singapore should instead connect to Tokyo. Master domain administration should preferably be local to the PDC so this function should move also.

Optimizing Number of Regional Master Domains

In stage 1 of the design we made an assumption that the network hubs would be the right locations for our master domain PDCs. This is sound, however we don't have to map a master domain onto every network hub. Taking a closer look at the WAN topology we can see that London has the same capacity direct WAN connection to each of the locations Paris might serve, rendering the need for the Paris based regional master domain on technical grounds redundant.

It would be natural for the WAN topology to be an abstract of the corporate structure, particularly in this case as the topology we are considering is a proposal for the new, re-organized MBI. Thus, we shouldn't dismiss the concept of a Paris based regional master domain out of hand as to have one might suit the planned corporate organizational structure. This decision should be made in conjunction with the business.

Need for an IT Support Domain

The concept of an IT Support domain was introduced during the discussion about different domain models. Its function is to group all computers running infrastructure services that don't directly serve a user, into one domain. This brings several advantages which are shown listed as justifications for the design principle below.

Design Principle 11-9—The Need for an IT Support Domain
All WINS, DHCP, SMS servers and management workstations will be members of a separate IT Support resource domain, trusting each master domain.
Justification
▪ By ensuring the infrastructure services run on computers in their own resource domain tighter control is allowed over who can do what to a computer. This makes it easier to maintain a consistent and predictable environment, keeping management requirements down. This supports MBI Business Principle 4. ▪ The objective of MBI is to run an integrated support group. By collecting all infrastructure servers together in one domain, allowing a clear differentiation between infrastructure servers and resource servers, this is made easier. ▪ Less senior or experienced IT Support staff may be granted greater rights in the IT Support domain than could safely be done in the production domains containing the resource servers. ▪ Heavy processing or IO access on the IT Support domain server will not impact users accessing general resource servers. ▪ Guarantees a single security environment for the services that need it.

continued▸

continued

Implications
▪ More trusts to administer. ▪ In a smaller location, the use of an IT Support domain server may result in more hardware being required.
Issues

MBI chose to use the IT Support domain primarily because it was seen as a way of keeping the infrastructure services organized and management requirements down.

Final Domain Design

For the final MBI domain design we shall assume that after consultation with the business it was decided that there was no reason to have a Paris based regional master domain in addition to the London one.

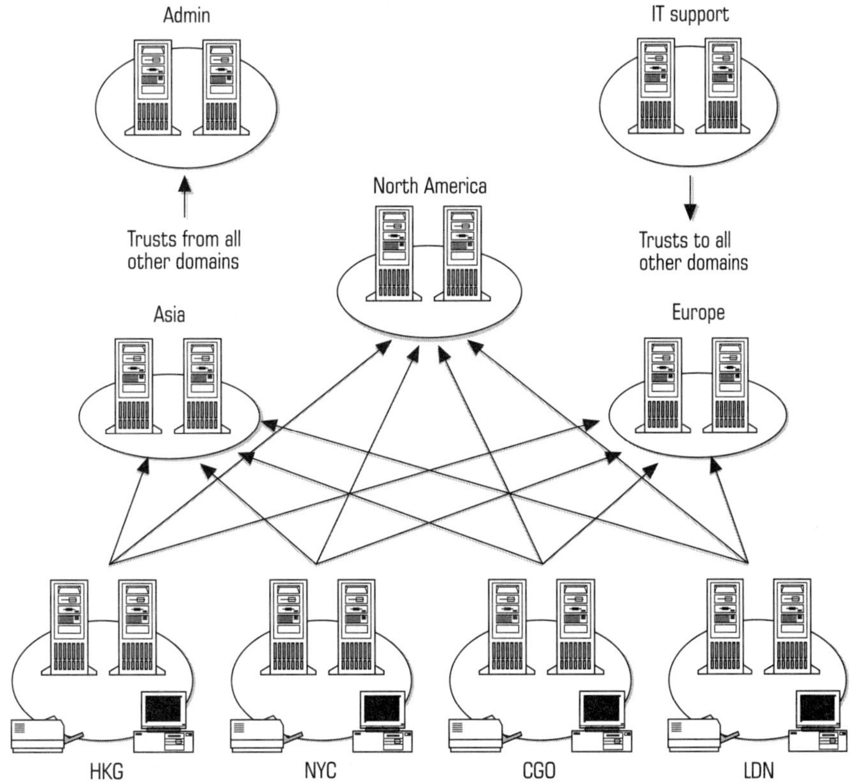

Figure 11.20 *Final Domain Design*

Note that for clarity Figure 11.20 only shows a selection of resource domains, the complete list matches the locations the MBI corporation has at present, as shown in Table 11.4, Population Distribution of MBI. Names of domains are as defined in Chapter 16, Naming Standards.

Coping with Locations of Different Size

The MBI example paid little attention to the fact that the user population varied considerably from location to location, instead treating all as if they were of the same size. Had we recognized different location populations we might have decided that different domain controller configurations were appropriate for different locations.

For example, a location with a large population might warrant a PDC and several BDCs. Whereas, a small location might warrant just a BDC, choosing instead to be part of another location's domain.

Clearly the population of a location will be just one factor among many in determining how a location participates in a domain. Other factors include:

- Money to pay for hardware
- Determination to be independent or willingness to be part of a larger structure
- The WAN connection to a location
- The skills available at a location for managing a domain controller

If the organization a domain design is being created for contains locations of significantly differing population then it is recommended that each be categorized according to some agreed criteria, defined in the design document, allowing the solution architect to treat every location in a category on an equal basis.

For example, in a simple case, an organization might define a *primary* location to be one where the population was over one thousand and there was the budget and political will to host a domain. A *secondary* location would be defined such that its population was less than one thousand and it had no inclination to host its own domain.

Clearly the criteria for categorizing locations need to be matched very specifically to the organization concerned, making it impractical to give general guidelines. The recommendation is that the solution architect define the categories and associated implications of belonging to each. However, representatives of the different locations should participate in deciding which category they belong to.

Migrating to Windows NT 5 Active Directory

The migration plan should have two aspects. One is a description of the target design and the other is a plan for getting there. Here we present an overview of the Active Directory migration plan for MBI. The full plan should be far more detailed than this. Note that at the time of publishing, Active Directory had yet to be released from Microsoft. Every effort has been made to ensure the accuracy of references to this technology, however the author cannot be held responsible for any discrepancy between this book and the product.

Planning the Creation of an Active Directory Design

Creation of an Active Directory domain design will require a far greater understanding of an organization's structure than was necessary for the creation of an NT 4 domain design. The reason for this is the substantially greater degree of flexibility offered by Active Directory. The advantage is that the Active Directory domain design may reflect more accurately how an organization uses and manages IT resources. The downside is that the scale of the task to produce a design is substantial. It is made even more difficult when we consider the effect of constantly changing organizational structures. The use of tools such as design principles will be even more valuable when planning for NT 5 as a means of managing the increased complexity of the design.

In an organization comprising thousands of users the task of designing the Active Directory configuration could be endless if the challenge were not broken down into discrete activities that could be carried out on demand and in parallel. Specifically, the approach to designing an Active Directory configuration for a large corporation should be broken down into the following steps:

1. The development of a top down domain architecture that includes high level organizational units.
2. The identification of policies for organizational unit and group creation. These policies would dictate naming standards, the authorization needed to have these objects created, position in the hierarchy and the identification of who is to administer them.
3. The identification of guidelines for configuring organizational units and groups. The purpose of this is to guide someone who may not be an expert in Active Directory technology to decide best how to group resources and users and delegate control.

The above three steps should be carried out by the Active Directory domain architecture design team. Once complete, the task of defining the implementation details of the organization unit and group configuration for each group within the corporation can be assigned to the local support groups. They would effectively work in parallel, exploiting their knowledge of the business users they support and working to the policies and guidelines laid out by the design team. This way, the task of configuring the Active Directory is broken down, with the components allocated to the most appropriate teams for each business grouping. This approach also copes more effectively with the constant organizational change prevalent in large organizations.

Design principles would be the recommended way to express the policies for organizational unit and group creation. They could also be used to express many of the guidelines for configuring organizational units and groups.

In summary, to design an Active Directory domain architecture it is recommended that a top down approach be taken to developing a high level domain and organizational unit architecture. This should then be followed by the detailed configuration of local organizational units and groups according to corporate policies and guidelines.

The next section summarizes the top down approach for the MBI case study, however, associated policies and guidelines are omitted.

Draft Active Directory Domain Architecture

The multiple master domain model chosen for MBI employed three master domains aligned with the three regional political units of the corporation and resource domains aligned to the various locations around the world. However, while a diagram of the domain architecture can be drawn to look hierarchical, there is very little about it that reflects any of the hierarchical aspects of an organization.

For this reason it is not recommended that the existing domain architecture be used as a starting point for an Active Directory design. The Active Directory domain architecture should instead be designed by taking a fresh look at the organization.

We know MBI to have three principle tiers to its organizational hierarchy, the top being the head office, the next one down being the regional reporting groups aligned to continent and the third being cities. Each of the upper two tiers is co-located with one of the city offices. For example, the Asia reporting group is co-located with the Hong Kong operational office. An Active Directory domain structure can be drawn up to match this hierarchy as shown in abbreviated form in Figure 11.21.

The first tier will be a single new domain which will host the few global organizations within MBI such as the IT Support group. Three regionally aligned second tier domains will be linked into the first tier domain and into each of these will be linked the third tier city domains. Organizational units will be used throughout to distinguish between business functions within each domain.

In developing the Active Directory design the MBI design team found that they could easily accommodate MBI Business Principle 4, which demands the flexibility to be able to set up a new office in another city, supported remotely by an existing office, by allowing a fourth tier to develop. The new office would be a domain in its own right but hierarchically subordinate to an existing tier three domain supporting it with IT management and administration capability. For example, suppose MBI was to open an office in Canberra, Australia, it may suit MBI to link that domain in under the Sydney domain making it easy for the existing resource and user management structures in Sydney to manage those in Canberra.

The flexibility offered by Active Directory would make it relatively easy to change the position of the new domain in the namespace if it were to be advantageous in the future.

Figure 11.21 *Partial MBI Active Directory Domain Structure*

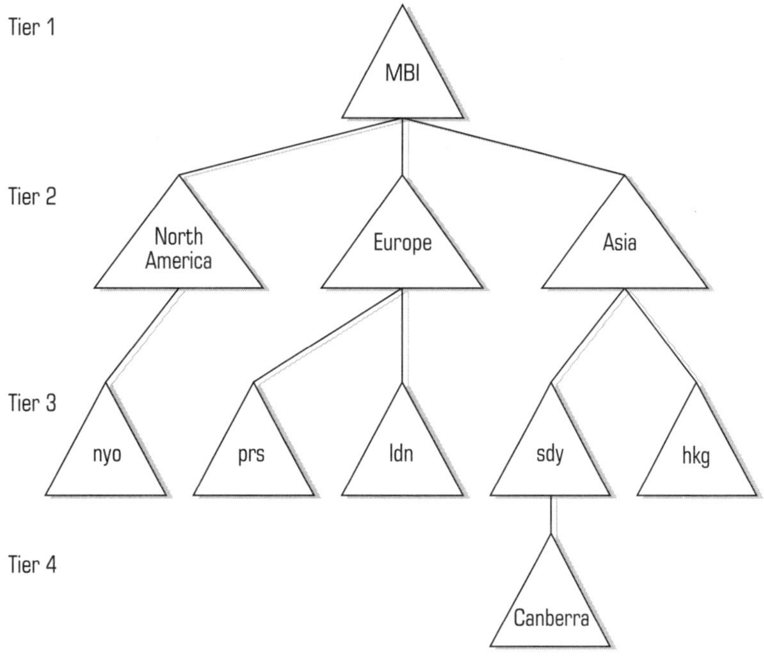

Among the advantages of this new structure are:

- Less domain process traffic on the WAN, only updates to the global catalog.
- Controlled devolution of user account and resource administration allowing a better balance of local needs within the context of a single organization.

Business groupings

Chapter 10, Naming Services, discusses how this domain architecture maps onto the proposed DNS namespace for MBI. The original NT 4 domain architecture for MBI employed a management master domain. We shall make the reasonable assumption for the sake of this case study that the management and operations users within this domain are migrated into the Active Directory user domain structure. The ability to group resources and inherit rights down the domain hierarchy will allow us to accommodate their needs without use of a separate domain.

Migration Strategy

Windows NT supports the incremental migration from Windows NT 4 domains to Windows NT 5 Active Directory. We shall exploit that in the plan that is outlined in Table 11.8. To put into effect this migration strategy would clearly need much more detail. Consult the latest Microsoft literature to confirm the most appropriate approach to migration and the best tools to use.

Table 11.8 *Steps for Migrating to Active Directory*

Step	Action	Explanation
1.	Create the tier one Active Directory domain called MBI.	This will be the root of the domain tree.
2.	Create trusts from the three regional and one management Windows NT 4 master domains to the MBI domain.	These trusts are created so that the correct structure is achieved after the upgrade process. It avoids the need to manipulate domains after upgrading.
3.	Upgrade the three regional and one management Windows NT 4 master domains to Active Directory domains.	An initial set of Active Directory domains are created subordinate to the MBI domain.
4.	Upgrade the Windows NT 4 resource domains to Active Directory domains.	The third tier of the Active Directory domain structure is now complete.
5.	Migrate the user accounts from the original master domains to the appropriate ex-resource domains.	This process should be easier using Active Directory tools.

Table 11.8 *Steps for Migrating to Active Directory (continued)*

6.	Re-allocate the old master domain BDCs to the role of catalog servers in the tier three domains.	BDCs from remote domains will not be required unless there is a high degree of user mobility or remote resource access.
7.	Create the organizational units within the domains.	Should be done by the support groups according to the policies and guidelines laid down by the design team.
8.	Decommission the old management master domain by first removing all trusts to it and from it.	There should be no user accounts left in it by now.

12

Windows NT Groups

A large user population will generate a constant flow of demands for changing rights on a user's account and permissions on resources. The same changes will often need to be applied to several accounts at the same time. Windows NT provides a convenient way to grant rights and assign permissions for several accounts in one operation by treating them as a group.

A Windows NT Group is an object stored in the account database of a domain (SAM) that enables a set of user accounts to be treated as a single entity. For example, by assigning to a group the right to be able to set the system time, all user accounts in that group receive the right. This is clearly very efficient when compared to assigning the right to each of the accounts in the group individually.

Similarly, the access control list on a resource object can include groups. Setting resource access permissions for a group in a single operation is more convenient than setting the resource access permissions for each account in the group.

Tests for group membership can be made in scripts or from a program, allowing actions to be taken dependent upon which groups a user is a member of. However groups are used it is critical that there is a convention associated with their usage or they will ultimately become a burden and not a benefit. As groups and group usage are closely related to the domain structure in which they are used it is recommended that Chapter 11, Windows NT Domain Design, is read before this one.

Figure 12.1 *Windows NT Groups as Part of Design Activity*

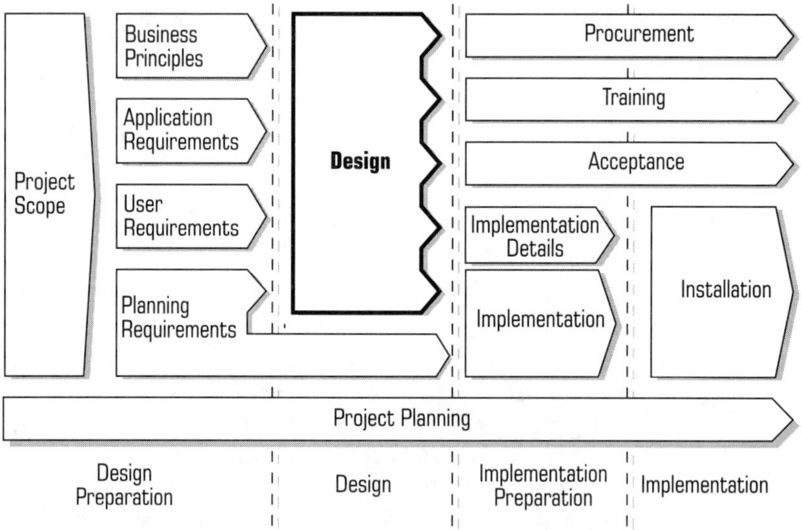

Chapter Structure

Table 12.1 shows the structure of Chapter 12.

Table 12.1 *The structure of Chapter 12*

Topic	Elements
Technology Review	▪ Using groups to control resource access. ▪ Making decisions in scripts that are dependent on group membership. ▪ The built-in groups and their membership relationships. ▪ Active Directory considerations.
Windows NT Group Design	▪ Scope of a Windows NT group design. ▪ How a group design can be characterized by the common attributes. ▪ Designing a group usage strategy for the MBI case study.
Migration Strategy for Getting to Active Directory	▪ A strategy for the use of groups under Active Directory. ▪ A strategy for migrating from NT 4 groups to Active Directory groups.

Technology Review

Windows NT implements two types of group, Global and Local. The characteristics of each are as follows:

- A global group may contain only users from the local domain as members.
- A local group may contain users and global groups from the local domain.
- A local group may contain users and global groups from trusted domains.

Local groups defined on a domain controller may be assigned rights to resources in the local domain. Local groups defined on a member server may be assigned rights to resources on that server only. The level of access to resources such as files and printers may be defined by groups, as well as individual users.

Windows NT has a small number of built-in groups to support fundamental aspects of the system. Otherwise, group creation and membership is the task of the system administrator. The basic group and account membership possibilities are summarized in Figure 12.2.

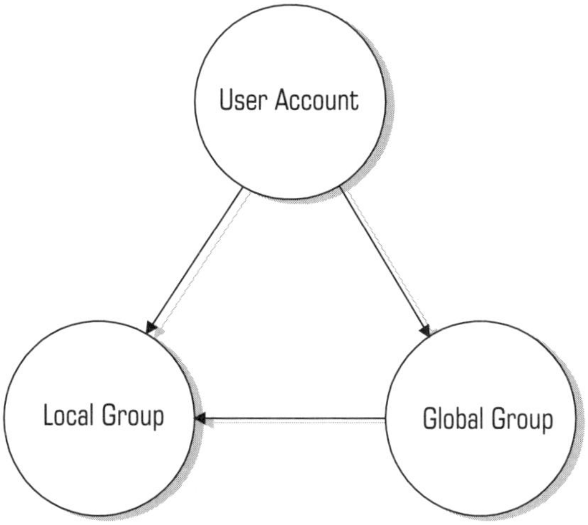

Figure 12.2 *Basic and Account Group Membership Possibilities*

Using Groups to Control Resource Access

Building on our basic knowledge of the two types of group, we will now describe a strategy for their usage that is appropriate for the complete trust, the master and multiple master domain models. This strategy is recommended by Microsoft.

Groups will be used in the two tiered manner for which they were designed. In the upper tier we use global groups solely for grouping user accounts and in the second tier we use local groups for governing access to resources (via permissions on objects) and the granting of rights. Using these two tiers or "dimensions" we have a convenient way of reducing the complexity of the many to many relationship between users on one hand and resources and rights on the other.

We can summarize the strategy for using global and local groups by the following rules:

1. Define user accounts in the master (account) domains.
2. Define global groups in the master domains.
3. Allocate users to global groups. A user may be a member of more than one global group.
4. Define local groups on domain controllers and member servers of the resource domains.
5. Place global groups from the master domains trusted by the resource domain into the local groups.
6. Assign rights to the local groups.
7. Assign permissions to resources in terms of local groups.

For this system to work we should not create user accounts or global groups in any other than master domains. Neither should we put user accounts from a master domain directly into a local group unless there is a specific reason for doing so or the discipline of the approach will break down and management overhead will increase.

A benefit of this system is that it avoids the need to create trusts to overcome resource access restrictions introduced by ad hoc placement of user accounts among domains. This way, the domain model remains as intended.

What makes this system appropriate for the master and multiple master domains models is that it maps global groups onto domains that contain user accounts and local groups onto domains that offer resources.

In the complete trust model we can't avoid mixing global groups with local groups in the same domain. However, the system still works well as we may need to grant access to a resource in one domain to a collection of users in another.

Figure 12.3
Group Strategy

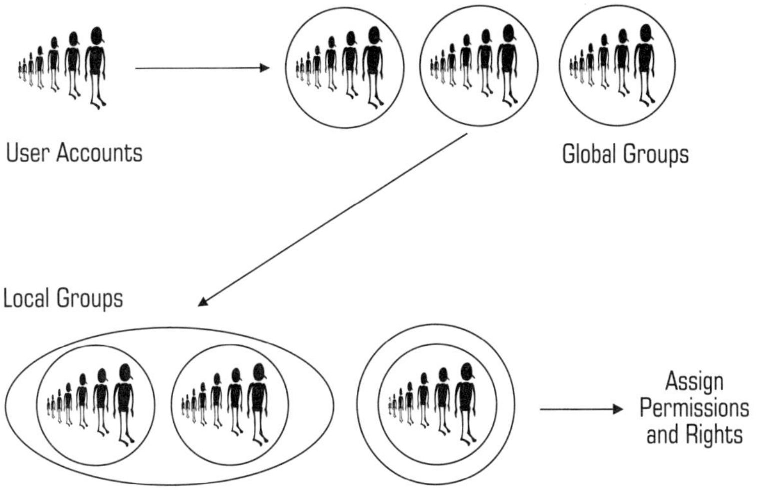

In a single domain model the need to use this two tiered approach is less compelling. However, the advantage remains that it helps structure use of groups, reducing complexity, and that it is a way of future proofing the design should the single domain ever trust or be trusted by another domain.

Using Group Membership to Control Decisions

The introduction mentioned that it is possible to check whether an account is a member of a group from a script or under program control. This presents the possibility that decisions can be made in the logic of a script depending upon which groups a user is a member of.

A simple example of this is the use of a logon script to connect users to different printers depending upon which global group they are members of. The advantage is that the printers a user is connected to upon logon can be changed using the *User Manager for Domains* utility by moving the user's account from one group to another group rather than having to edit the logon script.

Use of groups for determining printer connections (among other things) is shown in the MBI logon script in Appendix C. The design of the MBI logon script is covered in Chapter 14.

Built-in Groups

Windows NT includes a number of built-in accounts and groups created for well defined roles and categories of users. More information is available in the Windows NT Resource Kit, what follows is a summary.

The built-in local groups available on Windows NT Workstation and Windows NT Server computers are:

- Administrators
- Users
- Guests
- Backup operators
- Replicator

The additional built-in local groups available only on Windows NT Server computers acting as primary or backup domain controllers are:

- Account operators
- Print operators
- Server operators

Another predefined local group, power users, is available only on Windows NT Workstation computers or on Windows NT Server computers that are not acting as domain controllers.

The built-in global groups available on a domain controller are:

- Domain admins
- Domain users
- Domain guests

A small number of group memberships are automatically set up on a domain controller as illustrated in Figure 12.4. It is important that the membership of Domain Users and Domain Guests not be changed, however it is possible to remove Administrator from Domain Admins and to remove Domain Admins from Administrators. It is not possible, or desirable, to remove Administrator from Administrators.

The diagram is similar in the case of a domain member server except that the built-in global groups from the *domain* SAM are members of the built-in local groups in the *member server* SAM and of course there are no Print, Account or Server Operators local groups.

Each domain controller and member server has an additional group called Replicator to support the replication service that is used to replicate files from one computer to a set of others. The replicator service and replicator group are typically used to distribute logon scripts and default profiles. There is no need to consider this group when planning a user group usage strategy.

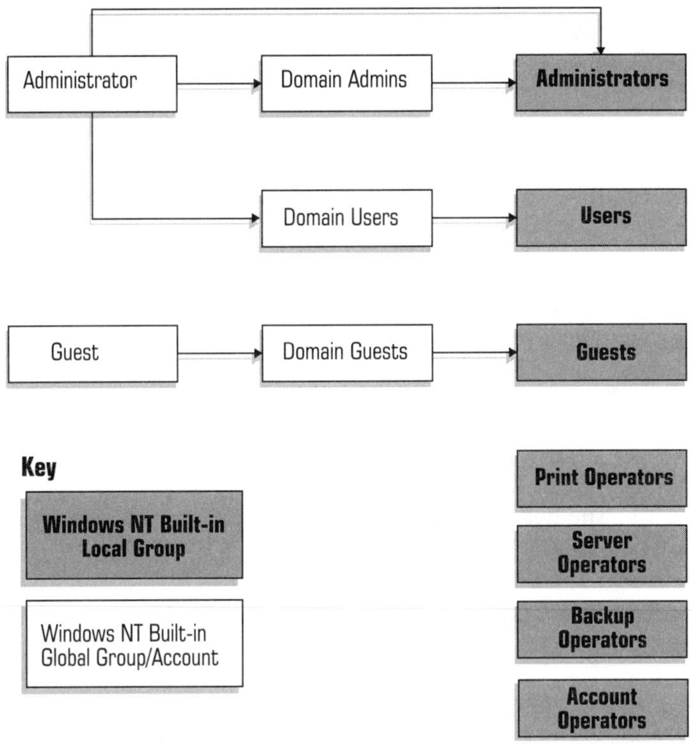

Figure 12.4 *Domain Controller Built-in Accounts, Global Groups and Local Groups*

Moving to Active Directory

Active Directory removes the distinction between global groups and local groups by offering a more flexible group capability. In summary:

- Groups may be members of other groups which in turn may be members of other groups and so on.
- Rights inherited through group membership are transitive.
- Any group may be assigned resource permissions in an access control list.

Indeed, with this added flexibility there is the danger that without a clear group usage strategy chaos could ensue. Until a suitable strategy is identified and there is the confidence that the administrative processes are strong enough to allow it to be adhered to, it is recommended that upon upgrading to Active Directory, the original usage strategy is retained. That is, keep the concept of user only groups (global groups) and groups that contain the user only groups (local groups). To that end, the Windows NT 4 based group naming convention chosen is important for when the icons used to distinguish one type of group from another disappear.

Note that the process of upgrading a master or multiple master domain model will probably result in user accounts being migrated to the ex-resource domains, away from the domains in which the global groups they are members of are defined. The details of such a migration should be addressed on a case by case basis, however in general we should look to create corresponding new groups in the ex-resource domains to act as the new "global" groups.

Note that Local Groups are retained through the upgrade process on Primary Domain Controllers and Backup Domain Controllers for backward compatibility. Local Groups are also retained on member servers.

Windows NT Group Design

Before applying our knowledge of groups to the creation of a design for the MBI case study, we must carry out the following preparation:

1. Define scope of a Windows NT group design
2. Review the requirements on the design
3. Analyze the factors affecting our choices in terms of the common attributes

Scope of a Windows NT Group Design

Before defining the scope of a Windows NT group design we should consider what it is our design should say. The technology review presented a straightforward way of using groups which will suffice for most situations. The difference from one environment to another is going to be the policy for who gets placed in what global group, which global group gets placed in which local group and how local groups are used for governing access to resources. In essence, what we are looking to define is a strategy for applying the standard method of leveraging Windows NT groups. Consequently, a Windows NT group design must include the following elements:

Table 12.2 *Windows NT Group Design Scope*

Topic	Elements
User Local Groups	▪ The local groups to be created ▪ Group membership policy ▪ Group usage policy ▪ Group rights

Table 12.2 *Windows NT Group Design Scope (continued)*

Topic	Elements
User Global Groups	■ The global groups to be created ■ Group membership policy ■ Group usage policy ■ Group rights
IT Support Groups	■ Use of built-in groups ■ Additional groups required
Group Creation Policy	■ Rules governing the creation of a new group
Group Names	■ Global and local group naming conventions (covered in Chapter 16, Naming Standards)
Migration Plan for Getting to Active Directory	■ Draft Active Directory based group strategy ■ Migration strategy

- **Note 1:** Resource object access permissions granted to groups are covered in Chapter 13, File and Print Services.
- **Note 2:** Naming standards are developed in Chapter 16. Although awkward in terms of having to cross reference, it remains important to keep naming standards independent from the subject of the standards. This argument is explained in more detail at the beginning of the Naming Standards chapter.

Requirements on the Design

A Windows NT Group strategy for a corporation should be aimed at supporting the domain structure and user environment—the domain structure because groups are the tool with which we realize the resource access and control intentions of a domain design, the user environment because they affect what the user can do.

For these reasons we shouldn't expect group usage to be driven by direct business needs. Rather, we look to groups to complement our plans for the domain structure and user environment.

Business Principles

The business principles for MBI place no explicit requirements on the group design.

General Requirements

For the purpose of the case study we will state some general requirements here which, under normal circumstances would have been derived from the requirements placed on the system by the existing infrastructure and the requirements for enhancing it:

1. Each business unit shall be restricted from accessing another business unit's data. Business units are confined to locations. So, for example, the foreign exchange business at one location is a distinct business unit to the foreign exchange business at a different location.
2. Only certain staff in each business unit shall be allowed access to sensitive data.
3. Users shall be able to logon at a workstation in any domain and have access to the local shared area for the business group they work in.
4. We know from Chapter 14, User Environment, that there will be a business unit specific shared directory per location.
5. Administrative and Operational staff may either have responsibilities for many domains or they might be local staff with responsibility for certain duties within their own domain. In the latter case, this staff must be restricted from exercising their responsibilities over any other domain.

This requirement touches on the important issue of user mobility and what services are available to a user logging on at a workstation different to the one normally used. User mobility is addressed in more detail in Chapter 14, User Environment.

Application Requirements

The case study has no explicit application based group requirements. However, for the purpose of the example we will declare that a particular application unique to the Foreign Exchange business line requires a special type of printer. We can then see how groups can help us manage that need.

Common Attributes

Of the common attributes we have chosen to use in this book only three have any significant relevance to groups:

- Scalability
- Manageability

- Security

Here we review how Windows NT groups can be characterized by these attributes.

Scalability

To fully understand the scalability of group usage we must study three relevant dimensions:

- **Users**—An increase in number of users does not by itself necessarily cause an increase in the number of groups, neither does it affect a group usage strategy. Indeed, the main rationale for having groups is to make the management of increasing quantities of users easy by grouping them according to common needs.
- **Groups**—An increase in the number of groups used is typically caused by the need to accommodate an additional business unit or the specific needs of a subset of users in a business unit. The group usage strategy should define when additional groups are necessary.

  The act of adding a new global group will require that it be populated by user accounts and made a member of appropriate local groups. Adding a local group will require global groups to be made members of it and permissions will have to be set up on resources for it to fulfill its role. The more groups in use the more complicated the addition of a group becomes. Strong, simple alignment between global groups and local groups can minimize the complexity of using large numbers of groups.
- **Domains**—The intimate relationship between groups and domains means that increasing the number of domains will inevitably cause additional groups to be created with the same consequences as illustrated above.

  Addition of a resource domain in a master or multiple master model will require that each local group created be populated with new and existing global groups from the master domain(s). Addition of a master domain will require the addition of global groups which need to become members of existing local groups. The above comments can be no more than generalizations. A more specific analysis will depend on the exact group usage strategy and domain model in use.

Manageability

Windows NT groups are a solution to the management challenge presented by a large user population. How they are used to solve that challenge is amply dealt with in the rest of this chapter. What we need to consider here, when examining how we can characterize NT groups in terms of the common attribute of manageability, is the straightforward administrative requirements of NT groups, which are:

- Moving users from one group to another
- Adding/removing users from groups
- Creating groups
- Assigning permissions and rights to groups

On balance, these tasks are trivial, particularly compared to the administrative savings of using groups. A point worth making again is that a strong and simple group usage strategy will make the management of groups both easier and safer.

Security

Groups make the administration of access to resources easier when there is a large population of users to deal with. However, we shouldn't forget that if the concept of groups did not exist, the Windows NT security model would not be any different.

It is very important that the way groups are used does not obscure the level of access users have to resources. Rather, we should try to enhance the management of security by making it very clear through group usage conventions and clear alignment of groups to needs, the level of resource access a user has as a result of membership to certain groups.

The main danger with group usage from a security standpoint is that through an oversight, an individual gets more rights or is granted a higher level of access to resources than they should have. For example, a group may have been created for the purpose of controlling access to a printer and subsequently given permissions on a directory containing sensitive information. The need to restrict access to that directory for some of the members of the group can easily be missed, particularly if the name of the group is misleading or there are no conventions regarding group usage.

An audit department will need to be able to establish the permissions each user has, as a result of group membership. With many groups in use this can become complicated and is a natural task for an automatic audit tool.

This example highlights a specific issue and that is using a group for a purpose it was not intended. Ultimately, changes made to satisfy one purpose end up conflicting with the other purpose, making group usage a constraint rather than a benefit.

Windows NT Group Strategy

In this section we develop a group usage strategy for MBI. We deal with local groups in the resource domains first, as the primary objective of the MBI group usage strategy is to allow control of access to resources by users. Global groups will be dealt with next and then we will look at groups for members of the IT Support organization.

Local Groups

Looking closely at MBI we can make the following observations:

1. Its business is effectively replicated from one location to the next.
2. Each location is broken down into several business units, foreign exchange, derivatives, etc.

Combining observations 1 and 2 from above with general requirements, is it clear we need a category of local group that can be used to govern access to the business unit specific shared directory at a location. Groups in this category should therefore contain a field to identify business unit.

We also know that in several cities, the resource domain at that location includes offices from more than one subsidiary of MBI. This is because the MBI domain design focuses on a structure suitable for the integrated organization of the future, making it undesirable to recognize the different subsidiaries by the use of a distinct domain for each.

The decision was therefore made during the design of the domain architecture to use Windows NT Groups to satisfy MBI Business Principle 5 stating that the authority of the subsidiaries be recognized during the process of transitioning to an integrated organization. Thus, to distinguish between different subsidiaries at each location we need an additional field in the group to identify the subsidiary it applies to, alongside the one for business unit.

This category of local group now contains two fields, one for business unit and one for subsidiary and will be used to govern access to the shared file service for a business unit of a particular subsidiary at each location. We shall call this category of groups *Local File Access*.

The third general requirement requires that a subset of users in each business unit will need to have access to sensitive data. To implement the general solution we shall include in the name of this new category of group the same fields used in the category *Local File Access* and add a Security Suffix, to arrive at a new category we will call *Local Restricted Access*. Granting suitable permissions on resources for this group only, will result in its members being given exclusive access to the sensitive data.

Note that if anyone has the right *Take Ownership* on their account or through membership of a group then they will be able to change ownership of a sensitive file and access it. Creation of a group for the purpose just described should of course be done in the context of implementing an overall secure environment.

Table 12.3 *Local Group Strategy*

Category of Local Group	Name Fields	Usage and Membership
Local File Access	Business unit + Subsidiary	For permissioning the shared area for a particular business group. The single member of this group will be the File Access global group corresponding to the location of the resource domain in which the local group is defined.
Local Restricted Access	Business unit + Subsidiary + Security	For permissioning the restricted shared area for a particular business group. The single member of this group will be the Restricted Access global group corresponding to the location of the resource domain in which the local group is defined.

Global Groups

MBI has chosen to use a geographic multiple master domain model with master domains aligned to region and resource domains aligned to locations. In line with the recommended Microsoft strategy, global groups will be defined in the master domains and local groups in the resource domains and on resource domain member servers. This design decision is captured by Design Principle B-22 entitled Global/Local Group Usage Policy in Appendix B.

To keep our group design simple we will create in the master domain a matching global group for each local group we identified in the previous section. The purpose of each global group will be to contain the user accounts of the people to whom the corresponding local group is designed to govern resource access.

Note that we can't use the same name for the global group as used for the local group or we would end up with many global groups of the same name in each master domain. It is recommended that the global group name include the same fields as used in the corresponding local group, to emphasize the pairing, however there needs to be an additional field to distinguish the location to which the global group applies.

We will therefore have a category of group called *Global File Access* and a category called *Global Restricted Access*, each with a field for location in addition to the fields used in their associated local groups.

All global groups will be created in the appropriate regional master for the location concerned. So, for example, the Global File Access group for the Zurich branch of the Red Bank foreign exchange unit should be created in the Europe master domain. This should be obvious as Europe is the domain where the user accounts for the staff in the Zurich offices are held. Thus, continuing the example with the group names defined in Chapter 16, Naming Standards, the local group ZRC\EFX2 would have as its single member Europe\ZRCEFX2.

Let us now consider the requirement for users of a particular application in the foreign exchange business unit to print to a special printer. We shall assume that they use this application most of the time and would wish for the special printer to be set as their default. However, they also use other applications for which the standard office printers are satisfactory so they should be able to select any of these as well.

There are, of course, several methods of achieving this arrangement. The way we are going to do it, as an example, is to set the default printer for this group of users in their logon script. The logon script for MBI illustrated in Appendix C shows how this can be done. All we need to do is define a global group, the members of which are users of this particular application.

It is recommended in situations like this to design a general solution to the need, so that if any other group requires access to a special printer, the naming standard can be used to determine the name of the new group name. In this case, it means treating the new category of group as a subset of the Global File Access group, meaning the printer group name must include the same three fields as Global File Access plus an additional field to identify its special purpose. We shall call this category of group Global Printer Access.

Table 12.4 *Global Group Strategy*

Category of Global Group	Name Fields	Usage and Membership
Global File Access	Location + Business unit + Subsidiary	This is the standard set of groups aligned by business at a location. The purpose is to govern file service access (to the local business unit specific shared area primarily). By default *every* user in that business is a member of the appropriate group.
Global Printer Access	Location + Business unit + Subsidiary + Printer	These groups are used to govern which printer is set to the user's default in their logon script. There does not need to be a corresponding set of Local Groups.
Global Restricted Access	Location + Business unit + Subsidiary + Security	For every group in the category Business there will be a corresponding group containing only those people who have access to sensitive information.

IT Support

We should recall that MBI has decided to use the Management Master version of the multiple master domain model, employing a master domain called *Admin* to host all the accounts and associated global groups for users with IT support roles. Reviewing general requirements we can see that we must be able to restrict staff in terms of which domains they can administer. Combining this with MBI's group usage strategy (represented in a design principle) of not putting user accounts from a master domain directly into local groups in trusting domains we find that we must create in the *Admins* master domain a global group for the administrators of each trusting domain.

Further, if we are to maintain the distinction between the standard roles suggested by the built-in local groups, we should create a matching global group per trusting domain for each built-in local group. The use of the standard built-in groups is important if we are not to grant more rights than are necessary to carry out a role (see the Design Principle 14-6, *Only Grant the Minimum Rights for the Role*, in Chapter 14, User Environment). Although the group usage strategy we are arriving at for administrative and operational staff is almost logically derived from previous design principles and the general requirements we would be wise to capture its essence in a new design principle.

Principle 12-1—A Global Group per Built-in Local Operators Group
The management master domain should contain a global group for each built-in local group in each domain.
Justification
▪ Use of built-in groups supports the design principle requiring that an account has the minimum rights necessary to carry out a role. ▪ Ensures all staff with a role in a domain matching that for which a built-in group exists can be managed together in a global group. ▪ No need to place user accounts from the management master domain directly in a trusting domain local group.
Implications
▪ For convenience the names of the global groups should make it clear which domain and which built-in local group they correspond to.
Issues

This structure is illustrated in Figure 12.5 for the management master domain *Admin* and the Hong Kong resource domain *HKG*. A diagram showing the complete set of accounts and groups in the *Admin* domain would include four global operators groups and associated accounts for every domain in the MBI system.

Note that Figure 12.5 shows the groups involved on a domain controller in domain HKG. A member server in the HKG resource domain would not have the Account Operators, Print Operators and Server Operators local groups. To set this group membership scheme up completely for a resource domain, the relationship illustrated needs to be configured once in the resource domain SAM and once in the SAM of each resource domain member server (omitting the three domain controller only local groups in the latter case).

In keeping with the design principle insisting that no user should share an account with another user (Chapter 14, User Environment), MBI chose not to use the built-in *Administrator* account but to populate each new global administrative group with the account of each person sharing the role of administrator for that domain, thus avoiding the security risk associated with need for a number of people to know the password. For example, a person with the role of administrator for the Hong Kong resource domain would have an account created for the purpose in the *Admin* master domain.

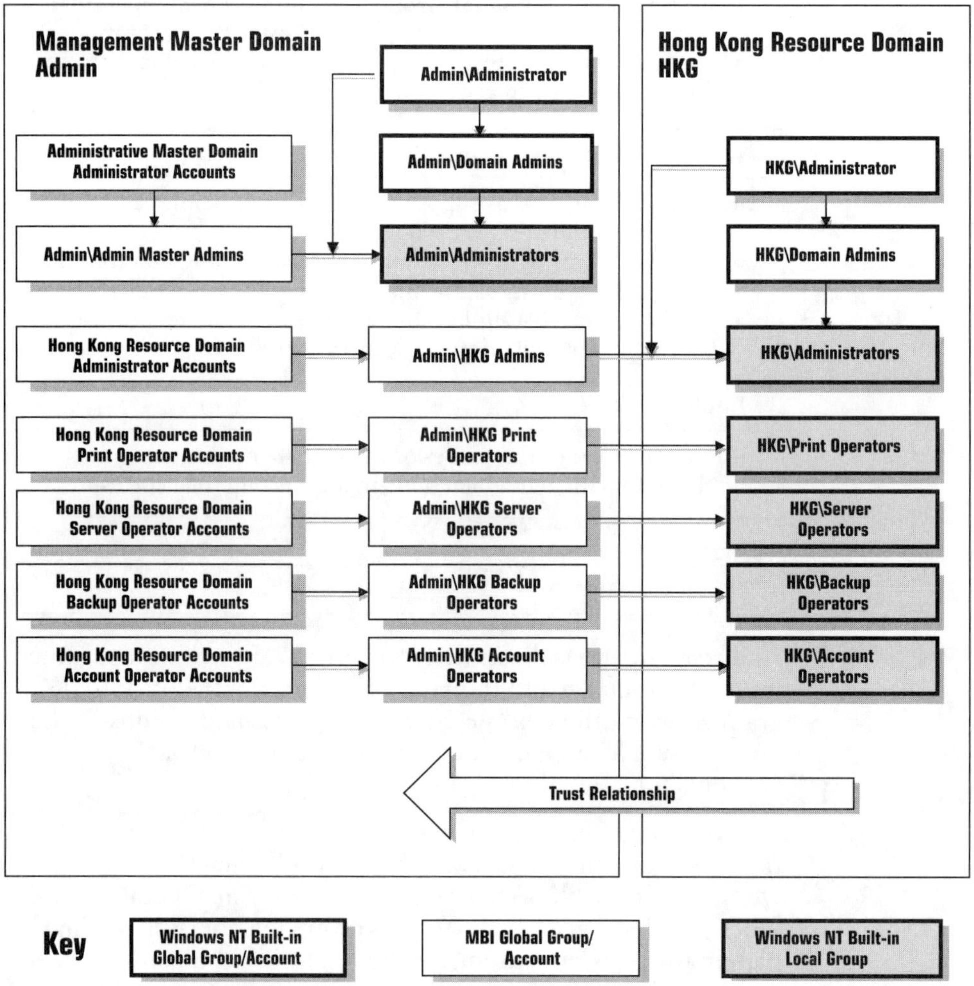

Figure 12.5 *IT Support Groups Overview for Hong Kong Office*

This account would be a member of the *Admin\HKG Admins* global group which in turn would be a member of the built-in local group in the Hong Kong resource domain *HKG\Administrators*. At the same time the same person might be a backup operator for the Admin domain itself, in which case they would have a separate account which would be a member of the global group Admin\Admin Master Backup Operators (or suitable abbreviated form!).

If the built-in *Administrator* account is not to be used then it can be removed from the *Domain Admins* group, which in turn can be removed from the *Administrators* group. Note that *Administrator* cannot be removed from *Administrators*. Figure 12.5 shows the relationship between administrator groups and accounts prior to any membership removals.

Clearly there is an issue here with some IT Support users needing to maintain several accounts. The risk is that a person will keep the password to each the same making them easier to remember.

The IT Support group strategy we have described for MBI is primarily designed to leverage the existing built-in groups and to guard against accidental and malicious actions on domains or resources. As MBI is a bank, a higher degree of security may well be appropriate. If it were we would expect to see explicit security requirements stated in the user or application requirements or guidance in the form of a business principle.

If higher security were necessary the group usage strategy would need to be complemented with measures to remove rights from users and groups. This is described in more detail in the Windows NT Resource Kit.

Group Creation Policy

There are two good reasons why it is important to keep the number of groups to a minimum and to make the group usage strategy as simple and straightforward as possible:

1. To avoid the management of groups becoming a liability
2. To retain control of which resources a user may gain access to

Management Overhead

For group usage to achieve its goals it must be easier to use than to not use. If a poor group usage policy is chosen that fosters the creation of a vast number of groups then the management of groups will rapidly become an overhead. This is a real danger in a large system so every effort should be made to keep group usage as simple and disciplined as possible.

To avoid accumulating too many groups, consider whether the chosen group usage strategy:

- is clear enough to avoid ambiguity. If it isn't, administrators will create groups they may not need to create.

- accurately addresses the resource access needs of the user population. If it doesn't, new groups will be created to compensate.

Control of Resource Access

The use of a large number of groups can present a security risk by making it difficult to establish exactly which resources users will gain access to when they are placed in a global group. This problem is particularly serious when the resource domains and global domains are managed by different administrators. Fortunately, tools are emerging that will scan SAM databases and create a report showing the level of access each user has to which resource.

There is no easy solution to this problem, however it is worth considering the following:

- Limiting the authority to create groups to a small number of administrators who fully understand the group usage strategy.
- Whether groups are being used for purposes they were not intended. If this is the case, assumptions about resource access based on the original group usage strategy will be invalid.

Migration Plan for Getting to Active Directory

The group and migration strategies recommended here represent the most appropriate plan based on the facts available at the time. They could easily change when more is known about the Active Directory implementation and its associated management tools. The important thing is that there is a plan that looks workable, increasing confidence that the Windows NT 4 design can be upgraded in a straightforward fashion.

Active Directory Group Strategy

The group strategy for use with Active Directory at MBI will be as recommended in the section on Active Directory considerations earlier in this chapter. That is, the existing two tiered group structure will be retained through the use of pseudo global groups created in the local domains where the accounts now reside (after the domain migration).

You should use design principles to support the approach taken to the migration strategy from Windows NT 4 to Windows NT 5 or where a new design is being created.

Active Directory Group Migration Strategy

This strategy should be created in conjunction with the domain migration strategy. For the group migration strategy we will assume that user accounts have been moved to the local domain as described in the MBI Active Directory domain migration strategy. The strategy is to:

1. Create new groups in the local domains to act as pseudo global groups. The list of groups will be the same as used in the Windows NT 4 structure.
2. Assign users to the pseudo global groups as before.
3. Assign pseudo global groups to the existing local groups.

Note that the naming standards used for the pseudo global groups will need to distinguish them from the local groups. MBI supported this approach with a design principle:

Principle 12-2—Two Layer Active Directory Group Structure
The two layer group structure used with Windows NT 4 will be retained with the Active Directory configuration.
Justification
▪ No experience of operating a group structure with more than two tiers (global and local). ▪ Operational procedures currently struggle to cope with the complexity of the existing two tier structure. More tiers would result in more complexity. ▪ More complexity will lead to errors which could amount to security holes as users are inadvertently granted more access rights than they should be.
Implications
▪ The two tiered structure may not allow the full exploitation of the capabilities of the Active Directory to organize users into groups. ▪ Guidelines should be drawn up governing the creation of new groups and their usage. ▪ If successful, additional tiers may be introduced at a later date in a planned manner.
Issues
▪ The naming convention for groups currently does not suit the Active Directory design.

13

File and Print Services

One of the original reasons for the emergence of the PC server, the provision of shared file and print services remains at the heart of a modern Windows NT technical infrastructure. These two services deal in the currency of computing, the file, so playing a fundamental role in any complete technical infrastructure. The success of file and print serving is rooted in the notion of data sharing and the more efficient use of computing resources.

The two services are dealt with together in this chapter because they have several things in common. They share the same protocol and are frequently hosted by the same server. More importantly, they are services that are used directly by users while at the same time being equally important to applications. File and print services depend on a common security environment and rely on a name resolution service.

Figure 13.1
Design Phase of Project

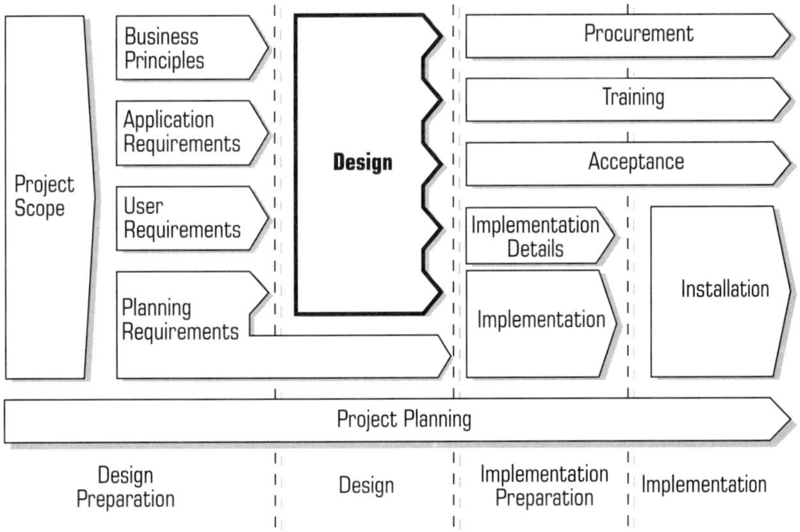

In addition to providing file and print services for homogeneous Microsoft environments, Windows NT provides tools for integrating other platforms into a Windows NT based file and print serving architecture. Software from third parties expands the number of platforms Windows NT can be integrated with to encompass most of the popular ones currently in use.

Design of the technical infrastructure file and print services is part of the design activity shown on the project roadmap in Figure 13.1

Structure of Chapter

This chapter is split into two main sections as shown in Table 13.1.

Table 13.1 *The Structure of Chapter 13*

Section	Overview
Technology Review	A review of the basic technologies involved in the provision of and access to file and print services in a Windows NT environment. Consideration is given to the common need to integrate with file and print services from other platforms. The role of Microsoft Distributed File Services is reviewed as a tool for simplifying the use of file services from the perspective of the user.
File and Print Service Design	In the course of developing a file and print service design for the MBI case study the following aspects are specified: ▪ File and print service protocols. ▪ Server sizing guidelines. ▪ File share mappings and visibility. ▪ File and print service permission settings. ▪ Use of Microsoft Distributed File Service. ▪ A server deployment strategy is also developed for MBI, guiding the number and capacity of servers at each location.

Technology Review

Windows NT File Service

There are two key concepts necessary to understand the Windows NT file service:

- File shares
- File systems

Both are introduced here along with an architectural view of how they are implemented within Windows NT.

File Shares

A file share is the means by which one computer may make available files in local storage to another computer. A computer acting as a client would make a connection to the file share on the server and until that connection is broken, it can access the files on the file share as if they were stored locally. Multiple clients may connect to the same file share providing a means of sharing files between several users.

The connection to a file share is made either through a Windows NT 4 utility such as Explorer or Network Neighborhood or through a command issued in a script or at the DOS window:

```
net use h: \\SNYO0003\apps$
```

SNYO0003 is the name of the computer offering the file service called apps$. Once the connection is made, the files will be accessible from the client's h:\ drive.

File Systems

A file system is the convention an operating system uses to store data on disks. The arrival of Windows NT brought with it a new file system called NTFS, which is more efficient at handling the large disks which are becoming more common and most importantly, it allows full security control over directories and files.

Windows 95 and Windows 3.x are unable to access an NTFS file sytem directly so Windows NT allows the use of FAT, which is the predecessor to NTFS, for backward compatibility. Systems that only understand FAT can access NTFS though a file share, however the security information held by NTFS is unavailable on that type of client.

Windows NT File Service Architecture

The provision of file and print services is implemented by the NT Server Service and connections to remote services are implemented by the NT Workstation Service. Both are implemented as Windows NT files systems allowing the distinction between local and remote resources to be as transparent as possible.

Figure 13.2 *Workstation and Server Services*

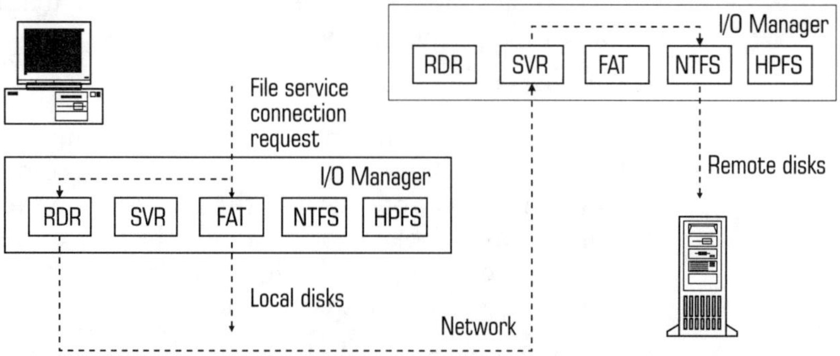

Note that both the NT workstation service and the NT server service are present on the Windows NT Workstation and the Windows NT Server products.

Table 13.2 *Abbreviations used in Figure 13.2*

Abbreviation	Explanation
RDR	Redirector (NT Workstation Service)—Undertakes the connection to the Server component of another computer as part of the remote file and print service access mechanism
SVR	Server (NT Server Service)—Takes connections from the Redirector component of another computer as part of the remote file service access mechanism
FAT	The original DOS based file system
NTFS	The new Windows NT file system
HPFS	File system provided for compatibility with OS/2

Windows NT Print Service

It is important that two basic Windows NT printing terms are understood from the outset:

- a *printing device* as the physical printer
- a *printer* as the system software entity between an application submitting a job for printing and the printing device itself. An icon is typically associated with a printer in the Printer Manager utility. (Note that on other computing platforms this term equates roughly to a print queue.)

The Windows NT print service enables printing:

- to a locally attached printing device,
- to a printing device locally attached to another computer,
- direct to a network attached printing device,
- to a served network attached printing device.

Figure 13.3 *Windows NT Printing*

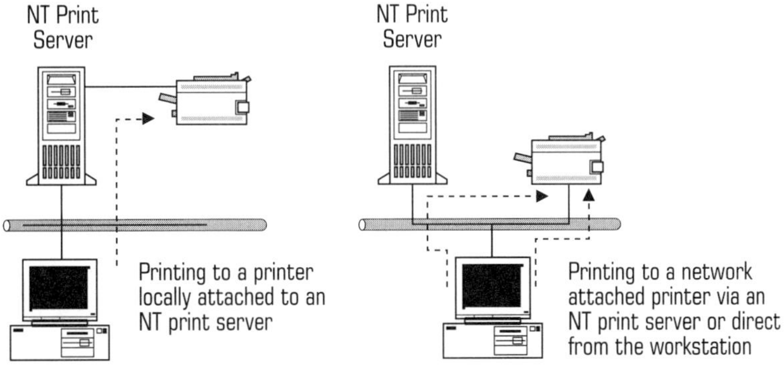

In the case where a printing device is served from a Windows NT print server, the printer driver software gets supplied to the client by the server if the local copy is out of date or missing. This means that printer drivers only need be maintained on computers serving printing devices, greatly simplifying printer driver management.

Figure 13.4 *Windows NT Printer Pools*

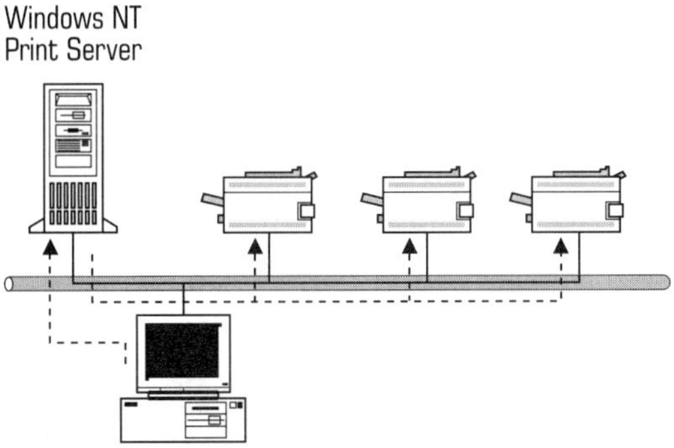

A Windows NT printer can be configured to treat a set of printing devices as a pool, spreading the print load among multiple equivalent printing devices. Operations such as pause on the printer will affect all printing devices.

Printer Shares

A connection can be made to a shared printer in a similar manner to that used to connect to a file share. A connection may either be made through the Windows NT utility such as Network Neighborhood or a command line. For example:

net use \\SNYO0003\laser15

The computer serving the printer is SNYO0003 and the printer is served as laser15.

UNIX Interoperability

File Service

UNIX environments usually include the equivalent of Windows NT's file serving capability using a technology called NFS or Network File System. Microsoft does not currently supply any software to implement an NFS server or client but a number of software companies do.

Figure 13.5 *Windows NT as NFS File Service Client and Server*

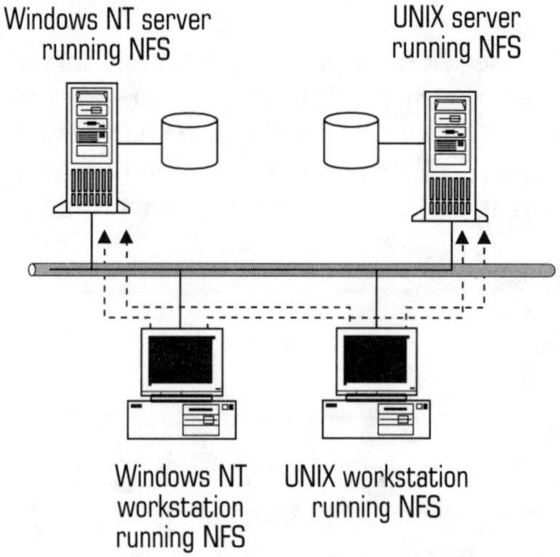

As can be seen from the diagram above, using NFS client software a Windows NT Workstation can access shared files on a UNIX host. Similarly, a UNIX computer can access files on a Windows NT server. Indeed NFS could be used between two Windows NT computers.

Print Service

LPD and LPR represent the server and client components of the UNIX printing system. Windows NT offers both components and can therefore act as a print server to systems running LPR and can print to a server running LPD.

Figure 13.6 *LPD/PR Print To and From Windows NT*

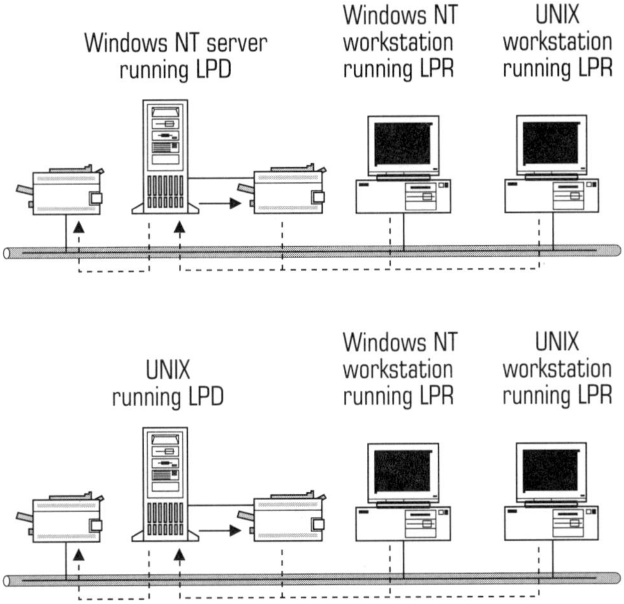

This capability would typically be used in the following circumstances:

- Windows NT workstations need to print to an existing UNIX print server.
- Windows NT needs to offer a print service to UNIX workstations.

Note that Windows NT Server running LPR (the client) can connect to a UNIX print server and re-offer the UNIX based printer to systems running only default Microsoft print client software.

Novell NetWare Interoperability

File and Print Services for Novell NetWare

Windows NT is able to act as a client or a server for Novell NetWare file and print services. Thus, a Windows NT system may access Novell NetWare file and print services offered from a Novell NetWare server and a workstation running Novell NetWare client software may use file and print services offered from a Windows NT system.

Figure 13.7
Novell NetWare File and Print

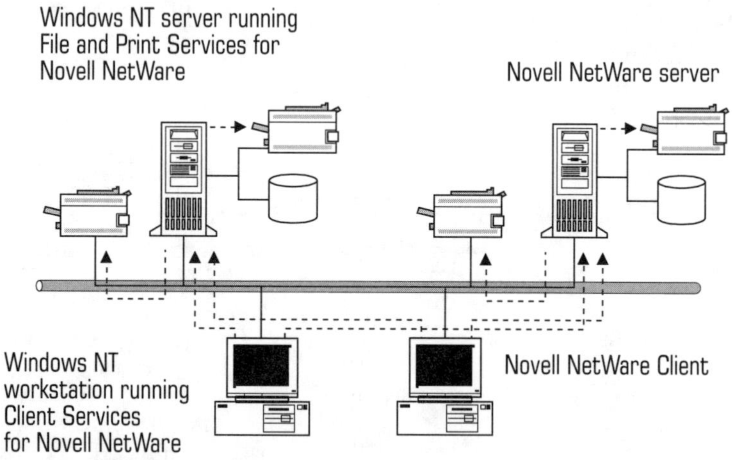

Gateway Service for Novell NetWare

Windows NT provides the ability for Windows NT clients to connect to file and print services offered by a Novell NetWare server via a Windows NT server acting as a gateway. The advantage of this is that the client computers need not run any Novell NetWare protocols. The most obvious observation on such a configuration is that care needs to be exercised over the load placed on the Windows NT server.

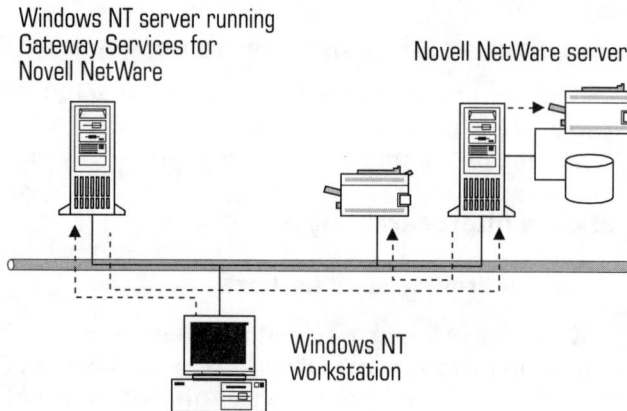

Figure 13.8
Gateway Service for Novell NetWare

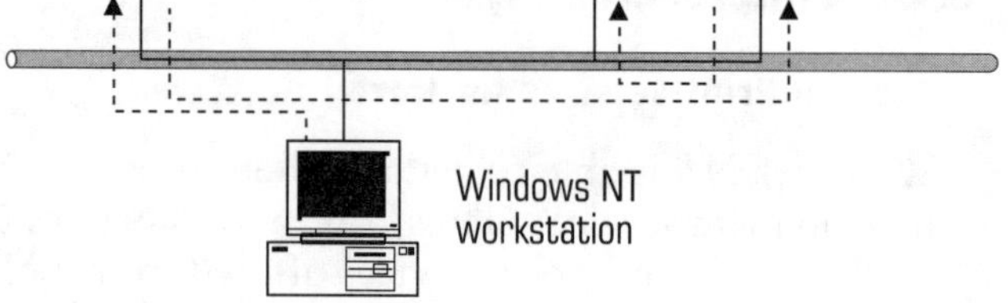

Distributed File Services

Microsoft DFS (Distributed File Services) provides a way of linking file shares on different computers together to create a single logical directory hierarchy. The objectives are to:

- Minimize the number of drive letters to which a user has to map.

By minimizing the number of drive letters required it becomes easier to introduce a consistent drive mapping convention throughout an organization. This will lead to greater uniformity of the infrastructure which brings ease of use and lower support costs.

- To provide a single directory hierarchy through which all network based files may be accessed.

  Presenting a single directory hierarchy allows the user to navigate directories without needing to know which actual file shares they are associated with.

A DFS volume (a directory tree) is created by declaring a file share to be the DFS root. This is the file share from which *links* to other file shares will be created. Each link is given a name which is mapped to the UNC name of the shared directory being linked to.

DFS allows multiple links each with the same name to be mapped to different shares. This is intended to facilitate the load balancing of users across a set of shares offering identical sets of read-only data. Note that DFS itself does nothing to synchronize data between these different shares; that must be the carried out by some other mechanism.

An example DFS volume logical directory structure is illustrated in Figure 13.9 based on the example link name to share mappings shown in Table 13.3. The example shows a DFS root called RootShare on Computer1 with three links, Public, Groups and Home. Each of these links maps to a different file share. These file shares could of course be mapped to directly by a client computer but by using DFS they can be accessed through the logical directory structure.

Table 13.3 *Example DFS Link to Share Mappings*

DFS Link Name (in bold)	Share the Link is Mapped to...
\\Computer1\RootShare	\\Computer1\RootShare
\\Computer1\RootShare**Public**	\\Computer2\PublicData
\\Computer1\RootShare**Groups**	\\Computer3\GroupData
\\Computer1\RootShare**Home**	\\Computer4\HomeDirs
Share	**Sub-directories**
\\Computer2\Public Data	None
\\Computer3\GroupData	EFX, CMK
\\Computer4\HomeDirs	User1, User2, User3

The three names Public, Groups and Home shown in bold are the names of the DFS links. When a user references the UNC path listed under the column DFS Link Name they will be directed to the corresponding share in the right hand column.

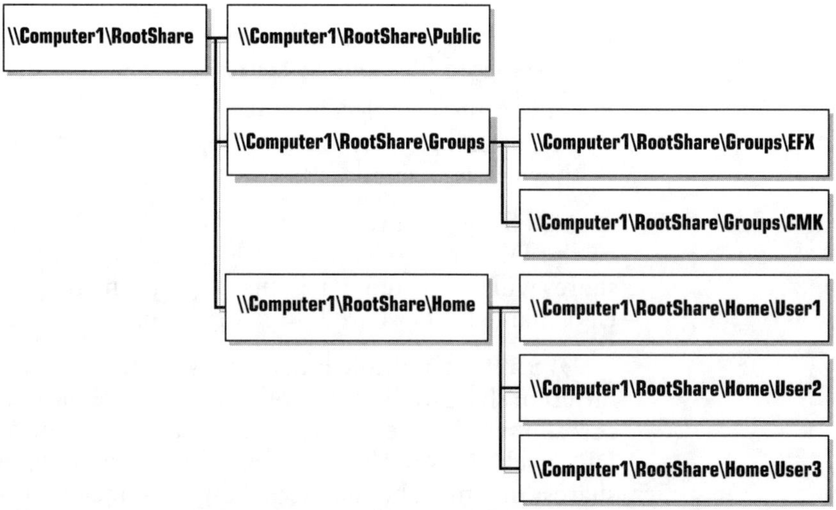

Figure 13.9 *Example Logical DFS Tree Based on Mappings in Table 13.3*

Access Control

Restrictions on the level of access and control a user can exercise can be set up for both file shares and served printers by setting permissions on the resources or objects. When a user logs on to a Windows NT domain they are granted a security-access token. This access token contains information about the user and the Windows NT groups they belong to. When an attempt is made to access one of these resources the information contained in the user's access token is compared against the list of permissions for that resource. If there is a match, the user is allowed to access the object in the manner requested.

Shared Files

Table 13.4 and Table 13.5 show the possible file share permissions and NTFS file and directory permissions respectively. Words are used to describe permissions for the benefit of humans, however, Windows NT uses a means of representing permissions more suited to a computer which is not illustrated here.

Table 13.4 *File Share Access Permissions*

Permission	Effect
No Access	▪ Can't see or use shared directory contents
Read	▪ Can see file and directory names ▪ Can navigate directory tree ▪ Can run executables ▪ Can read files and their attributes
Change	Read permission plus: ▪ Can write to files ▪ Create directories and files ▪ Remove directories and files ▪ Modify file attributes
Full Control	Change permission plus: ▪ Change file permissions ▪ Take ownership (set the file as owned by the person carrying out this command)

Table 13.5 *File and Directory Access Permissions*

Permission	Effect
No Access	▪ Can't see or use directory contents
List	▪ Can see file and directory names ▪ Can make changes to subdirectories
Read	List permission plus: ▪ Can run executables ▪ Can read files and their attributes
Add	Read permission plus: ▪ Can add files and subdirectories to a directory
Add + Read	▪ Add permission plus Read permission
Change	Add and Read permission plus: ▪ Write to files ▪ Remove directories and files
Full Control	Change permission plus: ▪ Change file permissions ▪ Take ownership (set the file as owned by the person carrying out this command)

To work out the effective permissions on a file available through a file share use the three steps in Table 13.6.

Table 13.6 *Deducing File Access Permissions*

Step	Action
1.	Determine the file's local permissions by adding together the user *file* permissions and the *file* permissions of any groups the user is a member of.
2.	Determine the file's share permissions by adding together the user *share* permissions and the *share* permissions of any groups the user is a member of.
3.	The user's resultant permissions through the file share are the most restrictive combination of these two.

For example:

File Permission	Share Permission
Through group membership = Read	Through user account = Read
Through User account = Change	
Total File Permission = Change	Total Share Permission = Read

Resultant file access permission = most restrictive of Change and Read
= Read

Note that it is easier to deduce resultant file access permissions if the underlying Windows NT representation of permissions is used rather than the word descriptions shown in the example. Refer to Microsoft documentation for a more complete description of how to calculate resultant file access permissions.

Shared Printers

The following permissions apply to shared printers:

Table 13.7 *Printer Share Permissions*

Permission	Effect
No Access	▪ No access
Print	▪ Can print ▪ Control settings for own print jobs ▪ Pause, restart and delete own print jobs
Manage Documents	As Print and additionally: ▪ Control settings for all print jobs ▪ Pause, restart and delete for all print jobs

Table 13.7 *Printer Share Permissions (continued)*

Permission	Effect
Full Control	As Manage Documents and additionally: ■ Set a printer as shared ■ Delete a printer ■ Change a printer's properties ■ Change the permissions on a printer

The printer share permissions are designed to match a type of need. The Print permission is intended for end users who need only be able to control their own print jobs. The Manage Documents permission is for those who have some level of responsibility over the print jobs of other people. Full Control is of course for IT support or administrative staff to carry out any task they need to on a printer.

File and Print Service Design

In this section we start the process of file and print service design using the MBI case study as a basis for examining the many configuration options available. First, the scope of the design is specified, followed by an examination of the factors affecting the attributes of a file and print service design. Finally a design for MBI is produced using several design principles.

Scope of a File and Print Service Design

The design for file and print services will include:

Table 13.8 *File and Print Service Design Scope*

Element	Aspect
File Service	■ Server sizing ■ Service allocation to servers ■ File sharing protocols ■ Directories and file shares ■ Server disk partitions and file systems ■ Directory and share permissions ■ File share visibility ■ Drive letter mappings ■ Migrating to Microsoft Distributed File Service ■ Naming standard

Table 13.8 *File and Print Service Design Scope (continued)*

Element	Aspect
Print Service	▪ Server sizing ▪ Service allocation to servers ▪ Printer sharing protocols ▪ Printing devices served ▪ Printers created ▪ Printer permissions ▪ Connecting users to printers ▪ Naming standard

Some aspects of print service design have been treated together with file service design to avoid unnecessary duplication. Where that is the case, their treatment will be found after the Specific Attributes section. The aspects dealt with together are:

- Server sizing
- Service allocation to servers
- File and print sharing protocols

We will include in the category of file server, a computer offering network based application binaries, as the considerations for each are similar. File and print service naming conventions are covered in part in this chapter and defined fully in Chapter 16, Naming Standards.

Requirements on the Design

This section summarizes a small number of requirements that will be used during the following case study design.

Business Principles

Before we begin the design of the file service we should take note of MBI Business Principle 2 which states that the new settlements system will be phased in and suggests that the technical infrastructure may also be phased in. This is important because we must ensure that the design we choose can be phased in instead of requiring a rapid switch over.

Application Requirements

Although not referred to in a business principle, it has been established during the application requirements gathering activity that the new MBI Settlement System requires a high availability print service.

Common Attributes

The common attributes all apply to file and print services, indicating that there are several important aspects to consider when designing these services. Ironically, they are two of the most trivial services to set up without needing to think about design. This can be a situation which leads to difficulties as the services have to undergo constant change to evolve towards a configuration that meets the business needs.

Scalability

The scalability of a file and print service is measured by the ease with which its capacity can be increased.

- *File Serving*

There are three ways of expressing a need for increased file serving capacity:

1. *A need for more storage capacity*—This can usually be satisfied by adding to the storage subsystem. To balance usage across sets of disks it would be normal to have to move directories from one disk to another depending on their usage, however this can all be done in a manner transparent to the client connecting to a file share.
2. *A need for higher throughput*—A need for higher throughput can usually be satisfied by either more IO adapters or more disks. In some cases it can demand additional computers to host the extra IO adapters and disks. When a new computer is commissioned to handle increased throughput it will be necessary to change the computer to which some users' drives are mapped. This can cause an administrative overhead. The use of DFS can alleviate this problem by presenting all file shares, regardless of which computer they are served from, as one logical directory hierarchy. For example, suppose that before the addition of a new server, DFS presented a user with a single share point providing access to their home directory and a public directory. DFS will allow the re-hosting of the public shared directory to another computer in a way that is transparent to the user as DFS maintains the same logical view to the client even though the physical location of part of the directory hierarchy has changed.
3. *A need to support more files and directories*—This will expand the directory tree offering file shares. The issue here is less one of whether a need for additional files and directories can be met, but one of whether the directory structure remains easy to use after a major expansion. This will be a matter of judgment.

- *Print Serving*

  A need for increased printing capacity will usually be expressed in terms of the need for either:

  - *Volume*—Increased volume will usually be met by using additional printers
  - *Speed*—Increased speed is best met by using a more powerful printer.

  This gives rise to two questions:

  1. How are the additional printers to be made available to users?

     Use of a pool of printers is the easiest way of making additional printers transparently available to users. If they are not added to a pool, the only way is to either connect to them through the logon script or for the user to manually connect

  2. Will this increased capacity require increased server capacity to drive the printer?

     Increased printing work will cause increased server usage as more files are transferred from clients to printers via the server. Beyond certain levels, gauged by server utilization, or where printing activity is intensive for periods of time it is common to use computers dedicated to serving printers.

Reliability and Availability

As users and applications alike depend on file and print services extensively, their unavailability can have a major impact on the ability of users to continue working.

We will consider how to offer resilient file services for two different types of file access:

- Read only
- Read and write

Offering resilient access to read only files is relatively straightforward as multiple copies of the file can be distributed across several computers for sharing, maintaining a path of access in the face of the failure of most types of system component. Of course, some type of automatic replication mechanism will be necessary for this to work well.

Resilient access to files that need to be written to is more difficult as there can only ever be one instance of this type of file. Until recently the only practical solution to the need for high availability for this type of file has been to build the file service out of reliable components such as high availability disks subsystems.

A recently available option is to use clustering, a configuration where two computers share the same storage subsystem. Under normal circumstances one computer in the cluster would serve a directory or directories and in the event of it being unable to continue to do so, the other computer would take over automatically. This mechanism relies on two main features:

1. That the set of computers in the cluster is known on the network by one name.
2. That the healthy computers can detect the failure of another computer in the cluster.

The single computer name for the cluster is sometimes referred to as the cluster alias and it is this name that is used in the UNC string to make a connection to the relevant file shares. The use of a single computer name for the cluster means that it is transparent to the client which computer is actually serving the shared directory. Windows NT Cluster technology, originally developed by Digital Equipment Corporation, is now licensed to the Wolfpack consortium and is available for several manufacturer's computers. Figure 13.10 shows a typical cluster configuration and how the directory serving path changes in the event of a failover.

Figure 13.10 *Windows NT Cluster File Share Failover*

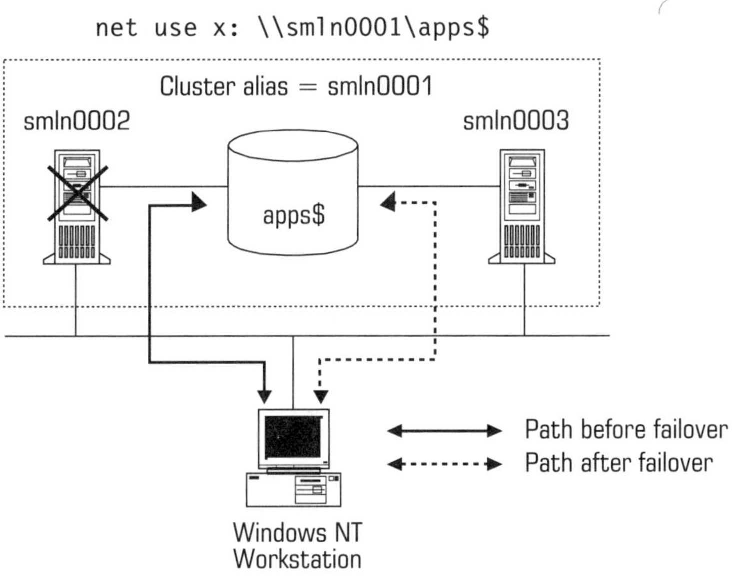

Clusters will also allow printers to be served using the cluster alias computer name, though the nature of served printers makes it practical to increase availability by serving several physical printers from different computers. Clusters offer a level of availability considerably in excess of that possible from a single standard computer, however it is not completely fault tolerant. A cluster would be used in situations where an interruption in service of greater than a few seconds cannot be tolerated. A cluster also has the benefit that failover from one computer to another is automatic, though restoring the cluster to a fully functional state where both computers are available will usually require manual intervention to fix hardware. Fault tolerant Windows NT servers are also emerging onto the market and these would typically be used in situations where no interruption to service can be tolerated.

As tolerance to faults is increased using clustering and fault tolerant computers the cost goes up, so which solution is used will be a clear business decision. It is also very important to bear in mind that in a networked environment, a fault tolerant computer may be used to serve critical files, but if the network becomes unavailable the fault tolerant benefit of such a server is eliminated. Similarly, if software faults or routine operations cause unavailability of service then the value of high availability hardware again needs to be questioned.

Manageability

The manageability of file and print services can be measured by the level of resources needed to manage a given user population. If the attributes of the file and print service match those required by the business it will help to minimize the management overhead. The tools within Windows NT (notably Server Manager) and the resource kit allow an administrator to:

- Determine how the various network resources are being used
- Set permissions on directories and shares
- Break client connections to network resources
- Set directories and printers as shared

File service management challenges usually arise from the need to manage the available disk space and to accommodate changes such as users moving from one business group to another or requiring new file shares and access permissions. Print service management challenges center around ensuring printers have appropriate drivers available, printers are restarted when stalled and are replenished with consumables.

Managing files in shared directories can be accomplished by scheduling batch files to tidy up and quota management software to limit volumes. Printer consumables, paper jams and routine maintenance can only be accomplished locally though the associated need to restart (software) printers can be done remotely.

Security

The security features of the operating system that can be applied to directories and shared resources are central to the control that can be applied to data, application binaries and any other resources that can be shared. The security of file and print services can be measured by the level of access a user has to file based resources. In practice this is whether someone can read, change or delete a file. It should always be possible to describe the security requirements in business terms as that is the ultimate driver for implementing security measures.

Security should always be approached in an integrated fashion to ensure that measures taken in one area aren't undermined by the lack of appropriate measures in another area. For example, suppose an application implements its own security system and stores all its data in text files on a file share. If the information in those files is restricted from some people through the application security, it would be bypassed completely if the underlying file permissions allowed those people to simply open the file outside the context of the application.

The NTFS file system available with Windows NT offers the level of capability needed to configure comprehensive security controls over the file and print services of the type required by a medium to large corporation. A good reason would have to be found for *not* using NTFS.

Capacity and Performance

At a given level of performance, the file and print serving capabilities of a server or set of servers will have a capacity that can be measured in terms of a rate of file and print operations. The spare capacity in a system is the increase in rate of file and print operations that can be sustained while still maintaining a minimum level of performance without needing to add hardware.

For example, a file service may be designed to cope with ten people loading a 100kb file into a word processor per second, with each operation taking no longer than one second. If there are only ever a maximum of five loads of this type in any second the service has the capacity to handle an increase in workload of 100%.

The section earlier on scalability discussed how to increase capacity. Increasing performance is related in that many of the measures used to expand capacity in the face of increased workload have the effect of increasing performance if the workload is kept static.

File service performance is measured in two ways:

- IO Request rate as IOs/second
- Throughput or MB/second

It is usual to find that disks and IO adapters are characterized by the manufacturer in terms of the maximum request rate and throughput they can sustain. Using these figures and knowledge of an IO subsystem configuration the net maximum request rate and throughput may be calculated.

To increase the request rate a system is capable of it would be normal to spread the IOs over more disks, though it is not uncommon to need to spread the load over multiple IO adapters as well. A crude redistribution of files across a set of disks is usually sufficient to spread the IO load in the same way. In rare cases, all the IOs may be directed at one file, in which case it may be necessary to spread that file over several disks. This can be done using two techniques, one called striping and the other mirroring. Striping breaks the file up and spreads it over the disks. Mirroring simply maintains multiple copies of the file on separate disks.

To increase the throughput we would again apply more disks or IO adapters but we should be careful to understand whether the throughput required is aggregate across access to several files or whether we need higher throughput when accessing a small number of files. If it is the latter then striping can again provide a solution as one IO request can cause data from the file to be supplied simultaneously from several disks.

To know when to increase maximum sustainable request rate and when to increase throughput demands that the IO needs of applications using a file server and the level of utilization of the current system are both known in terms of IO request rate and throughput. This data is best obtained through experimentation and observation, gathering system utilization statistics in the process and comparing them against manufacturers' stated figures.

Finally, we shouldn't overlook the fact that a file server is accessed over the network and so the network components will figure in the overall performance equation, in particular, the network adapters and the network infrastructure itself. Modern computers are capable of saturating a standard 10Mbit/second Ethernet segment so care needs to be taken that the network does not become a bottleneck to a high performance file server. Use of multiple network adapters can solve some problems, however the most likely area for a performance problem is not with the adapter but with the network itself. A popular solution is to either use multiple network segments to connect a server to the network or use a higher speed network technology such as 100MB/sec Ethernet, ATM or FDDI for the network segment used by the server.

Specific Attributes

In addition to the common attributes, examined in the previous section, the design of file and print services carries with it one specific attribute, that of platform dependency. Note that this specific attribute applies to all the technical infrastructure services to a greater or lesser extent. It is dealt with in this chapter as it is arguably most applicable to file and print services.

Platform Dependency

In an environment where there is more than one platform involved in the supply or consumption of file and print services, there can be a number of options for achieving the same objective. There will naturally be technical arguments in favor of one solution over another. However, which choice is made can have a significant bearing on the subsequent dependence a corporation has on particular technologies. The impact of this choice will be to determine:

- The level of security that can be implemented—Different platforms implement file and print service security in different and usually incompatible ways, compromising the overall solution.
- The manageability of the services—Different tools may be required to manage different components of the overall print or file service.
- The supportability of the services—A wider and hence more costly set of skills will be necessary to support a service comprising multiple platform technologies.
- The ability to exploit new functionality from a particular manufacturer—Frequently new functionality is only available within the context of a single vendor environment. Using multiple platforms can close off options for early adoption of new capabilities.

Let us take an example where file and print services are currently supplied to PC users by a Novell NetWare server and a Windows NT server. The options are to replace the Novell NetWare server with a Windows NT file and print server or to leave it in place. In either case, the solution can be characterized in terms of the platforms the services depend on. In one case, it was Windows NT and Novell NetWare, in the other it was just Windows NT.

Ideally, the platform dependency choice will be driven by a business principle with the justification and implications written in terms of the four items listed above. For an example, we can look to the MBI Business Principle 3, developed in Chapter 5, which asserts that duplicated systems should be avoided.

The use of this specific attribute is very simple, which belies the importance of the decisions behind it. If there is no business principle guiding the choice on this topic then one should be created and agreed on.

Server Sizing Guidelines

A file and print service design should specify server sizing guidelines. The problem is, how do we predict the capacity a particular server will offer and what the likely workload will be? It is possible to find tables illustrating guidelines for server sizing though these should be treated very carefully as they are likely to have been produced in artificial circumstances. In every case we should try to use existing knowledge about the likely workload and how computers of a given power perform. A design that states server requirements based on experience is likely to be more accurate than one based on an unjustified table from a publication.

A complicating factor is that servers are sometimes allocated several services to run, requiring the task of sizing to take into consideration more variables, reducing the accuracy of any results. If servers can be dedicated to a service, such as file serving, then sizing is much easier.

The MBI solution architect noted that the following observations are true about the MBI environment:

- there are a number of different sized locations
- the size of the locations will change over the life of the project
- the power available in a single computer will change over the rollout of the project
- there is a need to re-use a number of existing computers

Faced with these, the best thing to do is to determine the rules by which a server is sized. To do this it is necessary to make some assumptions. Here are those used for MBI:

1. Standard server = 200MHz Pentium Pro, 256MB memory, 10GB RAID 5

2. Power server = 440MHz Alpha, 512MB memory, 20GB RAID 5
3. Standard server can serve 300 light users, a power server 600
4. A medium user = 2.5 light users
5. A heavy user = 5 light users

Table 13.9 shows the calculation to determine the recommended file and print server capacity for a single example subnet.

Table 13.9 *Rule of Thumb File and Print Server Sizing Example*

User Type	Quantity on Subnet	Light User Equivalent
Light	100	100
Medium	50	125
Heavy	40	200
Total	190	425

The light user equivalent value of 425 implies the need for two standard servers or a single power server. The advantage of this approach is that experience can lead to adjustments to improve the user equivalent assumptions and new servers can be considered by assigning them a user rating. In practice, different user types may be more appropriate. It may be more useful to categorize users according to job type.

The implication of MBI Business Principle 4, that the technical infrastructure must have spare capacity, may be managed by adjusting the user equivalent ratings of the servers downwards to ensure they operate with capacity in hand. This type of decision is a good candidate for a design principle as it will probably be challenged. An example (B-26) is shown in Appendix B.

It should be borne in mind that the demands placed on a server by printing services are of a different nature to those placed on it by file services. Incompatibilities in service requirements will reduce the accuracy of the "user equivalent" sizing technique outlined above. A solution is to treat the two services separately for the purpose of sizing, particularly when there is the opportunity to dedicate a server to one service.

File and Print Service Allocation

The file and print service design should declare a policy for which computers in the infrastructure should be used to host the file and print services. Indeed, this should be part of a *service allocation policy* for governing how all the technical infrastructure services are allocated to servers. The MBI file and print service allocation policy is presented here in the context of a general service allocation policy for the MBI infrastructure.

The over-riding consideration for the MBI service allocation policy is to take into account MBI Business Principle 2, requiring a design that can be phased in. The ability to phase something in can be viewed as an aspect of scalability. The business principle says that groups of offices will be phased in at a time, though prudence would suggest that it should be possible to phase in the underlying technical infrastructure file service on an office by office basis or even business group by business group.

To facilitate this business principle MBI chose to adopt a simple design based on a policy of allocating a minimum of one computer offering file, print and application binary services dedicated to each IP subnet. This policy was captured as a design principle:

Design Principle 13-1—Basic File and Print Service Allocation Policy
A minimum of one computer offering file, print and application binary services will be present on each IP subnet hosting users.
Justification
▪ Supports MBI Business Principle 3 demanding a phased implementation. ▪ This approach is inherently scalable, supporting MBI Business Principle 4. ▪ No routers are involved between client and server, offering the possibility of using m-node type clients to speed up LAN communications. This should be satisfactory as the majority of client/server communications will be local to a subnet. (Note that the emergence of switched networking will reduce the value of this justification.) ▪ This principle broadly matches MBI's current service allocation policy.
Implications
▪ Some subnets may not be highly populated, making it less economic to dedicate one server to those users. (Note that one option would be to decide a cut-off user population for a subnet, below which they would have them share a server on another subnet.) ▪ Some existing servers will need to be moved to a new subnet.

The design principle above is a good starting point but the service allocation policy should be documented in detail in the form of a set of rules so it may be used to determine the deployment of servers. Table 13.10 shows the MBI service allocation policy.

Table 13.10 *Service Allocation Policy*

Rule	Details
1.	Each location will have a BDC from the regional master domain.
2.	Each location will have a PDC from the local resource domain (designated according to the server naming standard with the numeric portion of the name 0001).
3.	Each location will have at least one BDC from the IT support domain.
4.	Resource servers will host file and print services.
5.	Application servers will host applications.
6.	The resource domain PDC will be counted as a resource server.
7.	The first additional resource server added to the resource domain will be configured as a BDC.
8.	Subsequent resource servers will be configured as member servers of the resource domain.
9.	Application servers will be configured as member servers of the resource domain.
10.	Each additional IP subnet shall contain an additional resource server.
11.	The E:\groups and E:\public directories and shares will *always* be configured on the resource domain PDC. The logon script depends on it.
12.	The IT Support domain BDC will host WINS, DHCP, NTP, Management tools, on-line software kits, etc. It will also host DNS where determined by the DNS design.

Note that in cases where the need for availability demands it, resource servers will be clustered together in pairs. Table 13.10 assumes that file, print and application binary serving will all be co-hosted on the same resource server.

An example of the server deployment strategy is illustrated in Figure 13.11. The diagram shows the various infrastructure computers including the IT support domain server and master domain BDC.

Figure 13.11
Small Sized Installation

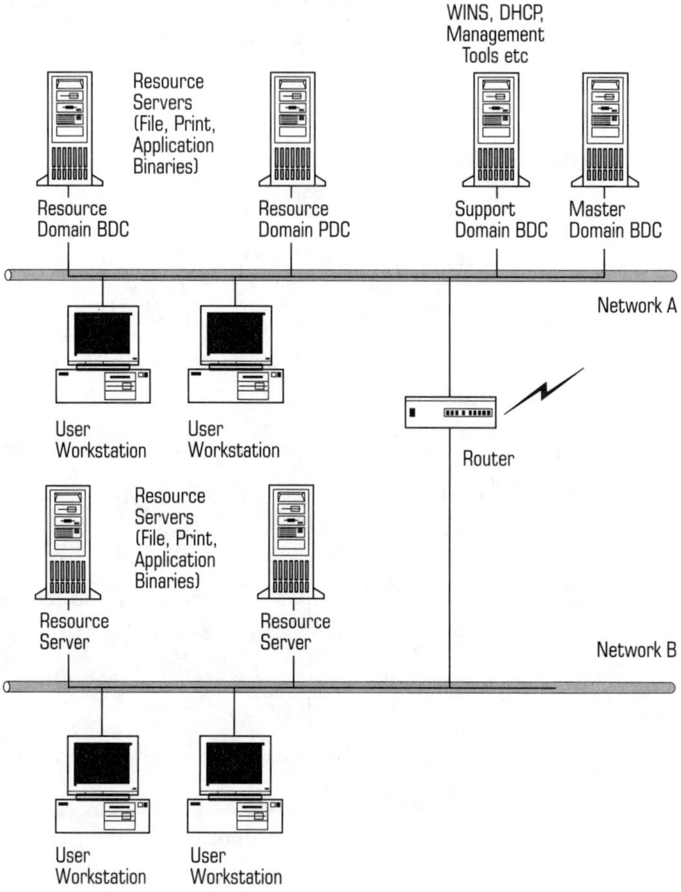

In a small location, Network B may not be present and the file and print serving functions, shown as using two computers per network in the diagram, could be combined onto one computer. In a larger location, additional networks (like Network B) can be added, each with file and print servers as members of the local resource domain. If more than one IT Support domain server is being used then each should be connected to a different network where they exist.

One strategy for increasing the overall availability of print services is to serve printers from more than one server. In most MBI locations there will be at least two resource domain servers that can be used for this purpose, however, the minimum server implementation as prescribed for a small location allows for just one resource server dedicated to file and print services. To provide an alternative for serving printers we can look to the master domain BDC or the IT Support domain BDC as potential hosts.

File and Print Sharing Protocols

The existing MBI technical infrastructure includes Novell NetWare servers and UNIX servers offering file and print services to a variety of client systems. The preceding sections of this chapter outlined some of the options for delivering these file services to the Windows NT client base. What we need is guidance from the business.

The main example used in Chapter 6, Design Principles, is directly applicable to this stage of the MBI design. The design principle statement is reproduced below.

Design Principle 13-2—Optimize Use of Windows NT File and Print Servers
The technical infrastructure will facilitate the use of existing Novell NetWare and UNIX file and print servers but will be designed to achieve maximum benefit when using Windows NT Server in this role.

The option this presents is to use a Windows NT server as a gateway to other servers confining the use of non-NetBIOS over TCP/IP protocols to the servers. Although the total number of file sharing protocols in use is not necessarily reduced by this design principle, use of a gateway does mean that the workstations need only run the one file and print service protocol that is optimized for Windows NT.

The question of which protocols to use is related to the choice of platform and should be examined closely when considering the platform dependency attribute.

A file and print service design should make it clear which protocols are to run where in the system. This is best shown using a summary architecture diagram like the one in Figure 13.12. The implementation detail for a particular location would require the diagram to list the actual computers.

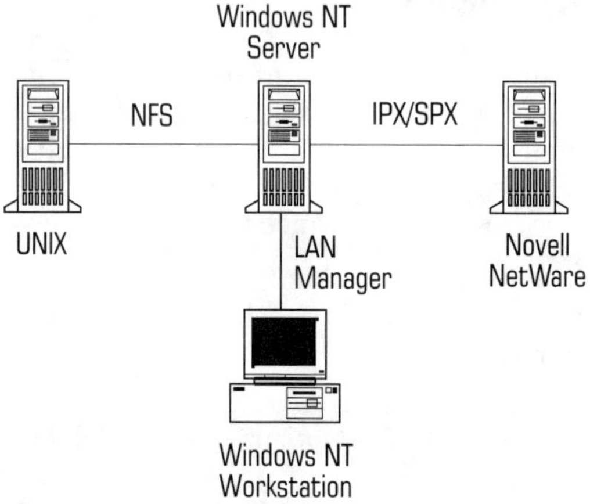

Figure 13.12 *MBI File and Print Service Protocol Use*

File Service Design

Directories and File Shares

In considering the design of the directory structures the MBI solution architect carried out a review of current server directory structures to establish how well they worked for the corporation. The principle findings were as follows:

- Products tended to be installed in their default directories. This meant some product directories were created in the *program files* sub-directory, others were created under c:\, a number of product installations created directories with the product version number embedded. For example, acme36 for version 3.6 of the acme product. This practice caused difficulties for logon scripts and other batch files when the product came to be upgraded, creating a new directory to reflect the new version.
- Some administrators had created sub-directories to reflect the usage of the computer, others hadn't. A significant observation was that because there was no standard directory structure it was difficult for anyone other than the computer's regular administrator to find their way around the directory structure of another computer.

The solution architect judged this state of affairs to be an impediment to the realization of a global technical infrastructure that would satisfy the various MBI Business Principles, particularly those concerned with making support easier.

It was therefore decided to create a standard super directory structure which could be implemented on each server and workstation. This is written as a design principle.

Design Principle 13-3—Use of a Standard Directory Structure
The standard directory structure shown in Figure 13.13 should be configured on every Windows NT workstation and server.
Justification
▪ Uniformity will reduce administrator error. ▪ Reducing administrator error will reduce support overhead, consistent with MBI Business Principle 4.
Implications
▪ Some parts of the directory tree will remain unused. ▪ A corporate wide convention will be needed to map application name onto directory name to ensure consistent installation of applications. ▪ Management must support user compliance with the standard directory structure. ▪ Management must support the migration to the standard directory structure with resources and clear deliverables.
Issues
▪ Certain old applications do not offer a choice as to where to install them so will end up outside the standard structure.

The directory structure used for MBI is as shown in Figure 13.13. It should never be assumed that by listing a directory structure that everyone will have the same understanding of the purpose of each directory. It will be necessary to supply a table detailing the directory usage conventions. Importantly, instructions for extending the directory structure should be given so the principles behind its construction will remain in force allowing administrators to benefit from the consistency.

Figure 13.13 *MBI Server General Directory Structure*

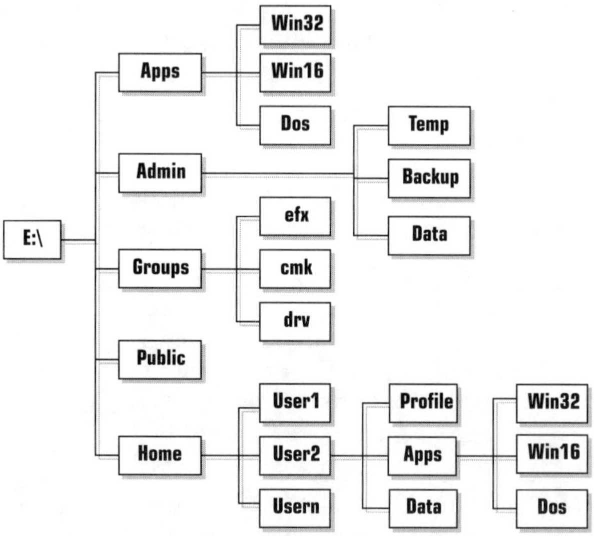

An extract from the MBI directory usage convention table is shown in Table 13.11.

Table 13.11 *MBI Directory Usage Conventions (extract)*

Directory	Usage	Extending the Structure
Apps	Under each of the three subdirectories will be directories for the applications installed on the server. In some cases these applications will run on the server, in others, the applications will be invoked on a client.	Add a directory under the appropriate sub-directory of Apps.
Groups	The purpose of each subdirectory under Groups is to provide a location for members within a particular business group to share data.	There should only be one level of subdirectory under Groups. Each sub-directory will be named using the three letter business code for the particular business group. (See Table 16.4, on page 497).

The super directory structure has been designed for sharing out so there is a simple relationship between directory and file share. Table 13.12 shows the mapping between the two.

Table 13.12 *MBI Directory to Share Mapping*

Directory	Share Name
E:\Apps	Apps$
E:\Users\usern	Usern$
E:\groups\efx	efx$
E:\groups\cmk	cmk$
E:\groups\drv	drv$
E:\public	Public

Server Disk Partitions and File Systems

A file service design should state how disks should be partitioned and which file system to use. This information would ultimately be reproduced in the server and workstation installation instruction documents but should be captured at the design stage. MBI mandated that every system disk (or disks) be divided into a 1GB C: partition containing the system files in the standard Windows NT directory structure and the remaining space on the disk formatted as partition E:. The E partition will host the super directory structure. To implement the super directory structure to maximum effect by applying suitable permissions to the directories to stop accidental or deliberate unauthorized access, implies the use of the NTFS file system. If this decision is at all contentious it could be represented as a design principle as follows:

Design Principle 13-4—Use of NTFS
All disk partitions will be formatted to use NTFS.
Justification
▪ Greater data protection ▪ Greater control over security ▪ More robust
Implications
▪ The partition will be unavailable from the local computer if the PC is booted from DOS.

Directory and Share Permissions

As an additional observation made during the directory structure review, the Solution Architect noted that where NTFS was in use, directory permissions were frequently more lax than they needed to be and in many cases were inconsistent with the file share permissions. In addition, new groups had sometimes been created with miscellaneous selections of user rights. Keeping track of security under such conditions is extremely hard, with so many variables involved, that MBI decided to adopt a strategy of keeping the directory and file share permissions as simple as possible. The use of built-in accounts and groups where possible would minimize "special cases" needing extra rights. Table 13.13 defines the MBI permission strategy, using a NorthAmerica resource domain as an example.

Table 13.13 *Directory Structure and Share Permissions*

Directory	Group or User	Directory Permission	Share Permission
E:\Apps	MTL\Users	Read (RX)	Read (RX)
E:\Groups\efx	MTL\EFX	Full Control	Full Control
E:\Groups\cmk	MTL\CMK	Full Control	Full Control
E:\Groups\drv	MTL\DRV	Full Control	Full Control
E:\Public	MTL\Users	Full Control	Full Control
E:\Home\Usern	NorthAmerica\Usern	Full Control	Full Control
E:\Admin	MTL\Administrators	Full Control	Full Control

All permissions in the table are in addition to the standard permissions applied to a new directory.

File Share Visibility

If browsing is enabled then there needs to be a policy to decide which file shares are visible and which are invisible. In general, users will only need to browse for commonly shared resources and not, for example, their own home directory. It, therefore, makes sense to limit the information available when browsing by listing only those resources that are commonly shared. Design Principle 13-5 shows how the MBI solution architect chose to describe this design decision.

Design Principle 13-5—Use Hidden File Shares
File shares will be created hidden unless there is a reason for them not to be.
Justification
▪ Minimizes length of the browse list shown in utilities such as Network Neighborhood. ▪ All file share connections except home drive are set up in the logon script, making the need to browse for file shares rare.
Implications
▪ In some circumstances users may need to be told of a hidden share to enable them to be able to connect to it.

The design principle does not reference any of the five MBI Business Principles created in Chapter 5 as none have a bearing in this case. A business principle requiring a certain level of security may support such a design principle. Alternatively, if it can be shown that by using hidden shares the number of support calls is reduced then that would be consistent with a business principle looking for a reduction in support overhead.

Based on the directory tree structures shown in Figure 13.13, MBI Server General Directory Structure, the shares created are listed in Table 13.14.

Drive Letter Mappings

The use of a consistent convention for drive mappings brings similar benefits to those of a consistent convention for directory names and file share names. Support costs are lowered as there are fewer mistakes through dealing with unfamiliar configurations. The actual letters used are arbitrary though of course they must avoid those used for built-in disks and local partitions.

Table 13.14 *Driver Mappings*

Share Name	Mapped to	Comment
Apps$	F:\	Shared application binaries
Usern$	H:\	Home drive
efx$	G:\	Foreign exchange group share

Table 13.14 *Driver Mappings (continued)*

Share Name	Mapped to	Comment
cmk$	G:\	Capital markets group share
drv$	G:\	Derivatives group share
Public	P:\	Public share
N/A	A:\	Floppy disk drive
N/A	C:\	Hard drive operating system partition
N/A	D:\	CD-ROM
N/A	E:\	Data and applications partition

The table only shows three group shares for clarity. The convention assumes that a user is not a member of more than one business group.

Coping with Driver Letter Conflict

The file share implementation for MBI we have just seen requires the user to work with eight different drive letters if we include A:, C:, D: (CD-ROM) and E:. This is likely to be quite manageable for most users, however, we have overlooked the fact that in many of the MBI offices there are already local drive letter usage conventions in place conflicting with our new design.

If complete uniformity of drive letter usage was desired it would have been necessary to find out exactly what everyone was using and to try to develop a compromise design. However, it would have inevitably led to some groups being asked to change. This can be a particular problem if applications and macros have been hard-coded to use certain drive letters.

For example, a Microsoft Excel macro may open a file from the directory k:\spreadsheets assuming k: was always mapped to the same file share. Changing where k: is mapped to by forcing a new convention will require that this macro is updated. Once known about it is usually easy to make the change. The difficulty is in establishing all the programs and macros that do make such references to make sure none are left to break when the change in drive letter is made.

Migrating to Distributed File Services

We know that the MBI locations vary in size considerably and will be likely to change in size in the future. For this reason the service allocation policy will lead to differences in the number of file servers at each location with the prospect of some locations requiring additional servers in the future. The introduction of a new file server will often lead to the redistribution of served directories among the servers to balance the load. This will cause some users to change their file share connections, causing an administrative overhead.

DFS presents the opportunity to hide these differing physical configurations by presenting one unchanging logical structure. Another benefit of Microsoft DFS is that is offers a possible solution to the problem of conflicting drive letter conventions by significantly reducing the number of drive letters required. It does this by linking several shares that would normally require separate drive mappings into one directory tree that can span multiple computers. One way to use the MBI directory and share structure with DFS would be to share out the directories Home, Groups, Public, Admin and Apps for the purpose of linking them into a DFS tree.

The directory and share structure designed for MBI earlier would require a different set of permissions for it to be used successfully with DFS. Without DFS, a file share connection made directly to the target directory meant that that directory was inherently protected from deletion, as were any other directories above it. Using DFS a user will be connected to a single point near or at the top of the DFS tree and would be expected to navigate down to the directory of interest. To do this they must be given at least List permission on all the directories in the hierarchy they need to be able to navigate through. The files and subdirectories in a given target directory must then have the appropriate permissions to allow the user to carry out their job. For example, the user should have Read, Write, Execute and Delete permissions in their own directory only and no one else's. They must also be restricted from deleting their own home directory and any other directory at the same level or above it.

A design that uses DFS should specify the following details:

- Which directories are shared and with what share names
- How the shares are linked into the DFS tree
- The permissions on all the directories and shares
- The share connections to be made by clients (we must not assume all connections will be made to the root of the tree)

Print Service Design

While too frequently the last thing to be considered in any design or implementation, printing can be of utmost business importance. It is also true that printing issues can consume a disproportionate amount of support time, so it is critical from a business and a support perspective that printing services should operate smoothly.

The recommended way to achieve an effective and supportable print service is to design for simplicity and uniformity. This way there is less to go wrong and IT Support staff are able to become more familiar with the specific technology employed and how it is configured.

Shared Printers

The design for shared printers should define:

- Printer connection method:
  - directly to a network attached printer
  - directly to a locally attached printer
  - to a shared printer on a server
- The allocation of printers (the software entity) to servers
- The allocation of printing devices (the hardware entity) to printers on servers

The choice of printer connection method should be a matter of policy. MBI chose to disallow workstations from connecting directly to network attached printers or local printers because of the support overhead of having to configure the correct printer drivers on each workstation.

Design Principle 13-6—Use of Print Servers
Workstations will connect to printers via a printer (the software entity) on a server.
Justification
▪ Appropriate printer drivers may be maintained on the server for automatic download to the workstation should the version not be up to date or the driver missing. This mechanism avoids the need to maintain the correct printer drivers on each workstation, so keeping support overhead down. This supports MBI Business Principle 4.

continued ▸

continued

Implications
▪ The ability for users to print to any particular printer will be dependent on the availability of the computer sharing the printer unless several computers share a printer for the same printing device.
Issues
▪ In cases where a high degree of security is needed or it is a method of enhancing the availability of the print service, locally attached printers will be required.

The allocation of printing devices to printers then to servers is best defined using a table as shown for the Milan office in Table 13.15.

Table 13.15 *Server/Printer/Printing Device Allocation*

Server	Printer	Model	Address
SMLN0001	PMLN1234	Laser 49/i	16.245.20.60
SMLN0001	PMLN1235	Laser 49/i	16.245.20.61
SMLN0001	PMLN1236	Laser 49/i	16.245.20.62
SMLN0001	PMLN8888	Laser 49/i	16.245.20.63
SMLN0002	PMLN1234	Laser 49/i	16.245.20.60
SMLN0002	PMLN1235	Laser 49/i	16.245.20.61
SMLN0002	PMLN1236	Laser 49/i	16.245.20.62

Note that Milan has two computers acting as print servers, each configured to serve each of the printing devices, with the exception of PMLN8888. The reason for this might be flexibility, however it does provide an opportunity to increase the availability of a printing device by eliminating the dependency on a single print server for access to that device, particularly if printing direct to devices from workstations is disallowed. A policy decision such as this should be captured as a design principle.

Design Principle 13-7—Redundant Network Attached Printers
▪ Each network attached printing device will be served by more than one computer.
Justification
▪ Supports the application requirement that the ability to print is critical. ▪ Eliminates dependence on a single print server computer. ▪ This is a better way of increasing availability than configuring workstations to print direct to network attached printing devices. ▪ Protects against printer (software entity) malfunction as well as server unavailability.
Implications
▪ To realize any increase in availability users must be connected to printers in an appropriate systematic fashion.
Issues
▪ How to load balance between the two print servers.

Printer Permissions

Because printers are one of the more unreliable components of a technical infrastructure, MBI decided that all printers at a location should be potentially accessible by all users so as to provide a basis for continued printing should any printer fail. It was also decided to go with the default security settings which allowed for Users to submit and manage their own print jobs and for Administrators, Print Operators and Server Operators to have complete control over the printer and its jobs.

If it ever becomes necessary to restrict access to a particular printer then this would be done as an exception. This may occur if, for example, a department buys an expensive color printer that would cost too much to run if it were a generally available resource.

Connecting Users to Printers

The topic of connecting users to printers is covered to an extent in Chapter 14, User Environment, and Appendix C containing the user logon script. To spread the load across a set of printers, the representatives of the business at MBI requested that different business groups be allocated to different default printers. This matched the layout of most offices with printers generally adjacent to the business group that used them.

To allow for automatic connection to the correct printers and selection of a suitable default, the solution architect chose to base the connection logic in the logon script on local Windows NT group membership. Table 13.16 shows the scheme that was used for three business groups only in the Milan office, EFX, CMK, DRV.

The special printer PMLN8888 is only to be connected to and set as default for the subset of users in the EFX group who are also members of the EFXP1 group. The logon script sets up PMLN8888 for members of EFXP1 after setting up the printers for members of EFX. Thus members of EFXP1 are connected to a total of four printers.

Table 13.16 *Printer to Group Allocation*

Printer / Windows NT Group	EFX	EFXP1	CMK	DRV
SMLN0001\PMLN1234	Default			1st
SMLN0001\PMLN1235	1st		Default	
SMLN0001\PMLN1236			1st	Default
SMLN0002\PMLN1236	2nd			
SMLN0002\PMLN1234			2nd	
SMLN0002\PMLN1235				2nd
SMLN0001\PMLN8888		Default		

1st = First reserve printer

2nd = Second reserve printer

Notice that a user will always be connected to at least one printer from each server. This enhances availability of the overall print service by ensuring a user can continue to print if one of the print servers fails.

14

User Environment

The nature of the user environment determines how a user interacts with the system. It is therefore important to how efficiently a user is able to work and the overall perception they gain of the system. Designed well, it should lead to productive and satisfied users. However, it is also an important factor in keeping support costs down.

Windows NT allows a considerable degree of customization of the user environment. It gives the systems administrator the power to control what a user can and cannot do from their workstation. Administrative control extends over settings for:

- Icons
- Menu structures
- Screen layout
- User environment operating defaults

To ensure a desire to customize or control doesn't lack business purpose, the goal of the user interface must always be kept in mind, which is to present an easily useable environment that allows the user to focus on their job. For example, we must trade off the degree to which users are allowed to customize their user interface against supportability, or administrative control of the desktop against flexibility for the user. This chapter is about creating a user environment that allows users to work effectively and the business to function efficiently.

The focus of this chapter is on the issues involved in the optimum design of a user environment. Throughout, it concentrates on the tools and functionality available with standard Windows NT 4 as this allows a "first principles" approach which offers a more complete insight into the subject. Emerging initiatives such as Microsoft Zero Admin Workstation should be seen as potentially alternative ways to achieve the same business objectives.

User Environment is a design activity and its position in the overall project roadmap is shown in Figure 14.1.

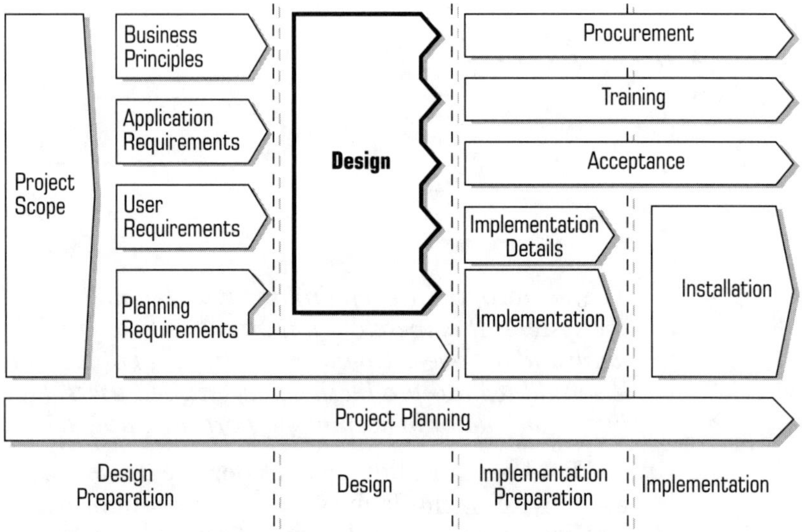

Figure 14.1 *Design Activity (highlighted)*

Structure of Chapter

Table 14.1 shows the structure of Chapter 14

Table 14.1 *The Structure of Chapter 14*

Topic	Contents
Technology Review	▪ Controlling the user environment with Windows NT user profiles. ▪ Controlling user accounts by setting account defaults and policies. ▪ Logon scripts as a means of configuring the user environment at logon time. ▪ Overview of a user environment control tool.
User Environment Design	▪ The scope of a user environment design. ▪ How user environment design can be characterized by common and specific attributes. ▪ Design of a user environment for the MBI case study that allows corporate-wide user mobility through use of design policies and logon scripts.

Technology Review

There are three main technology elements to the Windows NT user environment:

- **Controlling the user environment**—This is concerned with the balance between administrator customization and user customization of the user environment.
- **Controlling the user accounts**—As the foundation of the security mechanism the controls that can be applied to user accounts have a significant part to play in the implementation of security measures, in turn affecting what users can and cannot do.
- **Logon scripts**—A mechanism for configuring the user environment at logon time.

  Each of these are reviewed in the following sub-sections.

Controlling the User Environment

Here we will review the mechanism by which Windows NT allows administrators to control the extent to which users can customize their user environment. It is an important mechanism to understand because it has a strong bearing on the following:

- How users that need to work at several different workstations around the corporation may be presented with the same user environment at each one.
- The support implications of allowing users to customize their user environment.

User Profiles

A user profile is the collective term for all the user configurable items in a user's desktop environment. Windows NT treats it as three components, the important elements of which are summarized below.

1. A copy of the Current User section of the registry containing settings for:
   - Taskbar settings
   - Windows NT Explorer settings
   - Control panel settings
   - Accessory settings
   - Printer connections
   - Windows NT help bookmarks

2. The profile directory
   - Personal program groups and items
   - Shortcuts for start menu structure
   - Shortcuts for the desktop
   - Shortcuts to network neighborhood items
3. Common program groups and items
   - Shortcuts to common program groups and items

User profiles are saved by the system when a user logs off and are reloaded when they logon again, allowing the user to regain their customized desktop environment.

There are three types of user profile:

- **Local**—A local user profile is one stored on the Windows NT computer the user logged in at. It is stored in the profiles directory under the Windows NT directory and can only be used by that user at that computer.
- **Roaming**—A roaming user profile is one that is stored on a server and is loaded down to whichever computer a user logs on at. Upon log off, the profile is uploaded to the server and stored in the network location specified in the *Profile* dialogue box for the user account, set using the *User Manager for Domains* utility.
- **Mandatory**—A mandatory profile is one that cannot be changed by the user. This would be used for strict environments where the consequences of a change in the desktop could have an adverse effect.

System Policies

The principal means of controlling the settings of the user's desktop environment is using a system policy. System policies can be set on a per computer, per NT group or per user basis and have the effect of either:

- restricting what a user can customize, or
- setting values on behalf of the user.

The schematic in Figure 14.2 shows the effect of a policy on a user's environment.

Policies are created and modified using the *System Policy Editor*. This tool enables the administrator to control the settings in two sections of the computer's configuration database, commonly referred to as the registry. One is the Current User section, which forms the main constituent of a user profile and the other is the Local Computer section which controls settings that are independent of which user is using the computer.

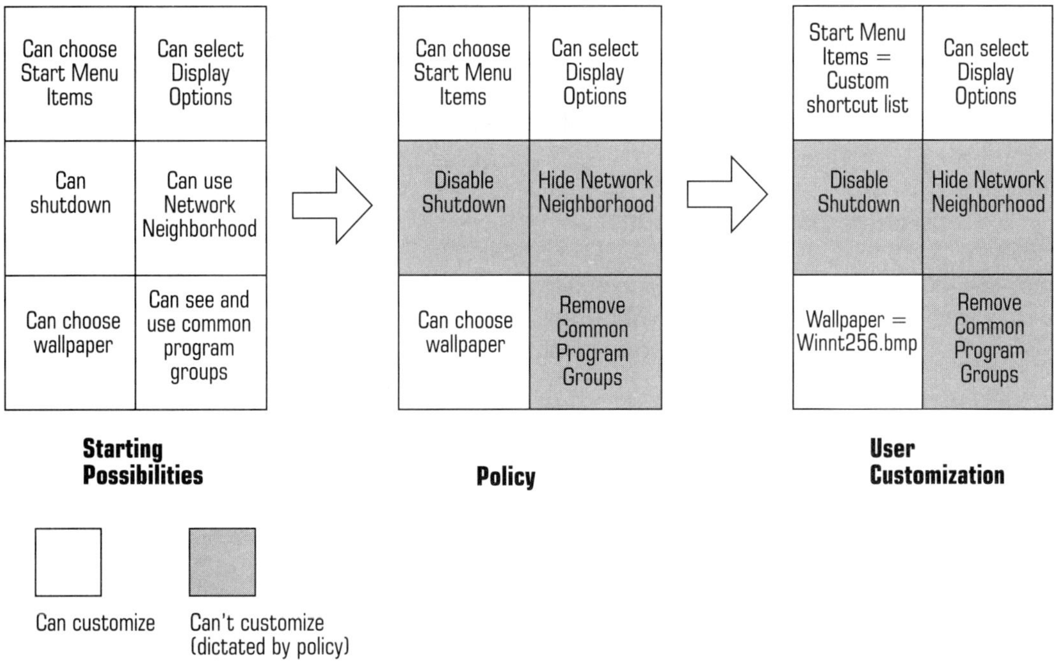

Figure 14.2 *Effect on a User Profile of Policy Setting*

As an example, the administrator may set a system policy that forces the wallpaper to a specific type for a particular user. This setting will form part of their user profile. Alternatively, the administrator may configure a system policy that sets the default logon id and password. This setting will apply to a specific computer and will not appear in a user profile.

Changes to the Current User section of the registry are essentially manifested as over-ride values for user profile settings a user might otherwise have made. Changes to the Local Computer section of the registry affect which aspects of the computer's desktop environment are available for use as well as the setting of default values.

Figure 14.2 shows the policy having been set, represented by the gray squares, controlling a user profile by either denying the user the ability to select an option or setting a value for them.

Policy Templates

A policy template is the starting point from which a policy is defined. Administrators or third party software vendors may construct new policy templates that allow policies to be set on behalf of users that were not available under the default built-in templates.

It would be rare to need to create a new policy template. The MBI case study later in this chapter uses the default policy template.

Controlling the User Accounts

Each user needs a user account to be able to access a Windows NT security domain. A Windows NT user account is very much like a user account on other operating systems. It has the following characteristics:

- User account name
- Full user name
- Description
- Password
- Flags and a date relating to password expiration
- Membership of groups
- Rights in the domain assigned to the account or groups to which the account belongs
- Hours account can be used
- Computers the account can be used to logon to
- Whether the account is local to the computer or in a domain
- Dial-in type (dial-in permission and callback strategy)
- User Environment Profile information (user profile path, logon script name, home directory)

In addition to these, a domain wide policy can be set for password restrictions including what conditions cause an account to be locked out. User related activity can be audited according to the settings in the Audit Policy dialogue box.

Logon Scripts

Invocation of the logon script is the last thing that happens automatically before a user begins work. A logon script is not absolutely necessary, however it gives us the opportunity to customize the user's environment and to carry out things we might not want to rely on the user to do. In the logon script we can:

- Connect to printers and set a default printer
- Connect to file shares (for both sharing files and accessing server based applications)
- Create personal program groups and program items
- Install applications (where no other method is favored)
- Set environment variables
- Start applications
- Customize the actions of the logon script according to environmental factors such as user group membership

Script Language

A logon script would typically be written in an interpreted scripting language though it may break out to compiled code for speed. The more established operating systems such as OpenVMS or UNIX have powerful interpreted scripting languages bundled with the operating system that typically provide features such as:

- Conditional loops
- Variables
- Functions for accessing the operating system
- The ability to execute a command line within the script

Windows NT is not blessed with such a built-in scripting language though there are a small number available via other sources. One such language is Perl, which has the advantage of being portable between Windows NT and UNIX. Another is KiXtart, both of which are available on the Internet or in the Windows NT Server 4.0 Resource Kit. KiXtart will allow the same script to be run on Windows 95 and Windows NT, though there are some unavoidable differences.

One of the particular advantages of KiXtart is its provision of built-in variables that are automatically set to useful values. For example, one is set to the name of the server that logged the user on. Another contains the name of the domain the user logged on from. This makes it easier to write a common logon script that simply uses conditional statements to change its behavior depending on a number of environmental parameters.

The MBI case study uses KiXtart as the script language.

Microsoft's response to the need for a fully functional and integrated scripting tool is the ActiveX Scripting Architecture. This architecture defines an environment in which a script may execute, the implementation of which is called a scripting host. Initially only Internet Explorer and Internet Information Server had scripting host capability. It is now available for the Windows NT platform.

The Internet Explorer scripting host allowed client execution of VB Script (a language based on a subset of Visual Basic) or Java script embedded in html pages. The Internet Information Server scripting host introduced the capability of running scripts on the server prior to download of an html page. Such pages are referred to as Active Server Pages. The scripting host for the Windows NT platform is called the Windows Scripting Host (WSH) and allows the execution of scripts from within Windows (e.g., double clicking on an icon to initiate script execution) or from the command line.

WSH will be built-in to Windows 98 and Windows NT 5 and will become available in Windows 95 updates. It is likely that support for other scripting languages will emerge over time.

A User Environment Control Tool

It is paradoxical that to control the user environment to the extent a user only has access to a very limited set of functionality requires a high degree of customization. It is, however, common to find that a group of users might only need access to one application or perhaps a small number of applications and a remote file service. To provide functionality over and above what is necessary can incur a greater than necessary support overhead.

The Microsoft Zero Administration Kit (ZAK), which is a component of the overall Zero Administration Initiative provides a set of tools, methodologies and guidelines based on Windows NT policies and profiles that are intended to ease the central configuration and management of a large workstation population. Policy templates are provided that can be customized to allow workstations to be built with functionality closely tailored to the user's needs. This provides a route to keeping support overheads down by only exposing to the users the functionality they need to do their job.

Note that to employ ZAK implies use of policies and policy templates to control workstation configuration. In a large organization there may be many groups of users with each requiring a different set of policy settings. This raises two issues which must be considered very carefully before committing to this approach for workstation configuration management:

- The quantity of different policies and policy templates will require management in their own right.

It will be important for guidelines to be laid down specifying under what circumstances new policies and policy templates can be created and a change control process be implemented governing the change in settings for a policy or template.

- The restrictions applied to any particular group of users need to be judged carefully.

  Too many restrictions and there will be hasty demands to de-restrict certain features. Too little restriction and the benefits of using ZAK may be diminished.

It is important to put a tool such as ZAK into context by recognizing that it is only after the business principles and requirements have been accounted for and the user environment design principles created, are we then in a position to decide whether the Zero Admin Kit is an appropriate tool for meeting our need.

User Environment Design

This section of the chapter looks at how to design a Windows NT user environment. First we examine how the user environment relates to the common and specific attributes of our technical infrastructure and in particular, how differing business intentions imply differing implementations. We then look at the various design options for a user environment using the MBI project as a case study. Note that the design of a user environment involves a large amount of detail. The case study omits that detail for the sake of clarity though it does mean that in some instances the design produced for MBI is incomplete.

Scope of User Environment Design

From a user's perspective, the user environment comprises the desktop environment and the facilities it makes available to the user. Although the statement is straightforward, if we are going to design a user environment for users this is not a very helpful definition to work with. Instead, we shall define it in terms of the technology involved:

Topic	Elements
User Mobility	▪ File service access policy ▪ Print service access policy ▪ Application access policy

continued ▸

Topic	Elements
System Policies	■ Policy templates used ■ Policy settings ■ Policy distribution
User Account Details	■ Account details ■ Account policy ■ Audit policy
Desktop Configuration	■ Desktop shortcuts ■ Menu structures
Logon script design	■ Structure ■ Usage guidelines ■ Logon script distribution ■ Script details

Note that the elements of the user mobility topic are closely related to the design of the file and print services. In this chapter we focus on the *policy for using those services*, whereas the chapter entitled File and Print Services concentrated on the *features of the services* themselves such as directory structures and share permissions.

Requirements on the Design

For the purpose of this case study we will draw on the business principles developed for MBI in Chapter 5 for most of our requirements, as it is their role in the design process we want to illustrate. The user requirements and application requirements listed below have been created for the purpose of this exercise.

User Requirements

The most important user requirement with respect to the user environment is the degree to which users need to work from different computers in the corporation. We will refer to this as user mobility and deal with it as a specific attribute of the user environment.

For the case study we will state that the requirement is for users to be able to:

- Logon at any other workstation in the corporation.
- When logging on at another workstation have the following facilities available:
  - Access to home data
  - Share data with members of same business group at home office

  - Share data with any local users
  - Print locally
- Use of a word processor, e-mail, spreadsheet, and a core business application.
- These will be referred to as a *core* set of applications.

Note that it would be appropriate to express the degree of user mobility that will be implemented in a corporation in the form of a business principle. See Business Principle A-1 in Appendix A for an example.

Application Requirements

Although arbitrary, the following requirements allow the illustration of a technique for ensuring local versions of network applications are used wherever a user logs on.

- MBI serves the binaries of in-house applications from file servers because it is easy to frequently update them.
- The MBI network based applications (application binaries available on a file share) demand the performance of a LAN to operate satisfactorily.

Common Attributes

In the following sub-sections the way the common attributes can be used to characterize the design of the user environment is examined.

Scalability

To see why a user environment might not be able to scale up we must look at whether an increase in workload or number of users will cause:

- Performance problems or
- Management problems.

Performance problems will tend to stem from two causes. One is the demand placed on the network and the other is the demand placed on servers caused by user profile downloads or application and file usage policy. In each case it must be recognized that the user environment does not inherently have scalability problems. The key to ensuring the user environment can be deployed for increasing numbers of users is to ensure the network and server infrastructure it is being asked to operate over is sufficient.

The degree to which a user environment can be customized by the user will have an impact on the support overhead. The more customization allowed, the higher the overhead as users experience difficulties such as accidentally deleting items from the desktop. Training can overcome much of this but in general, the more users there are, the higher the support requirements.

A poorly structured set of logon scripts can also be a brake on expansion as they become increasingly complex and unreliable in the face of constant updates. It is important to note that it is not an increase in users that will put pressure on the logon script as a useful tool, it is an increase in diversity which has the effect of increasing its complexity and making it more difficult to maintain. The way to address this is to:

- Develop a clear understanding of the diversification the logon script will have to cope with and design it appropriately.
- Rigorously enforce standards for modifying the logon script.

Reliability

The main element of the user environment that can have a measure of reliability applied to it is the logon script. This is clearly something that can have bugs and can fail. The principle way of tackling this is to ensure the logon script is as clearly structured and documented as possible, minimizing the likelihood of bugs being introduced when it is modified and aiding diagnosis if problems are seen.

Availability

There are several aspects to the way a user environment can be set up that can contribute to higher availability of the technical infrastructure. They can be split into two categories, those that are built in to the Windows NT user profile mechanism and those that are possible through administrator or designer configuration.

If a user has a roaming (server based) user profile that can't be accessed at the time of logon, the workstation will try to use a cached version of the user profile. If a cached version isn't available then a default user profile will be used instead. Indeed, a user's account can be set up to use a cached copy of the user profile if the logon is over a slow network link. Thus, Windows NT ensures that access to the remote server based profile is not essential to the availability of a desktop environment.

Configuration of:

- Server based network shares, including server based home drive
- Server based printers
- Server based applications

for availability is a challenge that needs to be addressed by the design of the underlying file and print service. If designed well, these services should meet the user's needs for availability and be implemented in a manner transparent to the user environment.

Such a level of service is not always possible or practical. In cases like that the solution lies in examining exactly what is critical for the user to carry on working and designing the user environment in conjunction with the file and print services to meet that need.

Manageability

The manageability of a user environment is measured by the ease with which problems are solved and changes implemented. Broadly, the less customization a user can do, the fewer problems they will have with their environment, although a bounded environment could cause a management overhead with some users complaining they can't customize something they feel they should be able to. User training has been shown to have a big impact on the supportability of a user environment so should be carried out if a new user environment is planned. How much the user environment deviates from the defaults could impact manageability as new staff (users and support) come to terms with a configuration they may not be familiar with.

The logon script gives us the possibility of rebuilding part of the user environment every time a user logs on. Thus, if a user gets into difficulties with, for example, file share connections or icons, one of the first things they would be asked to do would be to log off and logon again, returning their desktop to a known state.

Security

The user environment is where the computer meets the user and is therefore the critical boundary between security as a facet of human behavior and prescriptive security measures implemented in computer technology. Conventions regarding such things as who, according to their job, is allowed what level of access to a resource must ultimately be reflected in the assignment of rights to users and permissions on those resources. For example, it is no good saying that someone is restricted from reading a particular file if the user environment isn't set up to enforce that dictate. While this aspect of security is an important part of the user environment, we have covered it in the chapters dedicated to Windows NT Groups and File and Print Services as they allow a more thorough examination of the subject.

The user environment extends the model further by giving the administrator the opportunity to configure in a degree of "security through obscurity." While not a reliable security measure in its own right, security through obscurity can enhance the overall level of security by hiding key aspects of the system. For example, using hidden shares users would be less likely to connect to a share out of curiosity or, by not displaying icons for applications that would not be used by a particular user it discourages but does not bar that person from invoking the application. Use of system policies allows the administrator to deny a user from running certain applications explicitly.

The File and Print Services chapter identified the need for a business principle on the topic of access to data. The one chosen, listed in Appendix A as Business Principle A-3, Access to Data, asserts "Access to data is minimum necessary to carry out job." Security through obscurity supports this principle and we will see how this is executed in the System Policy for users and the logon script, later in the chapter.

Performance

Users are particularly sensitive to a computer apparently taking a long time over doing something. Two examples of where this occurs are the logon process and application invocation. The user environment has a bearing on both of these.

It is worth paying attention to good programming practices for increasing efficiency when creating the logon script. For example, rather than deriving the same value in several places in the script, derive it once and store the value in a variable.

Use of network based applications or network based data can cause significantly slower application startup than if the files were local. It should be a matter of experimentation and judgment as to whether the logon script starts applications for the user prior to terminating.

Specific Attributes

Two specific attributes apply to the user environment:

- Usability
- User mobility

Usability

The usability of the user environment influences the effectiveness with which a user interacts with the computer. An aspect of this is that if the user is not comfortable with the user environment, support calls to the help desk will go up.

To avoid these negative effects it is important to ensure that the tools a user needs are clearly available and the operations they need to carry out simplified. A simple example would be to ensure that there is a desktop shortcut for a frequently used application or that file shares are already mapped to ease a regular manual transfer of data files.

Usability is mainly subjective and trial and error is the optimum way to develop a highly usable user environment. If help desk statistics are recorded, the relative usability of a user environment can become measurable as the impact of changes can be measured in terms of the problems they cause or solve.

Usability is one of the key attributes of a user environment. Effort expended measuring and striving for usability will be rewarded with greater user satisfaction.

User Mobility

Two aspects of user mobility need to be considered:

1. Which workstations (including laptops) in the corporation a user or group of users need to be able to logon to and work at.
2. The functionality available to a user after logging on at a different workstation.

This information should be established during the user requirements gathering activity in the Design Preparation phase of the project.

User mobility requirements (assuming they are to be implemented) can have a significant impact on the design of not only the user environment but other technical infrastructure services as well. The subject is dealt with here in one place rather than have it dispersed throughout several chapters.

- *Co-located Users*

Consider the requirement for a user to be able to logon to the workstation at the adjacent desk and have access to exactly the same user environment they were used to having at their usual workstation. A server based Windows NT user profile can be implemented to ensure the user has the same desktop environment. If there is no bandwidth problem loading it down to the user at their usual workstation then there are unlikely to be any at this adjacent system. Access to any server based applications can be provided in exactly the same way as usual. Indeed, the user profile may be set up to automatically reconnect the file shares and printers so all usual network applications, served directories, and printers are available over the same network as usual. If there are applications on the workstation the user usually logs on at then these must be available from the adjacent workstation either from a server or installed locally. Thus, assuming server based user profiles are used, we can state that user mobility within a group of co-located users requires that each workstation offer the same applications.

- *Campus Mobility*

  Let us now extend the scenario to users requiring mobility within a group of adjacent offices. This type of environment is generally referred to as a campus environment. We will assume that the network is good and that user profiles download fine no matter where on the campus the user logs on. For the same reason we can also assume that any file share connections and network based applications work equally well. One problem has arisen though. A user might logon at a computer in a different building or on a different floor than usual, yet their user profile connects them to the printer(s) local to their common place of work. A solution to the need to print locally must be found.

- *Regional Mobility*

  Extending the user mobility region further to remote offices that have their own file servers may call for the need to share files with users of the site the mobile user is visiting. This means additional or alternative file share connections need to be set up in the case where the mobile user logs on at a different office. As a rule, remote network based application should not be used even over a good WAN as the performance is unlikely to be satisfactory. We shall assume that the network is good enough between these offices to ensure that the user profile transfer is still not a problem.

Finally we can consider the situation where the WAN link is poor. In this case we may find that a user profile transfer is impractical so an alternative needs to be found. Table 14.2 summarizes these deductions.

Table 14.2 *Characterizing a Technical Infrastructure in Terms of User Mobility*

Requires	Server based user profile	Local user profile	Local file sharing	Local printing	Local applications
User mobility region					
Co-located	✓				
Campus	✓			✓	
Regional (good network)	✓		✓	✓	✓
Regional (bad network)		✓	✓	✓	✓

The deductions that have been made form an adequate starting point for planning to support a degree of user mobility in a typical distributed organization. We should recognize that it may not be necessary to make all applications available from every workstation. For example, it may be sufficient to offer a subset of core applications which might just include an office suite and e-mail, throughout the corporation.

There is a price for user mobility which is the inflexibility introduced by the element of uniformity necessary to make it work. Maintaining any level of uniformity is a challenge in business environments where users get what they want. For example, suppose the standard spreadsheet is Microsoft Excel and to enable user mobility it has been installed on every workstation. A user who has Lotus 1-2-3 installed on their workstation for a valid business reason cannot expect the corporation to install it on every workstation on the off-chance it will be visited by that person.

This raises another issue with an implication on the need for user mobility. Making certain applications available at every workstation can incur a license cost for each seat regardless of whether the software is used. This can be a high price to pay for user mobility, particularly where the software may only be used by a minority of users.

One solution to the adverse licensing issue and the need to maintain uniformity is to introduce the concept of a "touchdown" workstation. In each office a small number of workstations would be dedicated for use by mobile users. Every touchdown workstation would be configured in exactly the same way with the same applications installed. This provides the uniform, predictable facility required to support mobile users without the need for complete uniformity throughout the workstation population. Another solution is to provide mobile users with laptop computers, although the challenge of how to make local file share and printer connections still remains.

User Mobility

To design the user environment to support user mobility we must:

1. Determine the facilities users require at different workstations throughout the organization.

2. Decide the best way to make these facilities available.

Determination of the facilities required by users at different locations can only be done by thorough user requirements gathering. The earlier section entitled Requirements on the Design specified a set of requirements for MBI that amounted to global user mobility with all facilities available to a mobile user except non-core applications.

Before we can determine the best way to make user mobility facilities available it is important to note that in most cases where user mobility is required, the user environment needs to be set up differently depending on where the user logs on relative to where they usually logon. This has an important implication for the role of the Windows NT user profile.

Although a Windows NT user profile effectively solves the problem of providing a user with an appropriate user environment when the user only needs mobility between a set of adjacent workstations, its value is far less when the user needs to move around in a campus or regional environment. This is because a user profile is unable to adapt settings automatically to accommodate the different printers and servers found in different offices. Another method needs to be found to complement user profiles. There are only three realistic alternatives for how to make the correct network share and printer connections needed to provide for user mobility:

1. Support the user in making those connections manually.
2. Use a logon script to make the connections.
3. Use a logon script to make a basic set of connections and then rely on support for the user to set up any additional connections manually.

Which approach is chosen will depend on:

- The diversity of the file and print share environment at each location.

  A more diverse environment will make use of a logon script less practical as it will rapidly become unmanageable, introducing reliability problems.

- The ease with which visiting users can be supported by telling them which connections to make.

  This has serious implications for the IT Support group who will need to ensure they have adequate staff and network resource knowledge on hand to enable a speedy response to the needs of a user.

- The skill of users in being able to make connections themselves is also important.

  In some cases users will not want to have anything to do with making file share or printer connections. In others, they will be comfortable with browsing for connections or typing UNC strings in.

Assuming the needs of mobile users are to be provided for, the primary impact of choosing one way of meeting those needs over another is the administrative overhead. The key is to match the method chosen to the abilities of the workforce and the IT Support organization.

MBI Business Principle 4 has as an implication the need to keep management overheads down. We also know the MBI technical infrastructure project is designing a highly consistent environment that lends itself to use of logon scripts to support user mobility. The decision on which approach is being used should be recorded as a design principle. The design principle MBI used to support the use of logon scripts is shown below.

Design Principle 14-1—Use of a Logon Script
A logon script will be used to satisfy user mobility requirements.
Justification
▪ A logon script allows changes to be made easily and remotely, supporting MBI Business Principle 4. ▪ All user mobility requirements can be satisfied in a logon script, eliminating the need to make the system more complex by using additional methods.
Implications
▪ The logon script will be critical to the successful configuration of the user environment wherever a user logs on, including at their usual workstation. It is therefore important it is protected, and fully tested in all scenarios. ▪ There needs to be a rigorous change control procedure applied to maintenance of the logon script. ▪ Resources not connected to by the logon script will need to be connected to manually by the user, supported by the local IT Support group.
Issues

Please refer to the section later in this chapter entitled Logon Script Design to see how this was implemented.

The need to have the same limited set of applications available at whichever location the user was working in gave rise to a very specific requirement that MBI chose to capture in a design principle.

Design Principle 14-2—Availability of Applications
Each application required to support user mobility must be available either installed on the workstation or on a local application server.
Justification
▪ Running applications over the WAN is not advisable for performance and bandwidth usage reasons hence the need for local versions of the applications. ▪ Any user should be able to work at any location and have available to them local versions of these core applications.
Implications
▪ Non-core applications cannot be guaranteed to be available at all locations. ▪ A means of ensuring the same version of an application is available at each location is required.
Issues
▪ During a corporate application upgrade, some locations may get out of synchronization temporarily. ▪ For technical reasons some applications will not allow installation and usage in this manner.

This design principle is achievable for well behaved applications such as Microsoft Office. However, for some applications it is more difficult. In one case, MBI found a particular market data application in use in some offices that required the user's application profile to be stored on their local workstation and matched user ID against IP address of workstation as a security check. User mobility within a location would be hard enough to achieve with this software let alone inter-location mobility.

System Policies

MBI Business Principle 4 impresses the need to minimize support requirements so we should approach designing the system policy with this in mind. The MBI solution architect, in consultation with user representatives, settled on allowing the users the ability to customize the cosmetic aspects of the user environment but their ability to access data and run applications would be restricted to that which was essential.

Clearly the system managers and operators could not be restricted in such a way so an alternative policy was created for the users while the administrator policy was left at the default settings. The table below summarizes the key aspects of the user policy.

Table 14.3 *MBI Per User System Policy Settings*

Attribute	Policy Setting
ControlPanel.Display.RestrictDisplay	▪ Hide Settings Tab
Shell.Restrictions	▪ Remove Run Command from Start Menu ▪ Hide Drives in My Computer ▪ Hide network neighborhood
System.Restrictions	▪ Disable registry editing tools ▪ Run only allowed Windows applications

A user environment design should include specification of all policy templates and how they are combined into policies. This is particularly important where the Microsoft Zero Administration Kit is used as these files will characterize how the whole user environment is configured.

Policy Distribution

The system policy file needs to be present in the standard location on each PDC and BDC in the infrastructure so the Windows NT replication service should be used to distribute it from a single location. A point to note is that if more than one version of the system policy file is in use in a domain structure, then it is conceivable that system policy files with different Local Machine settings could be loaded onto the same computer, depending upon who is logging on and which server their system policy file came from.

This could have the effect of changing local computer settings such as the logon warning message. In general this effect will be undesirable and could arise if two parts of the organization replicated their own system policy file to other PDCs and BDCs.

MBI chose to use a design principle to record the importance of using a single version of the system policy file throughout the corporation.

Design Principle 14-3—Single System Policy File
Only one version of the System Policy File should be used throughout MBI.
Justification
▪ Ensures that the local workstation settings aren't dependent on who logs on. ▪ Ensures consistent user environment behavior wherever a user logs on.
Implications
▪ Must define administrative procedures to govern maintenance of a single system policy. ▪ The system policy must satisfy all local legal and corporate regulations.
Issues

User Account Details

Selecting user account details is less a matter of design than a matter of policy. The policies will center around the allocation of accounts and rights to users and relate to the way user accounts are used to contribute to the required level of security throughout the technical infrastructure. Design principles lend themselves well to capturing these policies. Three examples are illustrated below.

Design Principle 14-4—No Account Sharing
No account should be used by more than one person.
Justification
▪ Accountability for actions will be lost. ▪ The account may temporarily be unavailable to someone if the password was changed by someone else who had failed to communicate the change. ▪ By grouping individual accounts, permissions may be applied to resources for a group just as easily as they can be for a single account.

continued▸

continued

Implications
■ More accounts need to be created. ■ Groups must be used to ensure rights remain consistent from user to user. ■ Need a clear naming convention for the accounts to identify their purpose.
Issues

Design Principle 14-5—A Separate Account for Each Different Role
Each user should have a separate account for each role they perform.
Justification
■ Encourages a sense of purpose and caution.
Implications
■ Some users will have to remember passwords to multiple accounts. This may end up posing a security risk as users either write them down to aid memory or keep them all the same.
Issues

Design Principle 14-6—Only Grant Minimum Rights for the Role
■ A user or member of administrative or operational staff should not be granted more rights or permissions than is necessary to carry out their role.
Justification
■ Greater rights or permissions than are necessary introduce the risk of accidental or deliberate abuse. ■ Easier to audit.

continued ▸

continued

Implications
▪ Need to work out clearly what necessary rights and permissions should be. ▪ In some cases, rights or permissions granted for a specific purpose will need to be revoked. ▪ There is likely to be a support overhead dealing with requests for additional rights and permissions.
Issues

Choosing Account and Audit Policy

The account and audit policy for MBI has been dictated by the IT Audit Department and reflects a reasonably secure environment. Users forgetting passwords and having to have accounts unlocked will be a fact of life. However, this was seen as a modest price to pay for the required level of security. To convey the importance of the need to conform to the MBI standard security rules, the project manager chose to create a business principle to that effect. The business principle is listed in Appendix A as number A-4, asserting "Conformance to corporate security requirements is mandatory." The account policy settings are as follows:

Table 14.4 *MBI Account Policy Settings*

Category	Attribute	Value
Password Restrictions	Max Password Age	Expires in 30 days
	Min Password Age	Allow Changes Immediately
	Min Password Length	At Least 8 Characters
	Password Uniqueness	Remember 10 Passwords
Account Lockout	Lockout After 3 Bad Logon Attempts	
	Reset Count After 60 Minutes	
	Lockout Duration	Forever

The IT Audit group require that computers automatically audit activity that should not occur very often. The result is that an NT auditing failure event is particularly important as this could indicate a violation attempt. The same activities are audited for success as a means of tracking in the case where they correlate to prior audit failure events.

Table 14.5 *MBI Server Audit Policy*

Audit Type	Success	Failure
Logon and Logoff	✓	✓
File and Object Access		
Use of User Rights		
User and Group Management	✓	✓
Security Policy Changes	✓	✓
Restart, Shutdown and System	✓	✓
Process Tracking		

Desktop Configuration

The desktop configuration will be a matter of policy concerning itself with the shortcuts available on the desktop and the menu structures available from the Start button. As such it lends itself to the creation of design principles to state how it should be configured. We shall illustrate two design principles used by MBI, each supporting a different business principle.

The user requirements stated at the beginning of the User Environment Design section called for a high degree of user mobility. If expressed as a business principle, one of the implications might be to require that a familiar desktop environment be presented to the user wherever they log on to make it easy for them to orient themselves.

A difficulty arises with this implication if shortcuts are used to access network applications. The network applications must be local to the workstation to deliver best performance but that means using a different application server depending on where the workstation is. One solution to this is to create the shortcuts at logon time within the logon script for that location. Another solution is to create them as common shortcuts on that computer (shortcut located in the All Users \ Desktop profile folder), in both cases causing the network application to be invoked from the correct location.

While implementing shortcuts to network applications using common shortcuts keeps the complexity of any logon script down, the management overhead may still be significant, particularly if the properties of a particular shortcut ever need to be changed on several hundred computers at once. The logon script for MBI discussed later in this chapter illustrates how to create shortcuts at logon time. The solution chosen should be recorded as a design principle.

Design Principle 14-7—Create Shortcuts at Logon Time
Shortcuts to (all/core/list of) applications should be created at logon time in the logon script.
Justification
▪ Supports user mobility by ensuring all applications are available wherever the user logs on. ▪ Allows new applications to be made available via a shortcut automatically upon logon with only a change to the logon script required. ▪ If shortcuts are moved or corrupted in any way they can be restored by the user logging off and re-logging on.
Implications
▪ The logon script must allow for site specific locations of applications.
Issues

Windows NT comes with several shortcuts already on the desktop. It is usual for some not to be required and for it to be preferable to deny the use of others. This would be the case where the desktop was being configured specifically for simplicity or safe usage. An example might be where the Briefcase utility was judged likely to cause too many support calls. Removing the shortcut would avoid user experimentation and difficulty. The policy for how to create a simple and safe desktop should of course be captured as a design principle. An example business principle demanding simplicity of the user environment can be found in Appendix A.

Design Principle 14-8—Keep Desktop Environment Simple
Remove all shortcuts from the desktop and Start menu that are not required.

continued ▸

continued

Justification
■ Keeps user environment as simple as possible. ■ The simplicity should lead to ease of use of the desktop and start menu. ■ Less risk of users getting into difficulty with a utility they have no need to use.
Implications
■ Utilities that have had their shortcuts removed will still be available through other means such as double clicking through Explorer or from the Run command on the Start menu unless these methods have been denied using system policies. ■ Removal of shortcuts is an administrative overhead unless it can be done as part of the automatic initial system installation process. ■ Unless considered carefully, unilateral removal of shortcuts may generate support calls and subsequent non-standard configurations as they are re-instated.
Issues

The exact desktop configuration will be highly project specific so the details for the MBI case study will not be recorded here.

Logon Script Design

The logon script design for MBI is based on the user and application requirements stated earlier in this chapter. The design uses a single master logon script that gets run whenever anyone logs on and a location specific logon script that is branched to dependent upon where the user is logging on. The scripts carry out the following actions.

In the Master script:

1. Connect to local public share
2. Connect to home group share
3. Connect to local application share
4. Call local logon script

In the local logon script:

1. Connects to local printers
2. Sets default printer
3. Creates program groups and icons
4. Starts applications

Logon Script Usage Guidelines

A logon script is similar to a software program and as such we should expect it to be modified in the future. To minimize the chance of future modifications introducing errors the script should be well documented and clearly structured. In many cases, a basic script template will be taken and customized for a new environment, in which case there should be clear instructions on how to customize the script to achieve the new functionality. For example, suppose members of a particular global group needed to be connected to a specific printer. A well written script should make it clear exactly where in the script logic, the test for group membership, and subsequent printer connection is made.

Exact guidelines are going to depend on the functionality of the basic script. MBI drew up a list of guidelines, two of which are shown in Table 14.6, to assist the support staff at each location in the task of updating their location specific scripts.

Table 14.6 *Location Specific Logon Script Usage Guidelines*

Modification	Guidelines
Any user specific need that only applies when the user is at their normal location.	Create a logon script called <username>.scr for that user and place it in the netlogon shares at the location (use replication locally if necessary). Any user specific processing should be carried out in this new script.
A group of users needs to have exclusive use of a new printer.	Request the creation of a new global group in the master domain which can then be placed in local groups at the relevant location. After the printer connection section add a specific check for membership of the new group and if true, set up a connection.

Logon Script Distribution

As with system policies, the master logon scripts will be distributed from the domain PDC to the netlogon shares of all the logon servers (BDCs and PDC) in the infrastructure using the Windows NT replication mechanism. The location specific script will be distributed from wherever it is maintained using the same replication mechanism to the same netlogon shares as the master logon script. If there is a strong local IT support group it may be maintained locally, if there isn't the central IT support group will maintain it.

Logon Script Details

The MBI logon scripts, shown in flow chart form Figure 14.3 and in full in Appendix C make several assumptions about the technical infrastructure for their correct functioning. The development of the features supporting these assumptions is covered in other chapters, in particular the chapter on File and Print Services. They are summarized here for convenience:

- Group and public shared directories and shared network applications are on the computer SAAA0001 where AAA is the three letter location code.
- Global groups are named beginning with the three letter location code followed by a three letter business group code.
- The user's home drive is located on a server at their usual working location.

Table 14.6 provides a more detailed explanation of the script logic and its dependence on a standard, consistent infrastructure for its successful functioning.

Figure 14.3
Logon Scripts Flow Diagrams

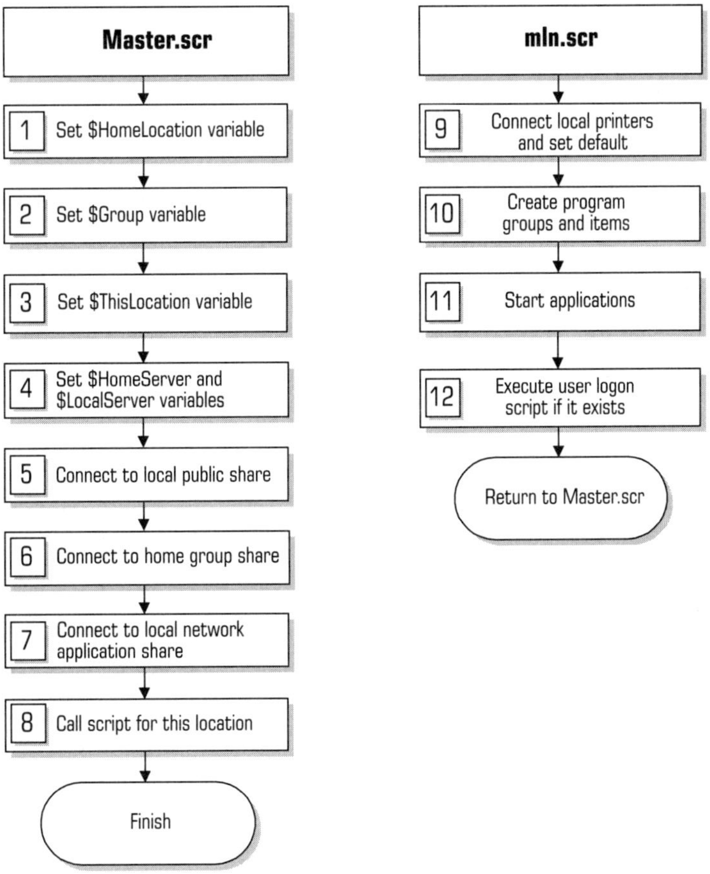
Master.scr
1 Set $HomeLocation variable
2 Set $Group variable
3 Set $ThisLocation variable
4 Set $HomeServer and $LocalServer variables
5 Connect to local public share
6 Connect to home group share
7 Connect to local network application share
8 Call script for this location
Finish
mln.scr
9 Connect local printers and set default
10 Create program groups and items
11 Start applications
12 Execute user logon script if it exists
Return to Master.scr

The MBI logon script has been written using the KiXtart language, details about which can be found in the Windows NT resource kit.

Table 14.7 *Key to Figure 14.3, Logon Scripts Flow Diagrams*

Step	Explanation
1.	The $HomeLocation variable is used whenever there is a need to connect to the user's normal location. The home drive is mapped by default by Windows NT, however MBI also chose to map a drive to the user's group shared directory on their home server. The variable $HomeLocation is derived from the KiXtart built-in variable @HOMESHR which is set to the UNC string for the home drive. The MBI computer naming conventions use the first three characters of the server name to denote the location code and it is this sub-string that is extracted.
2.	The $Group variable is used to identify the business group the user is in. The group shared directory and the name and contents of a personal program group depend on this variable. The variable is set by finding which global group of the format AAABBB the user is a member of. AAA = $HomeLocation BBB = Three letter business group code
3.	The $ThisLocation variable is used to select the correct local logon script. There is a separate logon script per location, each named with the three letter location code. The variable is derived from the first three characters of the workstation name the user is logging on at. By MBI convention these are the three letter location code.
4.	Set variables matching the names of the local file and application server and the home (potentially remote) file server. Note that the actual script in Appendix C assumes the remaining portion of the server name is S0001. This scheme therefore does not cope with situations where there are multiple servers at a location supplying the apps$ share. This would be a good reason to move the connection to the apps$ share into the local logon script for each location.
5.	The MBI file and print design calls for a shared directory at each site that everyone has mapped to their P: drive. This is specifically for ad hoc file sharing and temporary disk space. Even if a user is from another location they are still connected to the local public share.
6.	The MBI file and print design calls for each business group at each location to have a group shared directory. This is for a more orderly and secure type of file sharing. Users are always connected to their usual home location group share even if they are working at a different location. It would be straightforward to map the appropriate local group share as well if that were necessary.

Table 14.7 *Key to Figure 14.3, Logon Scripts Flow Diagrams (continued)*

Step	Explanation
7.	Some applications are only available on a file server, thus the F: drive is mapped to the local file server's application share.
8.	Call correct local logon script. The construct used in the actual script depends on there being a script per location as the target of the Call statement is constructed from the $ThisLocation variable.
9.	Assuming printers are created on servers and connected to by workstations, this section connects to printers on the print server at the local site. This is done on the basis that people generally want to print out local to where they are working. It would be here that the script connected certain user groups to different printers and set a different default printer to load balance across a set of printers.
10.	The MBI user environment requires that commonly used applications be available as shortcuts in a personal group. Broadly, each business group has a different set of shortcuts (with some in common) and the same business group at different locations may have differing sets of shortcuts. Being a personal group, users can change its contents. Thus, every time a user logs on, the group is re-created. This was done to minimize the support overhead of rescuing people who might accidentally delete shortcuts from the group.
11.	To minimize the need for a user to set their environment up, certain applications are automatically started.
12.	The user specific logon script is called to address any unique needs of a user. Note that user specific logon scripts would be the exception rather than the rule.

Script Options

MBI made the choice to use a common script that called a specific, location dependent script. Exactly what goes into each of the two types of script is dependent on where it is most practical to code the logic in a reliable, general fashion. The MBI environment is relatively highly organized, particularly as far as groups and directory structures are concerned and so these aspects can be dealt with in the common script (master.scr). As the various locations differ in size and to some degree business marketplace, the setting up of printer connections and shortcuts to network based applications has been left to the location specific script.

If it were ever necessary to distribute users at a location among several application servers then this logic should move into the local scripts as the number of application servers would be likely to vary from site to site. In the end, the split of logic between the two types of script is only there to introduce some structure to the logon process, making it easier to understand and modify safely.

A significant aspect of the MBI logon scripts is that they depend on location information being available in the names of workstations and servers. If the naming scheme for the corporation does not have this information in the computer name then an alternative would have to be found. One solution is to use system environment variables. Each computer would have a system environment variable set with the relevant location code.

Environment variables may also be used for specifying on a per computer basis which printers are local. The logon script would then need to examine a set of well known environment variables for their value and proceed to make printer connections on that basis. This approach has the advantage of making printer connections highly specific to each workstation. Though, as a workstation is moved to another desk, the environment variables may need to be changed.

A Generic Logon Script

It is very difficult to avoid being led towards a large set of complex scripts when the design approach is to determine which printer shares to connect to based on the results of environment tests. This complexity is even harder to avoid if we are aiming to support user mobility as it substantially increases the permutations the scripts have to cope with.

So, even while the MBI logon script only provides basic support for user mobility, we can see that if it were listed in its full form, including all business groups and locations, it has already become complex and cumbersome to change. Suppose, for example, we had to add another business group? This would entail updating the master script to check for membership of an additional group and potential changes for each location specific script. It is not difficult to envision scripts that start out simple ending up in an unmaintainable state after several modifications.

Ideally, we would use a single logon script that was applicable in every location and that did not need updating just to cope with the run of the mill change we should expect to see in a large corporation. This can only be done if the information determining who gets connected to what is held in a more easily maintainable form separate from the logon script. The logon script would then reference the information at execution time to carry out the appropriate actions.

One way of doing this is to use a table driven approach. For example, to make network share connections for a user, the script would parse a table in a text file looking for the record corresponding to that user and then extract a list of share connection information from the table. Thus, any changes are now made to the table and not the script.

The file containing the table can be distributed to servers local to the workstations where logon script executes using Windows NT replication, just like the logon script. Clearly, it is important to understand exactly what changes are likely to occur in the future to be able to design a table driven logon script that will stand the test of time.

Now we have a simple, universally applicable logon script that is purely table driven. All modifications are carried out to a table in a file. While this is an improvement, the maintenance problem has shifted from the logon script code to the table. A table driven approach could itself become cumbersome to manage if it contains information for several thousand users. Indeed, questions such as who has the right to update the table and how can it be done safely become very important in a large scale system. If such a method is used it is essential that a simple to use management interface be provided to make it easy to update without risk of error.

An improvement on a straightforward table would be to use an SQL database such as Microsoft SQL Server. This would allow better security and management, though at the cost of increasing the complexity of the logon script as it will need to generate SQL queries.

An important advantage that can be realized through use of a database driven logon script is that the database can contain fallback values for things such as printer connections or flags telling the logon script what to do in the event of an error. Thus, the whole logon script system becomes more robust, scalable, and manageable. To take the system one final step, the logon script does not need to be written in a script language any more. It can be written in a high level language such as C, enhancing its performance, and reducing its size.

Logon Script Rules of Thumb

1. If the logon script is being used to solve the needs of a mobile user population determine precisely how those needs must be met.
2. Be clear what the purpose of the logon script is.
3. Be comfortable that the logon script is the best means of achieving that purpose.
4. Specify precise script modification rules.
5. Ensure the responsibility for script modification is clearly identified.
6. If a table or database driven system is used, clearly identify those who can update user information.

15

Time Services

Ensuring that a set of computers have a consistent notion of time is the function of a time service. Often overlooked or relegated to the bottom of the list of things to implement, the importance of a time service usually only becomes apparent with hindsight.

It is now common for applications to be distributed across many computers, with each using its own system clock. Typically the value of that clock is used to timestamp transactions, entries in log files, and events. It is also used to sequence the execution of remote applications and batch jobs. If the clocks on different computers tell a different time then it is possible for an analysis of timestamps to present a misleading chronology of events or jobs to start out of sequence, potentially leading to financial, legal or processing consequences.

Figure 15.1
Design Phase of Project

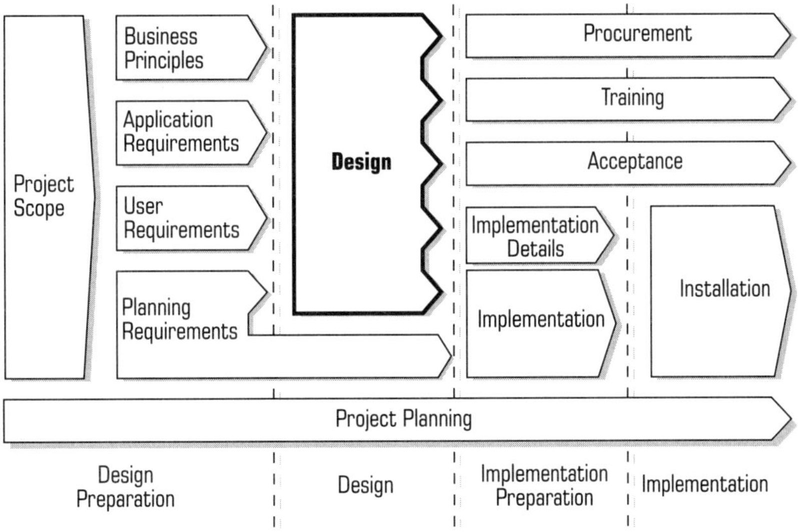

The goal of a time service is to provide a consistent value for time throughout the technical infrastructure. Of all the services, time more than most needs to pervade the whole technical infrastructure, synchronizing clocks among a diverse set of platforms. A time service needn't be complex to design and install, with a number of technology options offering robust, tolerant client/server architectures. Design of the technical infrastructure time service is part of the design activity shown on the project roadmap in Figure 15.1.

Structure of Chapter

The chapter is structured in two main sections as shown in Table 15.1.

Table 15.1 *The Structure of Chapter 15*

Section	Overview
Technology Review	A review of the basic time synchronization technologies involved in the provision of time services in a Windows NT environment including: ▪ Time service concepts ▪ NTP and OSF DTS ▪ Use of native operating system commands for setting time
Time Service Design	In the course of developing a time service design for the MBI case study the following aspects are specified: ▪ The source used to obtain accurate time ▪ Which time service synchronization mechanisms are used for which platforms ▪ Which computers will act as time servers

Technology Review

After starting with a brief introduction to time service concepts this section goes on to review the following time service technologies:

- Network Time Protocol (NTP)
- OSF DCE Distributed Time Services (DTS)
- Net Time Command

Time Service Concepts

Before reviewing time service technology it is worth describing several important time service concepts:

- Time of Day Clock
- Synchronization
- Drift
- Epoch Date
- Universal Time, Coordinated
- Strata
- Use of an External Time Source

Time of Day Clock

Every computer has a time of day clock so that the operating system and applications that run on it can keep track of time. It is implemented in hardware and will keep going under battery power when the computer is powered down. The time of day clock is usually just referred to as the clock or the computer's clock.

Computer clocks use a crystal to keep them reasonably accurate, however it is not unusual for them to drift (see below) from the correct time by several seconds per day. It is this clock that time service software will adjust when synchronizing.

Epoch Date

Time of day clocks keep time by incrementing a number stored in a binary register. For this number to have meaning we must be able to say that when it had a particular value the time was so many hours, minutes and seconds on a certain date. UNIX systems for example equate the number zero in the clock register with the start of January 1st, 1970. Thus, the value in the register represents the number of seconds since that date and time. The date equating to zero in the register is referred to as the epoch date.

Drift

Drift is the rate at which two clocks deviate from each other. It is measured in *time per unit of time*. For example two clocks may drift by 200 ms per day. It is usually used in the context of a time service client's system clock drifting relative to a time server.

Certain time services will force clocks to drift back into synchronization rather than adjusting them in one operation. By drifting a clock into synchronization we can avoid clocks appearing to go backwards, which would have the effect of invalidating log files and disrupting the scheduling of jobs.

Synchronization

This is the process of setting the time of one clock to be as near to the same as the time of another clock as possible. The purpose of synchronization is to ensure a set of clocks all have the same time. As discussed below, several challenges have to be overcome by any time synchronization solution.

- *Time Delays*

  It is difficult to synchronize two clocks accurately because several indeterminate physical phenomena get in the way. For example, the time a synchronization message takes to travel over a network link means that the message arrives at a later time than when it was constructed. Working out the length of time the message took to travel from the server to the client in order to compensate, can only ever be done to within a certain degree of error.

- *Dealing with Excessive Drift*

  If, when attempting to synchronize, a clock discovers that it has drifted from the time it is receiving from the time server by greater than a set limit, the synchronization software may refuse to set the clock on the client. The reason it may not synchronize is because the excessive drift may be the result of a more fundamental problem that will require manual intervention.

- *Ensuring Time Source Being Synchronized*

  Another issue with synchronization is how the time service client works out which time server is telling the real time. It is likely that a query to several time servers will reveal each to have a slightly different time even if the servers are synchronizing among themselves. Smart synchronization software will employ algorithms to deduce a best estimate for a time value based on several samples.

Universal Time, Coordinated (UTC) or Universal Coordinated Time

Time services that synchronize the clocks of computers in different time zones need to use a convention for exchanging the value for time that allows the correct calculation of the local time. Universal Coordinated Time answers this need by providing a standard representation of time that is based on Greenwich Mean Time (GMT). Thus, computers around the world only need to know the number of hours they deviate from GMT to be able to translate UTC into local time.

Strata

The concept of strata is used to indicate time server accuracy. Stratum 1 represents the most accurate level and is usually those systems connected to external reliable time sources. Stratum 2 is less accurate and so on down the strata. A server at a higher numbered stratum is therefore a slave to a server at a lower numbered stratum. Servers within the same stratum are known as peers.

Use of an External Time Source

It may be important for a set of computers to not only all have the same time, but that the time they have be accurate to an internationally accepted standard time. The normal way to achieve this is to use one or more computers to make a periodic connection to a recognized provider of standard time so the computer clock can be synchronized to this ultimate source. Computers that connect to such a source of time are referred to as stratum 1 time servers. Other computers would then synchronize their clocks with the stratum 1 time servers. Connection is usually made over the Internet or a dial-up connection.

The Time Services department of the U.S. Naval Observatory has the responsibility of providing an accurate publicly accessible time service to the United States. A number of other nations have an equivalent public time service. Such services are usually based on highly accurate atomic clocks that would be impractical for a commercial organization to own and maintain. Third parties may obtain time from these accurate sources or they may choose to connect to one of the many stratum 1 servers that are publicly accessible on the Internet run by public bodies such as a university. The Windows NT Version 4.0 Resource Kit provides a utility for enabling a computer to perform an external synchronization, either over a modem connection or the Internet.

Network Time Protocol

The Network Time Protocol (NTP) is an Internet Standard Recommended Protocol for maintaining consistent time among a set of different types of computer on an internet. NTP uses a flexible client/server architecture allowing a number of different configurations. In one configuration, NTP systems all act as clients and servers, synchronizing among themselves. In another, a multi-strata system can be built up where NTP systems will act as clients to lower strata and servers to higher strata. The computers in the highest strata would only act as clients.

NTP servers broadcast time messages at regular time intervals. When the message is received at another NTP system the offset between the value in the message and the local system clock is calculated and stored in the NTP database. A recalculation of what is the correct time is then performed and the local clock set to adjust itself. By using the time messages from several time servers an NTP client uses algorithms to discard dubious data and to determine which time server clocks to trust.

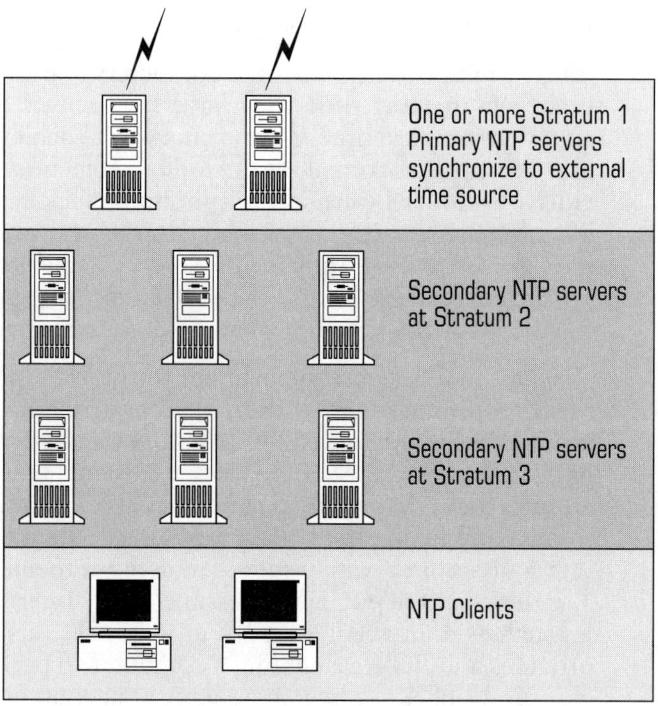

Figure 15.2 *Network Time Protocol*

OSF DCE DTS

The Open Software Foundation's Distributed Computing Environment (DCE) includes the Distributed Time Service (DTS) for providing time services in a heterogeneous network. DTS uses a client/server architecture with time servers synchronizing clocks among themselves on a regular basis and providing time to computers running the client component of DTS referred to as the clerk.

DTS time is reported by a server not as a single value but as an interval within which it has calculated the correct time lies. It does this on the basis that time can never be reported accurately to an instant, so an interval is used as a means of expressing the error.

To synchronize time, a DTS clerk contacts several DTS servers and computes a time from the set of responses by:

1. Matching up the intervals.

2. Rejecting any that fall outside the other overlapping intervals.
3. Calculating a new interval based on the overlapping ones.
4. Defines the time to be the mid-point of that interval.
5. The interval then becomes the measure of error for the value of time.

DTS can be used with external time sources to provide a highly accurate consistent time. DCE and hence DTS is available for a wide range of platforms including Windows NT, OpenVMS and many flavors of UNIX.

DTS provides an interface for obtaining time from an NTP source, presenting the possibility of linking the two types of time synchronization system together.

Figure 15.3 *Distribute Time Services*

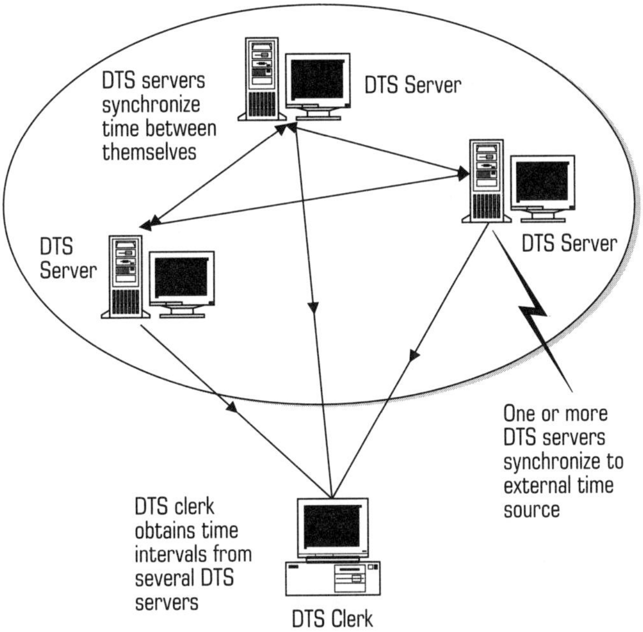

Net Time Command

A command available to Windows NT systems, `net time /set` allows a computer to set its clock to the value of time on either another computer or the primary domain controller of a Windows NT domain. This command would typically be issued in a script either:

- on system bootup

- at logon time
- as a regular scheduled job

Using the `net time /set` command a time synchronization hierarchy can be created as shown in Figure 15.4, Windows NT Time Sevices. The diagram shows a time server client which may be a workstation or server synchronizing its time with the PDC in the NorthAmerica domain. The PDC then sets its time explicitly with a computer in the IT Support domain that has been configured as the highest time authority in the corporation. This computer synchronizes its time with an external time source.

Figure 15.4 *Windows NT Time Services*

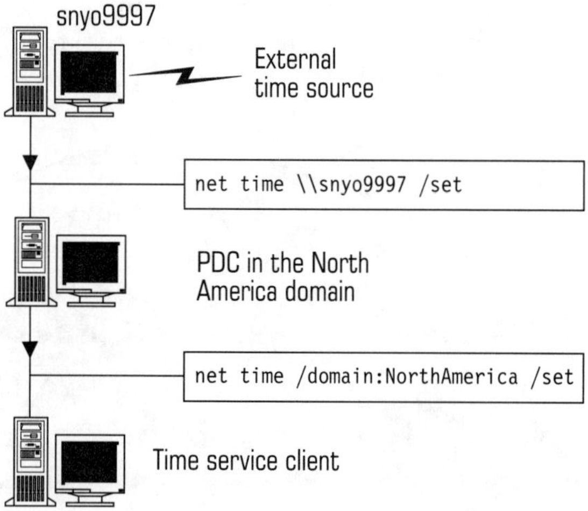

The `net time /set` command does no more than allow one computer's clock to be set the same as another's. It is up to the program invoking the command to determine:

- What action to take if the time difference is so great that something serious is wrong.
- How to deduce whether the time being received is accurate.
- How to adjust the clock on the local computer. It can be synchronized in one go or "drifted" into synchronization.

Several tools are available (mostly freeware or shareware) that add these extra capabilities to the use of the `net time /set` command.

Time Service Design

This section develops a time services design for the MBI case study.

Scope of Time Services Design

A time service design should include the following details:

Element	Aspect
Time sources	▪ The time source(s) used ▪ The method of obtaining time updates ▪ Choice of servers used to obtain time from the time source (stratum 1 servers)
Time Service Strata	▪ Organization of time servers into strata ▪ Synchronization protocol used between each adjacent strata ▪ Frequency of synchronization

Requirements on the Design

This section summarizes a small number of requirements that will be used during the case study design. These requirements complement the MBI Business Principles already developed for this case study.

Application Requirements

The new MBI Settlement System requires that time be synchronized across all computers hosting or accessing the application. Further, the time obtained by the Settlements System has to be within a certain degree of accuracy of that used by the Market Data System in use at MBI so trades and settlements can be logged in the correct chronological sequence by the two systems. Several additional MBI applications running on both UNIX and Windows NT platforms will require accurate time.

Business Principles

The three MBI business principles that will be seen to have a bearing on the time service design for MBI are:

- MBI Business Principle 2, suggesting it will be possible to phase in the technical infrastructure.
- MBI Business Principle 3, requiring no duplicate systems.
- MBI Business Principle 4, demanding scalability to support rapid establishment of an office at a new location.

Common Attributes

The common attributes of scalability, reliability, availability and manageability are all important characteristics of a time service. Security, capacity and performance less so.

Scalability

The scalability of a time service is measured by the degree to which the number of computers participating in time synchronization can be increased without allowing the time error between any two computer's clocks to go beyond the level of accuracy demanded from the time service. As each computer is synchronized with the next, the error in the value of time will increase in a cumulative fashion.

If the chain of synchronizing computers becomes too long then the error will eventually become unacceptably large. The OSF DCE Distributed Time Service and the Network Time Protocol address this by being designed for use in a hierarchical manner. Time values are then propagated down a small number of strata, with in each case, one or more computers providing time for many others in the next strata. Time synchronization is relatively infrequent and lightweight allowing a computer at one strata in the hierarchy to be capable of providing time to hundreds of computers one stratum down. This keeps the synchronization chain short for even very large organizations, resulting in a highly scalable service.

Reliability and Availability

The availability of a time server with which to carry out synchronization is roughly equivalent to the availability of the computer it is running on and the network over which it is accessed. If a time server is not available when a client tries to synchronize, the drift of the client computer's clock will cause an increasing difference between the time it has and the accurate time of the time server. The time service is still available because the client will continue to be able to respond to local requests for time by an application or user. However, the consequence of time server unavailability is a loss of accuracy at the client.

If a time service allows a clock to deviate from the correct time by more than a given amount, determined by the accuracy required for the clock to still be useful, it will be providing an unreliable service. It is easy to see that the natural drift of a computer's clock, compounded by non-availability of a time server can lead to an unreliable value for time. Indeed, the time can still be unreliable if the time service has difficulty keeping the error within the required limits even while synchronizing normally. In such a case, the time service will have been designed badly.

Manageability

The manageability of a time service can be judged by the level of manual intervention required to keep all computers participating in the service. Most time services are designed to require no management other than the regular examination of a log file to confirm there are no problems. The inherently tolerant nature of a time service ensures it can automatically survive temporary network and computer outages.

Occasionally, it may become necessary to alter the configuration of the time service running on a computer, in which case, an implementation that uses best practices for the platform it is running on generally makes the task easier. For example, a time service for Windows NT might be implemented as a Windows NT service, allowing remote configuration and control.

Specific Attributes

A specific attribute that allows a time service to be described in terms of whether it meets the needs of a time consumer is *suitability*. Consider being in an airport gift shop and you have forgotten your wristwatch and need to check how much longer you have before you need to go to the departure gate. The two things you need to know about the airport time service are:

- Can you see a clock? (Can you use the service?)
- Is the clock accurate? (To what degree can you rely on it?)

The same questions can be asked of a computer based time service. The ability to see the airport clock is equivalent to the availability of a time service on a computer.

The question of whether the clock is accurate is loaded because before we can answer it we need to decide what accurate means. Perhaps the airport clocks are all five minutes behind the airline's clock. The airport clocks would then be accurate with respect to each other but not with respect to the airline clock. Further, the plane will take off according to the airline clock time so it becomes unimportant whether the airport clocks are synchronized to an "accurate" external standard time source or not because the time they are telling has no value.

We could define being accurate as within six minutes. In which case the airline clock is accurate with respect to the airport clock. On the other hand we might reject this idea as an uncertainty of six minutes makes the time service unsuitable for the task as people may easily miss a plane.

We can conclude:

Regardless of whether a time service provides an accurate time or not, one aspect of what is important is whether the time it does provide is suitable for the purpose it will be used.

The MBI Time Service

Before making a start to the design of the MBI time service the user and application requirements along with the MBI Business Principles should be examined for anything they say about the nature of the overall service. MBI Business Principle 2 suggests that it should be possible to phase in the technical infrastructure. This provides an opportunity to phase in the time service though to be able to do so means it must be designed to perform its function as a time service across a subset of MBI computers. This is worth recording as a design principle as the implications have a bearing on the design and the implementation process.

Design Principle 15-1—Phase in the Time Service
At any phase of implementation the MBI time service must guarantee the required level of accuracy. (The required level of accuracy is that demanded by the MBI applications and users.)
Justification
▪ Supports MBI Business Principle 2, suggesting it will be possible to phase in the technical infrastructure. ▪ The value of a time service is the accuracy with which it can provide time. The fact that an implementation may not encompass all MBI computers should not mean that the time service is any less accurate.
Implications
▪ This design principle implies a scalable time service which supports MBI Business Principle 4. ▪ The implication of guaranteeing a level of accuracy from the time service is that computers not participating in the time service cannot guarantee the same level of accuracy. On this basis they should not be considered part of the time service. ▪ The time service technology must be able to function correctly across a limited set of computers. ▪ This design principle suggests that the time service is implemented with stratum one first, then stratum two and so on until the time service clients are able to use the service.

MBI Business Principle 3 states that there should be no duplicated systems within MBI. This can be translated straight into a design principle for the time service with two implications that between them form a useful working definition of how to recognize a time service when it has been created.

Design Principle 15-2—All Computers Must Participate
All computers within MBI must participate in a *single* time synchronization system.
Justification
▪ Supports MBI Business Principle 3, requiring no duplicate systems. ▪ Ensures the clock of each computer is synchronized to the clock of any other computer guaranteed to within a known error so that the time service is able to provide time to the required level of accuracy.
Implications
▪ If there are multiple stratum 1 servers within MBI then they should all synchronize with the same external time source. ▪ If the design principle is true then it must be possible to determine that the clock of any computer is synchronized with the clock of any other computer to the required level of accuracy.
Issues
▪ There may be limited implementations of time services in different parts of the organization. It may not be practical to decommission them until the new time service is available.

Time Sources

The application requirements summarized earlier state the requirement for the MBI Settlement System to have the same time as the Market Data System and for all computers running the MBI settlement system to have the same time. At first glance this points to synchronizing the time on MBI Settlement System computers with the Market Data System computers so ensuring all the computers that need to have the same time are synchronized together. Unfortunately there are several disadvantages to this idea:

- How do we know that the time used by the Market Data System is accurate enough for any other application that requires accurate time? This is important because Design Principle 15-2 makes it clear that we cannot simply go and synchronize a different set of computers to a different time source if the need arises. The correct choice needs to be made by taking into account the requirements of all users of a time service from the outset.

- As market data is supplied to several MBI offices around the world, how do we know which is the best market data computer to synchronize with?
- How do we know that the Market Data System in one country has the same time as the Market Data System in another country?
- By choosing the Market Data System to synchronize time with MBI potentially loses the option to use a different Market Data System in a different country if the synchronization requirement is the same. The reason is that it would be impractical for the MBI Settlement System to synchronize time with two separate sources.

In practice, log files that combine timestamps showing Market Data System time and the local settlements computer time can overcome the problem as far as the audit department is concerned. A better option would be to synchronize MBI computer clocks with the same external time source the Market Data System uses. According to Design Principle 15-2 we would then be able to consider the time service spanning the Market Data System and the computers in MBI.

For the sake of this case study we will assume that the Market Data System synchronizes its time with a clock at the Time Services Department of the U.S. Naval Observatory. MBI therefore chose to do the same. The point of this example is to show that it is important to consider the *purpose* of having synchronized time when deciding what time source to synchronize with.

Stratum One

Having decided that the source of time will be the clock of the Time Services Dept. at the U.S. Naval Observatory (USNO) MBI needs to consider the best way of synchronizing with it. MBI considered two options:

1. One option would be to use a single computer in the United States to dial-in to the USNO and adopt the role of stratum 1 server for MBI.

   The implication of this would be that offices remote from the U.S. would need to synchronize with a single computer over many WAN hops. This is the sort of configuration that challenges a time service and why algorithms for compensating for network delay and clock drift encourage a tiered architecture to a time service.

2. An improved option would be to choose three MBI computers to act as stratum 1 servers, well distributed throughout the network and each dialing-in to the USNO.

   By dialing in, MBI avoids the indeterminate delays over the links in the communications chain that would be associated with a WAN connection via the Internet. Using three stratum 1 time servers means stratum 2 time servers would be able to compensate for any inaccuracy among the stratum 1 servers.

Examining the two options more closely we might deduce that had the Bank gone with the option 1 then to distribute time to the rest of the bank would probably require a set of stratum 2 computers placed in the same locations as option 2 had chosen for the additional two stratum 1 computers. Option 2 has not only presented a more reliable way of obtaining external time, it has involved fewer strata, which in turn will lead to less loss of accuracy.

In this case, minimizing the number of strata was a sensible thing to do. That is not to say the first option wouldn't have worked, just that the second option matched the MBI circumstances slightly better. An alternative argument could be constructed suggesting that the real problem is the number of network hops between the time servers at one stratum and the time servers at the adjacent strata. This might encourage an increase in number of strata. Either of these arguments could be captured as a design principle if there was difficulty getting to an agreement. Below is an example design principle advocating a minimization of the number of strata.

Design Principle 15-3—Minimize Number of Strata
The number of strata in the time service hierarchy should be minimized.
Justification
▪ The fewer strata there are, the fewer layers of synchronization between the time source and the consumer of the time service exist to reduce the level of accuracy. ▪ Less strata means a more simple system. A more simple system is generally easier to manage.
Implications
▪ The number of strata shouldn't be reduced at the expense of accuracy.

Additional Strata

We accounted for stratum 1 time servers when considering which time source to use. Here we decide what additional strata are needed and which computers will adopt the role of time server in which stratum.

A basic observation that can be made straight away is that communication between the stratum 1 time servers and any time server in another office will involve the WAN. In some parts of the world the performance of this WAN link will be good, in others poor. In some cases there will be a dial-up network link used where a leased line cannot be obtained. We should therefore expect that latency could approach 0.5 to 1 seconds or more on occasions.

For this reason, MBI decided that only a time synchronization service that is able to compensate for network latency and temporary unavailability of lower stratum (more accurate) time servers should be used over the WAN. The choice came down to either NTP or OSF DTS as both these have appropriate compensation mechanisms. Compared to a rudimentary means of synchronizing computer clocks such as the `net time /set` command use of a powerful system such as NTP or DTS seems an obvious choice for a global network of computers. However, with the large number of time synchronization tools available, each offering differing synchronization capabilities, the choice isn't always so clear cut. Choosing a tool with the right capabilities will be a principle of the design. The MBI design principle on this topic is as follows:

Design Principle 15-4—Automatic Service Only Over WAN
▪ Only a time synchronization mechanism capable of compensating for network latency and time server unavailability should be used over WAN links.
Justification
▪ The latency associated with a WAN link introduces an inaccuracy to any time message received. An automatic time synchronization mechanism should have the ability to compensate for that latency. ▪ Computers acting as time servers in another part of the world accessible over what might be an unreliable WAN link may temporarily become unavailable. An automatic time synchronization mechanism should be able to retry regularly or contact alternative time servers.
Implications
▪ The time synchronization mechanism will need to be configured specifically for the target environment.

For a decision as to which time synchronization tool to use, NTP or DTS, MBI should look to the business for guidance. Both tools meet all the technical criteria including the need to work equally well on Windows NT and UNIX. Additional criteria the business may judge important are:

- Conformance to corporate technology standards
- The level of support available from the manufacturer
- The ease with which consultancy is available
- Cost to purchase and maintain
- Conformance to technology strategy

As product selection is outside the scope of this book we will assume MBI made the choice to use NTP.

We now know that NTP will be used to distribute time to each of the local offices from the stratum 1 time servers at the hub sites. What isn't known yet is whether there will be more than one stratum at each local office or which computers will participate in each strata. As all communications within an office are over a LAN, MBI decided that a single time server stratum to serve all the computers at a location would be sufficient. Let us now look at the implications arising depending on which platform is chosen to be the stratum 2 time server, Windows NT or UNIX.

- *Windows NT*

  If the single stratum 2 NTP time server was running on Windows NT, then each Windows NT client could synchronize using NTP or a tool based on `net time /set`. On the other hand, a UNIX client would need to be able to synchronize using NTP.

- *UNIX*

  If the single stratum 2 NTP time server was running UNIX, then a Windows NT client would need to synchronize using NTP, though a UNIX client could use `rclock`, a `net time /set` equivalent. If the stratum 2 time service is to run on a Windows NT, server then it should be the IT Support domain computer.

In summary, if a single stratum 2 time server is used, then one type of client platform will be forced to use NTP. If two are used, one UNIX and the other Windows NT, then the option of time synchronization mechanism is open for each client platform type.

Final Stratum

If a decision is made regarding which platform the stratum 2 time servers run on then the time synchronization protocol that must be used on the clients is constrained. Before making that decision we should consider whether it is more important that we decide the protocol the clients should use and allow that to constrain choice for the stratum 2 servers. As the time service client population consists largely of workstations, the management of which is always an issue, MBI saw an argument in favor of the option that requires the least management.

In the case of a Windows NT client the use of a third party tool based on `net time /set` command that ran as a Windows NT service and offered several convenient benefits was chosen. NTP was seen as the most manageable option for the UNIX time service clients. Hence the stratum 2 servers could be either a single Windows NT server or a Windows NT server and a UNIX server. The time synchronization tool running on the Windows NT time service clients will need to be configured to synchronize with the local IT Support domain server SXXX9999.

The issue of whether the protocol used at the server level should constrain choice at the client level or vice-versa lends itself to a design principle. The one MBI used is as follows:

Design Principle 15-5—Choose Best Option for Time Service Client
The choice of time synchronization mechanism should be optimized for the type of time service client platform.
Justification
▪ Most time service clients are workstations which are the biggest management challenge. By optimizing the choice for the client, there is the opportunity to employ a tool that minimizes management overhead. This supports the MBI Business Principle 4 demanding low management overheads.
Implications
▪ Different tools may be chosen for different platforms, potentially leading to increased complexity.
Issues
▪ Certain client choices may force the use of an additional stratum 2 time server to match the time synchronization protocol required on the client.

Summary

Here is a summary of the time service design created for MBI:

- Use of the same external time source (USNO) as the market data provider was recommended so the settlements system will be in synchronization with the Market Data System.
- To keep the number of strata to a minimum and to provide a level of resilience, a time server from each of the three regional hub locations will connect to the Time Services Dept. of the USNO using a dial-up connection.
- NTP will be used to synchronize time over the WAN as it has the ability to compensate for WAN latency.
- Windows NT time service consumers will use a tool based on the `net time /set` command that runs as a service to synchronize with the local IT Support domain server.
- UNIX systems will synchronize with the Windows NT NTP time service by using NTP.

The final design is shown in Figure 15-5, MBI Time Service Design. Only the Chicago local office is shown for clarity.

Figure 15.5 *MBI Time Service Design*

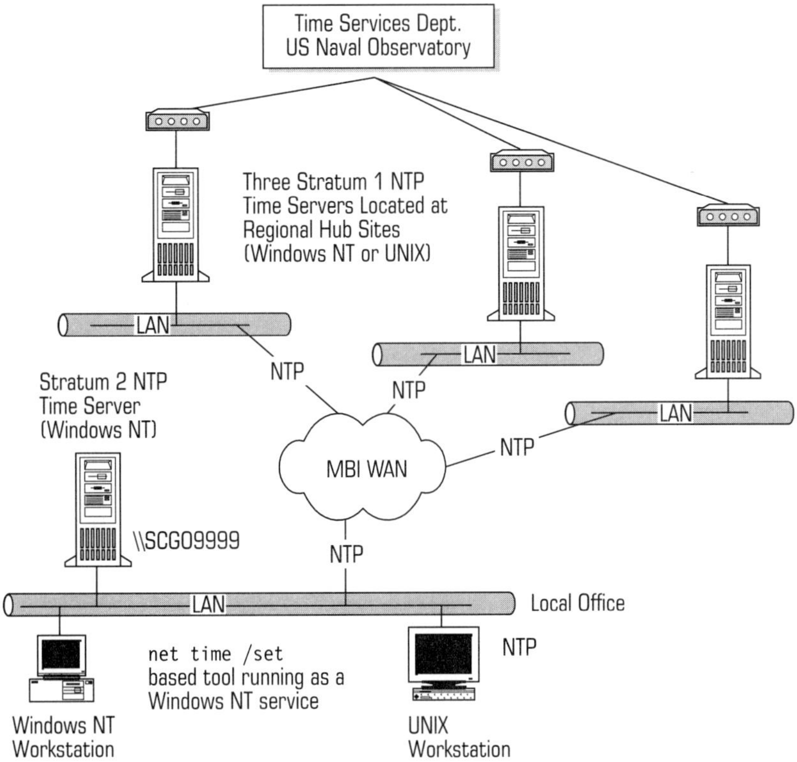

16

Naming Standards

Naming objects according to standards can bring several benefits to an organization including guaranteeing uniqueness, enhancing usability and lowering complexity. Each standard will incur an administrative overhead, which makes its choice a trade-off between the benefits of using it and the effort of managing it.

Choosing names or a naming standard for elements of a technical infrastructure can absorb a disproportionate amount of time, probably because it is one of the few opportunities to leave a lasting, visible impact on a design. There is, however, the chance to convey useful information in a name. For example, you may wish to name domains in such a way as to identify them with their geographic location, or perhaps the organizational group they service.

In this chapter we will use the MBI case study to examine the options for naming the following elements of the system:

- Windows NT domains
- Windows NT groups
- Computers
- User accounts
- File shares
- Printers

A valid question at this stage is "Why are the naming standards in a single chapter and not listed in their corresponding design chapters?" The answer to this question is not straightforward. Before we can attempt an answer, we need to define some terms and review the relationship between a naming standard and its corresponding design topic.

Table 16.1 *Naming Standard Term Definitions*

Term	Definition
Field	An element of a name. For example, a username might consist of two fields, family name and given name, collinsmike.
Standard Name	The ordered set of fields comprising a name.
Field Naming Conventions	These are the syntactical rules governing the construction of a given field. For example, the family name must be truncated to eight characters, must be lower-case, etc.
Naming Standard	A naming standard is the Standard Name and its associated Field Naming Conventions (hence the title of this chapter).

We can represent the relationship between the design task for a technical area and the work of defining the naming standard for it in diagram form as in Figure 16.1. The link between the two is represented by the ellipse, illustrating how the fields for a name are derived from fields fundamental to the design topic *and* from fields that aid usability in some way.

Figure 16.1 *Relationship Between Design Topic and Naming Standards*

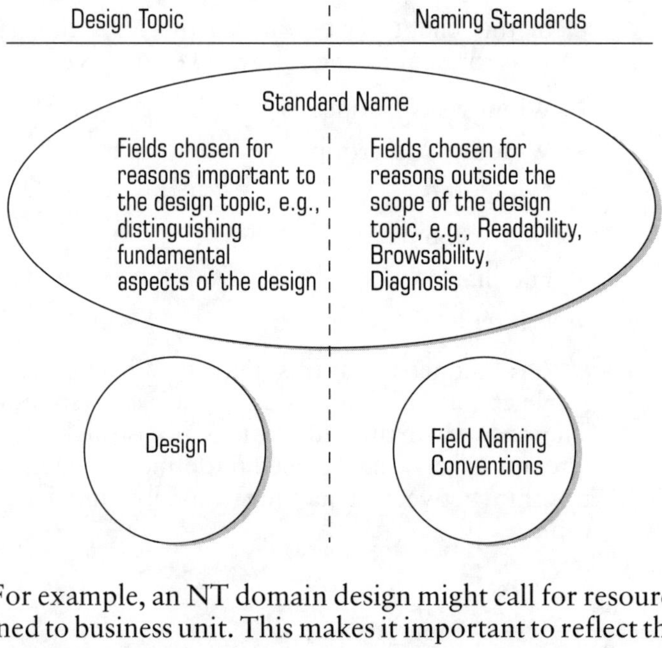

For example, an NT domain design might call for resource domains aligned to business unit. This makes it important to reflect that business unit in the name of each resource domain. For reasons outside the scope of the domain design there may be a need to identify the country the domain is in. We now have two fields in the standard name, one derived from the domain design and other derived from additional considerations. The creation of field naming conventions for both fields is treated as a naming standard activity and not part of domain design.

To answer the question posed above, the recommended approach is to keep naming standards in a separate chapter for the following two reasons:

- There will be field naming conventions used that are common to several naming standards (e.g., the abbreviations for cities may be part of both the domain and group naming standards). This allows lists of abbreviations to be kept in one place without the need to keep cross referencing between documents.
- Naming standards can take a long time to agree on. By separating them out from the subject of the names, design work can proceed at the same time standards are being agreed to.

Our treatment of naming standards in this chapter will be done in one of two ways depending upon which side of the dividing line the majority of the ellipse falls. If the ellipse falls mostly to the right, indicating a large discretionary element, the design of the naming standard will be examined from the perspective of the following interested parties:

- User
- IT support
- Logon scripts
- Organizational

If the ellipse falls mainly to the left of the line, indicating that the fields in the naming standard are determined largely by the corresponding technical design, the choices for the naming standard will be examined on a per field type basis.

Development of naming standards is one of the design activities. The position of the design activity within the overall project roadmap is shown in Figure 16.2.

Figure 16.2
Design Activity in Project Roadmap

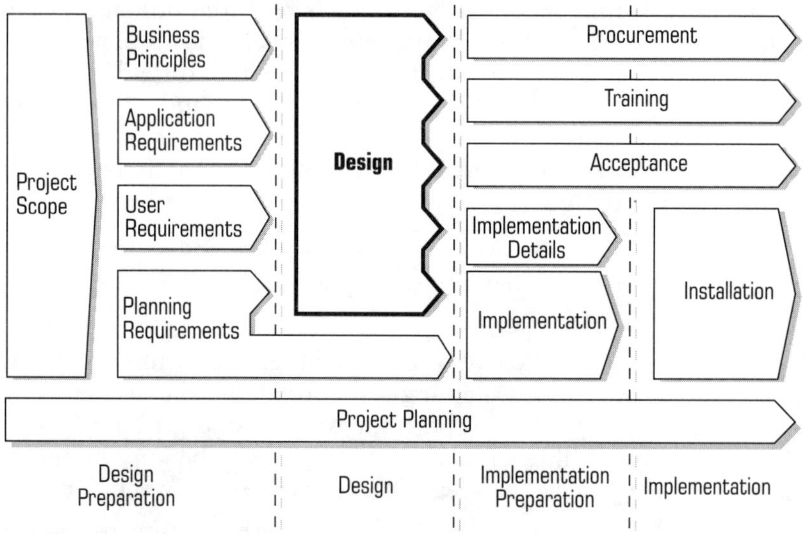

Structure of Chapter

The structure of this chapter is shown in Table 16.2.

Table 16.2 *Structure of Chapter 16*

Topic	Elements
Getting agreement on naming standards	Advice is given for getting to an agreement on naming standards with as little difficulty as possible.
Ensuring a complete naming standard	The importance of a complete naming standard is emphasized. Two methods of achieving that goal are offered.
A syntax for name definitions	Writing down a chosen naming standard clearly and unambiguously will help ensure its accurate usage. A simple syntax is proposed and then used throughout the chapter.
Domain names Group names Computer names User account names File service names Print service names	For each of these topics, the value of different items of information within a name is considered from several perspectives. Each topic concludes with a worked example using the MBI case study.

Getting Agreement on Naming Standards

Getting people from different parts of an organization to agree on a common set of naming standards takes work. Each person will have their own set of priorities, experiences and opinions which will provide ample opportunity for conflict, so you should plan for it to take a long period of time to reach a conclusion.

For the task to be successful it is essential you complete the following:

- Find out the naming standards already in use in the corporation and examine how well they have worked.
- Identify the groups who need to contribute to the development of new or revised naming standards.
- Define a process for reaching agreement.

The last point is particularly important as you will at times be faced with an impasse that needs escalation to be resolved. Plan ahead for this to happen so that when you need to invoke a process to reach agreement such as escalation or a vote, the argument doesn't spill over into the process itself.

Ensuring a Complete Naming Standard

One of the main objectives of a good naming standard is to ensure that it is possible to use it unambiguously in every instance. If it is open to interpretation, then you can guarantee that two different people will derive different names for the same object.

For example, suppose we were to include a two digit field in a computer name to indicate the floor of a building where the computer resides. If we overlook the fact that one of the offices in our organization has more than 100 floors we leave the creation of computer names open to interpretation for computers located on floor 100 or above.

Another problem might occur if we aren't clear about the other end of the building. For example, suppose the two digit field is defined as the building assigned floor number, how are we to name computers located on the mezzanine floor? We could define the mezzanine as zero but that leaves us a problem with numbering the ground floor, is it minus 1? How do we represent minus 1? How we solve the last problem doesn't really matter as long as an unambiguous convention is defined.

There is no easy way to determine when a naming standard is complete, particularly when it has to cope with unforeseen situations.

However, here are two strategies that can be employed to get as close as possible:

1. Have the draft standard reviewed by as wide an audience as possible.
2. Walk through the standard by applying it to all the different situations within the organization to check it works in every case.

A Syntax for Name Definitions

It is important to have a clear and understandable syntax for defining a naming standard. Using such a syntax reduces ambiguity and makes what can sometimes seem rather complex, more simple. A syntax is recommended here that is suited to the task of representing the types of names we are defining.

The overall structure of a name should be represented:

Name = **<Field1><Field2><Field3>...<FieldN>**

Each of the fields contains distinct information. The <> delimiters around the fields allow us to show any concatenation characters that might be used to make the name more readable. For example using an underscore

<Field1>_<Field2>

Each field should be given a meaningful name allowing the definition to be written as in the following example:

Computer Name = **<Location code>_<Floor number>**

Then each named field is defined in terms of its alphanumeric structure by a list, a set of rules or reference to a table showing all the possible values, for example:

Location code = LON, NYC, HKG, PRS, MLN
Floor number = nn

where nn = 00 for ground and mezzanine, floor number for other floors and 99 for floors higher than 98.

It is recommended that the letter **n** is used to denote a single numeric character and **a** used to denote a single alphabet character.

Example names are NYC_16, PRS_99, MLN_00

Windows NT Domain Names

This section examines possible Windows NT domain naming standards using the general case of a multiple master domain model. It is important to note that once a Windows NT domain is built it is not trivial to change its name, making it very important that the domain naming standard is correct from the outset.

User Perspective

Users are faced with domain names in two contexts:

- When browsing for resources
- When selecting a domain to logon from in the logon dialog box

We will examine both situations.

Browsing for Resources

From the users' perspective having domains named according to geography may be useful when browsing for resources, as the initial browse list displays a list of domains by name. Thus the user can quickly identify the domain containing resources at their location.

The use of organizational information in the domain name could also help the user home in on resources available to the business unit they belonged to. For example, if they knew that there was a file share they needed to connect to that had the same name in each location, knowing the name of the resource domain would be helpful in starting to locate the computer it was served from.

Often proposed is the use of a field in a domain name to explicitly identify it as a master or a resource domain. Thus, users would be able to identify from their name which domains had resources and which domains didn't. This argument has some appeal, though it would require users to understand the naming standard and to know that resources were unlikely to be found in master domains.

The need for a user to be able to distinguish between domains goes away completely if browsing is not used (with all network connections being set up in a logon script or manually by users who know the UNC name of the resource they need). Indeed, consider how likely it is, or whether you would want to encourage users to peruse the Network Neighborhood utility looking for something that might be "interesting" to connect to!

Selecting a Domain to Logon From

An argument supporting the use of a field to distinguish between a master domain and a resource domain is that it would aid the user in selecting which domain to logon from. For this to work the user would need to know that their account was in a master domain (without necessarily understanding what a master domain is) and not a resource domain, assuming a master or multiple master model was in use.

This argument can usually be dismissed quickly when it is recognized that a user will always logon from the same master domain (the one where their account is held), regardless of where they are in the world, unless in the unlikely circumstances that they had accounts in more than one domain.

Note that in the case of a master or multiple master model the *logon from* list comprises the local resource domain, the local computer and all trusted domains, so there will only be a maximum of one resource domain ever listed as an option to logon from. In the cases of the complete trust and single domain models there will be no resource domains listed.

IT Support Perspective

From a support perspective, information conveyed in a domain name could help provide context for a problem. However, in practice, support staff will get used to whatever domain names are used, making choice of name fields of low importance to support.

Organizational Perspective

Many of the factors affecting choice of domain model are organizational in that they deal with organizational structures and the control they exert. For this reason there is often a powerful need to label resources according to organizational association. For example, if a resource domain is aligned to a business unit, it can be useful to reflect that in the name of the domain.

Logon Script Perspective

It may be desirable to set options for a user in a logon script based on which master domain they are logging in from or which resource domain the computer they are logging on at belongs to. For example, a script may set up connections to local printers while connecting to a share in the user's home resource domain.

Use of domain names as parameters for making decisions in scripts can be done by using compare statements to match the name with those from a list. Constructing domain names or extracting fields from them in a script is helped by having the standard name consist of fixed length fields in a predictable sequence. So, for example, in the case of a field for location, rather than use the words London, New York, Chicago, the codes LON, NYC or CHG could be used. If this approach is used, it is often possible to use codes already in use for other purposes such as the internal post or e-mail.

MBI Master Domain Naming Standard

The MBI domain model is a multiple master variant which calls for three master domains aligned by region and one master domain for IT Support users. Although MBI has chosen to use a logon script that depends on certain naming standards, domain names are not among them so MBI is free to name their master domains descriptively. As the alignment is regional the names may reflect that:

Master Domain Location	Master Domain Name
New York	NorthAmerica
London	Europe
Singapore	Asia

The master domain for the IT Support users will be called **Admin.**

MBI Resource Domain Naming Standard

The MBI domain model calls for a single domain per location, making the choice of the following standard straightforward:

Resource Domain Name = **<Location>**

Location = values from Table 16.3.

Table 16.3 *MBI Location Code Table*

Location	Code	Location	Code
London	LON	Zurich	ZRC
New York	NYO	Singapore	SNP
Paris	PRS	Tokyo	TKO
Frankfurt	FRT	Hong Kong	HKO

Table 16.3 *MBI Location Code Table (continued)*

Location	Code	Location	Code
Milan	MLN	Sydney	SDY
Amsterdam	AMD	Chicago	CGO
Madrid	MDD	Montreal	MTL
Buenos Aires	BAS	Rio De Janeiro	RDJ

One of the domain design options MBI considered was to use a domain per subsidiary office at each location. Had that been the case it would have been necessary to introduce a second field to the domain name to distinguish subsidiaries. This might lead to a resource domain name such as SDY-RED which would be the name of the resource domain for Red Bank subsidiary of MBI in Sydney. Knowing the Bank to be on the road to integration towards a single organization, it would be a mistake to use the subsidiary name because it would become meaningless when the subsidiaries were amalgamated. If distinguishing between entities that will change in the future is important, the recommended approach is to use a numeric field in the domain name to make the distinction, for example, SDY-2. This may not be an ideal option but it would stand the test of time better.

Trust Relationship Names

Each trust relationship also requires a name. Trust relationships will only be of concern to IT administration staff and the primary need is to simply know which two domains are involved in any trust relationship. So, while any naming scheme could be used for trust relationships, the one recommended here uses the names of the two domains involved in the trust:

Trust name = <Name_of_trusting_domain>-<Name_of_trusted_domain>

e.g., NYO-NorthAmerica

Moving to Windows NT 5 Active Directory Services

The naming of domains takes on an extra significance with Windows NT 5 Active Directory as a domain name becomes a DNS name. For example, the fully qualified domain name for the Hong Kong resource domain could become hkg.asia.mbi.com.

Within a private organization there is no compulsion to use any particular standards for DNS names. However, if domains are aligned to countries then for consistency it is recommended that the codes employed by the NIC (ISO 1366) are used.

Group Names

Groups are an important part of managing a user population. By collecting user accounts together into groups according to administrative or security requirements, access to resources can be controlled efficiently.

The naming of groups is closely related to the way they are used, to the extent that a group usage strategy (the group usage strategy for MBI is defined in Chapter 12) will dictate nearly all of the fields of a group's name. Unlike other objects requiring names, adding fields not demanded by the group usage strategy will lead to confusion rather than clarity.

Business Unit and Location

Most group usage strategies demand that group names contain fields for either business unit, location or both. This should not be a surprise as these elements figure highly in the way organizations are structured.

In every case, the naming standard for a business unit field should allow the group to be clearly identified with its particular business unit. Whether the business unit is a division of a large corporation or a small department the actual business unit name or an accepted abbreviation should always be used.

In some cases it may be that there are two fields for business unit in a name, one relating to a business unit at a different level in the organizational hierarchy than the other. In such cases we have the opportunity to make the two fields adjacent and employ standards for the fields such that they concatenate into the common phrase for a department. For example, PC-SALES and SW-SALES.

There are several options for location field naming standards. As with business unit it is recommended that the field name standard uses values that will be easily recognized.

Distinguishing Between Local and Global Groups

An idea sometimes promoted is that the group names should convey information to improve the administrative interface of the *User Manager for Domains* utility. Such information might, for example, try to make the distinction between local and global groups more apparent by prefixing each with a G or an L.

Against this is that global groups and local groups have associated with them different icons in the *User Manager for Domains* utility and it is impossible to violate the rules regarding membership of groups such as putting a local group in a global group. For this approach might be to retain a distinction between the roles of different groups after a migration to Windows NT 5 Active Directory, where the concept of local and global groups goes away.

Arbitrarily Distinguishing Between Groups

We may be tempted to use a field to distinguish two or more groups that would otherwise have the same name, e.g., AccountsPayable1 and AccountsPayable2. In cases like this we should always ask two questions:

1. If these groups are similar, why can't we just use one group?
2. Can we think of a more meaningful method of distinguishing between the groups?

Fixed Length Fields

The chapter on groups illustrates the use of testing for group membership in a logon script as a means of making decisions about which shares and printers to connect to. This is very difficult to program with a scripting language unless the fields in a group name are of constant length and fixed order. Thus, when deciding the field naming standards we should be sensitive to the reason a field exists and what it is to be used for.

MBI Group Naming Standard

The MBI group usage strategy (Chapter 12) requires that the following name fields are used in the Windows NT Groups for users:

- location
- business unit
- subsidiary
- printer
- security

Not every category of user group contains all these fields. The MBI group usage strategy for groups used by the IT Support group requires an additional field to distinguish role. To make life easier for the IT Support group we should use the same conventions for fields in group names that are used by other naming standards. For example, the naming standard for Windows NT domains listed abbreviations for location which should be re-used in the naming standard for groups. This brings an immediate advantage because if we recall our group strategy, it is to put global groups from the master domains into local groups in the resource domains. By adopting resource domain name fields as part of the global group name an administrator can see straight away which resource domain that group was created for.

Although an obvious point, it is worth stating that where local and global groups share the same field they should also share the same naming convention for that field. If not, great confusion will ensue.

MBI User Global Group Naming Standard

We will now examine the different categories of group defined in Chapter 12, determining naming conventions for each new field introduced. The global group names are used in the logon script to check for group membership, so need to be in a fixed position and of fixed length.

- *File Access*

  This category of group introduces three of the five fields, Location, Business unit and Subsidiary. MBI chose to use the same field naming convention for Location as used in the other naming standards. Location codes are listed in Table 16.3. For Business unit code MBI chose to use the same three letter abbreviations used by the Human Resources department. These are listed in Table 16.4.

  The choice of convention for the Subsidiary field is less straightforward. We could easily use a code that closely resembled the subsidiary name such as BLU for the Blue Bank Subsidiary, however, based on the MBI Business Principles and what we know of the Bank, we would expect these names to become irrelevant in the future. More than that, by using the names we could actually hinder the process of integrating the subsidiaries into the Bank. Based on this argument the MBI team decided to use a simple numeric character to distinguish between subsidiaries, the benefit being that once the concept of the subsidiaries disappears, the groups can be re-used by adjusting membership. At that point the MBI group usage strategy document should of course be updated to reflect the change.

  Note that although the field for subsidiary is demanded by the Group design, for clarity the field isn't used in the chapters on User

Environment and File and Print Services or the case study logon script shown in Appendix C.

File Access Global Group Name =

<Location><Business Unit><Subsidiary>

Location = values from Table 16.3

Business unit = values from Table 16.4

Subsidiary = values from Table 16.5

e.g., MDDEQT2, SDYTRS1

- *Printer Access*

The printer access global group category introduces a new field called Printer which is used in the logon script to determine which printer should be set as the default for a user. This field should again be of fixed length and position. It should also be general enough to cope with a variety of different printers including ones that have yet to be deployed.

The standard chosen for MBI is to use a concatenation letter, P to introduce a numeric field Printer.

Printer Global Group Name =

<Location><Business Unit><Subsidiary>P<Printer>

Location = values from Table 16.3

Business unit = values from Table 16.4

Subsidiary = values from Table 16.5

Printer = n

e.g., MDDEQT3P3—Printer 3 used in Madrid Equities department of the Green Bank subsidiary.

Note that this field naming convention will break if more than 10 different default printers are required for any Location/Business Unit/ Subsidiary combination. Another point is that while the other fields in the group name provide some useful contextual information regarding who the default printers apply to, we are essentially using them as a means of constructing a unique group name without having to provide a unique number for every printer throughout the entire organization.

- *Restricted Access*

The final field we need to consider is one to identify a group as reserved for controlling access to certain sensitive files and directories. The MBI group usage strategy defines this category of group as having a one to one relationship with the File Access group. So, we only need look for a means of distinguishing the two categories of group. The simplest method is to include a suffix in the security group standard name thus:

Restricted Access Global Group Name =

<Location><Business Unit><Subsidiary>SEC

Location = values from Table 16.3

Business unit = values from Table 16.4

Subsidiary = values from Table 16.5

e.g., MDDEQT4SEC, SDYTRS1SEC

MBI User Local Group Naming Standard

The MBI local groups use the same fields as the global groups in every case except for the Location field. The Printer Access category of global group does not need a corresponding local group as it is only used in logon scripts. Thus, the two categories of local group we need to define are Local File Access and Local Restricted Access:

- *Local File Access*

  File Access Local Group Name = **<Business Unit><Subsidiary>**

  Business unit = values from Table 16.4

  Subsidiary = values from Table 16.5

  e.g., EQT2, TRS1

- *Local Restricted Access*

  Restricted Access Local Group Name =

  <Business Unit><Subsidiary>SEC

  Business unit = values from Table 16.4

  Subsidiary = values from Table 16.5

  e.g. EQT4SEC, TRS1SEC

Table 16.4 *Business Unit Codes for MBI*

Business Unit	Code
Default for shared resource domain	MBI
Capital Markets	CMK
Foreign Exchange	EFX
Treasury	TRS
Fixed Income	FIC
Equities	EQT

Table 16.4 *Business Unit Codes for MBI (continued)*

Derivatives	DRV
Research	RSC
Settlements	STL
Human Resources	HRO
Marketing	MKG

Table 16.5 *Subsidiary Codes for MBI*

Subsidiary	**Code**
Midas Bank International	1
Red Bank	2
Green Bank	3
Blue Bank	4

MBI IT Support Global Group Naming Standard

The last field type required by the group design is Role, which is used to distinguish between groups used by the IT Support organization. As the IT Support group design maps new global groups directly onto the built-in local groups, the field naming convention for the role fields has been deliberately chosen to match the built-in group names.

IT Support Global Group Name = **<Location> <Role>**

Location = values from Table 16.3

Role = Print Operators, Server Operators, Backup Operators, Account Operators, Admins

e.g. HKG Account Operators, NYC Admins

Moving to Windows NT 5 Active Directory Services

Following the recommendation in Chapter 12, Groups, new groups should be created in each ex-resource domain to take on the role each global group had in the previous master domains. These new groups should have names that distinguish them from any existing groups in the ex-resource domain.

Computer Names

The only demand placed on a computer naming standard is that it ensures a unique NetBIOS computer name for each system sharing the same network. Indeed, there is no aspect of Windows NT infrastructure design that will compel the use of any particular field in a computer name, however, there are a wealth of fields that could be used, a number which can bring some benefit.

As with the treatment of domain names earlier in the chapter, we will examine the various field possibilities from the user, IT Support, logon script and organizational perspectives, reflecting the fact that it is the need derived from these sources that is going to govern which fields are used in a computer naming standard.

As there are many potential computer name fields to consider it is clearer to introduce them all here at the beginning, rather than in an ad hoc fashion throughout the discussion of the four different perspectives. The fields we shall consider are listed in Table 16.6.

Table 16.6 *Potential Computer Name Fields*

Server	Workstation
Geographic region	Country code
City	Asset number
Office	Operating system
Type of server	Business unit
Role of server	
Operating system	
Floor number	
Business unit	

Where a conclusion is reached that a particular field should be included in the MBI computer naming standard the text is on a shaded background (as this is).

User Perspective

Before considering the fields in a computer name that might be important to a user, a basic question needs to be asked. "Does a user ever need to be able to determine anything about a computer by studying its name?" Unless browsing is used as a serious mechanism for directing users to resources, then the answer to the question has to be no. In which case, we do not need to consider the needs of users when deciding which fields to include in a computer name.

If browsing is relied upon for a user to be able to locate a resource, then we should consider the criteria used to home in on the correct server. Invariably they will include decisions related to location and business unit. In which case, putting several tiers of location information in the server name to aid navigation to where the resources lie would have merit.

In some cases users will routinely connect to a share on a well known server, one that's name can be constructed or remembered easily, and that always has the same role.

In the case of MBI, users will be connected to their network resources automatically by logon scripts, making it unnecessary to consider this perspective any further for the case study.

IT Support Perspective

The IT support community arguably has the strongest claim to need useful information in a server name, as they may be called upon to make swift judgments that can only be made with the benefit of knowledge about the server. Of the fields proposed above, the following have particular relevance to members of IT support:

- *Location* ▪ *Type* ▪ *Role* ▪ *Operating system* ▪ *Business unit*

We will examine each in turn in the following sub-sections.

Location Codes

Fields for location codes are among those most commonly employed in a server name. The two key considerations to bear in mind when deciding on location fields are:

- What is the location information going to be used for?
- How often is a change in location going to cause a name change?

The latter point is particularly important as changing a computer's name can have far reaching consequences. For example, if the name of a file server is changed, all computers that make connections to the file services offered on that computer will need reconfiguring to connect to the "new" computer. An often overlooked consideration is that as the name of a computer changes, the purpose or usage associated with it by humans will break.

Four fields of location information have been proposed. Taking a closer look at the value of each we can conclude the following:

- **Region.** Unless an administrator has responsibility for systems in more than one region, there is no use for this field.
- **City.** Unless an administrator has responsibility for systems in more than one city, there is no use for this field.
- **Office.** If an administrator has responsibility for computers in more than one office then this field would be useful. However, we should be aware that organizations are likely to move to new offices or move computers between local offices during the lifetime of that computer.
- **Floor.** Knowing which floor a server or workstation is on has some merit, particularly in a building of many floors. However, in such circumstances, computers are frequently moved from one floor to another to the extent that the floor field in the computer name would be certain to get out of synchronization.

The MBI administrative staff are grouped regionally although part of a single IT Support organization so the field of most value is City. MBI also plans to consolidate into a single office at most locations as the subsidiaries are absorbed into the organization. So, using a field for Office would be unwise as it will change in the near future.

Type of Server

Knowing what type of functions are carried out by a server just by looking at its name is an attractive proposition, potentially leading to a reduction in operational errors. However, in the case where each server runs many different services the use of a field to identify role is impractical as it has to convey too much information.

It was suggested by a representative of IT support that what they really wanted to know was whether the computer was one likely to be accessed directly by users, such as a file server or application server, or whether it was an infrastructure server hosting services such as WINS or Microsoft SMS. This would immediately help support personnel gauge the broad impact of any problem with a server. There are two practical ways of implementing this field. One way calls for a single character indicator field using one value for infrastructure server and another for user server, e.g.,

<Server Type > = U for user server or
I for infrastructure server.

Another way is to adopt a convention within the field that is included to ensure uniqueness. For example, infrastructure servers could be allocated numbers starting from the highest and user servers numbers starting from zero, e.g.,

<Uniqueness Number > = nnnn

which ensures uniqueness if all other fields in the name are the same. Infrastructure servers are allocated numbers 9999, 9998, 9997... and user servers are allocated numbers 0000, 0001, 0002...

MBI elected to use a convention in the unique number field to distinguish between user servers and infrastructure servers. Note that this effectively rules out the use of an asset number based system for ensuring unique names.

Role of Server

The role of the server is intended to indicate the environment the server is being used in. For example it could be a production server or a development server or perhaps a server used in the User Acceptance Testing laboratory. Various suggestions were put forward for how this field should be implemented. One proposed a three digit field as follows:

<Server Role > = aaa

Where aaa = PRD for production
UAT for User Acceptance testing
ENG for development engineering

The opposing view was that most people would be familiar with the role of a server without having this field, particularly the production servers.

MBI chose to place this field at the end of the server name and omitting the PRD value in the case of production computers. Thus, only user acceptance testing or engineering machines would have this field. It was also decided to use this convention for the workstations.

Operating System

A field indicating operating system was proposed in both server and workstation so it would assist users and IT support in understanding the capability of a computer. There were two main objections to this idea.

1. First, that users in particular would be unlikely to need to know the difference between a Novell NetWare and a Windows NT server.
2. Second, that it was common for computers to change operating systems, particularly Intel based systems. For example, a server could be changed from Novell NetWare to Windows NT Server or a workstation upgraded from Windows 3.1 to Windows NT. The result of embedding the operating system type in the computer name would be to cause a change to the computer name, requiring logon scripts to be changed and users re-educated as to the new name.

The imminent re-organization in MBI meant that such changes would be likely so the idea of using a field for operating system was dropped. On the workstation, the operating system name was agreed to be largely irrelevant and so was dropped for that as well.

Organizational Perspective

Organizational units within an organization are commonly aligned to location or business or both and it is common for the powers involved to demand that assets are labeled according to their business unit owners. We discussed the use of location fields earlier, here we examine how business unit information may be incorporated into a computer name.

Business Unit

Using a field for business unit within a computer name is clearly only practical if the computers are exclusively aligned to business units. In this case, such a field might be a useful addition to a field for location information to uniquely identify an organizational unit.

The design for the MBI case study shows several business units sharing the same file and print servers, making the use of this field for servers impractical. Workstations, however, are used exclusively by a single business so such a field could be used. Arguing against the use of a field for business unit in the workstation name was IT support, pointing out that workstations are frequently re-deployed from one business unit to another, making the use of that field a burden rather than a benefit.

Logon Script Perspective

We saw earlier how we may use group name fields from within a logon script to determine, among other things, which resources to connect to.

Here we need to consider the demands placed on a computer name by a script making connections to file shares and printers offered by a server.

The logon script must specify the servers resources are on. Here are three methods:

1. Hard-coding the server names. This could lead to a very large and cumbersome script in a large organization.
2. Use a database or lookup table which could be maintained independently of the logon script.
3. Create the server names dynamically in the script.

The first two methods can tolerate any computer naming convention, however the third method demands a well defined computer naming convention which ensures fixed length fields in a predictable order.

MBI chose the third method as the design of a new technical infrastructure offers the opportunity to implement the strict computer naming standards necessary. Appendix C illustrates how a logon script can be used to construct a computer name dynamically.

Note that environment variables are often a practical alternative to fields in a computer name when it comes to using scripts. Environment variables have the advantage that they can be changed more easily than computer names.

Ensuring Uniqueness

The NetBIOS computer name space is non-hierarchical and so demands a unique name for each computer, making it important that the naming system we use ensures it is possible to generate enough unique names. This can be done by embedding a numeric field in the computer name, the value of which is chosen to ensure the whole computer name is unique. In practice this means that if, for example, the computer name consists of a three character location field and a four digit numeric field, the numeric plus location code combination in total needs to be unique, e.g., **NYO1003**, **LDN1003**, and **NYO2439** are all valid.

There are two common approaches for generating values for the numeric field in such a way as to guarantee uniqueness in a name:

1. Systematic allocation where names are entered into a register or a database accessible from anywhere in the organization.

2. A system based on using the asset number of the computer.

Each system needs some careful consideration to ensure it achieves its objective.

Systematic Allocation

To make the systematic allocation of numbers as manageable as possible it is recommended that the rest of the name be examined to determine the extent of the set of names that are the same. Using the example above, if the field in a computer name standard is a code for a city, then we only need to ensure a unique number is allocated within each city on the basis that that is sufficient to ensure a completely unique name. This is preferable to using a system whereby the number alone is unique throughout the corporation.

The larger or more complex the set of computers requiring unique numbers is, the more difficult it is to put in place an administrative procedure that can reliably ensure their correct allocation. Consider if the set were European wide, requiring the administrator in one nation capital to coordinate with the administrators in all the other nation capitals in Europe just to be allocated a single number for installing a new workstation!

One solution is to pre-allocate batches of numbers out of the name space to the different administrative organizations, rather like the NIC does for IP networks. Once done, the allocation of numbers out of a batch is a local issue. For example, if the unique number field was six decimal digits then New York could be allocated 000000 to 040000, Chicago 040001 to 080000 and so on.

Another solution is to implement a number dispensing application that maintains a central record of numbers issued. Web technology would lend itself to such an application.

Asset Numbers

Asset numbering systems intrinsically generate unique numbers within the set of computers to which the system applies. At first glance this seems exactly what we need, however we should be cautious of encountering some common problems when attempting to use them:

- There may be several different asset numbering systems in operation so an additional field would be needed in the computer name to distinguish between differing asset numbering systems to maintain the guarantee of uniqueness should any two or more systems have numbers in common.

- The different asset numbering systems may differ in the number of digits used, making it necessary to pad out the shorter ones to arrive at a constant length asset number generated field.
- How to be sure whether all the asset numbering systems had been discovered.
- How to deal with the introduction of a new asset numbering system.

MBI chose to have the IT support organization maintain a database for systematic allocation of unique numbers to both servers and workstations.

MBI Computer Naming Standard

The MBI computer naming standard so far has no way of distinguishing between servers and workstations. The MBI IT Support group are keen that this distinction be possible as it means again, that the general impact of a problem with a computer can be gauged immediately. MBI chose to use a single character field with the letter S for server and W for workstation to distinguish category of computer.

The final MBI computer naming standard recommendation is as follows:

Computer Name =

<Category of Computer ><Location Code ><Unique Numeric ><Role>

where:

Category of Computer = **W** for workstation and **S** for server

Location Code = values from Table 16.3

Unique Numeric = nnnn

This number will be incrementally assigned on a per location basis beginning with 0001 for user servers and 9999 for infrastructure servers.

Role = UAT for a User Acceptance Test computer and ENG for an engineering computer.

Here are three example computer names:

SMTL0001, WSDY3256UAT, SMDD9998

User Account Names

The fact that this is one of the naming standards that is most easy to gain agreement to will probably be apparent from the existence of several account naming standards already in use (and disuse) within an organization. While it is not critical that there be only one user account naming standard in use, account names do have to be unique throughout a technical infrastructure. Therefore, as long as we can guarantee a method of producing unique account names the technical requirements will have been met.

User Perspective

The first priority for a user is that their account name, or account names if they have to use several, are not difficult to remember. If keeping track of account names is at all difficult, users will be tempted to write them down along with passwords, presenting a security risk.

A common system for producing account names that are easy to memorize is one based on the user's name. Three versions of such a system are as follows:

- Full family name concatenated with given name initials.
- Given name concatenated with family name.
- Family name concatenated with given name initials.

In each case a policy is required for ensuring uniqueness where more than one person has the same name. The usual approach involves using additional characters from the rest of the user's name until uniqueness is achieved.

IT Support Perspective

The IT Support group will be interested in two aspects of user account naming:

- That it be possible to generate unique user account names easily.
- That for a given user, their account names on different platforms be the same.

If an employee number based system is used (see Organization Perspective below) then generating unique account names is trivial, though it does require the employee to know their number when requesting a new account. Any other system relies on the administrator knowing the algorithm.

In practice, it is not so much the use of different account names that causes problems as the need for a user to remember several different passwords. However, keeping the number of different account names to a minimum, particularly when some are infrequently used, will assist in reducing support calls generated through user forgetfulness.

Note that there are tools available on the market designed to give users a "single logon" to a variety of systems. The effort of implementing such a tool is significant, however it can be worthwhile where the number of different platforms is low and the benefit is clear.

Organizational Perspective

One of the most common alternatives to account names based on the user's name is a system based on employee number. The argument runs that as account names need to be unique, why not use an existing system that already guarantees uniqueness?

The main operational benefit of this type of system is that it is possible to map a user name to employee uniquely, which makes auditing easier. Another point in its favor is that users are unlikely to have any difficulty remembering their user name. One area of difficulty might be electronic mail addressing though aliases can overcome that problem.

Logon Script Perspective

The user name is one parameter among several that are typically available as string variables to an executing script language. There are two ways of exploiting it. One is to use string manipulation to automatically generate values for, for example, share names, with the advantage that the logon script is applicable to any user. Another way is to simply use it as a cue to carry out user specific processing, though this should be considered carefully if we are dealing with a large user population. The MBI logon script does not make use of the user account name so there are no constraints imposed by the need to make the user account naming standard script friendly.

MBI User Account Naming Standard

As far as our case study is concerned we have identified no requirements on the user account naming standard so, what follows is a definition for a straightforward personal name based system:

User Account Name = **<Family Name><Given Initial>**

Where:

Family Name = Full family name, truncated to ten characters

Given Initial = Initial letter of the first given name

When the above system fails to generate a unique name, the second letter of the given name should be appended to the user name. If that fails to generate a unique name, then the third letter should be appended to the user name, and so on until the name is unique.

File Service Names

As with a naming standard for Windows NT groups, the fields in a naming standard for a file service will be driven by the design of that service. This is because the structure of the directories behind the file shares is important, as is the purpose of each file share and the only way to capture that purpose is through its name.

To structure our analysis of potential field naming conventions we will look at a set of typical uses for file shares and examine the options for naming them. The set are:

- Public and Group shares
- Home drives
- Network application shares
- Project shares

Before doing that we will note some aspects of file share naming that are important to our analysis.

Computers such as those running Windows for Workgroups will not be able to cope with the long share names available under NT. The name of the actual directory that is shared, however, need not be restricted to eight characters as this is never seen by the computer connecting to the share. This leaves the option of naming shared directories meaningfully while sharing the directory using an eight character version of the name.

One of the properties of a share is a comment, which is a text string that can be used to provide a browsing user more information about the share. While it is a useful feature it is not recommended that the comment property be used as a substitute for a well thought out share name, as once the share connection has been made, from the *explorer* type interface presented by various utilities, the share is only identifiable by its drive letter or actual share name. The comment is no longer accessible.

Public and Group Shares

These types of file shares are intended to allow groups of users to share a network directory for whatever purpose their business demands. The share will either be dedicated to a type of usage or to a group of users, or both.

In every case, unless there is to be some type of indexing system for cross referencing share name to purpose or group, shares should be named as descriptively as possible. The file service design will identify the fields necessary in the public and group share names as a result of describing their reason for use and what distinguishes one from another. If the group of users a file share is created for is the same as a group already identified in a field of another naming standard, then it makes good sense to re-use the field naming convention, not only because it saves work but it re-enforces the information a name carries.

Home Drives

Where a network home drive is used it is usual for the share connection to be made automatically via the user's NT profile. In which case, the user has no need to know the name of it. If home drives are to be used (they are essential for certain applications such as Microsoft Exchange) there has to be a separate share per user which means each must be named uniquely within the scope of a server. From the IT support point of view it is useful to be able to identify a particular home drive share with a particular user. Thus, the most obvious way to name home shares is to use a field the same as or derived from their user account name. It is recommended that the user account name is used in full as the share name except in cases where there would be too many characters in the string for the client system to handle.

Network Application Shares

Network application shares can be used for serving application binaries. The only sensible recommendation is that the application share be named after the application it is hosting.

Project Shares

Similar in concept to public and group shares, these are shares created to support projects. Typically there is one share created per project which provides access to a hierarchy of directories containing the project information. Again, the recommended approach is to name the share the same as the project name to avoid any confusion. A project share is one of the types of share most likely to be browsed or entered at the keyboard for the user to make a connection, making it important that the name means something to a user and is memorable.

MBI File Service Naming Standard

The file service design described in Chapter 13, File and Print Services, demands the following fields:

- Group name
- Application name
- User name

in addition to a name for a public share.

Share Type	Fields	Field Definition
Public	<Public>	"Public"
Group	<Group Name>$	Values from Table 16.4
Application	<Application Name>$	The name of the application
User home drive	<User Account Name>$	Same as user account naming standard

Note that for the shares hidden from the browser service (note the $ symbol at the end of the share name) there is no need to define the contents of their comment property. The Public share is not hidden and the name of it is self-explanatory.

Print Service Names

Many of the name fields that are candidates for inclusion in a computer naming convention are also candidates for print service names. In each case the arguments for and against their use are similar so they won't be repeated in this section. Instead we will consider three options each from the user, IT support, logon script and organizational perspective:

1. Employ the same naming standard as used for computers.
2. Include a field in the name for its location in the building so users can choose to print to a device near where they are situated.
3. Include a field in the name for identifying the type of printer, so users can choose printers based on a characteristic, such as color or monochrome, form type, capacity or even resolution.

First, we will review the way Windows NT 4 presents the print service name to a client computer and the alternative methods provided for communicating printer information.

Windows NT 4 offers a mechanism whereby printers shared from a server can have associated with them a comment property and a location property in recognition of the importance of providing useful information to the user about a printer. Unfortunately, the location property is only viewable on a client after the printer has been created (connected to) via the printer property tabs or the printing dialog. On the other hand, the comment property can be viewed from the browse information in addition to the printer property tabs and the printing dialog.

Another important point to note is that the share name assigned to a printer is only ever seen by the user of the client system during the browsing process. Once connected to, the client automatically uses a string describing the type of printer and where it is served from, not its share name. Thus, any information conveyed in the print service name is no longer accessible through the property tabs or printing dialog.

User Perspective

It is far more likely that a user will browse a set of printers and choose one to connect to than it is they do the same with file shares. For this reason it is useful to be able to convey two items of information about a printer through the browsing mechanism:

- what its capability is
- where it is located

We should also consider the case where a user is connected to several printers and needs to make a choice of printer using the options in the printing dialog. Here again we need to show capability and location information.

Presenting capability information is relatively straightforward as we can use the comment property which will get displayed both at browse time as well as print time. Presenting location information is more challenging. We should certainly use the location property, however we need to find a solution for displaying the information at browse time as well. One option would be to put the location information in the printer share name. Another, better option would be to put it in the comment property along with information about printer capability.

Location information should be relevant to the users. For example, in some buildings a system is used which would be suitable for describing where printers were located. In other cases location is expressed in terms of commonly recognized physical features of the building. MBI elected to place summary location information in the comment property and detailed location information in the location property.

As a result, from the user perspective, MBI has no need to put location or capability information in the actual print service name. This is good because both these types of information are best conveyed using free text, which is difficult to do in the constraints of a print service name.

IT Support Perspective

The primary tasks of IT support in respect of printers will be to carry out remote operations such as restart, pause or delete job or local operations such as changing toner or clearing jams. To do any of these tasks they need to be directed to the right printer either by knowing its name or knowing its location.

This information will need to be gained from the user via the help desk so it needs to be available either in the print dialog or through some other method such as a label stuck to the printer. Depending on the exact needs of the IT support organization we could consider adding special information in the comment property to be passed to the help desk in the event of a problem. For example, the print service name could be recorded there so a user could be asked by the help desk to read it out to help the IT support locate the offending printer.

Organizational Perspective

The organizational needs place the same demands on a print service naming standard as they do on a computer name standard. In the case of MBI, where most of the important user oriented information is being conveyed using the comment and location properties of a printer, there is a lot of freedom left to accommodate the organizational needs in the print service name. MBI decided to take this opportunity and declare the print service naming standard to be the same as the computer naming standard.

Logon Script Perspective

As with the logon script considerations for computer name, the need is to be able to construct a printer name under script control, which is easier to program if the fields are of fixed length, fixed order, and predictable content. This demand tends to suggest that location information and capability information shouldn't be fields in the printer share name as it would be compromising to convey them with fixed length fields of predictable content.

MBI Print Service Naming Standard

In summary, MBI chose to adopt a print service naming standard that was based on the standard defined for computer names. The letter P, used to signify a printer will be added to the definition of the field used to distinguish between server and workstation. Both printer capability information and summary location information will be carried in the general comment property. Detailed location information will be carried in the location property. For a definition of the computer naming standard please refer to the section headed MBI Computer Naming Standard earlier in this chapter.

Example print service names are shown in Table 16.7.

Table 16.7 *Example Print Service Names*

Print Service	General Property	Location Property
PRDJ0001	Standard Laser Printer / Century House, Floor 11	F5 by pillar
PLDN8934	Standard Laser Printer / 243, John F Kennedy Avenue, Floor 3 North	Next to drinks machine
PNYC3621	Color Printer / Midas Court, Marketing Department	By assistant's desk

Coping with Multiple Operating Environments

It is common to need to choose names that are valid for multiple operating environments. However, different operating systems have different constraints on the number and set of valid characters that constitute a valid name. In particular this applies to names for the following:

- Computers or hosts
- User accounts
- Printers
- Files and directories

In mixed environments be sure to consult the relevant documentation regarding valid character sets before defining name standards.

Summary

The process of choosing naming standards requires knowledge of the environment and careful planning. In many cases there is no compelling reason for one choice over another, reducing the matter to one of negotiation.

One of the main objectives of a good naming standard is to ensure that it is possible to use it unambiguously in every instance. If it is open to interpretation, then you can guarantee that two different people will derive different names for the same item.

It is important to have a clear and understandable syntax for defining a naming standard. Using a syntax reduces ambiguity and makes what can sometimes seem rather complex, more simple.

Rules of thumb for naming standards:

1. If a field isn't necessary then don't use it.
2. Don't underestimate the number of people who will have an opinion on the subject. Include everyone who needs to be involved in the decisions at the start of the process.
3. If the value of a field in a computer name is likely to change without at the same time requiring a complete system rebuild then don't use that field.
4. Always consider alternatives to putting information in names. Possible alternatives might be:
   - Manually maintained lists cross referencing information to name
   - Manually maintained database cross referencing information to name
   - Environment variables
   - Built-in variables in a scripting tool
   - Properties (where available)

17

Implementation Preparation

The ease with which Windows NT software can be installed is in stark contrast to the complexity of its configuration into a technical infrastructure. For this reason we can safely say that the effort spent preparing for an implementation will pay handsome dividends as problems fixed at this stage will be less costly than if fixed later.

Once the design is complete, focus moves to preparing for implementation of the technical infrastructure. This chapter describes the basic activities and tasks involved in the implementation preparation phase including the development of an implementation plan.

The main activities constituting the implementation preparation phase (in bold) are shown in the context of the overall project roadmap Figure 17.1, Implementation Preparation Activities.

Figure 17.1 *Implementation Preparation Activities*

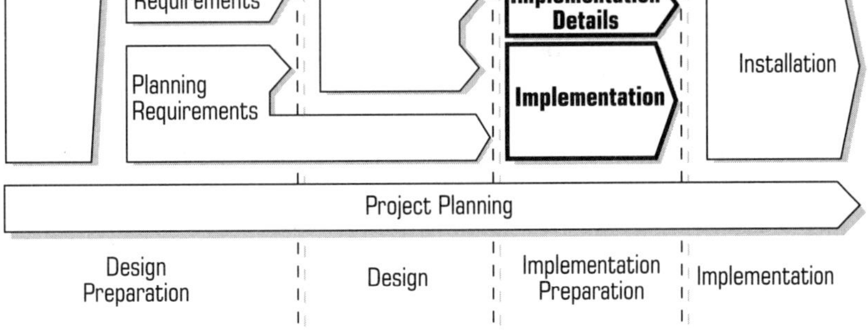

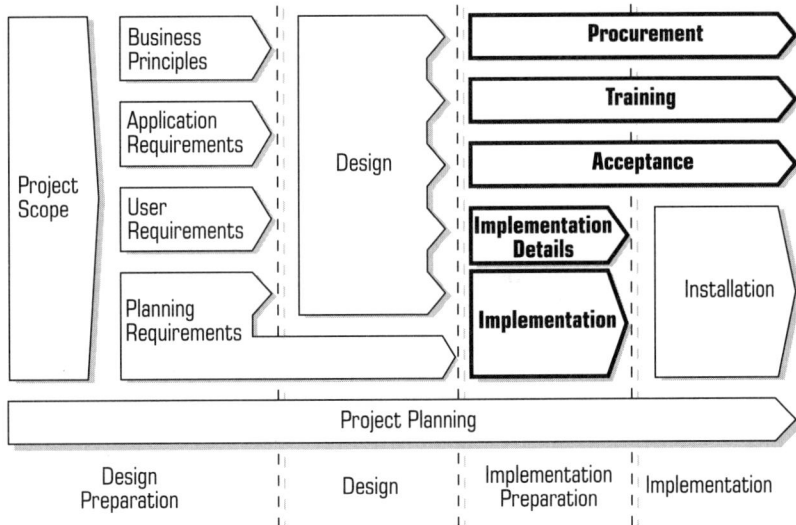

Chapter Structure

The five activities are addressed in the order shown in Table 17.1.

Table 17.1 *The Structure of Chapter 17*

Topic	Contents
Procurement	A project to design a technical infrastructure will require hardware and software to be purchased. How to choose the correct products and when to purchase them is discussed.
Training	Training for users and IT Support staff is essential if the new technical infrastructure is to be introduced smoothly. Recommendations are provided for identifying and satisfying the training needs of individuals.
Acceptance	The deliverable of a technical infrastructure is targeted at users and IT support. The different needs of both parties are examined to show how they determine the nature of the acceptance tests that need to be carried out.
Implementation Details	The steps involved in taking a design through to a tested set of products are explained.
Implementation Planning	The planning of an implementation involves the co-ordination of many involved parties. Correctly scoping the project, setting expectations correctly and appropriately resourcing it will all contribute to success.

Procurement

A technical infrastructure project will call for the evaluation, selection, and purchase of many items of software and hardware. Purchases will need to be made both for the testing environment and for the production environment. The procurement process can often be a source of delay which should be identified as a risk on the project plan.

The key to being able to manage the risk associated with procurement is to understand all the steps involved in the process. Once understood, measures can be taken to ensure things happen on time and accurate estimates of contingency time are made. To develop that level of understanding requires the following questions to be answered:

Table 17.2 *Initial Questions on Procurement*

Step	Questions to ask
Secure Funding	■ Has a budget been proposed? ■ What is the budget approval process? ■ Who is involved in the approval process? ■ How long is it going to take to gain approval? ■ Has the budget been approved? ■ Who needs to sign-off purchases?
Product Evaluation and Selection	■ Have products been selected? ■ When will products be selected? ■ Who needs to be involved in product selection? ■ Who has the authority to make product selection?
Product Purchase	■ Are product lead times known? ■ Is it known exactly how much product to purchase? ■ Does the budget cover the required cost of purchase? ■ Has a supplier been chosen? ■ Has a discount been agreed on?

The following sections examine product evaluation and selection and purchasing for the testing environment and the production environment in more detail as these are the aspects of procurement the technical infrastructure project will need to focus on.

Product Evaluation and Selection

It must be possible to justify the use of any product deployed as part of the technical infrastructure. To do this we must have considered all the important aspects of the product and judged it to be the most suitable in the context of our objectives.

At times a product is chosen after a lengthy evaluation involving other candidate products. In other cases, perhaps when time is short, only one product is evaluated with the objective of confirming it will meet the requirements. In the latter case, it is important to have a contingency plan should the single product under evaluation not measure up.

A product evaluation should consider the following areas:

- *Commercial*
  - Availability, is it pre-release, etc.?
  - Does it have a future?
  - Cost of license

  - Types of license available (e.g., site wide, corporate or per seat)
  - Cost of maintenance
  - Is it available in all the countries it needs to be used?
  - Viability of manufacturer
  - Can it be purchased from one global location for all sites or does it have to be purchased separately in each country?
- *Technical*
  - Does it have the required functionality?
  - Is it a good fit with the existing technology strategy?
  - Does it comply with corporate technology standards?
  - Can it be upgraded?
- *Support*
  - Availability of support in the countries it will be used
  - Availability of competent consultants from the supplier
  - Skills and resources required to use it
  - Does it comply with local safety standards?

It is essential that the right people in the organization are called on to judge the different areas of evaluation. The commercial area should be judged by the IT group that owns the decision on whether to use the product. If the corporation employs a supplier manager or purchasing manager then that person should be in a position to strongly support and advise on the commercial decisions.

The technical areas should be judged by the IT group that owns the decision, with the support areas judged by representatives from IT Support.

It is important to ensure that any product selection decision is made with the correct level of authority. That means the right people need to be fully involved and supportive of the selection process. The risk is that decisions may be overturned or delayed if the interests of a more powerful group in the corporation are overlooked.

Buying for Testing

At the point testing in the laboratory is necessary, it is only the work that is done in the laboratory that stands in the way of an installation. This means that if there are delays in testing then the overall project could slip. Two of the main reasons for testing delays are:

- Lack of suitable equipment
- Faulty equipment awaiting repair or replacement

Lack of suitable equipment can mean either that the right equipment couldn't be afforded or it simply hasn't arrived in time. The process of purchasing test equipment should begin in the early stages of the design phase, as soon as enough information is known about what will be needed.

Delays caused by faulty equipment are equally frustrating. The solution lies in ordering early and ordering spares. For example, if already ordering three workstations, order a fourth if being reduced to two seriously threatens the project.

In some cases problems will be experienced with a component of the system, leading to a need to replace it with an alternative. This occurrence is rarely foreseen and can again introduce delays if an alternative can't be found quickly. To minimize the impact of these risks the following measures should be taken:

- Test equipment should be ordered as soon as possible
- Spares should be ordered as a contingency measure
- There should be a budget for speedy purchase of unforeseen items

Buying for Production

Pre-release or trial versions of software will often be used during the Implementation Preparation phase of a project, either for evaluation purposes or until the purchased version arrives. It is particularly important not to overlook this when building the systems for transfer to their target sites. For example, a trial version of an anti-virus program might be included in the build. Apart from the fact that unlicensed software should not be used, it could have a time bomb in it causing a considerable impact to the production environment should it stop working after a fixed time.

This type of risk is best addressed through use of a quality procedure built in to the software release process. Checks for such a situation would then be carried out automatically, rather than relying on individual vigilance.

In most organizations the process of purchasing is well established, leaving the responsibility of the project team as specifying exactly what will need to be purchased in enough time for it to be ordered and delivered. The project team should also specify target delivery dates.

A number of things can stand in the way of the ordering process from the point of view of the technical infrastructure project team:

- Key design decisions influencing equipment requirements not made. For example, whether the WINS service should be a dedicated computer or whether it can reside on the DHCP and SMS server.
- Functionality or reliability problems with trial equipment causing a delay until a resolution is found.
- Insufficient or unprepared budget for funding purchases.

To minimize the impact of these risks the following measures should be taken:

- Ensure the purchasing budget is approved as early as possible. Delays in securing budget can extend to months.
- Factor in contingency time for coping with product problems.
- Ensure the full impact of delaying any design decision is understood in terms of the project's ability to deliver on time.
- Finally, do not underestimate the capacity of the purchasing process to delay a project!

Training

Training end users in the use of a new computer system is about ensuring they are able to use the new system effectively. User effectiveness may be measured by how many errors they make or how quickly they are able to work. If one of the main objectives for creating a new technical infrastructure is to operate more efficiently, the level of user effectiveness will significantly influence the degree to which that project achieves that objective.

IT Support staff also need training to understanding the workings of any new system. Lack of training can adversely impact the time it takes to fix a problem or administer a change; in the worst case, new problems are introduced by one erroneous fix. This costs money, so whether a reduction in support costs is a primary or secondary objective of introducing a new system, it is equally important to focus on the effectiveness of the IT Support staff.

The aspect all such projects have in common is the need to develop a training plan to maximize the chance of the exercise being successful. Table 17.3 shows the initial outline action plan for creating the MBI user and IT Support staff training program. This was developed into a detailed plan and subsequently a series of training classes, training materials and tests.

Table 17.3 *MBI Plan for Creating User and IT Support Staff Training Program*

Step	Details
Determine areas of training that will be required	Consider all aspects of planned technical infrastructure that will be new to users and IT Support. As a starting point, assume that training will be required for all these aspects.
Identify trainers	It will be unlikely that trainers with the required expertise will be available even from within a very large corporation. The best source of trainers will be training agencies that can offer a breadth of training skills and courses.
Establish individual training needs	Confirm on an individual basis who will need what training.
Determine style of training	The trainer should advise on whether the training should be: ▪ laboratory based ▪ classroom based ▪ self-paced
Develop training material	Training material should be carefully targeted at specific audience. Make sure the current aptitude and skills of the students are understood and that training material is geared towards the level of competence needed for each student to carry out their job.
Plan logistics and execute training	Plan who will be trained, when, where and by whom.
Confirm effectiveness of training	Ensure each person trained completes a questionnaire evaluating the training exercise. This way, the effectiveness of the training program can be enhanced as it progresses.

The next two sections highlight the differences between a training program for IT Support staff and a training program for users.

IT Support Training

For the IT Support staff to carry out their job they will need to understand two aspects of the technical infrastructure:

1. *The underlying product technology, (e.g., Windows NT, DHCP, DNS).* This can best be satisfied using standard training courses, many of which lead towards a professional qualification.
2. *The way the technical infrastructure is configured.* Training in the way the technical infrastructure has been configured can

only be done as an internal process drawing on the design documentation and support from the design team.

The wealth of technology and potential complexity of the technical infrastructure may lead to a long list of items for training. The recommended approach for coping with this complexity is to analyze the needs in terms of the roles the IT Support staff will carry out. By doing this, training on the technical infrastructure can be tailored appropriately and it then becomes a straightforward matter to work out what standard course will be needed. The three initial steps required to establish IT Support staff training needs are shown in Table 17.4.

Table 17.4 *Defining Objective of Training of IT Support*

Step	Details
1. Find out how things work today	Obtain from IT Support a list of job descriptions and associated responsibilities. Determine the types of tasks a person in each job category would typically undertake.
2. Confirm the business objectives	What the expectations of IT Support staff are (e.g., Will they have to meet new aggressive response times or fix times? Do they have a service level agreement? Will they have to reduce costs in some way? Where do their priorities lie?).
3. Define new list of tasks for each IT Support job category	Liaising with the technical infrastructure design group, find out what tasks the support staff will be expected to carry out with respect to the new system. Make sure it is understood why each task is done in a particular way. For example, if a file becomes corrupt on a workstation, the task might be to replace the hard disk and install a new workstation build, not to repair the file as that would take more time.

User Training

The most important thing to be clear on is exactly what is within the scope of technical infrastructure training for users. MBI determined that it certainly included the graphical user interface features such as shortcuts, folders and the taskbar. In addition they chose to include the core applications supplied to everyone, which includes the office suite, world-wide web browser and an anti-virus package.

MBI found that of the user population, a number of users currently had no PC (used to using a UNIX workstation instead) and those that did used Windows 3.*x* or Windows NT 3.51.

The new technical infrastructure will call for Windows NT 4 on the PC, introducing a graphical user interface style that will be new to all. The decision was taken to use the same training material for every class but to arrange attendance so that classes contained either all novice students or all advanced students. This allowed the pace of the class to be adjusted to suit all students. Thus, the most important question that needed to be asked of the users in the training needs checklist was whether they were familiar with PCs.

Acceptance

Agreement must be gained from the recipients of the new technical infrastructure that it meets their requirements before it can be handed over from development into production use. The best way of doing this is to create a set of acceptance tests to prove the system meets the requirements of the recipients.

To make sure acceptance testing is a meaningful process we must therefore be clear:

- Who should accept the system
- Who should create the acceptance tests
- What the acceptance tests are intended to prove

Who Should Accept the System?

Business users will use the technical infrastructure, both directly and via applications. IT Support will have the responsibility of managing the technical infrastructure. In the design preparation phase of the project we asked both of these two communities what their requirements were and we have designed the technical infrastructure to accommodate both their needs. We must therefore look for both communities to formally accept the technical infrastructure.

While it will usually be clear who the business is, the IT Support organization is likely to comprise several different groups, among which will be:

- Application support
- Database administration
- Production systems support
- Network support
- Telecommunications support

The production systems support group and the network support group are the two that will have most interest in formally accepting a new technical infrastructure, though as organizational structures differ between corporations you should look to identify those groups who will need to support the technical infrastructure components and the systems they run on. For convenience, the various support groups are referred to as IT Support.

The acceptance test for the IT Support group is termed a *System Acceptance Test* (SAT) and its objective is to ensure the technical infrastructure was configured and working as planned. The test for users is termed a *User Acceptance Test* (UAT) and its objective was to ensure the technical infrastructure offered the correct user features. Both types of test should be derived from the Technical Infrastructure Functional Specification.

Who Should Create the Acceptance Tests?

The UAT should be created by the IT Support group on behalf of or in conjunction with the business users. The UAT should be version controlled, just like the software it is there to test, with a new major version being released as the corresponding software is moved into user acceptance test status.

The SAT should be created by the engineering group as it is they who designed the technical infrastructure and are in the best position to know how it should be configured. IT Support should run the SAT to confirm the infrastructure is configured and works as planned.

What Acceptance Tests are Intended to Prove

The complexity of a technical infrastructure is such that to gain a satisfactory answer to the question "Does it work?" is often difficult. Even if we can be satisfied the technical infrastructure works, how can we be sure that it is configured as designed?

Consider the situation where two name servers are being used to resolve all computer name requests in a region. For a given workstation, according to the design, one will be configured as the primary name server and the other the secondary. Clearly both should be able to resolve names to addresses. However testing, for example, the ability to connect a remote file share from a workstation will not be able to reveal whether:

- The two servers have been configured in the right order as primary and secondary.
- Both the servers are functioning correctly. Only one might be working and that was the one used to resolve the name in the test.
- Failover to the other server works correctly (i.e., that it is running and the IP address has been entered correctly on the workstation).
- If configured correctly as primary and secondary whether the secondary can indeed be accessed.

Thus, a simple test like this may show the technical infrastructure working but it cannot prove it has been configured correctly. A better test would exercise several scenarios with the objective of proving the system behaved in the way it had been designed to in each.

It is very easy to fall into the trap of testing basic product functionality, which reveals very little, rather than testing how the products have been configured. For example, a test for whether the word processor can be invoked on a workstation tells us very little about whether a user will be able to edit their documents located on a file share.

We now know we must test the technical infrastructure to ensure it:

- Is configured as designed.
- Works as designed, which includes:
  - System environment—failover, capacity, security, etc.
  - User environment—file share connections, user directory structure, etc.

An example from the MBI SAT is shown in Table 17.5.

Table 17.5 *Extract from MBI SAT*

Test	Expected Result	Pass
1. WINS Replication	SMTL9999 should have a full push/pull relationship with the SNYC9999 WINS server located in New York.	
2. Replication settings	Replication settings on both computers as per design document.	
3. Add a new computer to the Montreal network	DHCP should provide the newly added computer with IP parameters and it should register its NetBIOS computer name with SMTL9999.	

Table 17.5 *Extract from MBI SAT (continued)*

Test	Expected Result	Pass
4. Propagation	Confirm that after the propagation time calculated in the design document the NetBIOS name/IP address mapping has propagated to all other WINS servers.	
5. Name resolution	Make a network share connection to the newly added computer by specifying the NetBIOS computer name. A connection will only be possible if the computer name has successfully been mapped to an IP address.	
6. Removing a computer from the Montreal network	Remove the computer and repeat test 4 checking that the name is purged from the WINS servers after the anticipated amount of time.	

An example from the MBI UAT is shown in Table 17.6.

Table 17.6 *Extract from MBI UAT*

Test	Expected Result	Pass
1. Power up workstation	Background bitmap is MBI logo	
2. Log on as NYCEFXUSER, password testefxuser from regional master domain and check user environment:	▪ Start menu contents = <shortcut list> ▪ Desktop icon/shortcut list = <shortcut list> ▪ H:\ connected to \\SNYO0001\nycefxuser$ ▪ G:\ connected to \\SNYO0001\efx$ ▪ P:\ connected to \\SNYO0001\public ▪ F:\ connected to \\SNYO0001\apps$ ▪ Can create a file and then delete it in each of H:\, G:\ and P:\. ▪ Can read files in F:\ ▪ Connected printers list in Print Manager = <Printer list> ▪ Default print set to EFXPrinter ▪ Print a MS Word file to EFXPrinter ▪ FAX MS Word file to EFXFAX ▪ EFX Application Group contents = <shortcut list> ▪ Do each of the applications in EFX Application Group startup OK? ▪ Is the time set correctly? ▪ Invoke each of the following applications = <Application list>	
3. Log on as NYCCMKUSER, password testcmkuser from regional master domain	Repeat NYCEFXUSER test substituting CMK for EFX where appropriate.	

Table 17.6 *Extract from MBI UAT*

4. Log on as NYCDVRUSER, password testdrvuser from regional master domain	Repeat NYCEFXUSER test substituting DRV for EFX where appropriate.	
5. Log on as LDNEFXUSER, password testefxuser from regional master domain	Repeat NYCEFXUSER test with the difference: ▪ H:\ connected to \\SLDN0001\ldnefxuser$ ▪ G:\ connected to \\SLDN0001\efx$	

Regression Testing

When testing systems of great complexity it is to be expected that there will be areas where the system will fail. It is usual to rank the severity of a failure indicating its impact. Possible ranks might be:

- **Critical**—Must be fixed for product to be released.
- **Medium**—Does not stop product being released but must be fixed within a time limit.
- **Low**—Fix in next patch or release.

Problems will also be identified during beta testing and production usage and each should be treated in the same way, as above, as a UAT or SAT highlighted problem.

Once problems are fixed, the UAT or SAT should be updated to include a test to confirm the problem remains fixed. This way, the problem can't re-enter the product chain without it being detected. We should apply the same process to functionality enhancements to ensure that they do not introduce new problems. This is known as regression testing.

Implementation Details

The objective of the Implementation Detail activity in the overall project model (illustrated at the beginning of the chapter) is to take a logical design through to a detailed design sufficient for implementation to begin.

That is a straightforward concept but it can be difficult to envision all the tasks that make up this activity. Chapter 4, Project Planning, lists a typical set of tasks for this activity along with a brief description for each. Here we examine the detail behind them.

In this phase of the project, when progress is becoming more visible, it is common to find that aspects of design you thought were agreed on and set in stone are being brought into question by parties you never knew existed, or who had not responded to requests for comment in the design phase. If the influence of these parties is not checked it may lead to disruption as work is scrapped and time is diverted to design matters again, drawing on resources when they can least be spared.

The usual method of removing the risk of revisiting earlier design decisions is to declare a design freeze. The freeze should be aligned with the delivery and sign-off of the design documentation and supported by the signatories.

Once underway, the implementation detail activity will involve:

- Development of a software delivery mechanism for loading software onto workstations
- Development testing to prove the design
- Pilot implementation (optional) to learn from the production environment
- Software release management to support the production of systems that are of high quality and stability

These topics are covered in the following sections.

Software Delivery

There are two types of challenge involved in installing software on a large scale.

1. The automatic initial installation of Windows NT on a workstation that may have no operating system installed or needs a new installation because confidence has been lost in configuration of the software currently installed.
2. The automatic remote upgrade of all installed components including operating system, service packs, drivers and applications on a workstation of a known configuration.

The latter challenge is extremely important if the technical infrastructure is to be maintained in a consistent state after the initial implementation is complete.

The two challenges need to be treated differently because automatic software upgrade and installation tools depend on an agent to be running on the client system. If there is no operating system on the client or it is of the wrong type or cannot be trusted, an agent cannot be used and some other method needs to be found. For an end user organization the choice usually comes down to methods involving boot floppy disks and server resident software kits.

For example, in an environment with diverse user needs, one approach might be to automate the installation of Windows NT and to install all necessary applications remotely on a per workstation or group of workstations basis. Thus, the initial installation does not depend on highly skilled technicians and applications can be installed remotely. The strategy in this case is to automate in a flexible fashion so differing user application requirements can be accommodated easily.

Another approach in an environment with little diversity might be to include several applications with the initial workstation installation kit, eliminating the need to install them separately. This is a good approach if, for example, everyone gets the same common set of applications.

Several tools and products are available for implementing a software delivery strategy.

Table 17.7 *Software Delivery Tools and Product Types*

Tool	Description	Comments
Computer Profile Setup (CPS)	A Windows NT Resource Kit tool for creating a clone of an installation. It does this by copying everything from a reference installation to a server based file which can then be downloaded to other computers.	*Designed for doing an initial installation.* ▪ Suitable for a modest degree of diversity among target hardware. Can require detailed knowledge of .inf files to reduce operator input during install. Major advantage is that it can include applications installed on the reference computer in the kit.
Unattended Setup	This is essentially the use of a special file prepared in advance, containing the answers to the questions posed in a normal installation. Use of this file allows the automated installation of any number of workstations to the same configuration. Tools for creating Unattended Setup and UDFs can be found on the Windows NT Resource Kit.	*Designed for doing an initial installation.* ▪ Can be complemented with Uniqueness Database Files (UDF) to cope with diversity in target hardware. Becomes cumbersome if too many UDFs.

Table 17.7 *Software Delivery Tools and Product Types (continued)*

Tool	Description	Comments
Software Delivery	Typified by Microsoft SMS, this type of tool is first and foremost a mechanism for delivering kits to target computers.	*Designed for getting software kits to target computers in very large installations.* ▪ Suitable for use with *operating system upgrades*, service pack installations and application installations and upgrades.
Software Installation	Typified by a product such as WinInstall or to a lesser extent Sysdiff, a software installation product creates a packaged kit for dispatch by a Software Delivery tool (see above).	*Designed for making the creation of installation packages easier.* ▪ Most work on the basis of comparing before and after snapshots of a system and then creating all the necessary information for a Software Delivery tool to be able to deliver the package and initiate its operation.

Now let us look at the MBI technical infrastructure project to see what delivery strategy suited them. We should recall that the MBI technical infrastructure project is guided by a number of business principles that we ought to refer to in situations like this. The key statement in this case is the recognition of the need to minimize support requirements in offices with limited local support capability (MBI Business Principle 4, Implication 4).

While not spelling out anything about the nature of software delivery, they have guided the analysis within MBI towards some key design decisions that are necessary to reduce support costs:

1. Workstation software installations should be disposable. If the software on a workstation gets into a faulty state it should be possible to re-install the entire build quickly and easily with minimum loss of configuration information.

2. It should be possible to control the installation, upgrade and de-installation of software products remotely.

3. Workstations should be of a standard configuration. This will mean there are fewer different drivers to manage and therefore fewer configurations to test new software against. This is extremely difficult to achieve in practice though the benefits make it worth having as a goal. To be realistic it will be necessary to settle for supporting a small number of different configurations.

4. Distribution of software should be restricted to the LAN as a WAN is unlikely to have sufficient spare capacity to cope with the large amounts of data without impacting business traffic.

The above points are recorded fully as Design Principles in Appendix B. The technical solution MBI chose based on these principles is as follows:

- An unattended build of Windows NT Workstation 4 and Microsoft Office 97 Standard Edition capable of supporting the three main types of workstation found in MBI.
- Distribute the build on CD-ROM to all locations.
- Create installation and de-installation packages for Microsoft Office 97 Standard Edition and all other software products that might be required.
- Use Microsoft SMS where installed to deliver software packages.
- Use CD-ROM to deliver packages to locations where Microsoft SMS is impractical due to support issues and low speed communications links.

Thus, re-installing a workstation amounts to downloading the unattended setup build and then installing the necessary software packages either using a local distribution share or using Microsoft SMS. Although the subject of software delivery is dealt with in the Implementation Preparation phase it has little dependency on deliverables from the design phase and is frequently started at the same time as the other design activities. Indeed, the benefit from doing this is that the tools for initial installation and upgrades may be available for use in the testing activity, reducing effort involved in test system re-installations.

Note that computer vendors are usually willing to undertake the initial workstation installation on a new computer for a particular customer. While this can be very cost-effective, the facility to re-install workstations on-site must not be lost.

Product Deliverables

Once we know the delivery strategy it is usually clear what the deliverables of the implementation detail activity should be. They will fall into two categories, software and documentation.

Software

This category of deliverable is applicable when some sort of preconfiguration, packaging or software creation, for example utilities or scripts is the output. We would not normally include standard software products passed on from a supplier such as Microsoft Office Professional in this category, though a Microsoft SMS package to install and de-install the product would be.

In the case of MBI, the following software deliverables were defined:

1. CD-ROM containing unattended setup build for Windows NT4 and Microsoft Office 97 Standard Edition.
2. Microsoft SMS installation and de-installation packages for all applications.
3. Logon scripts.

Note that each of these software deliverables should be designated with a version number and be subject to the project's software release management process.

Documentation

The Implementation Detail phase moves our theoretical design forward by introducing many more design details. These details must be captured if we are to stand a chance of either reproducing the system or maintaining consistency between several sites.

It can be tempting to put these design details into an updated version of the original design documents produced in the Design Phase of the project. That would be a mistake for the following reasons:

1. The quantity of additional detail would obscure the clarity of the original design.
2. Any change of design detail would render the design document out of date.

So how do we best capture the work done in this activity? Let us look at the MBI case study for what was done on that project.

The MBI technical infrastructure design project is developing a system that must be installable and supportable by the IT Support group anywhere in the world. Written instructions for installation are therefore essential. IT Support is also going to provide first and second line support for the system and therefore has a need to know how the system works to the extent it can be repaired. In recognition of the IT Support group as the main consumers of the Implementation Detail activity deliverables, they were asked to state the types of document they would require to be able to fully support the system.

Five types of document were identified:

1. *Installation and setup guides*—Guides to the installation and setup of technical infrastructure software and hardware is essential if the IT is to be installed according to the design.
2. *Operational procedures*—If the characteristics of the technical infrastructure are to be maintained then operational procedures must be carried out within certain guidelines. For example, the procedure for adding a new user to the system must ensure the user account has the correct rights, the home drive is created on the correct computer and is shared with the correct permissions. Getting some of these wrong could prejudice the security of the system or might deny the user some functionality.
3. *System guides*—The system guides show how the software product deliverables are created. For example, one might be written to show how to create the SMS packages required by one of the installation and set-up documents. Their purpose is to document the engineering work providing an explanation of how it's all put together.
4. *Recovery procedures*—To enhance technical infrastructure availability the Recovery Procedures documents a list of instructions for returning the computers and technical infrastructure services back to their original operational state.
5. *A document describing the detail of the implementation per site*—A document that may be produced as part of an installation at a location is one describing all its unique aspects. A title for it might be Site Overview and it would describe aspects of the configuration that are at the discretion of the particular location such as IP address allocations per subnet, special accounts and passwords or Windows NT groups particular to that location.

All documents should be written to a level that assumes the reader has passed the relevant Microsoft Certified Professional exams or has had equivalent experience. This meant they could be concise documents that complemented any existing manuals or on-line help. For example, an instruction in an MBI installation and setup guide for a server might be:

Table 17.8 *Example Installation Instruction*

#	Item	Explanation
1	Re-label the FAT utilities partition to U:	Re-labelling this partition will allow us to keep it and free up label C for the 1GB NTFS partition.

There is no further detail as to which utility to use or how to operate that utility. The explanation section is intended to explain why the item is being carried out, not how to carry it out.

Development Testing

The Implementation Detail activity is inherently practical, mandating the use of computers for the development and testing of the designs produced in the Design phase of the project. The purpose of development testing is to confirm the technical infrastructure will work as designed.

Essential as it is, the nature of testing is such that on occasions unpredictable things happen, such as saturation of the network. It is therefore essential that the production systems are guarded from anything that might impact their ability to serve the business. The recommended way to address this is to create a laboratory environment that is isolated from the production network. In cases where it is absolutely necessary to connect the laboratory to the production network a firewall may be acceptable.

Testing in a Laboratory

A laboratory environment should be used for:

- Developing scripts
- System setup procedure development and documentation
- Applications installation and configuration for testing and documenting
- Initial installation package production
- Application package production for the automated software distribution and installation tool
- Performance testing
- Trial installations of complete system for a site
- Testing of builds prior to release from development

The storing of all on-line software kits, documentation and software produced by the lab development activity should be done on a production server that is backed up regularly. Storing this kind of data on a lab server, which could be re-built with no notice, may result in its loss adversely impacting the project.

For it to be of most use, the lab should have enough equipment for the key production configurations to be replicated for testing. For example, if a site is going to consist of two domains, one master and one resource, then it should be possible to set that up. The equipment used should be the same as that planned or already in use in production as any differences will introduce factors that are hard to test.

The diversity and intensity of development testing can frequently lead to conflicting demands on testing hardware. Planning the development testing tasks will pay dividends when there is greatest demand on facilities.

WAN Simulation

The MBI production environment will consist of several slow WAN links so it is important we are in a position to replicate these in the lab to test whether our design will deliver the required level of performance over the WAN. Thus, we will need at least two servers, one for each end of the WAN link and a WAN simulator device to achieve the effect of a low bandwidth communications line. This is shown in Figure 17.2.

Figure 17.2 *Use of WAN Bandwith Simulator*

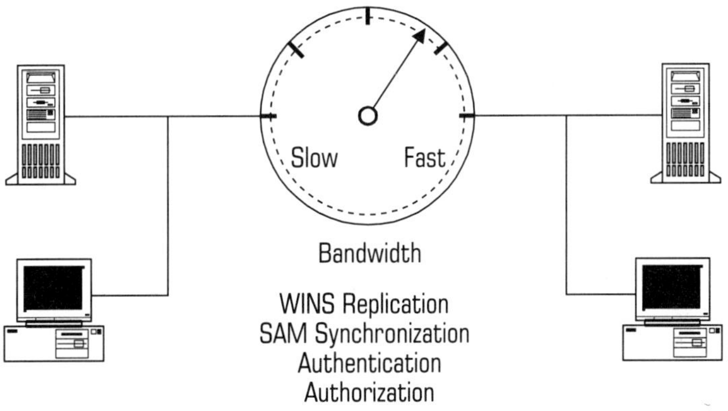

Reference Machines

In the lab environment it is common to find the development machines get into an unknown state very quickly as software is added, configured, de-installed and tweaked. This makes it impossible to carry out any tests on them with confidence as it is impossible to be certain whether the configuration is as it should be or not.

To overcome this it is useful to designate an example of each type of machine as a master. Thus, MBI designated one workstation as a reference and one server as a reference. Now experiments can be performed on these reference computers with confidence. If an unattended installation kit is one of the deliverables from this phase of the project then it can be useful to make available early releases of the build to enable the reference computers to be rebuilt quickly and consistently.

MBI Laboratory Inventory

The laboratory is going to be an important project resource and its creation should be treated like a small project. In addition to all the computer equipment it may require the requisitioning of office space, the installation of power and network cables. You should draw up an inventory for the laboratory as well as a diagram for how it is to fit together. As examples, the MBI inventory and diagram follow.

Table 17.9 *MBI Laboratory Inventory*

Item	Hardware	Software
Experimental Server (X 3 unless stated)	▪ 200MHz Pentium Pro ▪ 128MB memory ▪ 5 × 2GB Disks ▪ Dual Power Supply, Ethernet adapter ▪ 15" Monitor, CDROM ▪ Remote Server Manager ▪ Modem	▪ Windows NT Server ▪ Server Resource Kit × 1 ▪ Automated Software Installation ▪ Inventory database ▪ Capacity planner ▪ Performance management software ▪ Alert Management software ▪ Anti-virus software ▪ Terminal Emulator ▪ Office suite
Experimental Workstation (X 3 unless stated)	▪ 200MHz Pentium Pro ▪ 64MB memory ▪ 1 × 2GB Disks, ▪ 17" Monitor, CDROM	▪ Windows NT Workstation ▪ Workstation Resource Kit x 1
Laboratory Server	▪ As experimental server but with only 64MB memory and no remote server manager ▪ 10 × 2GB Disks mirrored ▪ 20/40GB DLT tape drive	▪ Backup Tools
Laboratory Workstation	▪ Same as experimental workstation	▪ Office suite ▪ Diagram package
Miscellaneous Hardware	▪ WAN Simulator ▪ 16 port hub ▪ 6 phone lines, 2 telephones ▪ Network attached printer	

Figure 17.3
MBI Laboratory Configuration

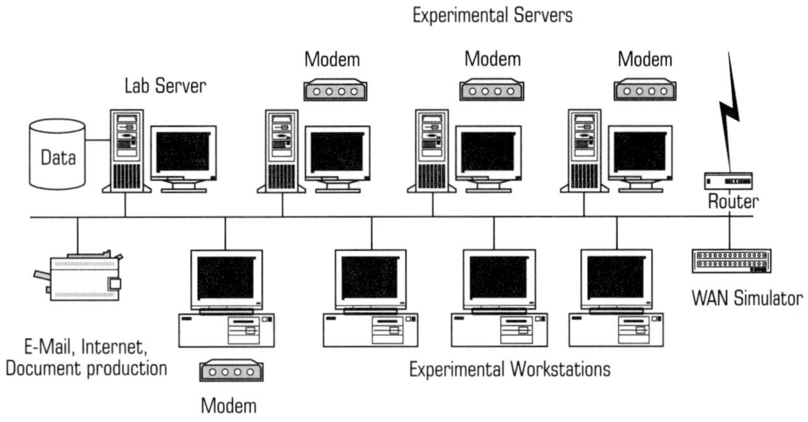

Testing in Stages

To make the task of testing the technical infrastructure services more manageable it is useful to take it in four stages:

1. Installation
2. Unit
3. Integration or system
4. Volume

Each stage is examined below.

- *Installation Testing*

Before any software can be tested for functionality it must be possible to install it correctly. Testing that this can be done is particularly important when software is packaged up for automatic distribution and installation. Installation testing checks the correctness of the installation and the installation instructions for their completeness and accuracy.

- *Unit and Integration Testing*

As components in a system interact, their behavior can be difficult to determine. If they are operated in isolation, their behavior can be measured more accurately. Thus, the separate components of a system should be tested individually, or unit tested, then tested in a system, or integration tested.

Now, if problems occur in the integration test but not the unit test then we know the problem lies with component incompatibility.

In a typical infrastructure project the following components of the system may be designed, developed and unit tested separately:

- Unattended Windows NT installation, including a small number of core components such as drivers and software such as an office suite or e-mail client.
- Software packages for layered applications.
- Server configurations.
- Logon scripts.

Integration testing should begin by re-running the unit tests to confirm that the components continue to work in the system as designed. Once the basic functionality has been proven the whole system should be tested for functionality that spans the software components. An example is resilience testing where the failure of a hardware component must be simulated, causing an effect on several system components simultaneously.

- *Volume Testing*

The purpose of volume testing is to ensure that the system behaves as designed under a load. In the laboratory environment a load has to be simulated using one of several tools that are available for subjecting a system to different types of artificial load. A difficulty with volume testing is determining the level of artificial load to apply.

In cases where the work profile of users is not likely to change much with the introduction of the new system, a good estimate can be arrived at. Where that is not possible the workload estimate can only be based on data from a capacity planning exercise. The results of volume testing should be used with great caution as real life production systems involve a greater number of variables than can be simulated completely under lab conditions.

Pilot Implementation

A pilot is a small scale deployment to a set of users who understand they are not receiving a final version of a system. It is useful to extend this notion of a pilot to include trial of non-application aspects of the system.

For example, the IT support organization might be a customer of the technical infrastructure as it will end up using the features and tools designed in to manage and operate the system. Thus, the decision might be taken to pilot the management and operations aspects of the technical infrastructure.

Other candidates for a pilot are:

- The general graphical user interface involving menus and user configuration options,
- Software distribution,
- Access to shares or resources, and
- The process for installing a new site.

A pilot can be used to:

- Gain experience in a relatively safe environment.
- Solicit feedback from users (any recipients of the system) to improve functionality.

The advantage of using a pilot is that its modest scale makes it practical to recover from a problem rapidly. It is also a lot cheaper to fix a problem early in its development cycle than later. Consider the benefits of uncovering a significant problem requiring a re-installation, while piloting the technical infrastructure to 20 users, instead of uncovering it after rolling the system out to 10,000.

The dividing line between a pilot and an initial rollout can be thin, so where a deliberate pilot is not favored, the support needs of the users in the first phase of deployment should be considered carefully.

It is essential that there are contingencies for if the pilot system fails in any way or is unable to deliver anticipated functionality. One approach is to run the pilot system in parallel with the system it will ultimately replace so ensuring users can revert to the old system if problems occur.

One of the problems that can arise with running the old system alongside the pilot system is that the pilot systems may not be used much if users cannot be encouraged off the system they are more familiar with. Lack of use will invalidate the pilot.

When to Pilot

A pilot would typically be considered when a group of people are likely to undergo a significant change in their working environment or be faced with completely new technology as a result of the new technical infrastructure. The pilot should begin at the point when the development is naturally complete, the same time deployment would start if a pilot was not being run. It should not be an excuse to start rolling something out before it is ready as the risk to the credibility of the project and those involved would be too high. A successful pilot is one where the users are content with its result.

Supporting a Pilot

By its nature there is an experimental element to a pilot. That usually means there is something that is not fully proven involved, creating the potential for difficulties. A well planned pilot should anticipate several scenarios where rapid corrective action might be needed, perhaps to the extreme of reverting back to the original systems. It should also offer the opportunity to pro-actively monitor performance and offer changes where necessary.

To support a pilot successfully:

- Users will need a quick and effective way to report problems or new requirements.
- Problems must be resolved speedily.
- New requirements must be evaluated to determine whether they should result in a modification to the pilot system or whether they should be rejected.
- Modifications must be implemented speedily.

Figure 17.4 *Supporting a Pilot*

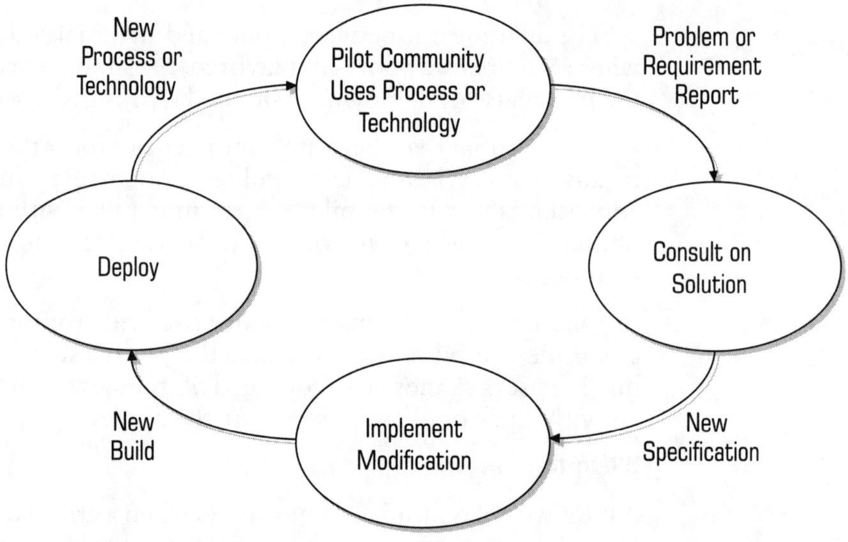

Key to the success of a pilot are the users. After all, they are going to use the technical infrastructure to do their job so it must work well for them. The pilot plan should therefore include steps to ensure the users are able to not only make a full contribution to the exercise but to keep working as well.

Elements to include in the plan to ensure users are a full part of it would be:

- Means of summoning speedy support
- Training on the new system or process
- An explanation of their role in the pilot

Learning from the Pilot

A pilot is a learning exercise so we must make a conscious effort to understand how successful it was. Our main aim must be to establish whether the system met the needs of the customer. This brings into question our original analysis, our design as well as our implementation. It may also bring into question some of the requirements supplied by the business.

To understand the success of a pilot it will be necessary to gather data that can support a judgment. That means having clear objectives for the pilot and practical means of measuring their achievement. The objective of the MBI pilot was to evaluate two things:

- The time taken to logon when being authenticated by a remote BDC.
- The file server capacity required for a population of users.

Logon performance over the WAN had been simulated by the MBI project team in the laboratory environment and it showed that performance could degrade quite badly over some of MBI's slower WAN links if they were already heavily utilized. To confirm this, MBI decided to implement a pilot incorporating a slow WAN link, taking the following measurements:

- Time taken from clicking OK box on logon screen to completion of logon process using *local* authentication at a set of planned times during the working day. Knowing the time taken to logon locally allows the time taken to logon remotely to be judged in a relative manner as well as an absolute one.
- Time taken from clicking OK box on logon screen to completion of logon process using *remote* authentication at a set of planned times during the working day.

To measure file service capacity requirements for the pilot population of users performance monitoring was configured on the file server to record counters applicable to file serving activity. As long as the pilot population comprises a typical cross section of users the result may be used with caution to estimate the file service capacity requirements for another similar group of users.

Reviewing the Pilot

To ensure the maximum benefit is extracted from the pilot it is important to hold a review. In the form of a meeting, the review would:

- Summarize and accept the data (should be written up and circulated prior to the review meeting)
- Evaluate the conclusions
- Make recommendations

It would be normal to include a representative of the user community in the review meeting as the pilot exercise is ultimately to do with making sure the users get a suitable system.

Software Release Management

As software builds and scripts are created various parties will want to have use of them for associated developments and general awareness. Without control over what is released, confusion can quickly develop regarding who has what version and which bugs were fixed when. A structured process for releasing product from the project team is critical if quality is to be maintained throughout the cycle of the project.

The subsequent sections describe the main aspects of a software release mechanism.

Phases of Release

A software product should make progress through to production in several phases, each one representing a higher state of readiness. Each release should have a designation that makes clear its phase and therefore what should be expected from it. MBI decided the three basic software product phases and their designations should be:

Table 17.10 *Phases of Release*

Phase	Designation	Description
Development	D0.0	Currently undergoing engineering work. Likely to change from hour to hour.
Beta	V0.0 Beta n	Intended to be complete but lacks user acceptance testing. Safe for use by all wishing to experience an early version of the new build. Several iterations may be gone through before submission to production test.
Production ready	V0.0	Passed the user acceptance test and ready for deployment.

Release Notes

It is important that released software products can be used with minimum support or resources will be diverted from the project to assist with installation and usage problems. The recommended way to address this is to include with the release of each software product a set of release notes containing useful information about it.

The MBI project team included the following information in the release notes:

- New features
- Installation details
- Configuration details
- Contacts for support
- Known problems
- Bugs fixed since last release
- The process for registering a bug report or feature requirement

Release Process

The transition from one phase to the next must be irreversible or the whole value of the process will be diminished. Equally important is the control over promoting a product from one phase to the next. Premature promotion risks lowering quality and reduces confidence in the product. The process MBI adopted for moving a product from one phase to the next involved the need to satisfy a broad set of prerequisites prior to it gaining the signatures of members of a release committee. For incrementing the beta level the prerequisites were less demanding and the release committee comprised IS staff only. For release to production the prerequisites included:

- Passed all user and system tests satisfactorily
- All documentation complete
- Software kits safely stored and reproducible
- No known show-stoppers
- Acceptable to the support organization

The release committee comprised representatives from:

- IS
- The help desk
- IT Support
- The business community

One of the dangers of a poor release process is that bugs fixed in one release can re-emerge in the next. To avoid this it is necessary to ensure that every time a bug is fixed a test to check the fix is included in the test suite.

Change Control

Depending on the nature of the production environment it may be necessary to apply fixes or features in the field, the time involved in producing another complete, fully tested build being too great. This doesn't mean efforts at quality can be abandoned. The MBI project manager recognized the need to cope with rapid enhancements and instigated the following procedure, designed to, above anything, register that a change had taken place:

- Test the enhancement thoroughly, if possible using the usual build test suite.
- Record the enhancement in a register maintained by engineering.
- The enhancement or suitable alternative should be considered for inclusion in the next version of the build.

Capacity Planning

Capacity planning is the process of managing the available power of a system to meet the demands placed on it by the business. It is an entirely pro-active discipline, the goal being to ensure that system capacity is available for when it is needed.

Capacity planning is used in two different situations:

1. To determine the hardware and networking requirements for the initial technical infrastructure installation.
2. To ensure the technical infrastructure, once installed, continues to meet the performance needs of a changing business workload.

The first activity is sometimes referred to as *system sizing* and the second is sometimes referred to as *capacity management*. The key difference is that capacity management can be carried out with more certainty than system sizing because the installed system provides valuable data from which to develop predictions of hardware need.

Capacity management should be an ongoing process that is an essential part of the job of managing and operating a technical infrastructure. System sizing is an important task in the preparation for an implementation. We shall focus on system sizing here, though it is closely related to capacity management.

System sizing presents two challenges, one is of a technical nature and the other business:

1. Translating the work of a user, or the processing of an application, into hardware requirements.
2. Determining how the number of users or processing needs will change over time.

To solve the first challenge we must look to estimates made with the best evidence available. To solve the second challenge we must look to the business to share its business plans. These two challenges are examined below, followed by a description of how to combine the answers to size a system.

Translating Workload into Hardware Requirements

Ultimately we are looking for a value for **n** in an equation of the form:

1 standard user requires n% of a computer system

From that relationship we can determine how many computers are required to support a given population. Unfortunately several factors complicate the matter:

1. Rarely is there such thing as a standard user. Each will differ in terms of the demand they place on a computer system.
2. Computers differ in their capacity so we will need to specify which type of computer we are referring to.
3. Computers are made from many different components, each of which is exercised to different degrees depending on the workload. Thus for the workload generated by one user, one component may be stressed while others are underutilized. The workload generated by a different user may cause a completely different distribution of work among the computer components.
4. The workload generated by a user will vary through the day or perhaps week.

These factors are capable of introducing a substantial error into such a simple equation. The process of capacity management would allow the development of a reasonably accurate equation through the study of how the system behaved for different workloads. In the case of system sizing we do not have historic observations and so must rely on estimates instead.

Before looking at how to use estimates to develop such an equation, let us look at how each of the factors above affects the accuracy of the equation. Point one may be addressed by taking a large enough sample of users so that the difference in demand each user places on a computer is averaged out.

Although computers differ in capacity, the commodity nature of computer hardware allows a computer to be crudely characterized by its:

- Processor power
- Memory
- Storage

So, rather than specifying a model of computer we can define the most appropriate commodity configuration to match the average way in which the three main components of a computer are exercised. This allows us to address points two and three.

Even taking a large sample population, cyclic demand will be clearly apparent as users logon at the beginning of the day, go for lunch and cope with any natural cycles in the business. The way to address point four is to develop an understanding of it. The system should be sized to cope with the periods of heaviest workload.

Now we understand the equation better we can now make some estimates. Estimates made from personal experience may be realistic but could be very inaccurate. There are several sources of information that can be used to strengthen an estimate:

1. **Manufacturers' Published Sizing Data**

   Make sure figures are interpreted carefully as they are likely to have been produced in laboratory conditions that do not accurately reflect a production environment.

2. **Other Corporations with Comparable Systems Already in Use**

   For competitive reasons the other corporation will need to be from a different industry. Contact can be made through industry bodies such as manufacturer sponsored user groups.

3. **Consultants**

   Moving from one company to another, a consultant may have experience of other installations that can add value to a system sizing exercise.

4. **Modeling Tools**

   Tools are emerging that allow the construction of a theoretical model of a production system. The model can be used to develop an understanding of the computer capacities needed to support different types and size of workload. The usual problem with these tools is the need to estimate how a workload stresses a system, which merely shifts the difficulty of system sizing from one part of the problem to another.

More recent modeling tools include definitions of standard workloads which can significantly help in the development of an accurate model. Skill is required to use these tools if a high degree of confidence in their output is required. Consider using consultants from the manufacturer of the tool to carry out the modeling exercise.

5. **Data Gathered from a Pilot**

   The MBI pilot detailed earlier in the chapter measured the load placed on the file servers by the pilot users. The purpose of this was to build up information that would enable the complete system to be sized with more confidence. Data gathered from representative users will always be more valuable than any type of estimate or model. If possible, develop estimates from more than one source of information so the results may be corroborated.

   The results of the MBI pilot are summarized here:

Table 17.11 *MBI System Sizing*

Server Capacity Requirements (Peak workload requirements, Maximum component utilization = 70%)		
Services: File, Print, FAX		
Business Group	**Component**	**Demand/User**
Foreign Exchange	266MHz Processor	4%
	Memory	15MB
	Disk IO	4/sec
	Disk Capacity	30MB
Swaps Back Office	266MHz Processor	5%
	Memory	20MB
	Disk IO	8/sec
	Disk Capacity	120MB

Using such a table we can see clearly that 25 foreign exchange users would require a 266MHz server with 375MB memory, a disk subsystem capable of handling 100 IO/sec with a volume of 750MB. These capacity requirements represent the peak over any chosen cycle and represent a system functioning at 70% capacity. If we know the foreign exchange group is going to expand to 50 within the planning horizon we can easily calculate the system configuration required using the sizing table.

Useful ways of presenting this data with more information would be to plot the requirements on a graph over the:

- working day
- natural business processing cycle
- system sizing horizon

(This is a more detailed form of the crude sizing technique used in the chapter dealing with File and Print services.)

Incorporating Plans of the Business

We need to know how many users are employed currently and how that user population is to change over time. We also need to know how the level of application processing the system carries out will need to change. You will find that clear user population plans are hard to come by because of their sensitive and in many cases uncertain nature.

Often the best that can be done is look for practical evidence of increases or reductions in workload. For example, knowing a new application is being introduced with the purpose of automating tasks once undertaken by users may support a judgment that the user population is unlikely to increase in the near future.

Although difficult to arrive at, knowledge of the future capacity requirements of a corporation is critical if the company's money is to be spent wisely. It is recommended that the business be required to sign-off the capacity plans as part of the business case for system purchase.

Sizing the Systems

Now we are nearly ready to calculate the computer requirements for the technical infrastructure by combining our understanding of the following:

- Capacity requirements of a given user population and level of application processing.
- User population and processing plans.

Before a final recommendation for computer requirements can be made we must:

1. Agree on the planning horizon.
2. Choose a practical level for maximum planned computer utilization.

The further out the planning horizon the more uncertain the workload estimates will be. In the case of a growing workload, a distant planning horizon might encourage the purchase of computer power far beyond immediate capacity requirements. A horizon too close might have the corporation upgrading hardware inconveniently soon. The recommended way to choose the correct horizon is to agree with the management purchasing the systems that either:

- Planning should be on the basis that no upgrades will be necessary within an agreed time period or
- Systems should be sized with an agreed percentage capacity for growth.

The reason for choosing a maximum computer utilization above which we plan not to go is based on the fact that a workload places fluctuating demands on the components of a computer system and that computers do not function efficiently at near full capacity. The best thing to do is adopt a rule of thumb that says no system component should be planned to be more than a certain percentage utilized (a value commonly used is 70%). This way a margin for error and workload fluctuation is built-in to the sizing calculations.

Reviewing the Design

Before work began on the system design a functional specification was drawn up defining what the system is to deliver. To ensure that the design work leads to a system that will meet the functional specification it should be reviewed at critical junctures. Two design reviews should be carried out:

1. After the initial design work has been done and key design principles have been developed. A design review at this stage will ensure work proceeds on a sound basis with buy-in from all concerned.
2. At completion of the design. The design review done at this stage will provide a mechanism for signing the design document off.

The purpose of a design review is to ensure that what is being designed will meet the requirements of the functional specification. Its purpose is not to provide a forum for carrying out any design work or the making of any design decisions. Both of these activities are for the designer to carry out during the normal course of design work.

Carry out the following steps to ensure an effective design review:

Step	Details
Choose the review panel	Members of the review panel should be capable of providing quality criticism both technically and in the context of the needs of the business. It should include: ▪ Technical experts in the field of the design (if the necessary expertise doesn't exist within the organization then external consultants should be used) ▪ Peers of the designer (probably other members of the design team) ▪ Technical representatives from IT Support ▪ Technical representatives from the business The attendee list should include all those people with an interest in the design. This includes those who will use it as well as those creating it.
Choose supporting attendees	Supporting attendees should include: ▪ Chair — Someone with authority but no investment in the design ▪ Someone with no other responsibility to the meeting to take the minutes ▪ A senior solution architect to facilitate the meeting by encouraging questioning and assisting the formation of conclusions
Arrange venue	Choose a venue that is convenient to as many attendees as possible. You may need to provide telephone or video conferencing facilities.
Send out invitations	A minimum of a week and preferably two weeks notice should be given of the design review. The invitation should state clearly the following: ▪ The purpose and subject of the design review ▪ The responsibility of each attendee ▪ Venue and time ▪ That comments on the review material should be directed at the Chair
Send out material for review	The latest design document should be sent out along with the Functional Specification and the invitations. It is this version of the design document that should be the basis for review even if a further revision is created prior to the actual review meeting. It is very important that everyone review the same version of the design.
Solicit comments	The Chair or designer should contact all attendees in advance of the design review to solicit comments and clarify any points or ambiguity in the documentation.

Convene design review meeting	The design review meeting should be planned to last one hour and follow an agenda such as:
	▪ Introduction — Chair
	    ▪ Introduce people
	    ▪ Explain purpose of meeting
	    ▪ Explain attendee responsibilities
	▪ Present design — Designer
	▪ Summarize conclusions — Chair
	▪ Summarize actions — Chair

Step	Details
Send out minutes	The minutes of the meeting should be sent out as soon as possible after the design review meeting. They should clearly state conclusions to discussions and actions.
Update design	The design document should be updated at the discretion of the designer to incorporate the input received at the design review.

The final design review for a particular technology may be positioned as a sign-off review. At the end the Chair would summarize and ask for agreement that the design be signed off contingent on the identified amendments being made.

The responsibility of an attendee is to provide constructive criticism and to question in such a way as to ensure the designer has considered all the options. It is not the responsibility of the attendee to come up with a better design or to discredit anyone. It should be emphasised by the Chair that the responsibility for the actual design rests with the designer at all times.

Apart from contributing to a quality design, a design review provides the opportunity to include many different parties in the design process ensuring ultimate buy-in to a design.

Implementation Planning

In the Implementation Preparation phase of the project focus begins to move to the actual process of implementing the system. The components of a technical infrastructure will need to be installed, according to the design, throughout the offices of a corporation. The nature of the project will change significantly away from design, development and testing to implementation, a completely different type of activity involving different skills and different people.

Planning for implementation should begin alongside the other activities that follow design:

- Procurement
- Training
- Acceptance Testing
- Implementation Detail

Scope of the Installation

Whereas until now it is likely that we have been concentrating on the development of an installable and supportable IT technical infrastructure, the installation activity may involve many other factors, depending on how radical it is. If, for example, nothing of an original system is being retained then the process of installing a new technical infrastructure will include the following:

- furniture
- cabling
- machine room refurbishment
- network equipment
- server computers
- workstations
- software

The first three have been beyond the scope of our technical infrastructure project up until now. It is important therefore that the project manager for the computer or IT technical infrastructure is able to understand clearly their role in the overall installation process.

In the case of the MBI project, the technical infrastructure product was being produced by a central technical infrastructure engineering group, for consumption by many different parts of the organization. Each had its own legacy infrastructure, languages and differing levels of capability. A decision was taken that the MBI technical infrastructure engineering group should restrict their responsibilities to the production of quality builds and designs, including documentation. Responsibility for all other aspects of site preparation and installation was to be assigned to a local site project manager.

A smaller organization, with a less diverse set of target environments, might find it more appropriate to extend the engineering team and assign them the responsibility of the complete infrastructure rollout. On the other hand it is common for organizations to split the engineering work from the installation work. So in most cases there will be some sort of handover before installation begins.

In summary, MBI chose to treat implementations projects as distinct from the technical infrastructure project. As such, the implementation projects shared a number of milestones, dependencies and risks with the technical infrastructure project. A number of common methodologies refer to a collection of projects all focused on a single ultimate goal as a program. In which case the technical infrastructure project and the implementation projects collectively amount to a technical infrastructure program.

Co-ordinating with Other Parties

It is very important that as the various parties begin working with each other for the first time on the planning and preparation for the actual installation, roles and responsibilities are clearly understood. The way an implementation project is structured will vary significantly from corporation to corporation making it very difficult to generalize. MBI used a tool called a *roles and responsibilities matrix* to ensure everyone had a clear understanding of where they fitted in to the project.

Table 17.12 shows an extract from the MBI roles and responsibilities matrix. The matrix is kept simple by only showing the four key groups involved. In other corporations there could be many more groups. More detailed versions of the matrix may be produced to identify the roles and responsibilities of individuals within the groups shown.

Key:

O - Owns Has responsibility

C - aCcepts Receives a deliverable — usually implies sign-off authority

S - Supports Provides data and resources

A - Advises Provides skills and experience

Table 17.12 *MBI Implementation Project Roles and Responsibilities (extract)*

Task	Local Project Manager	Local IT Support	Technical Infrastructure Project Team	Local Business
Specify local requirements	O	S	A	
System sizing	O	S	A	C
Training	S	O	A	C
Purchasing	O	S	A	C
Install systems		O		
Accept systems	C	C		C
Quality control	O	S	A	C

Broadly, the tasks listed in the matrix will correspond to tasks on the implementation project plan though the matrix need not be confined to tasks, it can also be used to show ownership of key responsibilities such as quality control.

Setting Expectations

The delivery of a new computer system is fertile ground for misunderstandings. If people don't have the whole picture they may leap to the wrong conclusions based on pre-conceived notions. This will naturally reduce the likelihood that the project will deliver what they expect it to.

The key to avoiding misunderstandings is to set everyone's expectations at the beginning of the project and at regular intervals throughout. Recommended ways of setting expectations in order of effectiveness are:

1. Personal meetings
2. Group meetings
3. Documents

In practice it is best to use all three ways, with documentation supporting the meetings. The areas to cover when setting expectations are:

- Project details
    - Objectives
    - Scope
    - Approach
    - Duration
    - Deliverables
    - People
    - Management commitment
- Benefits to be accrued from the project
- Support that can be supplied to the local office
- Local office
    - Responsibilities to the project
    - Costs that will be incurred
    - Resources that will be need to be sourced locally
- Anticipated training requirements

Milestones, Dependencies and Risks

Treating the implementation at each location as a project separate from the technical infrastructure project has the following implications for milestones, dependencies and risks:

- The implementation project will share some of the milestones of the technical infrastructure project. It will also have additional milestones for work being undertaken that is outside the scope of the technical infrastructure project. An example might be installation of new telephones or laying of structured cabling.
- Rather than share the same dependencies as the technical infrastructure project, the implementation project can identify dependencies on the deliverables from the technical infrastructure project. For example, the implementation project is dependent on the technical infrastructure project to deliver an automated workstation installation kit.
- Implementation project risks relating to the technical infrastructure project can again be expressed in terms of technical infrastructure project deliverables. The implementation project might have several other risks associated with matters outside the scope of the technical infrastructure project.

Resourcing

Implementation planning must include the identification of resources to carry out the implementation projects. Where the resources are drawn from depends on the approach to the project. Let us look at the two different types of approach MBI considered:

1. Maximize the use of local resources
2. Use an "implementation team" to travel to each location

There are several benefits and drawbacks associated with each approach:

- *Benefits of approach 1:*
  - Better appreciation of local customs which helps in getting things done
  - Easier to overcome language barriers
  - Potentially lower cost
  - Can execute more implementation projects in parallel

- *Benefits of approach 2:*
  - Concentrating technical skills in an implementation team leads to higher quality
  - Experience of implementation team leads to quality planning
  - Skills can be transferred from experts in the implementation team to the local IT Support groups
  - Less remote support required to assist local implementation resources

Use approach 1 when there is a need to implement the technical infrastructure in several offices very quickly, there are language difficulties or where there is the local political will and expertise. Use approach 2 when there is less urgency or when suitable resources cannot be made available in the local offices.

For each approach there will be a need for:

- A local project manager to own the success of an implementation
- A central project manager to co-ordinate central and local effort
- Local project staff to act as liasion with the technical infrastructure project
- People to physically prepare desks, computers and network
- Technical experts to carry out system installation, setup and testing
- Local user and IT Support training

Note that whichever approach is chosen, the project will create demands on resources over and above the routine operation of an office, so the management will need to be prepared in ample time to be able to prioritize personnel availability and retain contract staff if required.

Summary

The implementation preparation phase of the technical infrastructure program begins when the design is complete. It consists of five main activities:

- Procurement
- Training
- Acceptance
- Implementation details
- Implementation planning

Purchases will be made both for testing in the development laboratory and for the production environment. Unless managed carefully, delays in buying essential items can easily impact project schedules so some precautions are needed. It is important that we are able to justify the use of any product deployed as part of the technical infrastructure.

Training end users in the use of a new computer system is about ensuring they are able to use the new system effectively. Support staff also need training in understanding the workings of the new system. The most important thing to be clear on is exactly what is within the scope of technical infrastructure training for users. For the IT Support staff to carry out their job they will need to understand the underlying product technology and the way the technical infrastructure is configured.

The technical infrastructure must be tested to ensure it:

- Is configured as designed.
- Works as designed, which includes:
  - User environment—file share connections, user directory structure, etc.
  - System environment—failover, capacity, security, etc.

Both the business users and the IT Support are recipients of a technical infrastructure, therefore both parties must have responsibility for accepting the system. The objective of the implementation detail activity is to take a logical design, or equivalent functional specification through to a state where implementation can begin. Carrying out the implementation detail activity will involve:

- Determination of a software delivery strategy — how the initial software installation and subsequent upgrades are carried out
- Development Testing
- Pilot implementation (optional)
- Software release management

The most important aspects of implementation planning are:

- Scoping the installation to ensure all aspects are included.
- Co-ordinating with the many parties that will be involved.
- Setting expectations accurately to ensure satisfaction with the project.
- Planning and resourcing the project using the resources of the target site.

Appendix A

Example Business Principles

This appendix is a list of candidate business principles, some of which may be useful as they are presented here or in modified form. Several of the business principles here are referenced from the chapters dealing with the case study design. These are the business principles that the design process revealed as advantageous to the project but which were overlooked in Chapter 5 when the initial set as developed. These business principles are listed in the section Additional MBI Business Principles.

For convenience the remaining business principles are categorized according to which of three categories they relate:

- Application
- Technology
- Organization

Additional MBI Business Principles

Business Principle A-1—Pattern of Working
MBI IT systems must support a mobile workforce by allowing users ▪ to work at any office using an existing workstation or ▪ to use their laptop computer from any office or remote location connected by telephone.
Justification
▪ A mobile workforce is more flexible, allowing the organization to meet its customers on their terms, not the Bank's. ▪ As the nature of the banking business becomes more international, travel from one office to the next is likely to increase.
Implications
▪ Users must be able to log on at any workstation and gain access to all the facilities necessary to be able to carry out their job. ▪ Users must be able to connect their laptop computers to anywhere on the corporate network. ▪ Users must be able to participate fully on the corporate network from a dial-in connection.
Issues
▪ The security implications for connecting to the corporate network from non-MBI locations need to be examined and addressed.

Business Principle A-2—Minimize Non-Application use of WAN Bandwidth
Non-application use of WAN bandwidth should be minimized.
Justification
▪ Business traffic takes priority over infrastructure traffic. ▪ WAN bandwidth is scarce and expensive in some regions of the world.
Implications
▪ Need to define carefully what is application related traffic and what is not. For example, there will be cases where an application's ability to use the WAN depends on an infrastructure service functioning across the WAN as in the case of name resolution.

continued ▸

continued

Issues
▪ A certain level of WAN usage by infrastructure services cannot be avoided. When that is the case it is often very difficult to exercise any control over the level and timing of its usage in terms of prioritization against other services.

Business Principle A-3—Access to Data
User access to data must be no more than the minimum necessary to carry out their job.
Justification
▪ Data is a corporate asset and should be guarded from inadvertent or malicious corruption or usage.
Implications
▪ The level of access to data will need to be analyzed on a job by job basis. ▪ There will need to be some method of allowing staff to stand in for others by being granted temporary levels of access.
Issues
▪ Service to customers may be impacted if someone with the necessary level of access is unavailable.

Business Principle A-4—Corporate Security Requirements
Conformance to corporate security requirements is mandatory.
Justification
▪ Information is critical to the organization and should be protected. ▪ Loss of public confidence in the organization would impact business should knowledge of a security breach become public. ▪ Corporate security requirements are designed to put the interests of the corporation first.

continued ▸

continued

Implications
■ Implementing a system that conforms to the corporate security requirements may require additional security tools to those that are included with Windows NT. ■ Security operations procedures will have to be created to reflect the features of Windows NT and use of any security tools.
Issues
■ Use of third party integration tools, for example, to provide file access to other platforms may not be compatible with the security requirements.

Application Business Principles

Business Principle A-5—Use of Electronic Commerce
Electronic connections to business partners should be used for commercial transactions.
Justification
▪ Strong customer demand for electronic commercial transactions ▪ More cost effective ▪ Should decrease errors ▪ Reduction in manual, time-consuming data entry
Implications
▪ May demand integration of several incompatible IT systems. ▪ Must ensure the procedures for using electronic commerce meet regulatory requirements. ▪ A manual fallback mechanism needs to be maintained should the electronic system be unavailable.
Issues
▪ The level of security available with electronic commerce falls below that required by the organization.

Business Principle A-6—Human/Machine Interface
The human/machine interface should allow efficient and accurate usage. For example, re-keying of data should be eliminated.
Justification
▪ Errors introduce cost and impact service levels. ▪ An efficient interface means less time is taken over the fundamentally unproductive activity of operating the human/machine interface.
Implications
▪ Interface design standards will be required to enable consistency between applications. ▪ An application integration technique must be deployed if this principle is going to achieve its impact. ▪ Ability to re-key data will need to be retained for resilience purposes.

continued▸

continued

Issues
■ The diverse nature of the systems that will need to be integrated implies a high engineering cost.

Business Principle A-7—Availability
Operation of an application shouldn't depend on a single person.
Justification
■ Problems locating a single person to execute an application operation can impact customer service levels. ■ The ability for several people to operate an application lends more flexibility to how a service is delivered.
Implications
■ Advantageous if application can be operated from several different locations. ■ Security and control of data and application functions must be reconciled with the need for a number of people to use it
Issues

Business Principle A-8—Modify Existing Systems
When integrating existing systems with a new one under construction preference should always be to modify the existing systems.
Justification
■ By forcing any modifications to be done on the existing systems the risk of compromising an optimum design for the new one is reduced. ■ Most existing systems were engineered in-house so modifying them is practical as source code exists and knowledgeable engineers are available. ■ There is no long term strategy of system replacement.
Implications
■ Cost/benefit study needs to be carried out comparing modification of the existing systems against design changes to the new application. ■ Multiple existing applications may need to be modified. ■ System testing will be more complex where changes are made to several applications.

Business Principle A-9—Maximize Application Availability
The IT systems must maximize application availability.
Justification
▪ Applications are fundamental to the competitive nature of the organization. Unavailable applications mean an inability to service the customer, leading to lost revenue and profit. ▪ In many cases there is no alternative fallback system such as use of paper. ▪ Financial penalties can be incurred from external agencies if certain processing isn't carried out by fixed times.
Implications
▪ Potentially higher costs of providing high availability.
Issues
▪ Some applications are fundamentally unreliable. In such cases availability can only be achieved by re-architecting the application. It is not possible to solve all availability problems using hardware. ▪ Low skill levels among support staff make recovery from failure more time consuming than otherwise necessary.

Technology Business Principles

Business Principle A-10—Platform Consistency
All workstations and servers should be configured according to the corporate standard build definitions.
Justification
▪ By using a standard build, technical diversity is reduced, making support easier. ▪ Testing and deployment of applications is more economical with less diversity in the target environment.
Implications
▪ Features required in addition to the current version of the standard build should be considered for inclusion in the next version, in order to minimize diversity. ▪ Some parts of an organization may not be comfortable with having to use a standard configuration. To implement a standard build throughout a large organization will require strong management commitment. ▪ The definition of a standard build must be flexible enough to cope with the installed base of different computer configurations. ▪ It must be possible to audit systems for their conformance to a standard configuration.
Issues
▪ It must be anticipated that in the production environment enhancements and fixes will be implemented. These must be managed to ensure consistency across all installations.

Business Principle A-11—Enhancing Business with IT
Use IT to enhance the basic business processes, not replace them.
Justification
▪ The current business processes work. ▪ Timescales are too short to re-engineer business processes. ▪ Return on investment is adequate for the low level of risk.

continued▸

continued

Implications
▪ The existing processes must be understood accurately before enhancements can be made. ▪ Technology may not be used to its fullest extent.
Issues
▪ Denies the opportunity for revolutionary change of organizational structure that may lead to substantial benefits.

Business Principle A-12—Reliance on the Network
The technical infrastructure and the applications that run upon it must be designed to place minimum dependence on network availability.
Justification
▪ The current network infrastructure has a poor reliability record. ▪ There are no immediate plans to enhance the internal network.
Implications
▪ Applications may need to be designed to compensate for the unreliability of the network. ▪ Priorities for the different types of network traffic will need to be set to ensure optimum alternate path usage in the case of path failure. ▪ A study should be carried out to establish whether the cost of compensating for lack of network availability in the infrastructure and applications compares favorably with the cost of enhancing the network.
Issues
▪ Minimizing dependency on network availability may not yield the required level of service or application availability.

Business Principle A-13—Use of Existing Network
Any new systems or infrastructure developments must use the existing network.

continued ▸

continued

Justification
■ Minimize implementation costs. ■ Plans exist for network replacement in two years so tactical network enhancements should be avoided.
Implications
■ The current network offers poor international bandwidth and is known to be unreliable in some areas. Therefore, non-application use of the network will need to be strongly justified. ■ Mandating use of existing network will limit the number of technical options for systems and infrastructure services, potentially leading to a business compromise. ■ Should investigate whether use of temporary dial-up links are permissible (e.g., RAS).
Issues
■ It may not be possible to use some aspects of Windows NT functionality over some network links. ■ The quality of the existing network may preclude certain functionality necessary to meet a business need.

Business Principle A-14—Maximum Availability During Office Hours
The system must offer a high level of availability during branch office hours.
Justification
■ The main purpose of the new technical infrastructure is to support applications used by the personnel in the branch offices. ■ The system will be instrumental in increasing the level of customer service.
Implications
■ Routine operational activities should be scheduled for non-office hours. ■ To achieve high levels of availability during office hours the system must be monitored and managed closely. ■ Centralized systems supporting branch offices in multiple time zones will need to offer high availability all the time any branch office remains open for business.

continued▸

continued

Issues
▪ Remedial support in remote branch offices will be difficult due to lack of local technical expertise. ▪ Costs might be increased if certain availability methods are implemented (e.g., disk mirroring).

Business Principle A-15—Maximum Performance During Office Hours
The technical infrastructure must deliver maximum performance during office hours.
Justification
▪ Customer facing staff depend on the IT infrastructure to deliver a swift response for generating quotations and booking orders.
Implications
▪ The IT infrastructure should restrict nonessential processing and network traffic to out of normal office hours. ▪ It may be necessary to provide additional systems to cope with non-customer facing processing.
Issues
▪ The technical infrastructure is global, potentially requiring maximum performance 24 hours/day.

Organizational Business Principles

Business Principle A-16—Single Technical Support Groups
First and second line technical support for all business groups will be carried out by a single IT Support group.
Justification
▪ Provide cost effective support of small offices where there may be many business groups represented but few people from each. ▪ Much of the technical infrastructure is used by all business groups so a single problem could affect more than one. Having one group address the problem will be more productive than several working in an uncoordinated fashion.
Implications
▪ Key support staff will need to have the ability to access the majority (if not all) of the Bank's systems. ▪ The separate support groups that are operated today will need to be integrated into one group.
Issues
▪ Finding a satisfactory formula for allocating support group costs to the different business groups may prove difficult.

Business Principle A-17—Minimize Infrastructure Costs
IT Infrastructure costs must be kept down by providing only the minimum necessary level of service.
Justification
▪ The corporation is not in a position to make a large financial commitment. ▪ The corporation is planning a significant relocation in the near future. Investment in more IT infrastructure than necessary would be wasteful. ▪ The IT Infrastructure can be upgraded at a later date if more capacity is needed.

continued ▸

continued

Implications
▪ Minimum necessary levels of service must be defined. ▪ May mean users having to suffer downtime. ▪ System capacity may not be enough to deliver good response at times of peak demand.
Issues
▪ If the systems are of too low a specification, users will waste time waiting for a system response. ▪ Users may experience discontent if they perceive necessary IT resources are not being provided.

Business Principle A-18—Send Information, Don't Share it
Where necessary, information will be copied or e-mailed between different business divisions not shared on-line.
Justification
▪ The different business divisions operate in different markets with little or no synergy between them. ▪ Regulatory requirements can restrict what information can be openly shared between two divisions. ▪ The protection and management of data shared between different business divisions presents difficulties of responsibility. ▪ Technological incompatibilities make the sending of information easier than sharing it.
Implications
▪ There must be a secure message passing mechanism. ▪ A means of auditing information transfer will needed.
Issues
▪ Sending data can be slower and more cumbersome than having it automatically shared.

Business Principle A-19—Managing Windows NT Systems as Business Critical
▪ The Windows NT server systems should be managed as business critical systems, not as incidental PC servers.
Justification
▪ The business impact of losing a Windows NT system is substantial. By managing it as a system that is critical to the business uptime is maximized.
Implications
▪ A culture needs to be developed that recognizes that the Windows NT server systems need managing with the same level of rigor, discipline and process as the corporate mainframe systems are. ▪ Suitable practices need to be developed for managing and operating the Windows NT servers.
Issues
▪ Windows NT is seen as a "PC" operating system by many people. This carries an implication that it is a system of less consequence than a more traditional computer. ▪ Windows NT is by default more accessible than more traditional computers presenting a greater danger of inadvertent abuse.

Business Principle A-20—Not being Constrained by Existing Systems
The planned system management platform should not be constrained by the need to conform with any existing network or application management systems.
Justification
▪ There are no plans to retain the existing management systems beyond when it will be possible to replace them with Windows NT based management systems. ▪ Conformance to any existing management system could introduce conflict between the need to choose the best in class tools and compatibility.

continued▸

continued

Implications
■ There may be a slight overhead in management effort as a result of using another different management platform. ■ Effort will need to be directed at making sure that all systems can continue to be managed efficiently given the introduction of another management platform.

Business Principle A-21—Strategic Technology Direction
Where technology offers alternative choices, the one consistent with the corporate technology strategy should be chosen.
Justification
■ The strategic technology direction will have been set for reasons that are in the interests of the corporation.
Implications
■ On occasions the business imperative might demand the use of non-strategic technology. ■ Need to develop a corporate technology strategy if one doesn't already exist.
Issues
■ Different parts of the corporation have different technology strategies. There will be difficulty arriving at a single technology strategy.

Business Principle A-22—Common Language for the Systems
■ The common language for the new systems should be US/English.
Justification
■ A single language facilitates global support. ■ A single language facilitates global user mobility. ■ English is already the official business language of the corporation.
Implications
■ A means of accommodating existing systems that are implemented to use non-US/English local languages will need to be found. ■ There will be a need for staff language training in some countries.

continued ▸

continued

Issues
The Tokyo office will mandate Japanese language support.

Business Principle A-23—Simplicity of the User Environment
The user environment should be optimized for simplicity.
Justification
▪ Will be more efficient to work with. ▪ Should generate fewer support calls. ▪ Should make it easier to ensure commonality across all systems.
Implications
▪ Extensive consultation will be required to define the simplified user environment.
Issues
▪ The diverse needs and opinions in a large organization will make achieving simplicity difficult. ▪ An environment that is simple to the user may not be more simple to implement.

Business Principle A-24—System Capacity
Systems must be sized to accommodate planned business expansion over the corporate planning horizon (currently this is 100% over three years).
Justification
▪ No need to upgrade for three years. ▪ Spare capacity available during this planning horizon will allow expansion to carry on unconstrained by system capacity.
Implications
▪ Care must be taken to ensure that performance doesn't drop as capacity is taken up over the three years.

continued▸

continued

Issues
▪ Potential error factor in forecast.

Business Principle A-25—System Scalability
Systems must scale to support expansion into new countries.
Justification
▪ The business needs to be able to move into countries where there are commercial opportunities.
Implications
▪ Systems may have spare capacity until expansion is realized. ▪ Guidance will be taken from the corporate strategy for growth document.
Issues
▪ Without knowing which countries the corporation will expand into and the scale of any expansion it is difficult to know to what degree the systems will need to scale.

Appendix B

Example Design Principles

While any Design Principle should be directly relevant to a particular design, it is common to find similar Design Principles occurring on different projects. This Appendix provides a list of example Design Principles that are generally applicable to various Windows NT domain design projects. Use the list for ideas, but you should expect to have to modify any that you choose to use. For convenience they are categorized according to technical infrastructure service. Note that some of the Design Principles listed in this appendix are referenced from the chapters dealing with the case study design. Most, however, do not apply to the case study so may include statements that are inconsistent with it.

Network Services

Design Principle B-1—Dedicated DHCP Server
The DHCP service may share a server with other services.
Justification
▪ DHCP places a very low processing and storage overhead on a server. ▪ The DHCP service can tolerate brief periods of unavailability such as those caused by planned downtime.
Implications
▪ Makes economical use of hardware. ▪ Need to make sure that other services running on the server are not adversely impacted by the DHCP service.
Issues

Design Principle B-2—Use of Dedicated Hardware for Dial-up
Dedicated communications hardware capable of creating a wide area connection on demand over a dial-up link will be used as a temporary measure where a leased line is required but unavailable.
Justification
▪ Provides a secure mechanism for establishing a temporary wide area connection. ▪ Supports a wide range of protocols. ▪ Can be simply managed by the network group.
Implications
▪ Additional hardware needs to be purchased.
Issues
▪ Use of public networks for transferring Bank data is currently disallowed by the audit department.

Naming Services

Design Principle B-3—WINS Replication
The WINS implementation should not contain replication chains of greater than x links.
Justification
▪ The propagation delay would be unacceptable if there were more than x links. ▪ Too many dependencies if there are >x replication links, potentially affecting reliability.
Implications
▪ Key WINS servers will need to replicate with more partners than would be the case if the replication chain were longer. ▪ May demand additional WAN links if the same replication traffic is not to pass over the same WAN link more than once.
Issues

Design Principle B-4—Primary and Secondary WINS Servers
Each client should be configured with a primary and a secondary WINS server.
Justification
To enhance NetBIOS name resolution availability.
Implications
▪ The WINS servers configured as primary and secondary should each contain the same portion of the name database. ▪ The WINS configuration should be able to sustain the name resolution workload without significant degradation if the WINS server designated as the primary fails.
Issues

Design Principle B-5—Clients as H-Nodes
Clients will be configured as H-nodes.
Justification
▪ To allow broadcast based name resolution should WINS be unavailable or unable to resolve a name. ▪ Allows use of LMHOSTS file for name resolution to be avoided.
Implications
▪ Broadcast forwarding will need to be enabled on local routers to enable full site visibility.
Issues
▪ If the WAN link is functioning and the site does not have a local WINS server then all NetBIOS name resolutions will use WAN bandwidth.

Design Principle B-6—Backing up WINS
WINS databases will be backed up at regular intervals to both a tape device and another computer's hard disks.
Justification
▪ Restoring a WINS database from backup on a hard disk will be quicker than allowing it to build automatically through a natural or forced replication. ▪ Recovery through replication will place too great a load on the network WAN links.
Implications
▪ Operational procedures will need to be created and adopted for regular backups of the WINS databases. ▪ Local trained personnel will be needed.
Issues

Design Principle B-7—Exclusive Use of WINS
All NetBIOS names will be resolved through WINS.
Justification
▪ Use of dynamic IP addresses would make the maintenance of LMHOSTS files untenable. ▪ No LMHOSTS files to maintain. ▪ No broadcast traffic.
Implications
▪ WINS service needs to meet the reliability and availability (add any attributes relevant) requirements of the applications and services it supports.
Issues
▪ Busy WAN connections will impact performance where there is no local WINS server.

Design Principle B-8—Use of DNS
DNS name resolution will be enabled on all computers.
Justification
■ There is a need to use IP utilities such as Telnet and FTP. ■ There is a need to be able to access UNIX servers from another computer. ■ Eliminates maintenance of HOSTS files on all systems.
Implications
■ The DNS service needs to meet the reliability and availability (add any attributes relevant) requirements of the applications and services it supports.
Issues

Design Principle B-9—Use of HOSTS or LMHOSTS Files
The LMHOSTS or HOSTS files will not be used.
Justification
■ These files are impractical to keep up to date in the face of a high rate of computer population changes. ■ They are impractical to use when computers use dynamic IP addresses.
Implications
■ If the network won't support broadcasts for NetBIOS name resolution WINS must be used. ■ WINS service needs to be reliable and available (add any attributes relevant). ■ DNS service needs to be reliable and available (add any attributes relevant).
Issues

Design Principle B-10—Dual WINS Server Configuration
Only two WINS servers will be deployed. One will be the primary server to all clients and the other the secondary.
Justification
■ Low synchronization overhead ■ Low propagation delay for name changes ■ More resilient than using a single WINS server ■ Simple to manage
Implications
■ Each WINS server must be of sufficient capacity to handle the name resolution requests for the entire network to cope with the situation where one WINS server is unavailable. ■ The network links to the WINS servers should be sufficient to cope with the name traffic. ■ Should split the two WINS servers across two sites for greater availability.

Design Principle B-11—Sizing the WINS Servers
Servers will be sized so they will run at 25% capacity on average. Peaks will take utilization up to 50%.
Justification
■ Changes in workload of up to a factor of two will not noticeably affect performance. The workload is planned to increase by roughly this factor over the next three years.
Implications
■ Utilization will need to be monitored to ensure it matches predictions.
Issues
■ Sizings will be based on estimates that are hard to confirm.

Design Principle B-12—Use of Dedicated WINS Servers
Computers will be dedicated to running the WINS service exclusively.
Justification
▪ Need greater consistency and predictability of WINS service performance. ▪ Don't want to impact WINS service by operational requirements of co-hosted applications. ▪ Total computer capacity dedicated to the WINS service.
Implications
▪ Dedicating a computer to the WINS service may demand the use of extra computers, in which case the following implications apply: ▪ Cost of extra computers ▪ Management overhead of extra computers
Issues
▪ This principle won't completely solve the need for consistent and predicable performance but it will make it easier to manage.

Design Principle B-13—Clients as M-Nodes
Name service clients will be configured as m-nodes where >80% of references are made to other computers in the same subnet.
Justification
▪ Reduces the number of WINS servers needed ▪ Higher performance ▪ Minimizes name resolution traffic over the network
Implications
▪ Causes broadcast traffic on local subnet.
Issues

Design Principle B-14—Minimize Number of WINS Servers
No more WINS servers should be used than are necessary to provide sufficient name serving capacity.
Justification
▪ Fewer WINS servers leads to less replication traffic. ▪ Fewer WINS servers leads to a lower propagation delay. ▪ Fewer WINS servers to manage. ▪ Better utilization of hardware.
Implications
▪ Loss of a WINS server will cause an increase in load on one or more of the remaining servers. They should be sized to cope with this increase. ▪ Minimizing the number of WINS servers on this basis may mean that the network path to a WINS server from a given client is longer than it might otherwise have been, impacting name resolution performance as perceived by a client.
Issues

Domain Design

Design Principle B-15—Number of Backup Domain Controllers
Each location (LAN) will incorporate two backup domain controllers from each of the master domain(s).
Justification
▪ If one BDC fails there is another locally available. ▪ Loss of one BDC should not affect users or applications in any way.
Implications
▪ Cost of additional computers required. ▪ Additional management overhead. ▪ Higher proportion of bandwidth to that site is used up with SAM replication traffic. ▪ In circumstances where there is no reason for anyone at a location to logon from one of the master domains or access resources from it, the two BDCs will fulfill no useful function.
Issues

Design Principle B-16—The Power of the User Administrator
The resource domain administrator will be given an account with permissions to manage users and groups in the master domain(s).
Justification
▪ The resource domain administrator has responsibility for adding and removing users. ▪ There is a high staff turnover at this particular office. Control of user access to the systems should be a local responsibility to ensure accuracy.
Implications
▪ The resource domain administrator will have the ability to modify, add or remove accounts for any user in the entire master domain, potentially affecting users of other resource domains. ▪ A means of recording changes made to the SAM by whom would be necessary if it were ever necessary to audit user account administration.

continued ▸

continued

Issues
■ The risk to the integrity of the SAM as a result of giving a local resource domain administrator the rights to administer it may be deemed too high by certain business groups. Unless it is satisfactory to use a third party product that allows secure partitioned management of the SAM this principle may be unworkable.

Design Principle B-17—Adding Trust to Local Group
Where a trust does not exist to allow a global user/group to be added to a local group, its creation should be justified.
Justification
■ The absence of a trust is for security reasons. (The correct approach is for the users in question to gain approval for accounts in the appropriate master domain.) ■ Discourages ad hoc modification of the domain model.
Implications
■ Procedure must be made available for granting accounts. ■ Requires support from management to resist the creation of ad hoc trusts. ■ If the granting of accounts in additional domains is likely to become an administrative burden the suitability of the domain structure for the corporation should be reviewed.
Issues
■ Users will need to remember multiple passwords if they have multiple accounts, potentially leading to a security risk if they are ever written down to aid memory.

Design Principle B-18—New Accounts from Templates
New accounts should be created from template accounts.
Justification
■ Less risk of error ■ Quicker to create new accounts

continued ▸

continued

Implications
■ Documentation must make it clear which template to use for which type of user. ■ Templates must be available in each master domain.
Issues

Design Principle B-19—Sizing for Future Workload
Domain controllers will be sized to cope with a 100% increase in workload.
Justification
■ It is corporate policy to plan with a three year horizon. The projected increase in workforce will amount to 100% over this period. (Note that this could be represented as a business principle.)
Implications
■ Additional hardware investment up front. ■ A sizing exercise must be carried out to estimate the initial workload levels. ■ The network must be sized to cope with a similar workload increase or it will need upgrading in under three years.
Issues
■ The estimate of initial workload is difficult to substantiate. ■ The increase in workforce over the next three years is difficult to estimate.

Design Principle B-20—Local BDCs
Local BDCs from remote domains will be used to enhance speed of set up of remote cross domain resource access connections.
Justification
■ Users have a need to connect to resources in other, geographically remote domains.

continued▸

continued

Implications
▪ Additional computers will be required to act in the role of BDC. ▪ Additional SAM replication traffic will be caused by additional BDCs.
Issues

Design Principle B-21—Minimum Required WAN Bandwidth
Each WAN connection must provide a minimum of Nkb/s available bandwidth after business traffic (and voice if that too is carried over the WAN link) has been discounted. This assumes a total maximum planned utilization of 50%.
Justification
▪ N kb/s is the bandwidth required by domain synchronization traffic (may re-phrase to account for all technical infrastructure traffic).
Implications
▪ Some WAN links may need to be upgraded. ▪ The variable nature of business traffic over the WAN makes it difficult to arrive at a reasonable estimate for its volume.
Issues
In some countries: ▪ There is a long lead time for WAN upgrades. ▪ The cost of the required bandwidth is high. ▪ The required bandwidth will not be available.

Groups

Design Principle B-22—Global/Local Group Usage Policy
Group usage policy will be: ▪ All user accounts in master domains ▪ All users in global groups ▪ Global groups in local groups ▪ Allocate permissions specifying local groups ▪ Allocate rights to local groups
Justification
▪ Keep group policy simple to aid management. ▪ Policy matches that recommended by Microsoft. ▪ Users defined in resource domains would cause pressure to create additional trusts compromising the domain model.
Implications
▪ Strong management support needed to enforce policy. ▪ A standard group usage policy will make it easier to carry out a security audit.
Issues

File and Print Services

Design Principle B-23—Browsing
Browsing will be disabled on all computers.
Justification
▪ Nature of the computing environment is that users should have no need for browsing resources. ▪ Logon scripts will set up any file share or printer connections.

continued ▸

continued

Implications
▪ Users will need to be mapped to alternative resources by the login script to provide a backup should one resource be unavailable. Can't rely on browsing to locate an alternate printer for example. ▪ Logon scripts will need to be changed to enable users to automatically access new network resources, unless they are informed of the name of the new resource and how to connect to it themselves.
Issues
▪ IT Support staff have a case for needing browsing to enable the perusal and ad hoc access to file shares for maintenance purposes.

Design Principle B-24—Workstations Not Offering File Shares
Workstations shall not offer file shares.
Justification
▪ To ensure the corporate security standards are adhered to, the management of all shared resources should be under the control of the system administrators. ▪ Server disks are backed up regularly, ensuring data is protected. ▪ Concentrating shared resources on servers allows browser announcements from workstations to be turned off, keeping the browse list short and manageable.
Implications
▪ The administrative procedure for allowing someone to get a server based share created for their use should not be prohibitive. ▪ Management of the shared disk space will be an important factor in keeping the server based file service available. ▪ The server file share structure must be designed to meet the needs of the business to minimize pressure to create shares in an unplanned fashion.

Design Principle B-25—Workstations Not Offering Printer Shares
Workstations shall not offer printer shares.
Justification
▪ Support overhead of allowing users this capability would be too high. ▪ Support overhead of ensuring the workstation based printer drivers are up to date would be too high. ▪ To ensure the corporate security standards are adhered to, the management of shared resources should be under the control of the system administrators. ▪ Concentrating shared resources on servers allows browser announcements from workstations to be turned off, keeping the browse list short and manageable.
Implications
▪ Availability of server based printers should be high enough to eliminate any incentive for users to operate their own printers.
Issues
▪ It is difficult to maintain a high availability print service.

Design Principle B-26—Share Permissions
File share access should be controlled using file and directory permissions, leaving the share permission set to full control.
Justification
▪ Keeps things simple and predictable.
Implications
▪ A user will have the same level of access to a file whether accessing it remotely or from the server on which it is located. ▪ Requires a directory permissions strategy that satisfies the corporate security standards.
Issues
▪ There are likely to be exceptions necessary.

Design Principle B-27—Granting Permissions
Permissions should only be granted to users on an as needed basis.
Justification
▪ More permissions than needed create the potential for abuse and error.
Implications
▪ Administrative effort involved in the granting of permissions. ▪ Some groups will find this more restrictive than what they had been used to. ▪ Permissions must be authorized and granted swiftly to avoid business impact. ▪ A process to request and grant permissions must be created and implemented.
Issues

Design Principle B-28—Server Utilization
File, Print and Application servers should be sized to operate at no more than 50% capacity on average throughout the normal working day.
Justification
▪ An implication of MBI Business Principle 4 states that the system should operate with spare capacity to allow for business expansion. ▪ Operating within the capacity of a server is good practice as it avoids bottlenecks. ▪ Fewer bottlenecks means there will be fewer performance problems to address and less user dissatisfaction with system performance. ▪ Spare capacity will allow peaks in demand to be met without a significant degradation of service.
Implications
By leaving this amount of spare capacity the cost of server provision will be higher than if they were sized to run closer to capacity. ▪ A capacity management program should be initiated to ensure the servers can be maintained at that utilization goal.

continued ▸

continued

Issues
■ System sizing can only ever be based on estimates, making it difficult to guarantee that the 50% figure can be met with any accuracy.

Design Principle B-29—Use of DFS
Shared directories should be made available using Microsoft DFS.
Justification
■ Reduces number of drive letters required. ■ Management of the file service is easier as it allows changes to the physical directory structure without changing the logical structure seen by the file service clients. This means no client system drive re-mappings are necessary.
Implications
■ File and directory permissions need to be set up appropriately to allow the user the ability to navigate to and use the files they are permitted to but not those they should be restricted from.

User Environment

Design Principle B-30—Built-in Accounts
1. Administrator will be renamed to xxxx. 2. Guest account will be disabled.
Justification
■ While renaming the administrator account does not guarantee security it can contribute by obscuring the most powerful account on the system. ■ There is no compelling reason to use the guest account.
Implications
■ Any process that used the guest account will need to use an alternative method.

continued►

continued

Issues
■ If the administrator account is given the same new name on each computer then it will be difficult to avoid that fact becoming well-known throughout the organization, reducing the value of renaming it and reducing any barrier there might have been to hacking.

Design Principle B-31—Different Accounts for Different Roles
Where a user has more than one role, each requiring different rights and permissions, they will be as created different user accounts, one for each role.
Justification
■ More permissions than needed create the potential for abuse and error. ■ Can assign user to different groups depending on the needs of the role. ■ Easier to audit.
Implications
■ Administrative overhead
Issues
■ Users will need to remember multiple passwords which could present a security risk if a user were to write them down to aid memory.

Design Principle B-32—User Mobility
The following facilities must be available to a user at a workstation at any location they log on at: ■ The user must be presented with their usual applications. ■ The user must have access to their usual data. ■ The user must be presented with a familiar computer desktop environment.

continued ▸

continued

Justification
■ The business demands user mobility (this need may be represented by a business principle. For an example see Business Principle A-1 in Appendix A).
Implications
■ Application types must be the same at every location. ■ Application versions must be the same at every installation.
Issues
■ The level of standardization of the technical infrastructure necessary to support this business principle will be new to the corporation. ■ The license costs of providing certain applications on every workstation can be prohibitive, particularly when the software is only required by a minority of users and is only licensed per seat, not per active user.

Time Services

Design Principle B-33—Common Synchronization Protocol
■ The time service must support a common time synchronization protocol between the platforms that require the service.
Justification
■ Use of a common protocol keeps more technical options open for the future. ■ Consistent time service behavior throughout the technical infrastructure.
Implications
■ Choice of a common protocol might require the use of a less than optimal time service program on some platforms. ■ It will be necessary to design the time service to use more than one protocol if a common protocol can't be found.
Issues
■ Certain solutions may only be possible using shareware or otherwise unsupported software. If the corporate policy is the only use supported software in production then this might present a problem.

Naming Standards

Design Principle B-34—Resource Domain Names
The name of a resource domain will contain codes for the location and business unit to which it applies.
Justification
▪ Allows users to easily identify local resources through browsing. ▪ Allows users to easily identify resources associated with their business group.
Implications
▪ That there will be a single resource domain for each business unit/ location combination. ▪ Where a resource domain is not aligned to any particular business group, but shared between several, there needs to be a default code to use in the name.
Issues

Appendix C

User Logon Scripts

This appendix lists the basic logon scripts used by the MBI case study. They are designed to facilitate automated set up of several aspects of the user's environment and allow user mobility throughout the fictional organisation .

Notes on the logon script example:

1. For clarity only three business lines are illustrated in the example, Capital Markets, Foreign Exchange and Derivatives.
2. Please refer to Chapter 16, Naming Standards for detailed descriptions of computer names, group names and printer names that are used throughout the scripts.
3. The logon scripts listed here are described in full in Chapter 14, User Environment.
4. The MBI group design described in Chapter 12 and the group naming standard described in Chapter 16 demand a field in certain group names to distinguish subsidiary. For clarity that field is omitted in these logon scripts.

Master Command File (Filename: Master.cmd)

```
kix32 master.scr
```

Master Logon Script (Filename: Master.scr)

```
; Master logon script
;
; Author:     Mike Collins
; Date:       19th December 1996
;
; Change Control:
;
; Version     Who          Comments
; -------------------------------------------------------------------
; V1.0        Mike Collins   First version created
;
;
; -------------------------------------------------------------------
;
; General Notes:
; - KiXtart built-in variables are shown in upper case.
;
;
; ============================================================
; Extract user's home location from built-in variable set to home share and then
; search for which business group the user is a member of, setting the Group
; variable when its found.
;
; @HOMESHR = \\SXXXNNNN    XXX = location code
; ============================================================
;

$HomeLocation = SubStr(@HOMESHR,4,3)

If InGroup($HomeLocation + "EFX")
$Group = EFX
          Goto EndGroup
Endif
If InGroup($HomeLocation + "CMK")
$Group = CMK
          Goto EndGroup
Endif
If InGroup($HomeLocation + "DRV")
          $Group = DRV
          Goto EndGroup
Endif
```

```
:EndGroup

;
; =============================================
; Establish the location user is currently at from the built-in
; variable set to workstation name.
;
; @WKSTA = \\WXXXNNNN    XXX = location code
; =============================================
;

$ThisLocation = SubStr(@WKSTA,4,3)
? "This Location = $ThisLocation"


; ===================
; Connect File Shares
; ===================
;
; (i)     connect to the local office shared directory
; (ii)    connect to the user's group shared directory at home location
; (iii)   connect to the local network applications directory
;
; Note that the home drive is automatically mapped by Windows NT
;
; The variable $LocalServer could be set to whichever local server is offering
; the public share. Servers with number 0001 are used as an example, the
; mechanism below ensures a general approach.
;
; This approach depends on the use of "well-known" servers. If they vary from
; location to location then the connection to the local public directory
; and the local application server should be made in the location specific
; logon script.
;

$LocalServer = "S" + $ThisLocation + "0001"
$HomeServer = "S" + $HomeLocation + "0001"

Use P: "\\$LocalServer\public"
If @ERROR<>0
       ? "Error connecting to public share..."
       sleep 2
Else
       ? "Connected P: to local public share..."
Endif

Use G: "\\$HomeServer\$group$$"
If @ERROR<>0
       ? "Error connecting to $group group share..."
```

```
        sleep 2
Else
        ? "Connected G: to user's home group share..."
Endif


Use F: "\\$LocalServer\apps$$"
If @ERROR<>0
        ? "Error connecting to apps share..."
        sleep 2
Else
        ? "Connected F: to local apps share..."
Endif

;
;
; ====================================
; Call logon script for this location
; ====================================
;

Call $ThisLocation+".scr"

Exit
```

Logon Script for Milan (Filename: MLN.SCR)

```
; Logon script for Milan
;
; Author:     Mike Collins
; Date:       19th December 1996
;
; Change Control:
;
; Version      Who            Comments
; -------------------------------------------------------------------
; V1.0        Mike Collins    First version created
;
;
; -------------------------------------------------------------------
;;
; ================
; Connect Printers
; ================
;
; Connection is made to the local printers...connections and defaults
; are made depending upon $Group variable...Only EFX is shown
; below for clarity.
;
; Note the connection to pmln8888 and it being set as default if the
; user is a member of a special global printer group.
;
If ($Group = EFX)
          If AddPrinterConnection("\\smln0001\pmln1234")=0
                 ? "Connected to pmln1234 printer on mlns0001..."
          Else
                ? "Error making printer connection..."
                sleep 2
          Endif

          If AddPrinterConnection("\\smln0001\pmln1235")=0
                ? "Connected to pmln1235 printer on mlns0001..."
          Else
                 ? "Error making printer connection..."
                sleep 2
          Endif

          If AddPrinterConnection("\\smln0002\pmln1236")=0
                 ? "Connected to pmln1236 printer on mlns0002..."
          Else
                ? "Error making printer connection..."
                sleep 2
          Endif
```

```
        If InGroup(MLNEFXP1)
            If AddPrinterConnection("\\smln0001\pmln8888")=0
                 ? "Connected to pmln8888 printer on mlns0001..."
            Else
                 ? "Error making printer connection..."
            sleep 2
            Endif

            If SetDefaultPrinter("\\smln0001\pmln8888")=0
                ? "Default printer set to pmln8888..."
            Else
                ? "Error setting default printer..."
                sleep 2
            Endif

        Else
            If SetDefaultPrinter("\\smln0001\pmln1234")=0
                 ? "Default printer set to pmln1234..."
            Else
                 ? "Error setting default printer..."
           sleep 2
           Endif

      Endif

Else
;       Connect other groups to alternate printers
;       Set alternate default printers
;       If no match on variable $Group then connect user to a default printer
;
Endif
;
; ================================
; Create program groups and items
; ================================
;
; This is again done based on global group membership. First of
; all, the program group is deleted in case it has been customised...
;
; Microsoft Systems Management Server program group control would be
; alternative method of doing this.
;
DelProgramGroup("$Group Group Applications",0)
Sleep 5
AddProgramGroup("$Group Group Applications",0)

; Now populate the group...
```

```
If $Group=EFX
       AddProgramItem("f:\efxapp.exe","EFXApp","",0,"h:\")
Endif

If $Group=CMK
       AddProgramItem("f:\cmkapp.exe","CMApp","f:\CMKApp.dll",3,"h:\")
Endif

If $Group=DRV
       AddProgramItem("f:\drvapp.exe","DRApp","f:\DRVApp.dll",3,"h:\")
Endif
;
; ==================
; Start Applications
; ==================
;
If $Group=EFX
       Run f:\efxapp.exe
Endif

If $Group=CMK
       Run f:\cmkapp.exe
Endif

If $Group=DRV
       Run f:\drvapp.exe
Endif
;
; ==========================================
; Calls to user specific scripts can be made here if necessary
; ==========================================
;
Call @USERID+".scr"
;
Exit
```

Appendix D

Case Study Gantt Charts

This Appendix shows the project framework activities and many of their constituent tasks mapped onto a Gantt chart. Use the charts to gain a general insight into the relative sequence of tasks for this type of project, do not use them for guidance on how long each task will take as this will vary too much from one project to the next. To develop these Gantt charts further note the following:

- The work to produce each deliverable should be shown as a task or tasks, with a milestone for when the deliverable is finally produced.
- Where documents are deliverables it can be useful to show the general sequence of tasks—create document, review it, update it, and then sign it off—for each one to make it more easy to plan for the time it takes to get a document through to sign-off.
- Each task should show resources allocated to carry it out.
- Dependencies on factors external to the project should be illustrated as milestones that have (finish-start) links to project tasks.
- Dependencies should be added to allow the effect of constraints to be illustrated.
- Many of the tasks will need to be broken down further to reveal exactly what is involved in their execution. For example, the design tasks should be broken down to illustrate when design reviews will be scheduled and when documentation will be produced.

You will find that after using this general Gantt chart structure as a starting point your final Gantt chart will barely resemble this one as all the project and environment specific detail has been included. A Gantt chart makes an excellent planning tool that most people can adapt to quickly. However, using it to support the management of a project requires more skill. To learn about how to use a Gantt chart in the running of a project please refer to a standard text on project management.

Activities

ID	Task Name
1	**Planning and Project Management**
11	**Design Preparation**
12	**Scoping**
17	**Business Principles**
22	**Application Requirements**
26	**User Requirements**
34	**Planning Requirements**
42	**Functional Specification**
47	**Design**
61	**Implementation Preparation**
62	**Implementation Detail**
99	**Implementation Planning**
108	**Procurement**
116	**Acceptance**
123	**Training**
127	**Implementation**
128	
129	

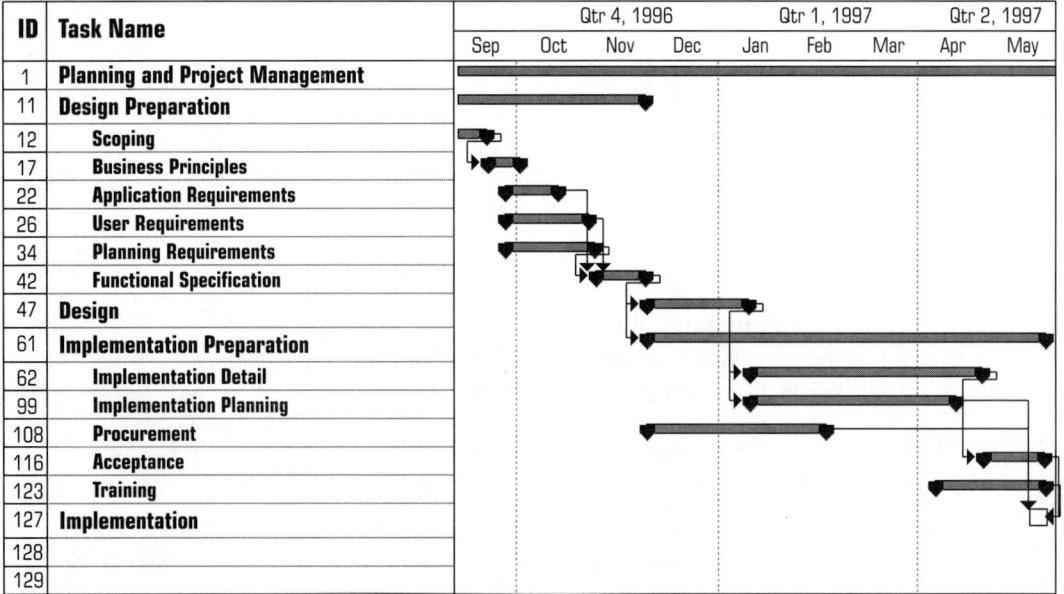

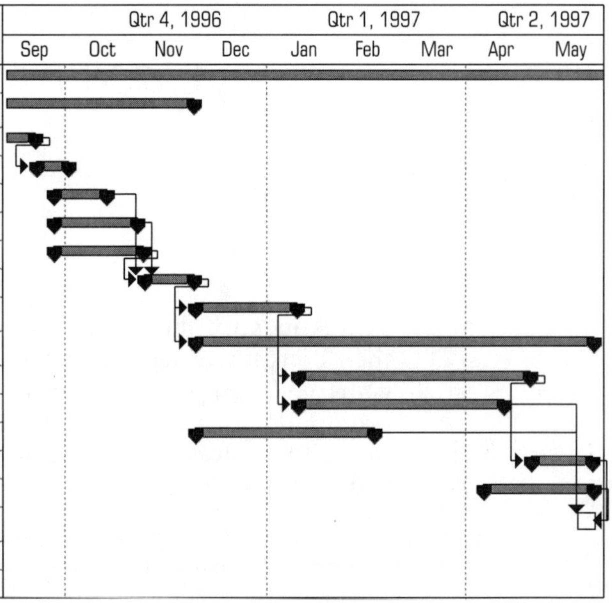

Design Preparation Tasks

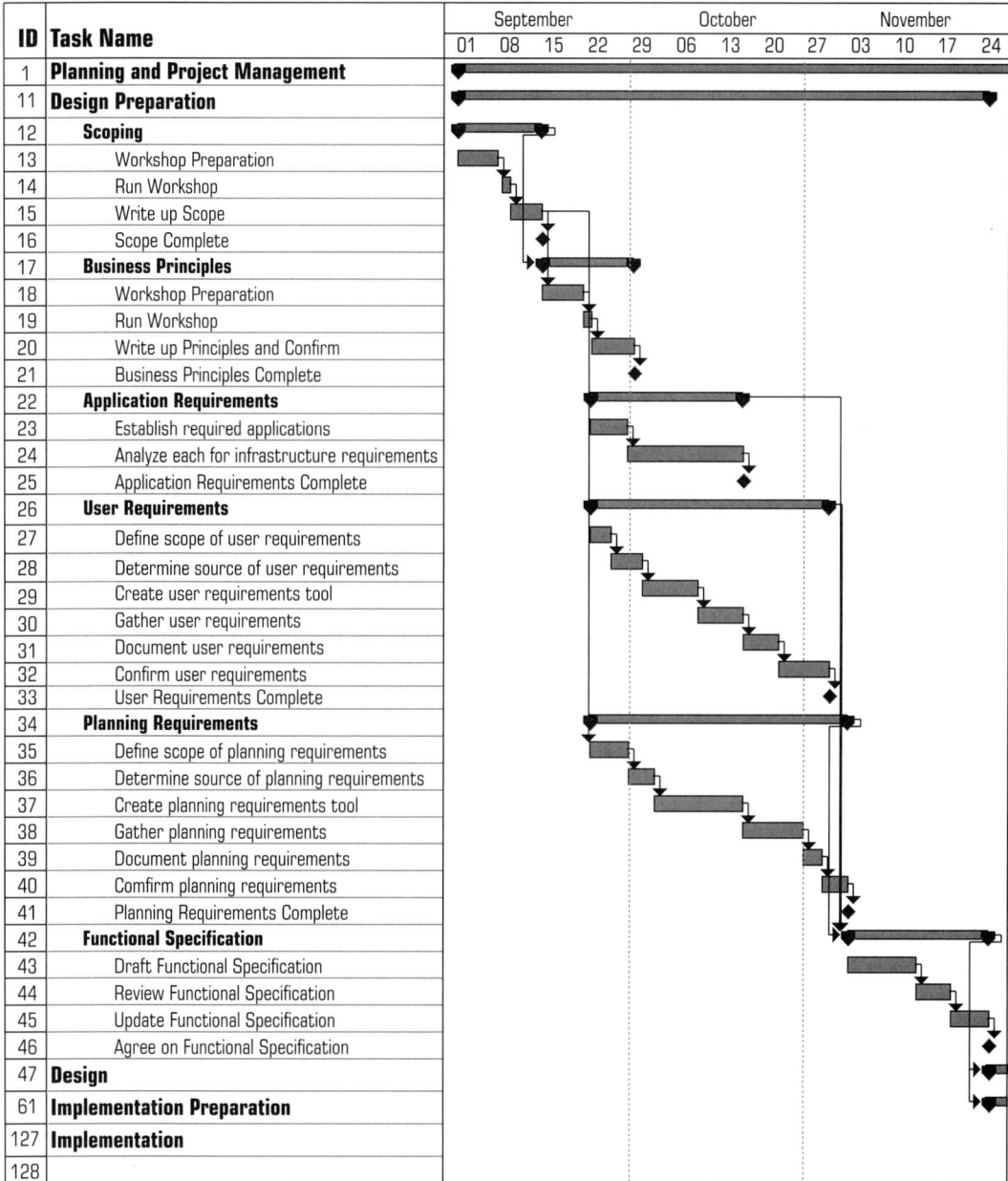

ID	Task Name
1	**Planning and Project Management**
11	**Design Preparation**
12	**Scoping**
13	Workshop Preparation
14	Run Workshop
15	Write up Scope
16	Scope Complete
17	**Business Principles**
18	Workshop Preparation
19	Run Workshop
20	Write up Principles and Confirm
21	Business Principles Complete
22	**Application Requirements**
23	Establish required applications
24	Analyze each for infrastructure requirements
25	Application Requirements Complete
26	**User Requirements**
27	Define scope of user requirements
28	Determine source of user requirements
29	Create user requirements tool
30	Gather user requirements
31	Document user requirements
32	Confirm user requirements
33	User Requirements Complete
34	**Planning Requirements**
35	Define scope of planning requirements
36	Determine source of planning requirements
37	Create planning requirements tool
38	Gather planning requirements
39	Document planning requirements
40	Comfirm planning requirements
41	Planning Requirements Complete
42	**Functional Specification**
43	Draft Functional Specification
44	Review Functional Specification
45	Update Functional Specification
46	Agree on Functional Specification
47	**Design**
61	**Implementation Preparation**
127	**Implementation**
128	

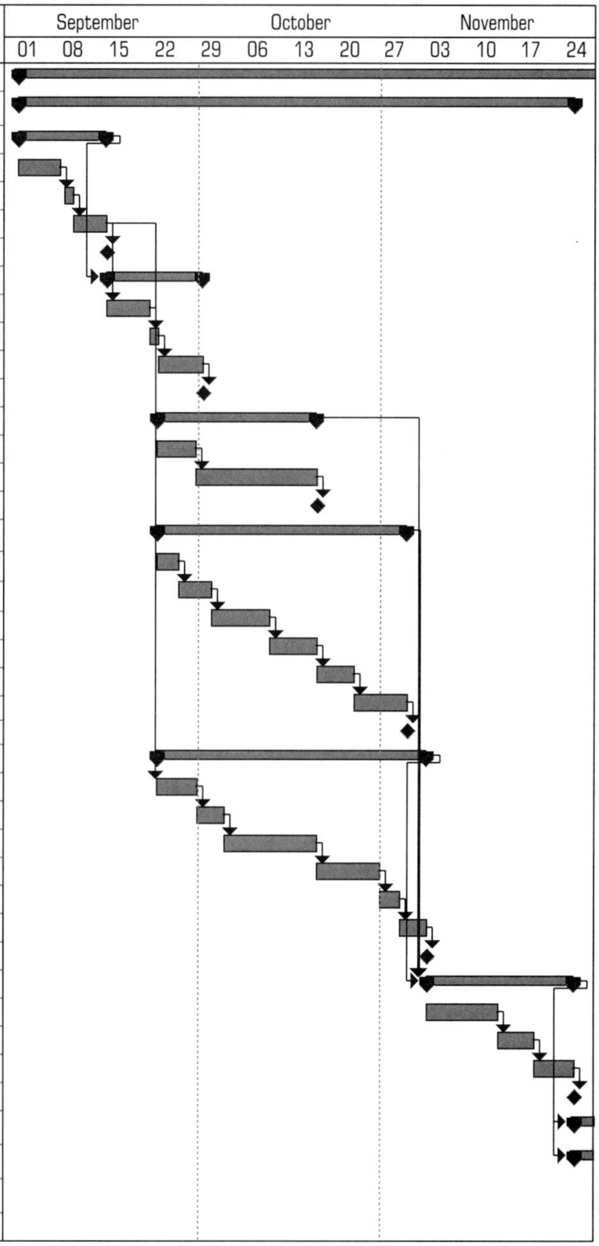

Note: Chapter 4, Project Planning, included the task of creating the Functional Specification with the application requirements and user requirements activities. This is reasonable; however, the Gantt chart shown here illustrates the creation of the Functional Specification as a distinct activity to ensure the effort is fully planned for at the outset.

Design Tasks

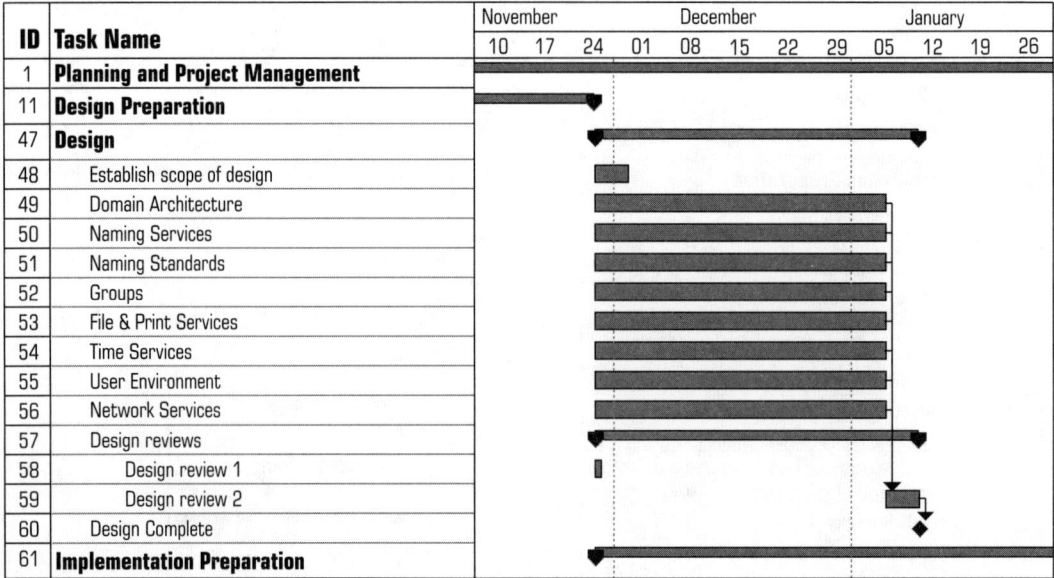

ID	Task Name
1	**Planning and Project Management**
11	**Design Preparation**
47	**Design**
48	Establish scope of design
49	Domain Architecture
50	Naming Services
51	Naming Standards
52	Groups
53	File & Print Services
54	Time Services
55	User Environment
56	Network Services
57	Design reviews
58	Design review 1
59	Design review 2
60	Design Complete
61	**Implementation Preparation**

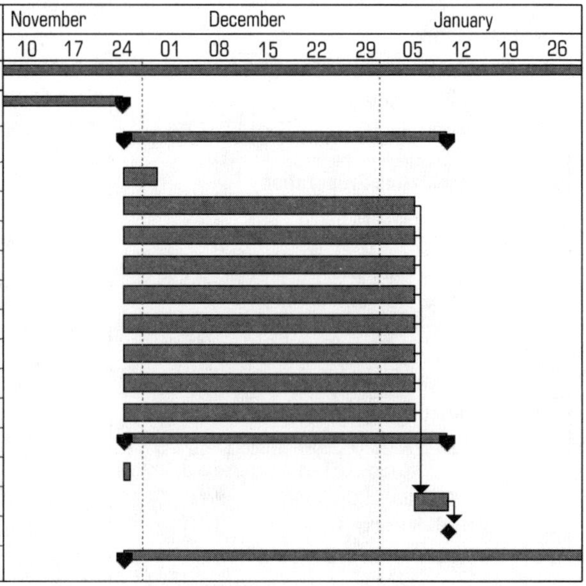

Implementation Preparation Tasks

ID	Task Name
1	**Planning and Project Management**
11	**Design Preparation**
47	**Design**
61	**Implementation Preparation**
62	**Implementation Detail**
63	Software Delivery
67	Product Deliverables
78	Development Testing
86	Pilot Implementation
91	Software Release Management
95	Capacity Planning
99	**Implementation Planning**
100	Define the scope of the installation
101	Identify roles and responsibilities
102	Recruit core project team members
103	Publish project terms of reference
104	Identify milestones
105	Identify dependencies
106	Identify risks
107	Identify and secure local resources
108	**Procurement**
109	Identify requirements
110	Organisation of equipment loans
111	Agree on evaluation criteria
112	Evaluate products
113	Recommend and agree on product
114	Purchase products
115	Products Delivered
116	**Acceptance**
117	Create User Acceptance Test (UAT)
118	Create System Acceptance Test (SAT)
119	Execute UAT
120	Passed UAT
121	Execute SAT
122	Passed SAT
123	**Training**
124	Needs analysis
125	Prepare training program
126	Deliver training
127	**Implementation**
128	

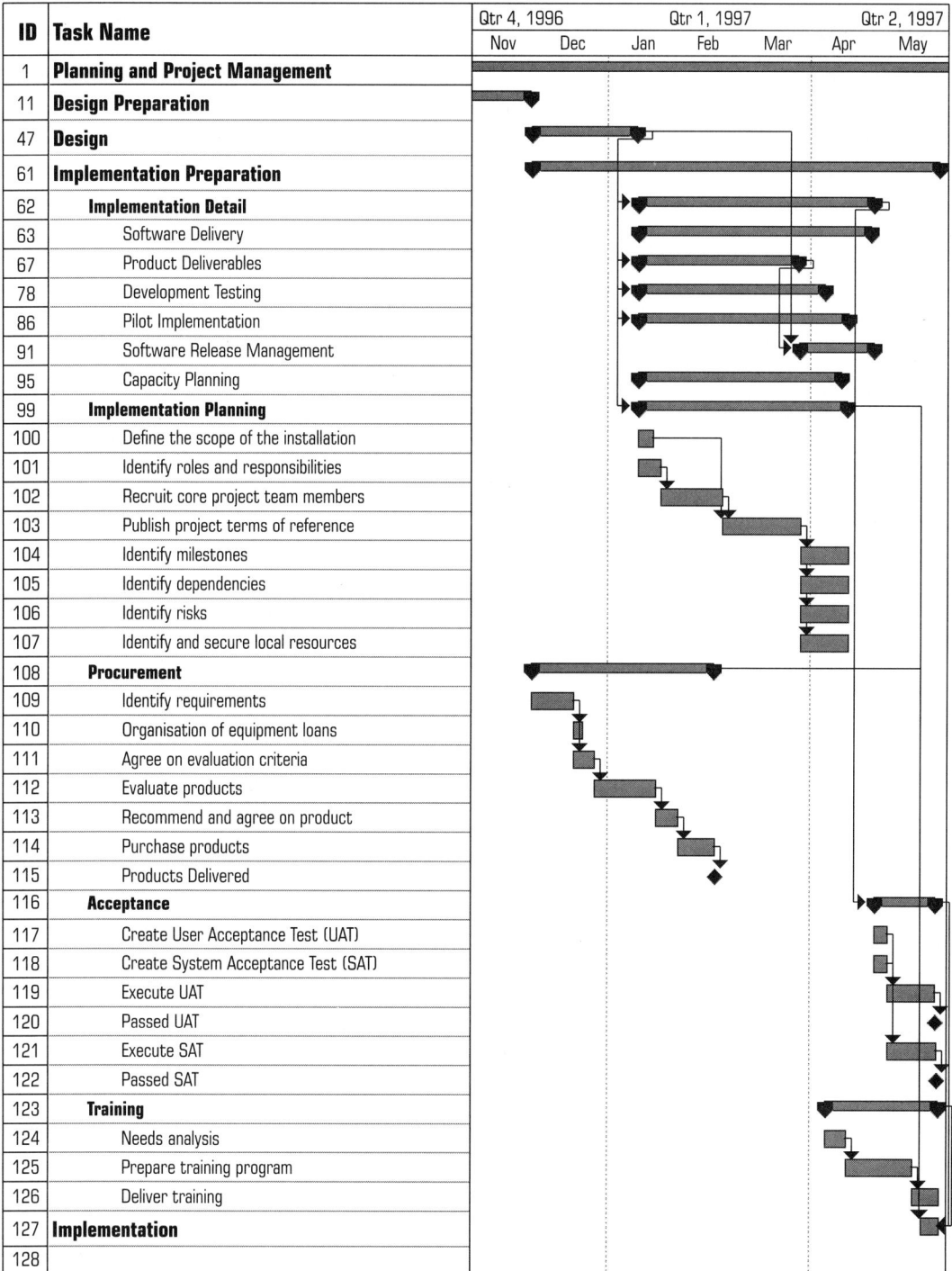

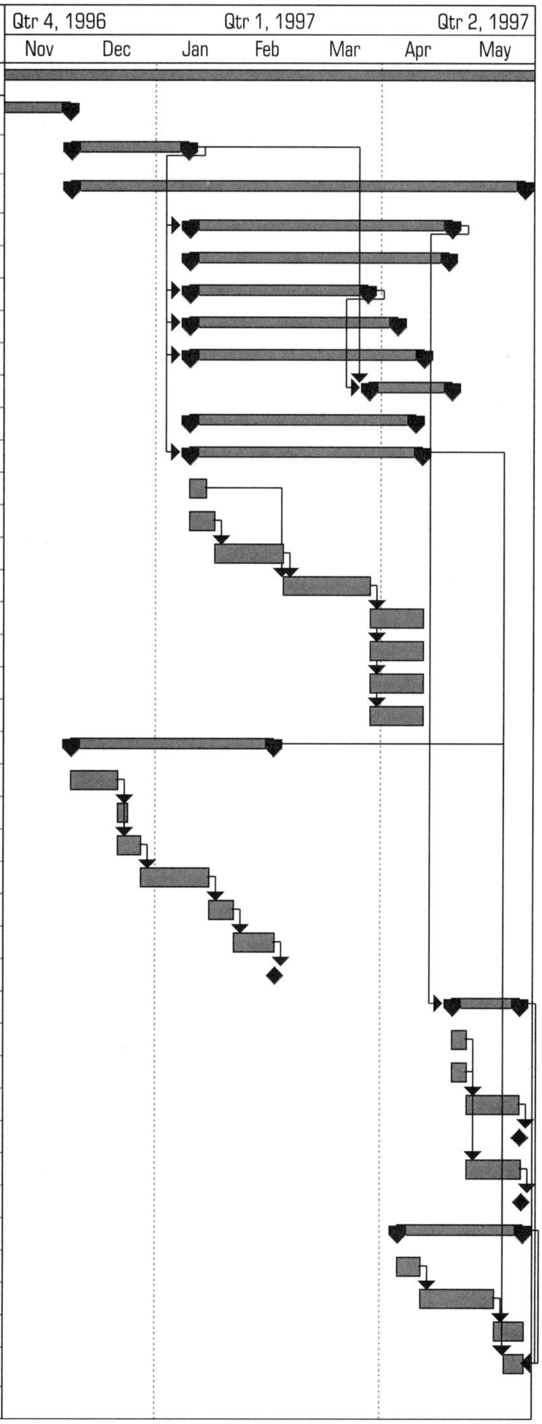

Implementation Detail Tasks

ID	Task Name
1	**Planning and Project Management**
11	**Design Preparation**
47	**Design**
61	**Implementation Preparation**
62	**Implementation Detail**
63	Software Delivery
64	*Create Software Delivery Strategy*
65	*Create Initial Installation Mechanism*
66	*Create Upgrade Mechanism*
67	Product Deliverables
68	*Create workstation installation kit*
69	*Create server installation kit*
70	*Create application installation packages*
71	*Create system guides*
72	*Application Porting*
73	*UNIX integration*
74	*Novell NetWare Integration*
75	*Recovery Procedures*
76	*Remote Computer Management*
77	*Create logon scripts*
78	Development Testing
79	*Set up development laboratory*
80	*Laboratory Ready for Use*
81	*Volume testing*
82	*Installation testing*
83	*Software unit testing*
84	*Software integration testing*
85	*Laboratory Management*
86	Pilot Implementation
87	*Identify suitable pilot*
88	*Plan the pilot*
89	*Manage the pilot*
90	*Review the pilot*
91	Software Release Management
92	*Run acceptance tests*
93	*Software release administration*
94	*Software Production*
95	Capacity Planning
96	*Translate workload into hardware needs*
97	*Incorporate plans of the business*
98	*Size the systems*
99	**Implementation Planning**

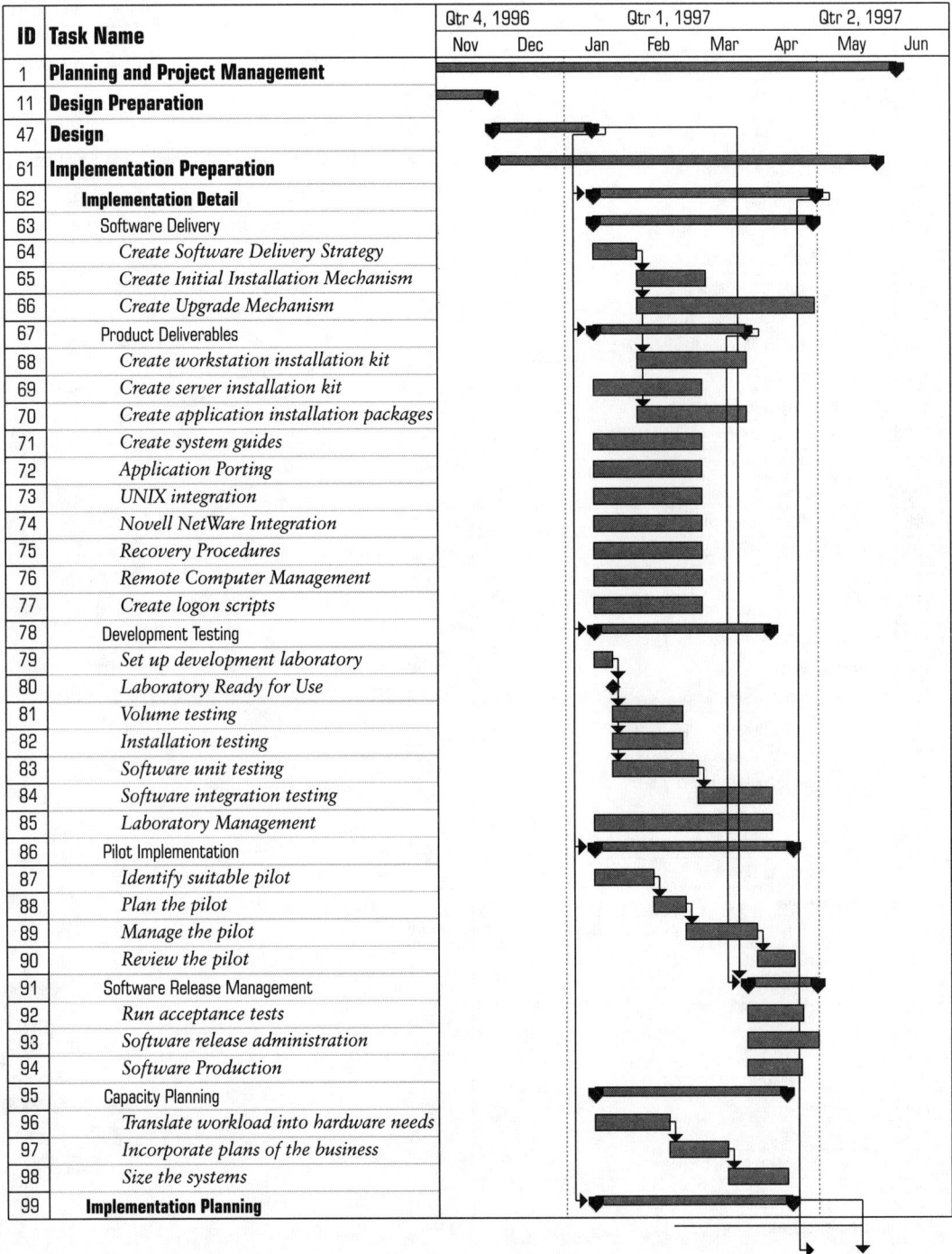

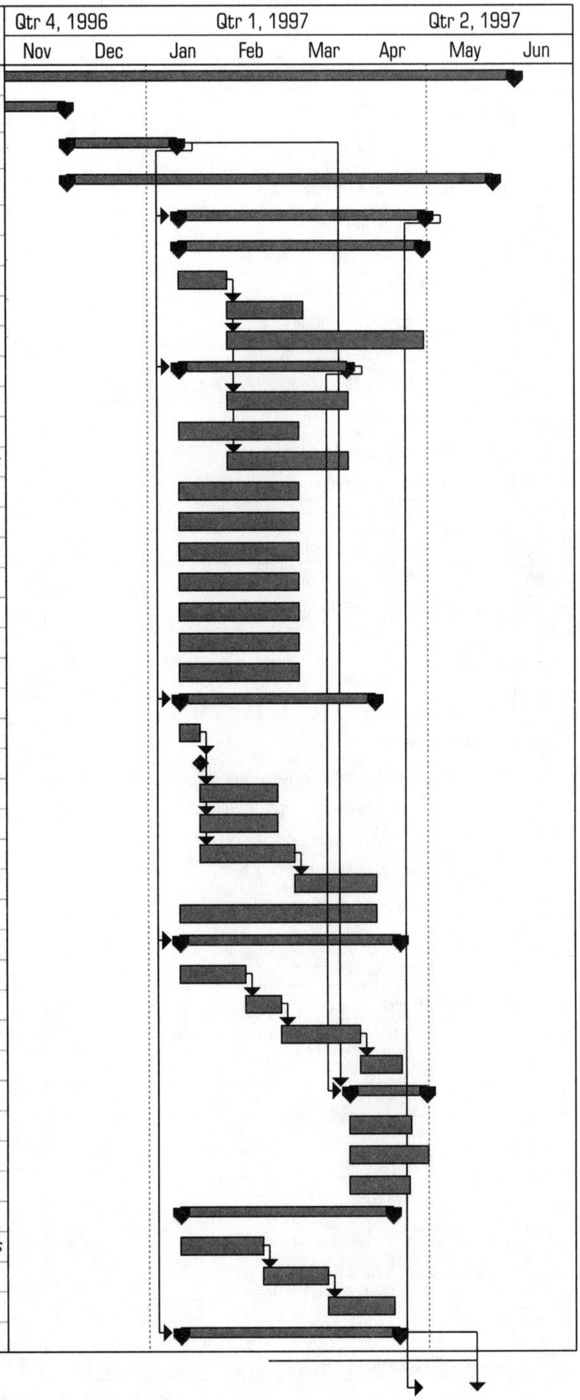

Symbols

A

B

C

D

E

K

L

M

N

O

P

R

S

T

V

W

Z